T0242855

The Enterprise Engineering Series

Explorations

More information about this series at
http://www.springer.com/series/8371

Marc Lankhorst et al.

Enterprise Architecture at Work

Modelling, Communication and Analysis

Fourth Edition

 Springer

Marc Lankhorst
BiZZdesign
Enschede
The Netherlands

ISSN 1867-8920   ISSN 1867-8939   (electronic)
The Enterprise Engineering Series
ISBN 978-3-662-57169-9   ISBN 978-3-662-53933-0   (eBook)
DOI 10.1007/978-3-662-53933-0

Printed on acid-free paper

This Springer imprint is published by Springer Nature
The registered company is Springer-Verlag GmbH Germany
The registered company address is: Heidelberger Platz 3, 14197 Berlin, Germany

Foreword to the Fourth Edition

Enterprise architecture faces many challenges as it attempts to gain and expand its foothold as a formally adopted discipline in organisations worldwide. One such challenge relates to an organisation's ability to coalesce myriad enterprise architecture concepts, approaches and frameworks, across diverse industry and geographic landscapes, into fully actionable strategies. A second challenge relates to the difficulty in articulating business value proposition, which stems from the perception that enterprise architecture is a technical discipline and not a business discipline. This second issue has resulted in business professionals and executives ignoring architecture concepts altogether and refusing to sponsor enterprise architecture in particular because it is viewed as a technical issue that benefits technologists.

This latest edition of *Enterprise Architecture at Work* takes steps to address these challenges by representing an expanded alignment of enterprise architecture with various business disciplines that include strategy, business models, business architecture and quality. In addition, the authors provide insights into how to align various views and frameworks to ensure that organisations adopting a cross section of frameworks and methodologies can leverage them in coordinated fashion.

The recent emergence of formal business architecture as a unique, yet complementary, discipline addresses one of the major challenges and misconceptions of enterprise architecture: that it is a technical concept that delivers limited business value. When business architecture is incorporated into enterprise architecture on equal footing, it enables organisations to clearly articulate the interdependencies among formal representations of the business and related IT solutions. Highlighting these interdependencies increases a business's ability to understand enterprise architecture's value while clarifying how all of the pieces fit together for practitioners within IT and within the business.

Business architecture is not the only element of business planning, strategy and execution as the authors demonstrate. But business architecture shares a pedigree with application, data, solution and technical architecture disciplines insofar as it is a robust, well-formed, clearly articulated discipline with defined integration points to the other architecture perspectives. Business architecture, therefore, becomes the lens through which to interpret and deliver strategy, align to various business models and link to operational business views, such as business process modelling.

Most important is the fact that the authors provide a gateway from business and other architecture perspectives to the comprehensive universe of enterprise architecture models and frameworks used in practice. As evidenced throughout the book, the authors share and detail a wide variety of modelling concepts within the enterprise architecture discipline. This book, while aimed at practitioners and students of the discipline, nevertheless provides insights for those business professionals that struggle to understand how the elements of enterprise architecture align.

Finally, enterprise architecture delivers value when it is widely applied and adopted. This requires not just technical architecture perspectives but also data, application, solution and business architecture perspectives. Without fully embracing this diverse view of enterprise architecture and ensuring that this view is easily digested by adopters, managers, sponsors and beneficiaries, the impact of the discipline is blunted. And while understanding the big picture is important, the details are equally critical. *Enterprise Architecture at Work* provides these perspectives for those that need to clearly see the big picture and also offers a wealth of detailed content for practitioners and students of the enterprise architecture discipline.

This book is a good reference point for those engaged in enterprise architecture directly and for those that benefit from its use overall. I trust readers will enjoy it and reference it as the discipline of enterprise architecture evolves.

Business Architecture Guild   William Ulrich
Soquel, CA, USA
September 2016

Foreword to the Third Edition

On January 31, 2012, The Open Group published version 2.0 of the ArchiMate® language for enterprise architecture modelling. This latest technical standard is now more aligned with TOGAF®, the world's most popular enterprise architecture framework. This is an important milestone in the development of the profession, and this book, now in its third edition, provides much of the background and foundations of this development.

When Novay and its partners started the ArchiMate R&D project in 2002, they wanted to develop better means for communicating enterprise architectures. Until then, architects expressed their architectures either in proprietary tools and frameworks, with all the ensuing problems of vendor lock-in, or in fuzzy PowerPoint pictures that you could only understand if the architect was present to explain what all the boxes and lines meant. A well-founded open standard for architecture description was sorely needed.

Shortly after the project, consultants and educators began using it, the first commercial tools started to appear, and an active user community emerged. In 2008, The Open Group had just created a working group to establish a description language to complement TOGAF, when it was contacted by the ArchiMate Foundation. Since ArchiMate was already developed with TOGAF as one of its inputs, the match between the two created a great opportunity. In 2008, the ownership of ArchiMate was transferred to The Open Group and became a standard in 2009.

This proved to be an all-important step. With the rising popularity of TOGAF and the professional support of The Open Group, ArchiMate adoption figures have grown rapidly. At the time of writing, The Open Group's ArchiMate Forum has some 70 member organisations, over 10 commercial and several open-source tools support the language, and its active LinkedIn group counts nearly 1700 members.

ArchiMate 2.0 provides a number of important extensions that make the fit between TOGAF and ArchiMate even closer. It improves collaboration through clearer understanding across multiple functions, including business executives, enterprise architects, systems analysts, software engineers, business process consultants and infrastructure engineers. The new standard enables the creation of fully integrated models of an organisation's enterprise architecture, the motivation behind it, and the programs, projects and migration paths to implement it. ArchiMate already follows terms defined in the TOGAF framework, and version 2.0 of the specification enables modelling through all phases of the TOGAF Architecture Development Method (ADM).

ArchiMate 2.0 provides enterprise architects with the tools and concepts necessary to create a consistent, integrated model that aligns more closely with TOGAF. It will increase interoperability and help enterprise architects establish a common language across the enterprise, raising the value and awareness of the discipline.

The growing use of models and standards is a sure sign of the maturation of any engineering discipline. This does not mean that enterprise architecture becomes a deterministic exercise, though. Rather, these instruments help managers and architects predict the effects of their actions, spot opportunities, and control risk, in the same way that navigational aids help a ship's captain steer an optimal course in the prevailing currents and winds.

The Open Group   Allen Brown
Reading, UK
February 2012

Foreword to the Second Edition

Have you ever built a new house, or rebuilt an existing one? If you did, most likely an architect has been involved guiding you through the whole process of permits, drawings and construction. In this process, the architect creates insightful two- and three-dimensional drawings, models and views of the house. These show the structure of the house, its division into rooms (like the kitchen, living, bedrooms, and bathroom), its windows with views of the light, the networks of electricity, gas and plumbing, etc. The architectural design process of a house is a well-established discipline, using internationally accepted standards for describing and visualising the design, and various ways to present the design and analyse and calculate the strength of the proposed construction. The architect is well trained in the design methods, the modelling language and certain supporting tools.

Building or rebuilding an organisation is a much more complex and challenging task. First of all because the steps one has to take in order to (re)build an organisation are not standardised. One could start by first (re)designing business processes, followed by the application (re)design. Or one could first design generic application services, followed by designing business processes on top of these. Since a few years, The Open Group Architectural Framework (TOGAF) defines a standard way to take these steps. This enables enterprise architects to (re)design an organisation and its supporting IT systems in a uniform and standard way. The release of the improved TOGAF 9 version in February 2009 will lead to an even more uniform and better way to do this.

Secondly, building an organisation is a complex and challenging task because of the multifarious dependencies within an organisation. Many (often unknown) dependencies exists between various domains, like strategy, products and services, business processes, organisational structure, applications, information management, and technical infrastructure. Besides a having good overview over these different domains, one needs to be aware of their interrelationships. Together, these form the *enterprise architecture* of the organisation. In many cases, different languages and concepts are used to describe each domain, with no support for describing and analysing relationships to other domains.

Until recently, a uniform and easy to use language for modelling and visualising enterprise architectures was lacking. ArchiMate, the modelling language described in this book, fills in this gap. It provides instruments to support enterprise architects in describing, analysing and visualising the relationships among domains in an unambiguous way. ArchiMate is supported by different tool vendors and service providers. Many organisations are using it already as their company standard for describing enterprise architecture and its value has been proven in practice!

Just like an architectural drawing in classical building architecture describes the various aspects of the construction and use of a building, ArchiMate offers a common language for describing the construction and operation of business processes, organisational structures, information flows, IT systems, and technical infrastructure. This insight helps stakeholders to design, assess, and communicate the consequences of decisions and changes within and between these business domains.

Moreover, ArchiMate is now The Open Group's open and independent modelling language for enterprise architecture. The specification of ArchiMate 1.0 has been released by The Open Group in April 2009. You can expect an even greater uptake of this language now that it has become a standard. Moreover, the synergy with TOGAF will provide enterprise architects with a very powerful approach, supported by methods, modelling languages and tools. Because ArchiMate is an open standard, it facilitates (model) interoperability and exchange of best practices. It is not a proprietary language from one tool vendor or service provider.

This book is about ArchiMate. It explains the background and the results of the research project that led to the realisation of the ArchiMate language. It also contains a description of the ArchiMate language itself, and many examples of its use for modelling, visualising and analysing enterprise architecture. The descriptions are based on the ArchiMate 1.0 specification published by The Open Group, and this second edition of the book adds more details on the relation between ArchiMate and TOGAF.

I cordially invite you to read this book. Reaching a second edition already proves its practical value. Convince yourself and start using ArchiMate!

BiZZdesign   H.M. Franken
Enschede, The Netherlands

ArchiMate Forum of The Open Group
Reading, UK
February 2009

Foreword to the First Edition

'Architecture', in a broad sense, is the synergy of art and science in designing complex structures, such that functionality and complexity are controlled. The notion of architecture is used in a wide range of domains, from town planning to building and construction, and from computer hardware to information systems, each being characterised by the types of 'structures' or 'systems' being designed. However, we can recognise some common concerns in all these approaches.

To begin with, architecture, and hence the architect, is concerned with understanding and defining the relationship between the users of the system and the system being designed itself. Based on a thorough understanding of this relationship, the architect defines and refines the essence of the system, i.e., its structure, behaviour, and other properties.

This representation of the system's essence, also called the 'architecture' of the system, forms the basis for analysis, optimisation, and validation and is the starting point for the further design, implementation, and construction of that system. The resulting artefacts, be they buildings or information systems, naturally have to conform to the original design criteria. The definition of the architecture is the input for verifying this.

During this process, the architect needs to communicate with all stakeholders of the system, ranging from clients and users to those who build and maintain the resulting system. The architect needs to balance all their needs and constraints to arrive at a feasible and acceptable design.

Fulfilling these needs confronts the methodology for defining and using architectures with demanding requirements. These can only be met if the architects have an appropriate way of specifying architectures and a set of design and structuring techniques at their disposal, supported by the right tools. In building and construction, such techniques and tools have a history over millennia. In information systems and enterprise architecture, though, they are just arising.

Important for an architecture description language is that the properties of the system can be represented in their bare essence without forcing the architect to include irrelevant detail. This means that the description language must be defined at the appropriate abstraction level.

If the architecture is concerned with the relationship between an enterprise and its IT support, the architect should be capable of expressing the structure, behaviour, and coherence of both the business processes and the IT support, such that one can use these specifications to get a thorough understanding of the architecture, to optimise it according to specific business goals, and to develop a strategy for introducing improvements in the current situation. This implies that the architecture description language should embrace easily understandable human notions of business processes and their IT support, far away from low-level implementation issues. It requires a level of comprehensibility of the description language by a broader audience than just the few specialists that are capable of understanding the obscurities of formal, mathematically oriented languages.

The very same applies to the methods that allow the architect to structure and manipulate architectural specifications such that their complexity can be controlled. Not in the least, the language and methods are the basis for unambiguous mutual understanding and successful collaboration between the stakeholders of the architecture. All stakeholders need to be aware about the implications of the choices in the architecture, and be capable of possibly influencing such choices.

This book presents the results of a research project that produced just that: a comprehensible, high-level design language for enterprise architecture, accompanied by a set of techniques and guidelines for visualisation and analysis of architectures. These results were validated in practice in real-life case studies in cooperation with several large, information-intensive organisations. Currently, various companies, ranging from vendors of architecture tools to consultants and other users of enterprise architecture, are implementing the results of the project.

This project is a prime example of the knowledge transfer for which the Telematica Instituut was founded. Both government and industry fund this Dutch national research institute. Its mission is to boost the innovative and competitive power of society by bridging the gap between academic research and its industrial application. The ArchiMate project, from which this book results, is a prime example of fruitful cooperation between these worlds. This proves the success of this knowledge transfer.

I hope and trust that the ArchiMate project not only proves to be an example of high-quality research in the important field of enterprise architecture, but also will have a considerable impact in practice.

Telematica Instituut   C.A. Vissers
Enschede, The Netherlands
December 2004

Preface

Many stakeholders within and outside the company can be identified, ranging from top-level management to software engineers. Each stakeholder requires specific information presented in an accessible way, to deal with the impact of such wide-ranging developments. To predict the effects of such developments and modifications of an organisation's business and IT, it is necessary but very difficult to obtain an overview of these changes and their impact on each other, and to provide both decision makers and engineers implementing the changes with the information they need.

This book is about *enterprise architecture*, the practice that tries to describe and control an organisation's structure, processes, applications, systems, and technology in such an integrated way. More specifically, we focus on methods and techniques for making and using integrated descriptions by means of architecture models, visualisation of these models for various stakeholders, and analysis of the impact of changes.

The unambiguous specification and description of components and especially their relationships in an architecture requires a coherent architecture modelling language. Such a language must enable integrated modelling of architectural domains and should be appreciated both by people from IT and by people with a business background. In this book, we present such an enterprise modelling language that captures the complexity of architectural domains and their relations and allows the construction of integrated enterprise architecture models. We provide architects with concrete instruments that may improve their architectural practice.

Furthermore, we provide techniques and heuristics for communicating with all relevant stakeholders about these architectures. Central to the communication of architectures is the notion of *viewpoint*. Viewpoints define abstractions on the set of models representing the enterprise architecture, each aimed at a particular type of stakeholder and addressing a particular set of concerns.

An architecture model is not just useful to provide insight into the current or future situation; it can also be used to evaluate the transition from 'as is' to 'to be'. We therefore provide analysis methods for assessing both the qualitative impact of changes to an architecture and quantitative aspects of architectures, such as performance and cost issues.

In order to make the approach we envisage practically feasible, architects require a tool environment, which supports the definition, generation, editing, visualisation, analysis, and management of architecture models and views. Moreover, such an environment should work in concert with existing domain-specific modelling tools, since we cannot expect architects to start using other tools, let alone other languages, than the ones they are used to. We therefore present the design of a viewpoint-driven enterprise modelling environment that can provide just this support and a vision on the future of model-driven enterprise architecture tooling.

The ArchiMate modelling language and the other techniques in the book have been proven in practice in numerous real-life case studies, and since its transfer to The Open Group, the language has become the de facto standard for enterprise architecture modelling. To put these instruments into context, the book also addresses the use of enterprise architecture models and techniques in governance, with a focus on alleviating the infamous business–IT alignment problem.

Audience

The intended audience of this book is twofold. On the one hand, we target enterprise, business, and IT architecture practitioners, especially those who are looking for better ways of describing, communicating, and analysing (enterprise) architectures. On the other hand, we aim for students of IT and (IT) management studying the field of enterprise architecture.

Overview of the Book

In the first chapter, we give an introduction to architecture in general and enterprise architecture in particular, outline its drivers, and describe the architecture process. Chapter 2 provides an overview of methods and techniques currently used in this field. Following this, we outline the foundations of our approach to enterprise architecture modelling (Chap. 3). We then describe our view of architecture as being primarily a means of communication with all the stakeholders involved (Chap. 4).

Architectures are fruitfully used both in requirements analysis and design for new applications, business processes, etc., and to gain insight into existing systems (in the broad sense). In our approach, the use of architecture *models* has a central role; the ArchiMate modelling language used throughout the rest of the book is introduced in Chap. 5. In Chap. 6, we show how this modelling language works together with other management, architecture and modelling standards and approaches. And having a language is not enough: the architect also needs to be guided in its use, which is the topic of Chap. 7.

Many stakeholders with different goals or concerns in mind can view architectures. Each of these requires its own depictions of (part of) an architecture model, and the creation, use of such views and viewpoints is the topic of Chap. 8. Given that we have accurate models of an architecture, we can subject these models to various types of analysis, to establish for example what the impact of a change might be, or whether the performance of the technical infrastructure is sufficient given the applications and business processes that use it. These analyses are discussed in Chap. 9.

The practical applications of these modelling, visualisation, and analysis techniques are the topic of the next three chapters. In Chap. 10, experiences and best practices from case studies regarding the alignment of business, applications, and infrastructures are presented. These provide the context in which architectures are designed. Chapter 11 describes our vision on software support for enterprise architecture. Chapter 12 presents our practical experience with applying ArchiMate in a number of real-life case studies. Finally, Chap. 13 provides a vision of the future: what is next; what comes 'after' architecture?

Acknowledgements

The first edition of this book was a result from the ArchiMate project, a Dutch research initiative that developed concepts and techniques to support enterprise architects in the visualisation, communication and analysis of integrated architectures. The project consortium consisted of the Telematica Instituut, ABN AMRO, Stichting Pensioenfonds ABP, the Dutch Tax and Customs Administration, Ordina, Centrum voor Wiskunde en Informatica, Radboud Universiteit Nijmegen and the Leiden Institute of Advanced Computer Science. Chapter 10 of this book results from the GRAAL project, a daughter project of ArchiMate that was cofinanced by the Telematica Instituut and the Centre for Telematics and Information Technology (CTIT) of the University of Twente, Enschede, the Netherlands.

Since this first version, ArchiMate was developed further under the aegis of The Open Group and is now in version 3.0. Our special thanks go to Henk Jonkers for his invaluable assistance in editing the third and fourth editions of this book, to make it compliant with new versions of the ArchiMate standard.

ArchiMate® is a trademark and standard of The Open Group. More information on the ArchiMate standard can be found at http://www.archimate.org and http://www.opengroup.org/archimate.

BiZZdesign   Marc Lankhorst
Enschede, The Netherlands
October 2016

Contents

List of Contributors

Chapter 1
Introduction to Enterprise Architecture

Marc M. Lankhorst

1.1 Architecture

It is often said that to manage the complexity of any large organisation or system, you need architecture. But what exactly does 'architecture' mean? Of course, we have long known this notion from building and construction. Suppose you contract an architect to design your house. You discuss how rooms, staircases, windows, bathrooms, balconies, doors, a roof, etc., will be put together. You agree on a master plan, on the basis of which the architect will produce detailed specifications, to be used by the engineers and builders.

How is it that you can communicate so efficiently about that master plan? We think it is because you share a common frame of reference: you both know what a 'room' is, a 'balcony', a 'staircase', etc. You know their function and their relation. A 'room', for example, serves as a shelter and is connected to another 'room' via a 'door'. You both use, mentally, an architectural model of a house. This model defines its major functions and how they are structured. It provides an abstract design, ignoring many details. These details, like the number of rooms, dimensions, materials to be used, and colours, will be filled in later.

A similar frame of reference is needed in designing an enterprise. To create an overview of the structure of an organisation, its business processes, their application support, and the technical infrastructure, you need to express the different aspects and domains, and their relations.

But what is 'architecture' exactly? Even in building and construction, the term is not without ambiguity. It can signify the art and science of designing the built environment, or the product of such a design. Thus, the term architecture can encompass both the blueprint for a building and the general underlying principles

M.M. Lankhorst (✉)
BiZZdesign, Capitool 15, 7521 PL Enschede, The Netherlands
e-mail: m.lankhorst@bizzdesign.com

© Springer-Verlag Berlin Heidelberg 2017
M. Lankhorst et al., *Enterprise Architecture at Work*, The Enterprise Engineering
Series, DOI 10.1007/978-3-662-53933-0_1

1

such as its style, as in 'gothic architecture'. There are different schools of thought on this. Some say we should reserve the term 'architecture' in the context of IT solely for such principles and constraints on the design space, as e.g. Dietz argues (2006), who uses the term 'enterprise ontology' for the actual designs. In this book, we will use the ISO/IEC/IEEE FDIS 42010:2011 standard (ISO/IEC/IEEE 2011) definition of architecture:

> **Architecture**: fundamental concepts or properties of a system in its environment, embodied in its elements, relationships, and in the principles of its design and evolution.

This definition accommodates both the blueprint and the general principles. More succinctly, we could define architecture as 'structure with a vision'. An architecture provides an integrated view of the system being designed or studied.

As well as the definition of architecture, we will use two other important notions from the IEEE standard. First, a 'stakeholder' is defined as follows:

> **Stakeholder**: an individual, team, or organisation (or classes thereof) with interests in, or concerns relative to, a system.

Most stakeholders of a system are probably not interested in its architecture, but only in the impact of this on their concerns. However, an architect needs to be aware of these concerns and discuss them with the stakeholders, and thus should be able to explain the architecture to all stakeholders involved, who will often have completely different backgrounds.

1.2   Enterprise Architecture

More and more, the notion of architecture is applied with a broader scope than just in the technical and IT domains. The emerging discipline of Enterprise Engineering views enterprises as a whole as purposefully designed systems that can be adapted and redesigned in a systematic and controlled way. An 'enterprise' in this context can be defined as follows (The Open Group 2011):

> **Enterprise**: any collection of organisations that has a common set of goals and/or a single bottom line.

Architecture at the level of an entire organisation is commonly referred to as 'enterprise architecture'. This leads us to the definition of enterprise architecture:

> **Enterprise architecture**: a coherent whole of principles, methods, and models that are used in the design and realisation of an enterprise's organisational structure, business processes, information systems, and infrastructure.

Enterprise architecture captures the essentials of the business, IT and its evolution. The idea is that the essentials are much more stable than the specific solutions that are found for the problems currently at hand. Architecture is therefore helpful in guarding the essentials of the business, while still allowing for maximal flexibility and adaptivity. Without good architecture, it is difficult to achieve business success.

The most important characteristic of an enterprise architecture is that it provides a holistic view of the enterprise. Within individual domains local optimisation will take place, and from a reductionist point of view, the architectures within this domain may be optimal. However, this need not lead to a desired situation for the company as a whole. For example, a highly optimised technical infrastructure that offers great performance at low cost might turn out to be too rigid and inflexible if it needs to support highly agile and rapidly changing business processes. A good enterprise architecture provides the insight needed to balance these requirements and facilitates the translation from corporate strategy to daily operations.

To achieve this quality in enterprise architecture, bringing together information from formerly unrelated domains necessitates an approach that is understood by all those involved from these different domains. In contrast to building architecture, which has a history over millennia in which a common language and culture has been established, such a shared frame of reference is still lacking in business and IT. In current practice, architecture descriptions are heterogeneous in nature: each domain has its own description techniques, either textual or graphical, either informal or with a precise meaning. Different fields speak their own languages, draw their own models, and use their own techniques and tools. Communication and decision making across these domains is seriously impaired.

What is part of the enterprise architecture, and what is only an implementation within that architecture, is a matter of what the business defines to be the architecture, and what not. The architecture marks the separation between what should not be tampered with and what can be filled in more freely. This places a high demand for quality on the architecture. Quality means that the architecture actually helps in achieving essential business objectives. In constructing and maintaining an architecture, choices should therefore be related to the business objectives, i.e., they should be rational.

Even though an architecture captures the relatively stable parts of business and technology, any architecture will need to accommodate and facilitate change, and architecture products will therefore only have a temporary status. Architectures change because the environment changes and new technological opportunities arise, and because of new insights as to what is essential to the business. To ensure

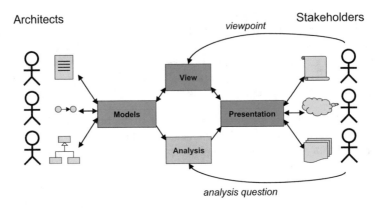

Fig. 1.1 Communicating about architecture

that these essentials are discussed, a good architecture clearly shows the relation of the architectural decisions to the business objectives of the enterprise.

To create an integrated perspective of an enterprise, we need techniques for describing architectures in a coherent way and communicating these with all relevant stakeholders. Different types of stakeholders will have their own viewpoints on the architecture. Furthermore, architectures are subject to change, and methods to analyse the effects of these changes are necessary in planning future developments. Often, an enterprise architect has to rely on existing methods and techniques from disparate domains, without being able to create the 'big picture' that puts these domains together. This requires an integrated set of methods and techniques for the specification, analysis, and communication of enterprise architectures that fulfils the needs of the different types of stakeholders involved. In this book, we will introduce such an approach. Architecture models, views, presentations, and analyses all help to bridge the 'communication gap' between architects and stakeholders (Fig. 1.1).

Of course, architects play a central role in this process. In this book, we will not go deeper into the various competencies and skills they need, but we refer the reader to Wieringa et al. (2008) and Op 't Land et al. (2008, Chap. 6) for more on this subject.

1.3 The Architecture Process

Architecture is a process as well as a product. The product serves to guide managers in designing business processes and system developers in building applications in a way that is in line with business objectives and policies. The effects of the process reach further than the mere creation of the architecture product—the awareness of

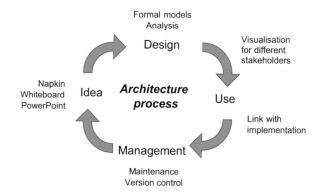

Fig. 1.2 The architecture description life cycle

stakeholders with respect to business objectives and information flow will be raised. Also, once the architecture is created, it needs to be maintained. Businesses and IT are continually changing. This constant evolution is, ideally, a rational process. Change should only be initiated when people in power see an opportunity to strengthen business objectives.

The architecture process consists of the usual steps that take an initial idea through design and implementation phases to an operational system, and finally changing or replacing this system, closing the loop. In all of the phases of the architecture process, clear communication with and between stakeholders is indispensable. The architecture descriptions undergo a life cycle that corresponds to this design process (Fig. 1.2). The different architecture products in this life cycle are discussed with stakeholders, approved, revised, etc., and play a central role in establishing a common frame of reference for all those involved.

1.4   Drivers for Enterprise Architecture

It need not be stressed that any organisation benefits from having a clear understanding of its structure, products, operations, technology, and the web of relations tying these together and connecting the organisation to its surroundings. Furthermore, there are external pressures to take into account, both from customers, suppliers, and other business partners, and from regulatory bodies. Especially if a company becomes larger and more complicated, good architectural practice becomes indispensable. Here, we briefly outline the most important and commonly recognised internal and external drivers for establishing an enterprise architecture.

1.4.1   Internal Drivers

Business–IT alignment is commonly recognised as an important instrument to realise organisational effectiveness. Such effectiveness is not obtained by local optimisations, but is realised by well-orchestrated interaction of organisational components (Nadler et al. 1992). Effectiveness is driven by the relationships between components rather than by the detailed specification of each individual component. A vast amount of literature has been written on the topic of alignment, underlining the significance of both 'soft' and 'hard' components of an organisation.

Parker and Benson (1989) were forerunners in using the term 'alignment' in this context and emphasising the role of architecture in strategic planning. The well-known strategic alignment model of Henderson and Venkatraman (1993) distinguishes between the aspects of business strategy and organisational infrastructure on the one hand and IT strategy and IT infrastructure on the other hand (Fig. 1.3). The model provides four dominant perspectives that are used to tackle the alignment between these aspects. One can take the business strategy of an enterprise as the starting point, and derive its IT infrastructure either via an IT strategy or through the organisational infrastructure; conversely, one can focus on IT as an enabler and start from the IT strategy, deriving the organisational infrastructure via a business strategy or based on the IT infrastructure. In any of these perspectives, an enterprise architecture can be a valuable help in executing the business or IT strategy.

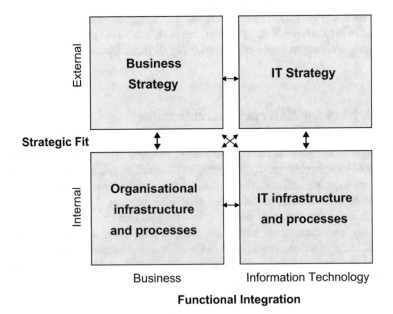

Fig. 1.3 Strategic alignment model (Henderson and Venkatraman 1993)

Nadler et al. (1992) identify four relevant alignment components: work, people, the formal organisation and the informal organisation. Labovitz and Rosansky (1997) emphasise the horizontal and vertical alignment dimensions of an organisation. Vertical alignment describes the relation between the top strategy and the people at the bottom, whereas horizontal alignment describes the relation between internal processes and external customers. Obviously, the world of business–IT alignment is as diverse as it is complex. In coping with this complexity, enterprise architecture is of valuable assistance.

In Fig. 1.4, enterprise architecture is positioned within the context of managing the enterprise. At the top of this pyramid, we see the mission of the enterprise: why does it exist? The vision states its 'image of the future' and the values the enterprise holds. Next there is its strategy, which states the route the enterprise will take in achieving this mission and vision. This is translated into concrete goals that give direction and provide the milestones in executing the strategy. Translating those goals into concrete changes to the daily operations of the company is where enterprise architecture comes into play. It offers a holistic perspective of the current and future operations, and on the actions that should be taken to achieve the company's goals.

Next to its architecture, which could be viewed as the 'hard' part of the company, the 'soft' part, its culture, is formed by its people and leadership, and is of equal if not higher importance in achieving these goals. Finally, of course, we see the enterprise's daily operations, which are governed by the pyramid of Fig. 1.4.

To some it may seem that architecture is something static, confining everything within its rules and boundaries, and hampering innovation. This is a misconception. A well-defined architecture is an important asset in positioning new developments

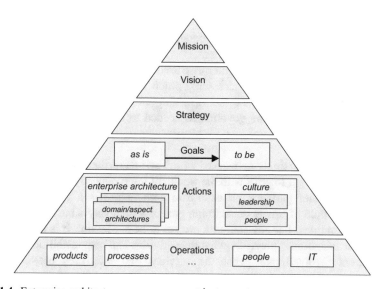

Fig. 1.4 Enterprise architecture as a management instrument

Fig. 1.5 Operating model
(Ross et al. 2006)

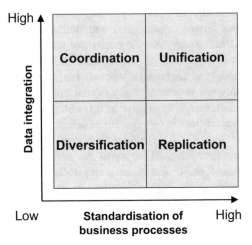

within the context of the existing processes, IT systems, and other assets of an organisation, and it helps in identifying necessary changes. Thus, good architectural practice helps a company innovate and change by providing both stability and flexibility. The insights provided by an enterprise architecture are needed on the one hand in determining the needs and priorities for change from a business perspective, and on the other hand in assessing how the company may benefit from technological and business innovations.

Moreover, architecture is a strategic instrument in guiding an organisation through a planned course of development. As Ross et al. (2006) show with numerous case studies, successful enterprises employ an 'operating model' with clear choices on the levels of integration and standardisation of business processes across the enterprise (Fig. 1.5). This operating model should fit both their area of business and their stage of development.

Ross et al. explain the role of enterprise architecture as the organising logic for business processes and IT infrastructure, which must reflect the integration and standardisation requirements of the operating model. They also describe the 'engagement model', i.e., the governance needed to ensure that business and IT projects meet local and corporate objectives and conform to the enterprise architecture.

Finally, in an increasingly networked world, no enterprise can focus solely on its own operations. To get to grips with the wealth of interconnections with customers, suppliers, and other partners, an enterprise architecture is a valuable asset. A prominent example of this is outsourcing part of a company's business processes and/or IT operations. For any sourcing project to be successful, it is paramount to have a clear insight into precisely what the activities and responsibilities are of all the partners involved, and what the services and interfaces between these partners are.

1.4.2 External Drivers

Next to the internal drive to execute effectively an organisation's strategy and optimise its operations, there are also external pressures that push organisations towards adopting enterprise architecture practice. The regulatory framework increasingly demands that companies and governmental institutions can prove that they have a clear insight into their operations and that they comply with the applicable laws on, say, financial transactions.

In the USA, the Clinger–Cohen Act (1996), also known as the Information Technology Management Reform Act, demands that every government agency must have an IT architecture, which is defined as: 'an integrated framework for evolving or maintaining existing information technology and acquiring new information technology to achieve the agency's strategic goals and information resources management goals'. Section 5125 (b) of the Act assigns the Agency Chief Information Officer (CIO) the responsibility of 'developing, maintaining, and facilitating the implementation of a sound and integrated information technology architecture.' The US Department of Defense even requires all IT to comply with this Act, including that in weapons and weapons system programmes.

The Clinger–Cohen Act has been an important stimulus for the development of enterprise architecture as a discipline, not just in a government context, but in general. Although most European governments do not impose such strict requirements on their agencies, these architecture practices are making inroads in Europe as well.

The capital adequacy framework known as Basel II (2004), endorsed in 2004 by the central bank governors and the heads of bank supervisory authorities in the Group of Ten (G10) countries, puts requirements on banking organisations with respect to their financial risk management, to promote stability in the financial world. The Basel II framework imposes strict regulations on banks in terms of risk measurement and management, with wide-ranging implications for both their organisations and their IT systems. The framework provides explicit incentives in the form of lower capital requirements for banks to adopt more comprehensive and accurate measures of risk as well as more effective processes for controlling their exposures to risk. This encompasses both credit risk and operational risk, the latter being defined as the risk of loss resulting from inadequate or failed internal processes, people and systems or from external events. Given this wide scope and the detailed requirements on risk management, compliance with Basel II can hardly be envisaged without a sound architectural approach.

Another US act, the Sarbanes–Oxley Act (2002), also has a major impact. This act, formally known as the Public Company Accounting Reform and Investor Protection Act, was drawn up in the aftermath of the Enron scandal, to force companies to adopt good corporate governance practices and to make company executives personally accountable. These accountability regulations make it very important for a company that it is clear what the responsibilities of each employee are. IT systems must provide the necessary accounting information to be able to perform the audits required by the Act, and should enforce their users to have appropriate authorisation. Again, enterprise architecture may be of assistance in providing the necessary insight, and many companies are improving their architecture practice to conform to these regulations. And given that this Act applies to all companies that have their stocks quoted on the US stock exchanges, it has a worldwide impact.

1.5 Summary

Architecture is the art and science of designing complex structures. Enterprise architecture, more specifically, is defined as a coherent whole of principles, methods, and models that are used in the design and realisation of an enterprise's organisational structure, business processes, information systems, and infrastructure. Architecture models, views, presentations, and analyses all help to bridge the 'communication gap' between architects and stakeholders.

Architecture is an indispensable instrument in controlling the complexity of the enterprise and its processes and systems. On the one hand, we see internal drivers for using an architectural approach, related to the strategy execution of an organisation. Better alignment between business and IT leads to lower cost, higher quality, better time-to-market, and greater customer satisfaction. On the other hand, external drivers from regulatory authorities and other pressures necessitate companies to have a thorough insight into their structure and operations. All of these drivers make a clear case for the use of enterprise architecture.

Chapter 2
State of the Art

Marc M. Lankhorst, Maria-Eugenia Iacob, and Henk Jonkers

First, we position enterprise architecture relative to a number of well-known standards and best practices in general and IT management. Second, we outline the most important frameworks and methods for enterprise architecture currently in use. Next, we discuss service orientation, the most important architectural paradigm that has emerged over the last few years. Finally, we describe a number of relevant languages for modelling organisations, business processes, applications, and technology.

Based upon this state of the art, in the next chapter we will describe what we see as missing in current methods and techniques, and how our own approach tries to fill some of these gaps.

2.1 Enterprise Architecture and Other Governance Instruments

Enterprise architecture is typically used as an instrument in managing a company's daily operations and future development. But how does it fit in with other established management practices and instruments?

Here, we describe how enterprise architecture is positioned within the context of corporate and IT governance by relating it to a number of well-known best practices and standards in general and IT management, as outlined in Fig. 2.1. In the next

M.M. Lankhorst (✉)
BiZZdesign, Capitool 15, 7521 PL Enschede, The Netherlands
e-mail: m.lankhorst@bizzdesign.com

M.-E. Iacob
University of Twente, Enschede, The Netherlands

H. Jonkers
BiZZdesign, Enschede, The Netherlands

© Springer-Verlag Berlin Heidelberg 2017
M. Lankhorst et al., *Enterprise Architecture at Work*, The Enterprise Engineering
Series, DOI 10.1007/978-3-662-53933-0_2

Fig. 2.1 Management
areas relevant to enterprise
architecture

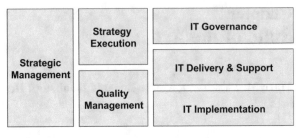

subsections, we will outline the relation of enterprise architecture with some
well-known management practices in each of these areas, not to be exhaustive but
to show the position and role of enterprise architecture in a management context:

- Strategic management: Balanced Scorecard
- Business model development: Business Model Canvas
- Business architecture: BIZBOK® Guide and O-BA
- Quality management: EFQM and ISO 9001
- IT governance: COBIT
- IT delivery and support: ITIL
- IT implementation: CMM and CMMI

Others have also written extensively on this role of enterprise architecture as a
governance instrument; see e.g. (Ross et al. 2006).

2.1.1   Strategic Management

Kaplan and Norton (1992) introduced the Balanced Scorecard (BSC) as a management system that helps an enterprise to clarify and implement its vision and
strategy. Traditionally, management focus has strongly been on financial aspects.
Kaplan and Norton argue that financial measures alone are inadequate to guide the
future development of an organisation, and that they should be supplemented with
measures concerning customer satisfaction, internal processes, and the ability to
innovate.

The BSC therefore suggests viewing an enterprise from four perspectives. The
Customer perspective asks how the enterprise should appear to its customers, with
measures like customer satisfaction. The *Financial* perspective is focused on the
business value created by the enterprise, entailing measures such as shareholder
value. The *Internal Business Processes* perspective looks at the effectiveness and
efficiency of a company's internal operations, paying special attention to the
primary, mission-oriented processes. Finally, the *Learning and Growth* perspective
addresses the corporate and individual ability to change and improve, which is
critical to any knowledge-intensive organisation. For each of the four perspectives
the BSC proposes a three-layered structure:

1. mission (e.g., to become the customers' preferred supplier);
2. objectives (e.g., to provide the customers with new products);
3. measures (e.g., percentage of turnover generated by new products).

To put the BSC to work, a company should first define its mission, objectives, and measures for each perspective, and then translate these into a number of appropriate targets and initiatives to achieve these goals. Strategy maps (Kaplan and Norton 2004) are often used as layered depiction of these elements and their relationships.

What is important in the BSC is the notion of double-loop feedback. First of all, one should measure the outputs of internal business processes and not only fix defects in these outputs but also identify and remedy the causes of these defects. Moreover, such a feedback loop should also be instituted for the outcomes of business strategies. Performance measurement and management by fact are central to the BSC approach.

If we look at the role of enterprise architecture as a management instrument, it is especially useful within the Internal Business Processes perspective of the BSC. Many operational metrics can be tied to a well-defined enterprise architecture and various performance analyses might be carried out. However, enterprise architecture has a broader use. In the Learning and Growth perspective, a company's ability to evolve, to anticipate, and to respond to a changing environment is vital. To determine an organisation's agility, it is important to assess what the impact and feasibility of future changes might be. Impact analysis of an enterprise architecture may assist in such an assessment.

In Sect. 6.3, we describe how the ArchiMate modelling language for enterprise architecture (The Open Group 2016a) introduced in Chap. 5 can be used to describe the Balanced Scorecard.

2.1.2 Business Model Development

The Business Model Canvas (Osterwalder and Pigneur 2010) is a template to create high-level descriptions of new or existing business models. It is conceptually rooted in the business model ontology described in Osterwalder's PhD thesis (Osterwalder 2004). The Business Model Canvas consists of seven parts:

- **Value proposition**: the centre of the canvas, describing what products and services an organisation has to offer to its different customers
- **Key activities**: what the organisation needs to do to provide its value propositions
- **Key resources**: the resources needed for these activities
- **Customer segments**: the typical customer groups the organisation distinguishes
- **Customer relationships**: the kind of links the organisation has with its customers
- **Channels**: how the organisation gets in touch with its customers.

Business model canvas

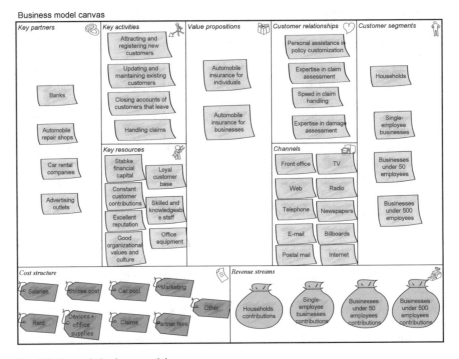

Fig. 2.2 Example business model canvas

- **Key partners**: others with which the organisation cooperates in delivering value to its customers
- **Cost structure**: the financial view of the means employed by the organisation
- **Revenue streams**: the way the organisation makes money from various revenue flows from its customer segments

The Business Model Canvas lays out these elements in a user-friendly, intuitive way. It is often used in a brainstorming or workshop context, sometimes using simple 'sticky notes', sometimes in a tool-supported fashion. Figure 2.2 shows a small example of such a canvas.

Enterprise architecture is typically used as a next stage in strategic development. Many of the elements in a canvas can be detailed out using enterprise architecture models. In Sect. 6.4, we describe how the concepts in the Business Model Canvas can be mapped onto those of the ArchiMate language introduced in Chap. 5.

2.1.3   Business Architecture

In recent years, business architecture has gained an increasing audience and has established itself as a distinct discipline. Partially fueled by often rather IT-focused enterprise architecture approaches and efforts, it has developed its own methods and body of knowledge, exemplified by "A Guide to the Business Architecture Body of Knowledge®" (BIZBOK® Guide) (Business Architecture Guild 2016) and the Open Business Architecture (O-BA) method being developed by The Open Group at the time of writing (2016c).

The Business Architecture Special Interest Group (BASIG) of the OMG has defined business architecture as follows:

Business architecture: a blueprint of the enterprise that provides a common understanding of the organisation and is used to align strategic objectives and tactical demands.

A business architecture provides a business-oriented abstraction of the enterprise in its ecosystem, which helps to translate strategy into action. The role of model-based support for design, analysis and decision making is becoming increasingly important in the business architecture discipline.

Key input for business architecture is the organisation's strategy, which includes its business model, for example, described using the Business Model Canvas (Sect. 2.1.2), and its operating model (Sect. 1.4.1). Commonly used design techniques in business architecture include, among others, describing its value network and value streams (Sect. 6.5), developing and improving customer journeys (Sect. 6.6) and creating service blueprints (Sect. 6.7). Analysis and decision making in business architecture are supported by, for example, risk analysis (Sect. 9.4), portfolio management (Sect. 9.5) and capability-based planning (Sects. 8.7.1 and 9.6).

Typical concepts and aspects that the domain of business architecture concerns itself with are shown in Fig. 2.3. Basically all of these can be represented directly or indirectly in the ArchiMate language, which will also be illustrated in Chap. 6 on combining ArchiMate with other standards and approaches.

In particular, the focus on the capabilities of the enterprise, with capability-based planning (Ulrich and Rosen 2011; The Open Group 2016b) as a core technique, is a key contribution of the business architecture discipline. This allows an organisation to focus on *what* the current and desired abilities of the enterprise are, before diving into the details of *how* it achieves these. This implementation- and technology-independent view provides a crucial connection between strategy and realisation: It links the often rather high-level, coarse-grained descriptions of an organisation's strategy and business model with more detail- and technology-oriented other domains within the EA scope, such as business process, application and infrastructure architecture.

In the context of this book, we consider business architecture to be an important domain within the broader scope of enterprise architecture, hence the inclusion of business architecture concepts such as capability, outcome and course of action in the current version of the ArchiMate modelling language for enterprise architecture described in Chap. 5. Others take a more IT-oriented view of enterprise architecture, considering it to be enterprise-wide IT architecture and position business architecture next to it as a separate discipline. A third group see business and enterprise architecture as largely synonymous. But no matter which stance you

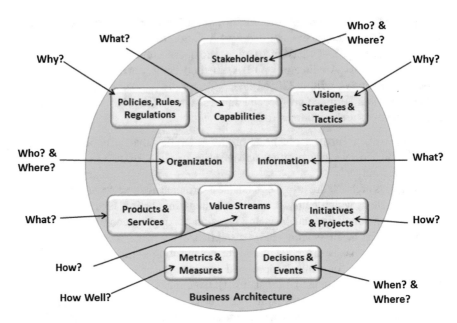

Fig. 2.3 The business ecosystem as represented by business architecture (Business Architecture Guild 2016)

take in this debate, the techniques used in the domain are an important addition to the toolbox you can use in designing and managing your enterprise.

2.1.4   Quality Management

Another important management approach is the EFQM (European Foundation for Quality Management) Excellence Model (EFQM 2003). This model was first introduced in 1992 as the framework for assessing applications for The European Quality Award, and was inspired by the Malcolm Baldridge Model in the USA and the Deming Prize in Japan.

The EFQM model has a much broader scope than ISO 9001 (discussed later in this section). It not only focuses on quality management, but provides an overall management framework for performance excellence of the entire organisation. The EFQM model consists of nine criteria for excellence, five of which are 'enablers', covering what an organisation does, and four are 'results', covering what that organisation achieves. These criteria and their mutual relationships are shown in diagrammatic form in Fig. 2.4. Leadership and Policy & Strategy determine the direction and focus of the enterprise; based on this, the People of the enterprise, its Partnerships & Resources, and its Processes make it happen; stakeholders of the results achieved are its Customers, its People, and Society in general; and these

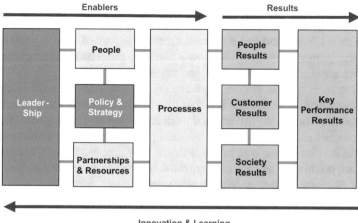

Fig. 2.4 The EFQM excellence model (EFQM 2003)

stakeholder results contribute to the enterprise's Key Performance Results, which comprise both financial and non-financial aspects. The EFQM model provides principles, measures, and indicators for assessing the performance of an enterprise in all of these aspects, and these measurements are the basis for continuous learning, innovation, and improvement.

All this also points to the main difference between the EFQM model and the BSC: whereas the latter is focused on developing effective strategic management, the former concentrates on measuring and benchmarking the performance of an organisation with respect to a number of best practices. Both are complementary: the BSC helps to make strategic choices, and the EFQM model assists in continuous improvement necessary to execute this strategy.

Positioning enterprise architecture with respect to the EFQM model, we view it especially as an important instrument for the Policy & Strategy and the Processes aspects. Based on its mission and vision, an organisation will determine the policies and strategies needed to meet the present and future needs and expectations of its stakeholders. An enterprise architecture is a valuable instrument in operationalising and implementing these policies and strategies. First of all, it offers insight into the structure and operation of the enterprise as a whole by creating a bird's-eye view of its organisational structure, business processes, information systems, and infra-structure. Such an overview is indispensable when formulating a coherent strategy. Furthermore, an enterprise architecture helps in developing, managing, and com-municating company-wide standards of operation, needed to ensure that company policies are indeed implemented. Finally, by providing a better understanding of the effects of changes, it is of valuable assistance in creating roadmaps for the future, needed to assess and execute the longer-term enterprise strategy.

Another important standard in the domain of quality management is the ISO 9001:2000   standard   (ISO   2000)   of   the   International   Organisation   for

Standardisation (ISO). This outlines criteria for a good-quality management system (QMS). Based on a quality policy and quality goals, a company designs and documents a QMS to control how processes are performed. The requirements of the standard cover everything from how a company plans its business processes, to how these are carried out, measured, and improved.

Starting from general, overall requirements, the standard states the responsibilities of management for the QMS. It then gives requirements for resources, including personnel, training, the facility, and work environment. The demands on what is called 'product realisation', i.e., the business processes that realise the company's product or service are the core of the standard. Key processes, i.e., those processes that affect product or service quality, must be identified and documented. This includes planning, customer-related processes, design, purchasing, and process control. Finally, requirements are put on measurement, analysis, and improvement of these business processes. Once the quality system is installed, a company can request an audit by a Registrar. If it conforms to all the criteria, the company will be ISO 9001 registered.

Although the standard has earned a reputation as being very 'document-heavy', this mainly pertains to its previous versions of 1987 and 1994. Notwithstanding these criticisms, the business value of a good QMS is universally acknowledged. In Europe, industrial companies increasingly require ISO 9001 registration from their suppliers, and the universal acceptance as an international standard is growing.

Looking at enterprise architecture from the perspective of quality management in general and ISO 9001 in particular, we see its main contribution in the integrated design, management and documentation of business processes, and their supporting IT systems. A well-designed and documented enterprise architecture helps an organisation to conform to the ISO 9001 requirements on process identification and documentation; conversely, the need for a QMS may direct focus to an enterprise architecture initiative, by putting the emphasis on those processes and resources that are critical for the company's product or service quality. In this way, quality management and enterprise architecture form a natural combination: the former is concerned with *what* needs to be designed, documented, controlled, measured, and improved, and the latter determines *how* these high-quality processes and resources are organised and realised.

2.1.5   IT Governance

The COBIT (Control Objectives for Information and Related Technology) standard for IT governance was initially published in 1996 by the Information Systems Audit and Control Association. Now in its fifth edition (Stroud 2012), COBIT is an internationally accepted IT control framework that provides organisations with 'good practices' that help in implementing an IT governance structure throughout the enterprise. It aims to bridge the gaps between business risks, control needs, and technical issues. The basic premise of COBIT is that in order to provide the information that the organisation needs to achieve its objectives, IT resources need to be managed by a set of naturally grouped processes.

The core of the COBIT framework is the control objectives and management guidelines for a set of IT processes, which are grouped into five domains:

1. Evaluate, direct and monitor
2. Align, plan and organise
3. Build, acquire and implement
4. Deliver, service and support
5. Monitor, evaluate and assess

Here, 'control' is defined by COBIT as the policies, procedures, practices, and organisational structures designed to provide reasonable assurance that business objectives will be achieved and that undesired events will be prevented or detected and corrected. The control objectives can help to support IT governance within an enterprise. For example, the control objectives of the 'Assist and advise IT customers' process consist of establishing a help desk, registration of the customer queries, customer query escalation, monitoring of clearance, and trend analysis and reporting.

Next to the framework of control objectives, COBIT provides critical success factors for achieving optimal control over IT processes, key goal indicators, which measure whether an IT process has met its business requirements, and key performance indicators, which define measures of how well the IT process is performing towards achieving its goals.

COBIT also offers a maturity model for IT governance, consisting of five maturity levels:

1. **Ad Hoc**: There are no standardised processes. Ad hoc approaches are applied on a case-by-case basis.
2. **Repeatable**: Management is aware of the issues. Performance indicators are being developed, and basic measurements have been identified, as have assessment methods and techniques.
3. **Defined**: The need to act is understood and accepted. Procedures have been standardised, documented and implemented. BSC ideas are being adopted by the organisation.
4. **Managed**: Full understanding of issues on all levels has been reached. Process excellence is built on a formal training curriculum. IT is fully aligned with the business strategy.
5. **Optimised**: Continuous improvement is the defining characteristic. Processes have been refined to the level of external best practices based on the results of continuous improvement with other organisations.

This maturity model closely resembles the Capability Maturity Model (CMM) for software development and its successor the CMMI (see Sect. 2.1.7).

According to COBIT, well-defined architectures are the basis for a good internal control environment. In many enterprises, the IT organisation will be responsible for establishing and maintaining the enterprise architecture. Whereas COBIT focuses on how one should organise the (secondary) IT function of an organisation, enterprise architecture concentrates on the (primary) business and IT structures, processes, information and technology of the enterprise. Thus, enterprise architecture forms a natural complement to COBIT. Relative to the maturity levels of COBIT, enterprise architecture will of course be most relevant in the upper level. At the Repeatable level, a first awareness of the value of architecture may arise, but there is typically no established architectural practice at the enterprise level. Only from the Defined level upwards is it recognised and used as an important instrument in planning and managing IT developments in coordination with business needs.

2.1.6   IT Service Delivery and Support

ITIL (IT Infrastructure Library) (Hanna et al. 2008) is the most widely accepted set of best practices in the IT service delivery domain. It was originally developed by the UK Office of Government Commerce (OGC), to improve management of IT services in the UK central government. The OGC's objectives were on the one hand to create a comprehensive and consistent set of best practices for quality IT service management, and on the other hand to encourage the private sector to develop training, consultancy, and tools that support ITIL. Over the years, ITIL has gained broad support and has become the worldwide *de facto* standard for IT service management. The ITIL users group, the IT Service Management Forum (*it*SMF[1]), actively promotes the exchange of information and experiences to help IT service providers manage service delivery.

ITIL comprises a series of documents giving guidance on the provision of good IT services, and on the facilities needed to support IT. ITIL has a process-oriented approach to service management. It provides codes of practice that help organisations to establish quality management of their IT services and infrastructure, where 'quality' is defined as 'matched to business needs and user requirements as these evolve.' It does this by providing guidance on the design and implementation of the various processes within the IT organisation. The core of ITIL consists of two broad groups of processes:

- Service Delivery, comprising service-level management, availability management, financial management for IT services, IT service contingency management, and capacity management;
- Service Support, covering problem management, incident management, service desk, change management, release management, and configuration management.

ITIL is complementary to COBIT. The high-level control objectives of COBIT can be implemented through the use of ITIL. Its help desk module, for example,

---

[1]http://www.itsmf.com

complements and provides details on the help desk process including the planning, implementation, post-implementation, benefits and costs, and tools. So, COBIT's control objectives tell what to do and ITIL explains how to do it, i.e., what the best-practice processes are to realise these objectives.

Management of the IT assets of an organisation is central to ITIL. This is where a well-developed enterprise architecture is very valuable. It provides IT managers with a clear understanding of the IT applications and infrastructure, the related business processes, and the various dependencies between these domains. Nearly all of the core processes identified by ITIL will benefit from this.

2.1.7 IT Implementation

The Capability Maturity Model for Software (Paulk et al. 1993), also known as the CMM and SW-CMM, is a model for judging the maturity of an organisation's software engineering processes, and provides organisations with key practices required to help them increase the maturity of these processes. In 2000, the SW-CMM was upgraded to CMMI (Capability Maturity Model Integration), which addresses the integration of software development with other engineering activities and expands the scope to encompass the entire product life cycle, including systems engineering, integrated product and process development, and supplier sourcing. The CMM's popularity has sparked off the development of similar maturity models in other fields, including enterprise architecture; see, e.g., the NASCIO Enterprise Architecture Maturity Model (NASCIO 2003).

In the CMMI maturity models in their most common form, there are five maturity levels, each a layer in the foundation for ongoing process improvement, designated by the numbers 1–5 (CMMI Product Team 2002):

1. **Initial**: Processes are usually ad hoc and chaotic. The organisation does not provide a stable environment. Success in these organisations depends on the competence and heroics of the people in the organisation and not on the use of proven processes.
2. **Managed**: The projects of the organisation have ensured that requirements are managed and that processes are planned, performed, measured, and controlled. However, processes may be quite different in each specific instance, e.g., on a particular project.
3. **Defined**: Processes are well characterised and understood, and are described in standards, procedures, tools, and methods. These standards are used to establish consistency across the organisation. Projects establish their defined processes by tailoring the organisation's set of standard processes according to tailoring guidelines.
4. **Quantitatively Managed**: Quantitative objectives for quality and process performance are established and used as criteria in managing processes. Quantitative objectives are based on the needs of the customer, end users, organisation, and process implementers.

5. **Optimising**: Process performance is continually improved through both incremental and innovative technological improvements. Quantitative process-improvement objectives for the organisation are established, continually revised to reflect changing business objectives, and used as criteria in managing process improvement.

The CMMI provides numerous guidelines for assessing the maturity of an organisation and the improvements needed in various process areas to proceed from one level to the next. Next to this familiar staged representation of the maturity model in terms of consecutive maturity levels, there is now a continuous representation as well.

In any software engineering project of substantial size, software architecture plays an important role. The context of this software architecture may be given by an enterprise architecture, which provides constraints and guidelines for individual software projects. As such, enterprise architecture is something that becomes especially useful (or even necessary) at CMMI Level 3 and beyond, where projects have to conform to organisation-wide standards and guidelines.

2.2   Architecture Methods and Frameworks

To provide more insight into the different aspects that an enterprise architecture model may encompass, we will outline a number of well-known architecture frameworks, standards and approaches. Frameworks structure architecture description techniques by identifying and relating different architectural viewpoints and the modelling techniques associated with them. They do not provide the concepts for the actual modelling, although some frameworks are closely connected to a specific modelling language or set of languages.

Most architecture frameworks are quite precise in establishing what elements should be part of an enterprise architecture. However, to ensure the quality of the enterprise architecture during its life cycle the adoption of a certain framework is not sufficient. The relations between the different types of domains, views, or layers of the architecture must remain clear, and any change should be carried through methodically in all of them. For this purpose, a number of methods are available, which assist architects through all phases of the life cycle of architectures.

2.2.1   The IEEE 1471-2000/ISO/IEC 42010 Standard

In 2000, the IEEE Computer Society approved IEEE Standard 1471-2000 (IEEE Computer Society 2000), which builds a solid theoretical base for the definition, analysis, and description of system architectures. IEEE 1471, which has since been subsumed by the ISO/IEC 42010 standard (ISO/IEC/IEEE 2011), focuses mainly on software-intensive systems, such as information systems, embedded systems, and composite systems in the context of computing. The standard uses the civil architecture metaphor to describe software system architectures. In this sense, it is similar to the framework of Zachman (see Sect. 2.2.2), although it does not try to standardise the system architecture by establishing a fixed number, or the nature of views (as in the case of the 36 cells of Zachman's framework). It also does not try to standardise the process of developing architectures, and therefore does not recommend any modelling languages, methodologies or standards. Instead, it provides, in the terms of a 'recommended practice', a number of valuable concepts and terms of reference, which reflect the 'generally accepted trends in practice for architecture description' and which 'codify those elements on which there is consensus'.

First of all, the standard gives a set of definitions for key terms such as acquirer, architect, architecture description, architectural models, architecture, life cycle model, system, system stakeholder, concerns, mission, context, architectural view, architectural viewpoint. As essential ideas we note a clear separation between an architecture and its architecture descriptions (defined as means to record architectures), and the central role of the relationship between architectural viewpoint and architectural view. The standard also provides a conceptual framework, which is meant:

- To explain how the key terms relate to each other in a conceptual model for architecture description (this model is shown in Fig. 2.5, using the UML notation for class diagrams; see also Sect. 2.3.3)

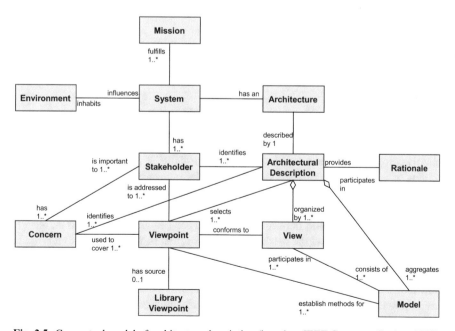

Fig. 2.5   Conceptual model of architecture description (based on IEEE Computer Society 2000)

- To explain the role of the stakeholders in the creation and use of an architecture description
- To provide a number of scenarios for the architectural activities during the life cycle: architectures of single systems, iterative architecture for evolutionary systems, architecture for existing systems and architectural evaluation

Furthermore, the standard gives six architecture description practices:

- Architectural documentation referring to identification, version, and overview information.
- Identification of the system stakeholders and of their concerns, established to be relevant to the architecture.
- Selection of architectural viewpoints, containing the specification of each viewpoint that has been selected to organise the representation of the architecture and the reasons for which it was selected.
- Architectural views corresponding to the selected viewpoints.
- Consistency among architectural views.
- Architectural rationale for the selection of the current architecture from a number of considered alternatives.

IEEE 1471 also provides a number of relevant architectural viewpoints together with their specifications in terms of concerns, languages, and modelling and analysis methods (see Annex D of the standard). It is important to note that architecture descriptions that are compliant with IEEE 1471 can be used to meet the requirements of other standards, like the Reference Model of Open Distributed Processing (described in Sect. 2.2.5).

2.2.2 The Zachman Framework

In 1987, John Zachman introduced the first and best-known enterprise architecture framework (Zachman 1987), although back then it was called 'Framework for Information Systems Architecture'. The framework as it applies to enterprises is simply a logical structure for classifying and organising the descriptive representations of an enterprise that are significant to the management of the enterprise as well as to the development of the enterprise's systems.

The framework (Fig. 2.6) in its most simple form depicts the design artefacts that constitute the intersection between the roles in the design process, that is, *owner*, *designer* and *builder*, and the product abstractions, that is, *what* (material) it is made of, *how* (process) it works and *where* (geometry) the components are relative to one another. Empirically, in the older disciplines, some other 'artefacts' were observable that were being used for scoping and for implementation purposes. These roles are somewhat arbitrarily labelled *planner* and *subcontractor* and are included in the framework graphic that is commonly exhibited.

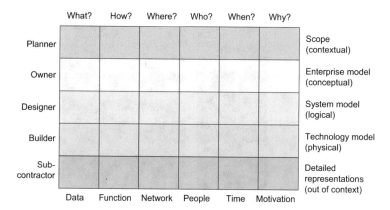

Fig. 2.6 The Zachman framework (Zachman 1987)

From the very inception of the framework, some other product abstractions were known to exist because it was obvious that in addition to *what*, *how*, and *where*, a complete description would necessarily have to include the remaining primitive interrogatives: *who*, *when* and *why*. These three additional interrogatives would be manifest as three additional columns of models that, in the case of enterprises, would depict: *who* does what work, *when* do things happen, and *why* are various choices made?

Advantages of the Zachman framework are that it is easy to understand, it addresses the enterprise as a whole, it is defined independently of tools or methodologies, and any issues can be mapped against it to understand where they fit. An important drawback is the large number of cells, which is an obstacle for the practical applicability of the framework. Also, the relations between the different cells are not that well specified. Notwithstanding these drawbacks, Zachman is to be credited with providing the first comprehensive framework for enterprise architecture, and his work is still widely used.

2.2.3   The Open Group Architecture Framework

The Open Group Architecture Framework (TOGAF) originated as a generic framework and methodology for development of technical architectures, but evolved into an enterprise architecture framework and method. From version 8 onwards, TOGAF (The Open Group 2011) is dedicated to enterprise architectures.

TOGAF has the following main components (Fig. 2.7):

- An Architecture Capability Framework, which addresses the organisation, processes, skills, roles, and responsibilities required to establish and operate an architecture function within an enterprise.

Fig. 2.7 TOGAF 9.1 (The
Open Group 2011)

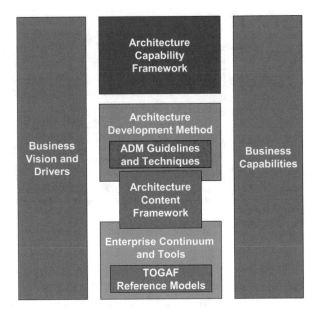

- The Architecture Development Method (ADM), which provides a 'way of working' for architects. The ADM is considered to be the core of TOGAF, and consists of a stepwise cyclic approach for the development of the overall enterprise architecture.
- The Architecture Content Framework, which considers an overall enterprise architecture as composed of four closely interrelated architectures: Business Architecture, Data Architecture, Application Architecture, and Technology (IT) Architecture.
- The Enterprise Continuum, which comprises various reference models, such as the Technical Reference Model, The Open Group's Standards Information Base (SIB), and The Building Blocks Information Base (BBIB). The idea behind the Enterprise Continuum is to illustrates how architectures are developed across a continuum ranging from foundational architectures, through common systems architectures and industry-specific architectures, to an enterprise's own individual architecture.

TOGAF's ADM (Fig. 2.8) is iterative, over the whole process, between phases and within phases. For each iteration of the ADM, a fresh decision must be taken as to:

- The breadth of coverage of the enterprise to be defined;
- The level of detail to be defined;
- The extent of the time horizon aimed at, including the number and extent of any intermediate time horizons;

Fig. 2.8 TOGAF
architecture development
method (The Open Group
2011)

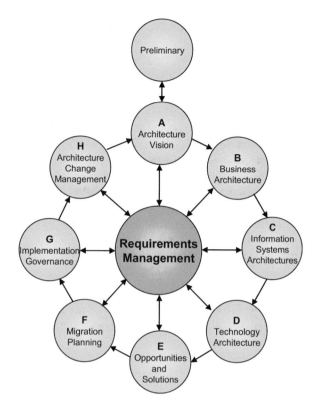

– The architectural assets to be leveraged in the organisation's Enterprise Continuum, including assets created in previous iterations of the ADM cycle within the
enterprise and assets available elsewhere in the industry.

These decisions need to be made on the basis of a practical assessment of
resource and competence availability, and the value that can realistically be
expected to accrue to the enterprise from the chosen scope of the architecture work.

As a generic method, the ADM is intended to be used by enterprises in a wide
variety of different geographies and applied in different vertical sectors/industry
types. As such, it may be, but does not necessarily have to be, tailored to specific
needs. For example:

It may be used in conjunction with the set of deliverables of another framework,
where these have been deemed to be more appropriate for a specific organisation.
(For example, many US federal agencies have developed individual frameworks
that define the deliverables specific to their particular departmental needs).

It may be used in conjunction with the well-known Zachman framework, which
is an excellent classification scheme, but lacks an openly available, well-defined
methodology.

In Sect. 6.13, we will provide more detail on combining the ArchiMate language
defined in Chap. 5 with the TOGAF framework.

2.2.4   OMG's Model-Driven Architecture

The Model-Driven Architecture (MDA) (Object Management Group 2014; Frankel 2003) aims to provide an open, vendor-neutral approach to interoperability. It builds upon the Object Management Group's modelling standards: the Unified Modeling Language (UML; see also Sect. 2.3.3), the Meta Object Facility (MOF) (Object Management Group 2015d) and the Common Warehouse Meta-model (CWM). Platform-independent application descriptions built with these standards can be realised using different open or proprietary platforms, such as Java, .NET, XMI/XML and Web services.

MDA wants to raise the level of abstraction at which software solutions are specified by defining a framework supported by a collection of standards that sets a standard for generating code from models and vice versa. Now, MDA-based software development tools already support the specification of software in UML instead of in a programming language like Java.

MDA comprises three abstraction levels with mappings between them (see Fig. 2.9):

1. The requirements for the system are modelled in a domain model or business model, historically called Computation-Independent Model (CIM) in MDA,

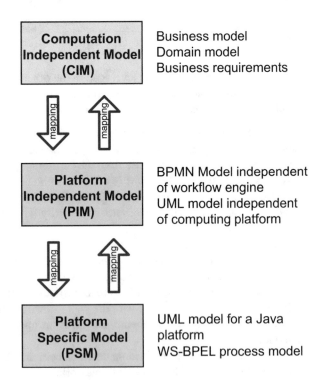

Fig. 2.9 MDA framework

which describes the situation in which the system will be used. It hides much or all information about the use of automated data processing systems.

2. The Platform-Independent Model (PIM) describes the operation of a system while hiding the details necessary for a particular platform. A PIM shows that part of the complete specification that does not change from one platform to another.

3. A Platform-Specific Model (PSM) combines the specifications in the PIM with the details that specify how that system uses a particular type of platform.

UML is endorsed as the modelling language for both PIMs and PSMs. At the CIM level, a language for business process specification such as BPMN (Sect. 2.3.2) may be used, and languages for the description of business rules and business models are also available.

One of the key features of the MDA is the notion of *mapping*. A mapping is a set of rules and techniques used to modify one model to get another model. In certain restricted situations, a fully automatic transformation from a PIM to a PSM may be possible, and software development tools will support these automated mappings. To what extent automation of mappings between CIMs and PIMs is feasible is still a topic of research. If these mappings are performed in a predefined (formal) way, relations between models of different abstraction levels can be assured. The ArchiMate language introduced in Chap. 5 would typically be positioned at the CIM level of the MDA. In Sects. 6.1.7 and 6.1.8, we describe how several ArchiMate concepts can be mapped to BPMN and UML, respectively.

The Meta Object Facility (MOF) (Object Management Group 2015c) is a standard for repositories that plays a central role in the MDA framework. A MOF-compliant repository makes it possible to manage models in an integrated fashion, even when the models are expressed in different languages. In order to make a repository effective for EA, it must be possible to model relations between models in the repository. MOF in itself does not offer a solution for this, but models in a modelling language like ArchiMate can be added in order to model these relations. In addition to MOF, OMG has developed the QVT (Queries, Views, and Transformations) specification (Object Management Group 2016b), which addresses the way mappings are achieved between models whose languages are defined using MOF and defines a standard way of querying MOF models and creating views of these models.

2.2.5 Other Frameworks

DoDAF/C[4]ISR The Command, Control, Communications, Computers, Intelligence, Surveillance, and Reconnaissance (C[4]ISR) Architecture Framework (C4ISR Architecture Working Group 1997) was originally developed in 1996, for the US Department of Defense, to ensure a common unifying approach for the commands, military services, and defence agencies to follow in describing their various architectures. The framework was retitled Department of Defense Architecture Framework (DoDAF) in 2003 (Department of Defense 2007). Although DoDAF has a rather specific target, it can be extended to system architectures that are more general. DoDAF sees the architecture description as an integration of three main views: operational view, system view, and technical view. A number of concepts and fundamental definitions (e.g., architecture, architecture description, roles, and interrelationships of the operational, systems, and technical architecture views) are provided. Some framework-compliant guidelines and principles for building architecture descriptions (including the specific product types required for all architecture descriptions), and a Six-Step Architecture Description procedure, complement them.

RM-ODP The Reference Model for Open Distributed Processing (RM-ODP) is an ISO/ITU Standard (ITU 1996) which defines a framework for architecture specification of large distributed systems. The standard aims to provide support for interworking, interoperability, portability and distribution, and therefore to enable the building of open, integrated, flexible, modular, manageable, heterogeneous, secure, and transparent systems (see also Putman 1991). The standard has four parts:

- *Part 1: Reference,* containing a motivational overview of the standard and its concepts (ITU 1996).
- *Part 2: Foundations,* defining the concepts, the analytical framework for the description of ODP systems, and a general framework for assessment and conformance (ITU 1995a).
- *Part 3: Architecture,* describing the ODP framework of viewpoints for the specification of ODP systems in different viewpoint languages (ITU 1995b). It identifies five viewpoints on a system and its environment: enterprise, information, computation, engineering, and technology.
- *Part 4: Architectural semantics,* showing how the modelling concepts from Part 2 and the viewpoint languages from Part 3 can be complemented in a number of formal description techniques, such as LOTOS, Estelle, SDL, and Z (ITU 1997).

GERAM The Generic Enterprise Reference Architecture and Methodology (GERAM) (IFIP-IFAC Task Force 1999) defines the enterprise-related generic concepts recommended for use in enterprise engineering and integration projects. These concepts can be categorised as:

- *Human-oriented concepts* to describe the role of humans as an integral part of the organisation and operation of an enterprise and to support humans during enterprise design, construction, and change.
- *Process-oriented concepts* for the description of the business processes of the enterprise;
- *Technology-oriented concepts* for the description of the supporting technology involved in both enterprise operation and enterprise engineering efforts (modelling and model use support).

The model proposed by GERAM has three dimensions: the life cycle dimension, the instantiation dimension allowing for different levels of controlled particularisation, and the view dimension with four views: Entity Model Content view, Entity Purpose view, Entity Implementation view, and Entity Physical Manifestation view. Each view is further refined and might have a number of components.

Nolan Norton Framework (Zee et al. 2000) This framework is the result of a research project of the Nolan Norton Institute (which involved 17 Dutch large companies) on current practice in the field of architectural development. Based on the information collected from companies the authors have defined a five-perspective vision of enterprise architecture:

- *Content and goals*: which type of architecture is developed, what are its components and the relationships between them, what goals and requirements has the architecture to meet? More precisely, this perspective consists of five interconnected architectures (they correspond to what we have called architectural views): product architecture, process architecture, organisation architecture, functional information-architecture, and technical information architecture.
- *Architecture development process*: what are the different phases in the development of an architecture, what is their sequence and what components have to be developed in each phase?
- *Architecture process operation*: what are the reasons for the change, what information is needed, and where do the responsibilities lie for decision making?
- *Architectural competencies*: what level of expertise should the organisation reach (and how) in order to develop, implement, and use an architecture?
- *Cost/Benefits:* what are the costs and benefits of developing a new architecture?

2.3   Description Languages

In subdomains such as business process design and software development, we find established description languages for modelling these domains. For software modelling, UML (described in Sect. 2.3.3) is of course the single dominant language. In organisation and process modelling, on the other hand, a multitude of languages are in use: there is no standard for models in this domain.

Here, we describe a number of languages for modelling business and IT We do not describe 'languages' that are merely abstract collections of concepts, such as the RM-ODP viewpoint languages, but focus on languages that either find widespread use or have properties that are interesting from the perspective of our goals in developing an enterprise architecture language.

2.3.1   IDEF

IDEF is the name of a family of languages used to perform enterprise modelling and analysis (see http://www.idef.com/ and Mayer et al. 1995; IDEF 1993; Menzel and Mayer 1998). The IDEF (Integrated Computer-Aided Manufacturing (ICAM) DEFinition) group of methods have a military background. Originally, they were developed by the US Air Force Program for Integrated Computer Aided Manufacturing (ICAM). The numbers of participants in the meetings of the IDEF user group are evidence of the widespread usage of IDEF.

Currently, there are 16 I.E. methods. Of these methods, IDEF0, IDEF3, and IDEF1X ('the core') are the most commonly used. Their scope covers:

- Functional modelling, IDEF0: The idea behind IDEF0 is to model the elements controlling the execution of a function, the actors performing the function, the objects or data consumed and produced by the function, and the relationships between business functions (shared resources and dependencies).
- Process modelling, IDEF3: IDEF3 captures the workflow of a business process via process flow diagrams. These show the task sequence for processes performed by the organisation, the decision logic, describe different scenarios for performing the same business functions, and enable the analysis and improvement of the workflow.
- Data modelling, IDEF1X: IDEF1X is used to create logical data models and physical data models by the means of logical model diagrams, multiple IDEF1X logical subject area diagrams, and multiple physical diagrams.

There are five elements to the IDEF0 functional model (see Fig. 2.10)**: the** *activity* **(or process) is represented by boxes,** *inputs, outputs, constraints,* **or controls on the activities, and** *mechanisms* **that carry out the activity. The inputs, control, output and mechanism arrows are also referred to as ICOMs.** Each activity and the ICOMs can be decomposed (or exploded) into more detailed levels of analysis. The decomposition mechanism is also indicated as a modelling technique for units of behaviour in IDEF3.

The IDEF3 Process Description Capture Method provides a mechanism for collecting and documenting processes. There are two IDEF3 description modes: process flow diagrams and object state transition network diagrams. A process flow

Fig. 2.10 IDEF0 representation

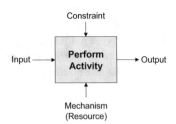

description captures knowledge of 'how things work' in an organisation, e.g., the description of what happens to a part as it flows through a sequence of manufacturing processes. The object state transition network description summarises the allowable transitions an object may undergo throughout a particular process. The IDEF3 term for elements represented by boxes is a Unit Of Behaviour (UOB). The arrows (links) tie the boxes (activities) together and define the logical flows. The smaller boxes define junctions that provide a mechanism for introducing logic to the flows.

The IDEF family provides support for the modelling of several architectural views. However, there are no communication mechanisms between models. The fact that they are isolated hinders the visualisation of all models as interrelated elements of an architectural system. This also means that a switch between views is not possible.

IDEF is widely used in the industry. This indicates that it satisfies the needs of the users within acceptable limits. The IDEF family is subject to a continuous process of development and improvement. Still, IDEF0, IDEF1X, and IDEF3 are rather stable and rigid languages, and IDEF0 and IDEF1X have been published as standards of the National Institute of Standards and Technology.

2.3.2 BPMN

The Business Process Modelling Notation (BPMN) was developed by the Business Process Management Initiative (BPMI), which has since merged with the Object Management Group. The BPMN standard (Object Management Group 2013) specifies a graphical notation that serves as a common basis for a variety of business process modelling and execution languages.

As the name already indicates, BPMN is restricted to process modelling; applications or infrastructure are not covered by the language. The main purpose of BPMN is to provide a uniform notation for modelling business processes in terms of activities and their relationships (Fig. 2.11).

The first version of BPMN only defined a concrete syntax, i.e., a uniform (graphical) notation for business process modelling concepts. However, there is a formal mapping to the XML-based business process execution language WS-BPEL. BPMN 2 (Object Management Group 2013) provides a semantics for execution of these models, and many business process management tool suites now support this.

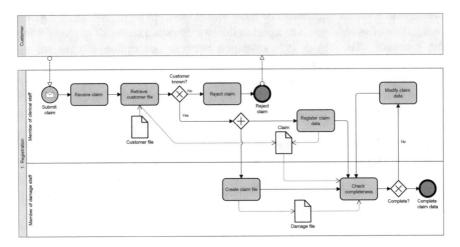

Fig. 2.11 Example model in BPMN

2.3.3 UML

The Unified Modeling Language (UML) (Booch et al. 1999; Object Management Group 2015a) is currently the most important industry-standard language for specifying, visualising, constructing and documenting the artefacts of software systems. The language's development is managed by the Object Management Group (OMG). It emerged from the combination of three existing notations, Booch, OMT, and Objectory, authored by the 'three amigos' Booch, Rumbaugh, and Jacobson. Other influences came from Harel's state charts and Shlaer-Mellor's object life cycles.

UML is intended to be used by system designers. Consequently, UML models are only clear to those who have a sound background in computer science, in particular in object orientation (see Fowler and Scott 1999). However, leaving out the more technical details, UML models should be sufficiently understandable for illustrative and explanatory purposes to business engineers and organisation specialists. Although UML was originally developed for the design of object-oriented software, its use has expanded to other areas, including architecture modelling. In its current version, UML 2 (Object Management Group 2015a), several architectural concepts are included.

Through object orientation, UML covers all possible modelling domains one can think of. From the point of view of UML, the world consists of only one kind of component-like thing, called *object*, together with a connection-like thing, called *link*. Examples of objects are persons, organisational units, products, projects, archives, and machines. The objects consist of a static part and a dynamic part. The dynamic part is a description of *how* such an object does what it should do.

The links reflect any kind of connection or relation between objects, varying from concrete ('is-boss-of') to abstract ('might-be-relevant-for'). In this way links can express relations, connections, dependencies, relevancies of a physical, logical, temporal, structural, behavioural, similar, or complementary character, to mention a few examples.

UML is a disturbingly rich combination of 13 sublanguages each having its own (sub)scope of the complete UML scope, and each with its own diagram to model a specific aspect of a (software) system. The 13 diagrams can be grouped in three categories:

- structure: package diagrams, class diagrams, object diagrams, composite structure diagrams;
- behaviour: use case diagrams, state diagrams, sequence diagrams, timing diagrams, communication diagrams, activity diagrams, interaction overview diagrams;
- implementation: component diagrams, deployment diagrams.

Each diagram type describes a system or parts of it from a certain point of view, and contains its own symbols. However, the diagram types and UML meta-model are interrelated; no strict separation between views and meta-model concepts has been made. Consequently, the relations between modelling concepts in different diagrams are often ill-defined. We will not show the notation of all these diagrams and modelling concepts here; a good overview is given in Fowler and Scott (1999).

Moreover, apart from the package, component, and deployment diagrams, each of the other languages is in itself a disturbingly rich combination of visual building blocks. Some of these languages have large mutual overlap, e.g., activity diagrams and state chart diagrams. The advantage of such richness is the expressiveness of the language; a serious disadvantage is the readability and accessibility of the language. The large numbers of symbols and diagrams make the learning curve of UML pretty steep for new users.

Next to the graphical notation, UML contains the Object Constraint Language (OCL), a textual language for specifying constraints on model elements. The meaning of UML diagrams is not always very intuitive and sometimes requires quite careful study. For an experienced UML user, however, the language is not too difficult to use.

To extend the modelling vocabulary or give distinctive visual cues to certain kinds of abstractions that often appear, UML offers three kinds of mechanisms:

- A 'stereotype' is an extension of the vocabulary of UML that allows the creation of new kinds of building blocks, based on existing ones. A stereotype is used to define specialisations of existing elements of UML meta-model.
- A 'stereotype attribute' is an extension of the properties of a UML element that allows the creation of new information in that element's specification. Stereotype attributes can be added to all existing meta-model elements.
- UML offers the possibility to define so-called profiles attuned to certain problem domains. A profile is a kind of dialect of the original modelling language, better suited to reflect the characteristics of a certain problem domain. A profile uses tagged values and stereotypes to express a specific and precise model.

Although these extension mechanisms give UML considerable flexibility, they also are a weak point of the language. Stereotypes, especially when applied too much, can confuse readers who are not familiar with them. In such cases stereotypes take away one of the strong points of UML, which is standardisation.

UML partially has a formal basis. Semantics for individual diagram types exist, in a more or less formal manner. However, a formalised integrated semantics for the whole language is still lacking. This lack of an integrated semantics makes it difficult to define rigorous analysis techniques.

Perhaps UML's most important asset is its broad tool support: there are many commercial as well as public domain modelling environments. As many of these environments offer means to translate a model into executable code, e.g. Java, some form of analysis is being provided: through the execution. Often also other means of analysis and verification are being provided, through partial consistency checking, or forms of animation or explicit translation to a different domain where a particular verification can be performed.

2.3.4   Architecture Description Languages

The term 'Architecture Description Language' (ADL) is used to refer to a (usually formal) language to describe a software architecture in rather general terms. A wide variety of ADLs exist, with several differences in the exact concepts that they offer: some focus on structural aspects of an architecture, while others pay more attention to the dynamic aspects. In general, their concepts are defined at a rather generic level: although they are usually intended for modelling the application level, the use of the concepts is not restricted to this. As a result of this high abstraction level, constructing and reading ADL specifications may be difficult for non-expert users. An advantage is the precise definition and formal foundation of the languages, which may make them suitable as an underlying language for more specific concepts. In Medvidovic and Taylor (2000) the basics of ADLs are described, and a large number of ADLs are compared.

Although the concepts used in ADLs are very generic, they are mainly applied in the field of software architecture. In addition to ADLs with a general applicability, there are ADLs with a much more specific application area (e.g., MetaH, for the guidance, navigation, and control domain). Because of the formal nature and high abstraction level of the concepts, ADLs are mainly suitable for users with a technical background. They are unsuitable as a means for communication at the organisational level.

In principle, ADL concepts are sufficiently flexible to create models in several domains. However, they are mainly applied, and are most suitable, for the application domain (i.e., to describe software architectures). As Acme (1998) is claimed to be suitable as a general architecture description and interchange language, we believe its concepts can be used as a representative for ADLs. The core concepts are:

- component;
- connector;
- system (a configuration of components and connectors);
- port (a point of interaction with a component);
- role (a point of interaction with a connector);
- representation (used to model hierarchical composition);
- rep-map (which maps a composite component or connector's internal architecture to elements of its external interface).

ADLs like Acme generally have an academic background, and limited usage. However, some of these concepts have been included in UML and SysML (Object Management Group 2015e). In this way, these concepts are made available to a large user base and will be supported by a wide range of software tools.

2.3.5 Suitability for Enterprise Architecture

In the previous sections, we have given an overview of several languages for modelling in the area of organisations, business processes, applications and technology. It is clear that none of these has succeeded in becoming 'the language' that can cover all domains. In general, there are a number of aspects on which almost all of these languages score low:

- The relations between domains (views) is poorly defined, and the models created in different views are not further integrated.
- Most languages have a weak formal basis and lack a clearly defined semantics.
- Most languages miss the overall architectural vision and are confined to either the business or the application and technology subdomains.

In contrast to organisation and business process modelling, for which there is no single dominant language, in modelling applications and technology UML has become a true world standard. UML is the mainstream modelling approach within ICT. This makes UML an important language not only for modelling software systems, but also for business processes and for the general business architecture. However, UML is not readily accessible and understandable for managers and business consultants; therefore, special visualisations and views of UML models should be provided.

2.4 Service-Oriented Architecture

The emergence of the service-oriented computing (SOC) paradigm and Web services technology, in particular, has aroused enormous interest in service-oriented architecture (SOA). Probably because such hype has been created around it, there are a lot of misconceptions about what SOA really is. Numerous Web services evangelists make us believe that if you could divide the world into service requestors, service providers and a service registry, you would have an SOA (e.g., Ferris and Farrell 2003). Others emphasise that SOA is a way to achieve interoperability between distributed and heterogeneous software components, a platform for distributed computing (e.g., Stevens 2002).

Even though dynamic discovery and interoperability are important benefits of Web services, a purely technological focus would be too limited and would fail to appreciate the value of the (much more general) service concept. SOA represents a set of design principles that enable units of functionality to be provided and consumed as services. The interesting thing is that the service concept applies equally well to the business as it does to software applications. Services provide the 'units of business' that represent value propositions within a value chain or within business processes. This essentially simple concept can and should be used not just in software engineering, but also at all other levels of the enterprise architecture, to achieve ultimate flexibility in business and IT design.

The idea of systems (applications or components) delivering services to other systems and their users has really caught on in software engineering. Moreover, in other relevant disciplines there is also an increasing focus on services. In fact, economic development is to an increasing extent driven by services, not only in traditional service companies but also in manufacturing companies and among public service providers (Illeris 1997). In the service economy, enterprises no longer convert raw materials into finished goods, but they deliver services to their customers by combining and adding value to bought-in services. As a consequence, management and marketing literature is increasingly focusing on service design, service management, and service innovation (e.g., see Fitzsimmons and Fitzsimmons 2000, or Goldstein et al. 2002).

Another area in which the service concept plays a central role is IT service management. This discipline is aimed at improving the quality of IT services and the synchronisation of these services with the needs of their users (Bon 2002). The ITIL approach described in Sect. 2.1.6, for example, puts great emphasis on services and service-level agreements.

The service concept is the result of a separation of the 'external' and 'internal' behaviour of a system. As such, it should be self-contained and have a clear purpose from the perspective of its environment. The internal behaviour, on the other hand, represents what is required to realise this service. For the 'consumers' of a service, the internal behaviour of a system or organisation is usually irrelevant: they are only interested in the functionality and quality that will be provided.

2.4.1   Service-Oriented Technologies

Web services are a large body of industry standards developed and managed by organisations such as W3C, UN-CEFACT, OMG, The Open Group and OASIS.

Next to these 'classical' and rather heavy-weight standards-based Web services, lighter service-oriented protocols based on Representational State Transfer (REST) have become widely used.

A parallel development in service orientation is the ability to access ICT resources, such as computing power, storage capacity, devices, and applications as services over the Internet. This provisioning of commoditised computing and storage capabilities over the Internet is collectively called Cloud Computing, with Software-as-a-Service (SaaS), Platform-as-a-Service (PaaS) and Infrastructure-as-a-Service (IaaS) as important categories. This gives large and small organisations access to ICT resources otherwise out of reach and provides advantages regarding cost and scalability. This development has its origin in e-science environments (computing grids), but has found extensive usage for a variety of other application areas like healthcare, education, finance, life sciences, industry and entertainment.

These service developments strengthen the impact of service orientation on business architectures, because they extend the application of service-oriented technology to the domain of utility computing and ASP, while its focus on sharing of ICT resources has additional impact on the way ICT infrastructure services are managed within organisations.

Several tool vendors recognise the importance of integrating real-time IT service management with operational business processes and customer services. They provide tools that propagate events at the IT level to process owners and customers; conversely, problem reports from users and customers can be propagated to the IT service level. Such integration should offer operational business–IT alignment giving insight into real-time performance and service levels. These developments create a strong case for service-oriented methods, since they apply service orientation in real-time operational service management allowing services to be used for on-line decision making and problem solving.

2.4.2   *Relevance and Benefits for Enterprise Architecture*

One might ask why we should focus on services for architecting the enterprise and its IT support. What makes the service concept so appealing for enterprise architecture practice? First, there is the fact that the service concept is used and understood in the different domains making up an enterprise. In using the service concept, the business and IT people have a mutually understandable 'language', which facilitates their communication. Second, service orientation has a positive effect on a number of key differentiators in current and future competitive markets, i.e., interoperability, flexibility, cost effectiveness, and innovation power.

Of course, Web services and the accompanying open, XML-based standards are heralded for delivering true interoperability at the information technology level (Stevens 2002). However, service orientation also promotes interoperability at higher semantic levels by minimising the requirements for shared understanding: a service description and a protocol of collaboration and negotiation are the only requirements for shared understanding between a service provider and a service user. Therefore, services may be used by parties different from the ones originally perceived, or used by invoking processes at various aggregation levels.

Interoperability and separation of internal and external behaviour provide new dimensions of flexibility: flexibility to replace or substitute services in cases of failure, flexibility to upgrade or change services without affecting the enterprise's operations, flexibility to change suppliers of services, flexibility to reuse existing services for the provision of new products or services. This will create new opportunities for outsourcing, rendering more competition and more efficient value chains.

By focusing on services, many opportunities for reuse of functionality will arise, resulting in more efficient use of existing resources. In addition, outsourcing and competition between service providers will also result in a reduction of costs. From a macroscopic point of view, costs will be reduced as a result of more efficient distribution of services in value chains.

The ability to interoperate and collaborate with different partners, including partners not familiar with the enterprise, provides new opportunities for innovation. Existing services can be recombined, yielding new products and services, ad hoc liaisons with new partners become possible that exploit emerging business opportunities, and newly developed services can easily be advertised and offered all over the world, and integrated in the overall service architecture.

Finally, service orientation stimulates new ways of thinking. Traditionally, applications are considered to support a specific business process, which in turn realises a specific business service. Service orientation allows us also to adopt a bottom-up strategy, where the business processes are just a mechanism for instantiating and commercially exploiting the lower-level services to the outside world. In this view, the most valuable assets are the capabilities to execute the lower-level services, and the business processes are merely a means of exploitation.

Some organisations have already started to implement service-oriented enterprise architectures, but the future will determine whether service orientation really can deliver on all its promises of increased interoperability, flexibility, and innovation power.

Chapter 3
Foundations

Marc M. Lankhorst, Leon van der Torre, H.A. (Erik) Proper, Farhad Arbab, Frank S. de Boer, and Marcello Bonsangue

3.1 Getting to Grips with Architectural Complexity

Companies have long recognised the need for an integrated architectural approach, and have developed their own architecture practice. Nevertheless, they still experience a lack of support in the design, communication, realisation, and management of architectures. Several needs can be categorised as follows with respect to different phases in the architecture life cycle:

- **Design**: When designing architectures, architects should use a common, well-defined vocabulary to avoid misunderstandings and promote clear designs. Such a vocabulary must not just focus on a single architecture domain, but should allow for the integration of different types of architectures related to different domains. Next to a common language, architects should be supported in their design activities by providing methodical support, general and organisation-specific guidelines, best practices, drawing standards, and other means that promote the quality of the architectures. Furthermore, to facilitate the design process, which is iterative and requires changes and updates to architectures, support for tracking architectural decisions and changes is desirable.

M.M. Lankhorst (✉)
BiZZdesign, Capitool 15, 7521 PL Enschede, The Netherlands
e-mail: m.lankhorst@bizzdesign.com

L. van der Torre
University of Luxembourg, Luxembourg, Luxembourg

H.A. Proper
Luxembourg Institute of Science and Technology, Luxembourg, Luxembourg

F. Arbab • F.S. de Boer • M. Bonsangue
University of Leiden, Leiden, The Netherlands

© Springer-Verlag Berlin Heidelberg 2017
M. Lankhorst et al., *Enterprise Architecture at Work*, The Enterprise Engineering
Series, DOI 10.1007/978-3-662-53933-0_3

– **Communication**: Architectures are shared with various stakeholders within and outside the organisation, e.g., management, system designers, or outsourcing partners. To facilitate the communication about architectures, it should be possible to visualise precisely the relevant aspects for a particular group of stakeholders. Especially important in this respect is to bring about a successful communication on relations among different domains described by different architectures (e.g., processes vs. applications), since this will often involve multiple groups of stakeholders. Clear communication is also very important in the case of outsourcing of parts of the implementation of an architecture to external organisations. The original architect is often not available to explain the meaning of a design, so the architecture should speak for itself.

– **Realisation**: To facilitate the realisation of architectures and to provide feedback from this realisation to the original architectures, links should be established with design activities on a more detailed level, e.g., business process design, information modelling, or software development. Companies use different concepts and tools for these activities, and relations with these should be defined. Furthermore, integration with existing design tools in these domains should be provided.

– **Change**: An architecture often covers a large part of an organisation and may be related to several other architectures. Therefore, changes to an architecture may have a profound impact. Assessing the consequences of such changes beforehand and carefully planning the evolution of architectures are therefore very important. Until now, support for this has been virtually non-existent.

3.1.1 Compositionality

In current practice, enterprise architectures often comprise many heterogeneous models and other descriptions, with ill-defined or completely lacking relations, inconsistencies, and a general lack of coherence and vision. The main driver behind most of the needs identified above is the *complexity* of architectures, their relations, and their use. Many different architectures or architectural views co-exist within an organisation. These architectures need to be understood by different stakeholders, each at their own level. The connections and dependencies that exist among these different views make life even more difficult. Management and control of these connected architectures is extremely complex. Primarily, we want to create *insight* for all those that have to deal with architectures.

The standard approach to dealing with the complexity of systems is to use a compositional approach, which distinguishes between parts of a system, and the relations between these parts. To understand how a car functions, we first describe the parts of the car such as the engine, the wheels and the air conditioning system, and then we describe the relationship among these parts. Likewise, we understand the information system of a company as a set of systems and their relations, and we understand a company as a set of business processes and their relations.

Compositionality also plays a central role in the architectural approach. For example, the IEEE 1471 standard defines architecture as the fundamental organisation of a system embodied in its components, their relationships to each other, and to the environment (together with principles guiding its design and evolution). Moreover, compositionality also plays a role when varying viewpoints on a system are defined. The latter type of decompositions are usually functional, in the sense that the functionality of an architecture is decomposed in the functionality of its parts and their relations.

3.1.2 Integration of Architectural Domains

The main goal of our approach is the integration of architectural domains, to deal with the complexity of architecture as a discipline, and to provide insight for all those that have to deal with architectures. There are many instances of this integration problem, of which we discuss two examples below. These examples also play their role in the remaining chapters of this book. In general, some integration problems can be easily solved: for example, by using an existing standard; others are intrinsic to the architectural approach and cannot be 'solved' in the usual sense. These hard cases are intrinsic to the complexity of architecture, and removing the problem would also remove the notion of architecture itself. We cannot get rid of the integration problems; we can only develop concepts and tools to make it easier to deal with these issues. This is illustrated by Example 1 below.

Example 1 As a first example of an integration problem, consider Fig. 3.1, which contains several architectures. The five architectures may be models expressed in UML, or models from cells of Zachman's architectural framework, or any kind of combination. For instance, there may be a company that has modelled its applications in UML and its business processes in BPMN. In all these cases, it is unclear how concepts in one view are related to concepts in another view. Moreover, it is unclear whether views are compatible with each other.

The integration of the architectures in Fig. 3.1 is problematic because these five architectures are developed by distinct stakeholders with their own concerns. Relating architectures means relating the ideas of these stakeholders, most of which remain implicit. A consequence is that we often cannot assume to have complete one-to-one mappings, and the best we can ask for is that views are in some sense consistent with each other. This is often called a problem of *alignment*, and the UML–BPMN example is called a business–IT alignment problem.

In complex integration cases that involve multiple stakeholders, it is clear that integration is a bottom-up process, in the sense that first concepts and languages of individual architectural domains are defined, and only then is the integration of the domains addressed. We can summarise Example 1 by observing that the integration of architectures is hard due to the fact that architectures are given and used in

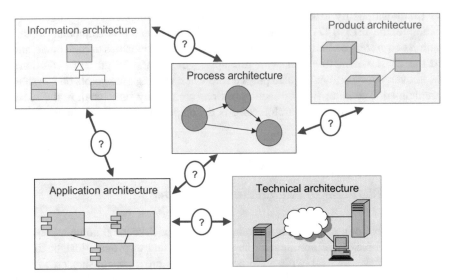

Fig. 3.1 Heterogeneous architectural domains

practice, and cannot be changed. It is up to those who integrate these architectures to deal with the distinct nature of architectural domains.

When we talk about the integration of architectural domains, we need a language in which we can describe these domains. For example, some sources refer to entities and relations, as in entity–relationship diagrams. Others refer to classes and objects, like in object-oriented modelling and software engineering. And yet others refer to concepts and instances; for example, in the area of conceptual modelling. These abstract concepts have been defined at a high level of abstraction, but often they also contain some implicit assumptions. For example, entities and relations are assumed to be finite, because databases are finite, which is not the case with concepts. There are many architecture languages, some of which we have discussed in Chap. 2, but here also terminology varies.

An architecture language is not only needed for the description of integrated architectures, but also a prerequisite for linking the different tools used in the various architectural domains (Lankhorst et al. 2005). Furthermore, an integrated language facilitates the analysis of architectures across domains and the reuse of analysis results from specific domains on an integrated level.

It would be foolish to suggest an entirely new architecture language that is built from scratch and ignores already existing developments. In this book we therefore take a pragmatic approach, and reuse elements from other languages, approaches, and techniques whenever possible.

When looking at everyday architectural practice, it is clear that some integration problems occur more frequently than others. A typical pattern is that some architectural models describe the structure of an architecture at some point in time, whereas other models describe how the architecture changes over time. The second example that we discuss in this chapter addresses this issue.

Example 2 As a second example of an integration problem, consider the first two viewpoints of the IEEE 1471 standard (IEEE Computer Society 2000): the structural viewpoint and the behavioural viewpoint. How are structure and behaviour related?

The second example touches on a problem that has been studied for a long time: the integration of structural and behavioural models. One instance of this problem is how structural concepts like software components are related to behavioural concepts like application functions. Another area where this issue has been studied is in formal methods and in simulation.

The enterprise modelling language described in Chap. 5 shows a strong symmetry between the behavioural and the structural aspects. A service is an 'external' reflection of the 'internal' behaviour that realises it, analogous to the way in which an interface is an 'external' reflection of the 'internal' structure behind it. For the internal behaviour, we distinguish between individual behaviour assigned to an individual structural element and collective behaviour assigned to a collaboration of structural elements.

In the next sections, we will go deeper into the foundations of our approach to modelling enterprise architectures, and in particular into the integration of architectures. However, just like architectural diagrams are often misinterpreted due to the fact that each stakeholder interprets the picture in its own way, architectural concepts also are often misinterpreted. This has led to the IEEE 1471 standard which had the ambition to resolve these ambiguities. Despite the fact that there seems to be increasing consensus on the terminology used, in practice one still finds many distinct definitions of relevant architectural concepts, such as model, meta-model, and view.

In this chapter we define the notions we need in the remainder of the book. These definitions are based on several standards, most importantly the IEEE 1471 standard, the conventions in UML, and other conventions used in daily practice. In general, we develop a language to talk about the integration of architectural domains, and we have to be precise as all concepts have been used in other areas too, and typically are already overloaded. In the architectural definitions we incorporate fundamental notions of architecture; for example, that an architecture never refers to reality, but only to some abstraction of it.

3.2 Describing Enterprise Architectures

To cope with the complexity of enterprise architecture, the representation of the essence of an architecture in the unambiguous form of a model can be of great value. We do not want to define the details of the individual architectural domains themselves. That would be the task of the architecture discipline within that particular field. Instead, we concentrate on what is essential for *enterprise* architecture, and therefore we limit ourselves to the core elements of these domains and focus especially on the relations and interactions between them. Precise definitions and constraints will help us to create insight into the complexity of the enterprise architecture and to evade conflicts and inconsistencies between the different domains. For this, we use *models*.

A model is an abstract and unambiguous conception of something (in the real world) that focuses on specific aspects or elements and abstracts from other elements, based on the purpose for which the model is created. In this context, models are typically represented using a formalised graphical or textual language. Because of their formalised structure, models lend themselves to various kinds of automated processing, visualisation, analysis, tests, and simulations. Furthermore, the rigour of a model-based approach also compels architects to work in a more meticulous way and helps to dispel the unfavourable reputation of architecture as just drawing some 'pretty pictures'.

Different stakeholders, however, have a different view of the world. Not everyone's needs can be easily accommodated by a single model. Let us therefore first consider what happens if some viewer observes 'the universe' around him or her.

3.2.1 Observing the Universe

We assume that any viewer that perceives the world around him or her first produces a conception, i.e., a mental representation, of that part he or she deems relevant. The viewer cannot communicate directly about such a conception, unless it is articulated it somehow. In other words, a conception needs to be represented. Peirce (1969a–d) argues that both the perception and conception of a viewer are strongly influenced by the viewer's interest in the observed universe.

In our case, the viewer is a stakeholder of (part of) the organisational, technical, or other systems that make up the enterprise, i.e., the universe that the viewer observes. The conception of this universe then is the architecture of the enterprise. The representation of this architecture is an architecture description, which may contain models of the architecture, but also, for example, textual descriptions.

The underlying relationships between stakeholder, enterprise, architecture and architecture description can be expressed in the form of a tetrahedron, as depicted in Fig. 3.2, which is based on the FRISCO tetrahedron (Falkenberg et al. 1998).

3.2.2 Concerns

So in conceiving a part of the enterprise, stakeholders will be influenced by their particular interest in the observed enterprise, i.e., their concerns. Note that stakeholders, as well as their concerns, may be regarded at an aggregated as well as at an individual level. For example, a single business manager conceiving an information system is a stakeholder. The collective business management, however, can also be seen as a stakeholder of the information system.

Fig. 3.2 Relationship
between enterprise,
stakeholder, architecture,
and architecture description

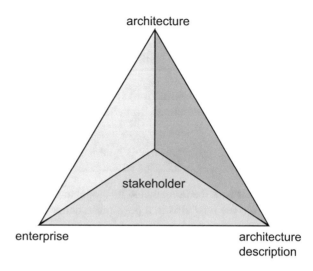

Yet concerns are not the only factors that influence a stakeholder's conception of a domain. Another important factor is the preconceptions a stakeholder may harbour as they are brought forward by his or her social, cultural, educational, and professional background. More specifically, in the context of system development, architects will approach a domain with the aim of expressing the domain in terms of some set of concepts, such as classes, activities, constraints, etc. The concepts an architect is used to using (or trained to use) when modelling some (part of a) domain, will strongly influence the conception of that architect. As Abraham Maslow said: 'If the only tool you have is a hammer, you tend to see every problem as a nail.'

We therefore presume that when architects model a domain, they do so from a certain perspective. In general, people tend to think of the universe (the 'world around us') as consisting of related elements. In our view, however, to presume that the universe consists of a set of elements is already a subjective choice, made (consciously or not) by the viewer observing the universe. The choice being made is that 'elements' (or 'things') and 'relations' are the most basic concept for modelling the universe. In this book, we will indeed make this assumption, and presume that an architect's conception of the universe, i.e., an architecture, consists of such elements.

3.2.3   Observing Domains

Viewers may decide to zoom in on a particular part of the universe they observe, or, to state it more precisely, they may zoom in on a particular part of their conception of the universe, in our case the enterprise. This allows us to define the notion of a domain as:

Domain: any subset of a conception (being a set of elements) of the universe that is conceived of as being some 'part' or 'aspect' of the universe.

In the context of (information) system development, we have a particular interest in unambiguous abstractions from domains. This is what we refer to as a model:

Model: a purposely abstracted and unambiguous conception of a domain.

Note that both the domain and its model are conceptions harboured by the same viewer. We are now also in a position to define more precisely what we mean by modelling:

Modelling: the act of purposely abstracting a model from (what is conceived to be) a part of the universe.

For practical reasons, we will understand the act of modelling also to include the activities involved in the representation of the model by means of some language and medium. We presume architects not only to be able to represent (parts of) their conceptions of the enterprise, but also to be able to represent (parts of) the perspectives they use in producing this conception. This requires architects to be able to reflect on their own working process. When modelling a domain in terms of, say, UML class diagrams, we presume that they are able to express the fact that they are using classes, aggregations, associations, etc., to describe the domain being modelled.

3.2.4   Views and Viewpoints

Very often, no stakeholder apart from perhaps the architect is interested in the architecture in its full scope and detail. As we observed in Sect. 3.2, different viewers have different conceptions of the universe they perceive. Their concerns dictate which parts of an enterprise architecture they deem relevant.

Stakeholders therefore require specific *views* of an architecture that focus on their concerns and leave out unnecessary information. Since we put models central in our description of architectures, this implies that we have to provide different views of these models to accommodate the stakeholders' needs.

A view is specified by means of a *viewpoint*, which prescribes how views that address particular concerns of the stakeholders are constructed, given the architecture under consideration. What should and should not be visible from a specific viewpoint is thus entirely dependent on the stakeholder's concerns.

The ISO/IEC/IEEE 42010:2011 standard (ISO/IEC/IEEE 2011) defines views and viewpoints as follows:

> **View:** expresses the architecture of the system of interest from the perspective of one or more stakeholders to address specific concerns, using the conventions established by its viewpoint
> **Viewpoint:** a specification of the conventions for constructing, interpreting, using and analysing one type of architecture view

Simply put, a view is what you see, and a viewpoint tells from where you are looking. For example, you might define a 'financial viewpoint' that tells you how to show, say, the costs for building certain applications. Applying that viewpoint to a model of the new customer relationship management (CRM) system of your company results in a financial view of that system which shows its costs.

3.2.5 Ways of Working

Creating and using architecture models typically involves several related 'ways of working' (Wijers and Heijes 1990):

- A **way of thinking**: articulates the assumptions about the kinds of problem domains, solutions, and modellers involved.
- A **way of modelling**: identifies the core concepts of the language that may be used to denote, analyse, visualise, and/or animate architecture descriptions.
- A **way of communicating**: describes how the abstract concepts from the way of modelling are communicated to human beings, e.g., in terms of a textual or a graphical notation (syntax, style, medium).
- A **way of working**: structures (parts of) the way in which a system is developed. It defines the possible tasks, including subtasks, and ordering of tasks, to be performed as part of the development process. It furthermore provides guidelines and suggestions (heuristics) on how these tasks should be performed.
- A **way of supporting**: the support that is offered by (possibly automated) tools for the handling (creating, presenting, modifying, etc.) of models and views. In general, a way of supporting is supplied in the form of some computerised tool.
- A **way of using**: identifies heuristics that:
  - define situations, classes of stakeholders, and concerns for which a particular model or viewpoint is most suitable;
  - provide guidance in tuning the viewpoint to specific situations, classes of stakeholders, and their concerns.

In this book, we try to give attention to each of these 'ways', since in our view they are all essential to the effective use of architectures.

3.2.6 Enterprise Architecture Models

In an ideal situation, we would have a single model for an enterprise architecture, to ensure coherence and consistency between all its different parts. In reality, such a model will probably never exist, especially when we talk about multiple architectural domains. However, it is something we may 'think into existence' without actually constructing the model. In practice, an architecture (and especially an enterprise architecture) will arise in a bottom-up fashion. Partial models from different domains will be constructed according to the needs in those domains. Where these touch upon each other, inconsistencies may appear, which need to be resolved eventually since the real-world system being designed must of course be consistent. In this way, we slowly move towards this Platonic underlying model, and the partial models from which it is constructed can be seen as views of the total architecture.

Having such a single underlying model makes it possible to create powerful techniques for visualisation and analysis of enterprise architectures, even if this model is incomplete and not fully consistent. Currently, if a stakeholder requires information on some aspect of an architecture that crosscuts several domains, a specialised view of the architecture will probably be patched together manually by integrating information from many different sources in these domains.[1] If we suppose that there is this single underlying model of an architecture, a view of this architecture can be expressed as a projection or subset of this model. Appropriate software tools can then automatically generate these views.

Consider the example in Sect. 3.1 on the integration of structural and behavioural views. To relate the two, we have to consider models and transitions of models. But in relating static and dynamic aspects, a new distinction appears. Are we talking about changes within a model, or changes of the modelling concepts, i.e., the conception of the universe? That is, is the change exogenous or endogenous? This distinction reveals itself only when we relate the structural and behavioural descriptions, not when we consider them in isolation.

As another example, consider the change from batch processing systems to service-oriented architectures. Someone working with batch processing systems 20 years ago could not explain to us today why they do not use service-oriented architecture, because the concept of service-oriented architecture did not yet exist. Since the concept had not been invented yet, it is not just a structural change within the model, but a change at the meta-level of the concepts underlying the model.

The importance of the set of concepts which are used to describe an architecture is acknowledged in the frequent use of 'ontology' within modelling. In our case, we refer to the set of concepts as the *signature* of the architecture. Moreover, the change of signatures and models leads to our notion of *actions in views*. This is explained in more detail in Sect. 3.3.

---

[1] One of the ArchiMate project partners has in the past invested more than one man-year in creating one specific view of an existing architecture. . .

3.3 Pictures, Models, and Semantics

In many engineering disciplines, modelling a system consists of constructing a mathematical model that describes and explains it. In the fields of enterprise and software architecture, however, there is an overwhelming tendency to see pictures and diagrams as a form of model rather than as a form of language, or, to be more precise, as a form of structure that helps in visualising and communicating system descriptions. In other words, in architecture there is a tendency to replace mathematical modelling by ad hoc visualisations.

In this book we follow the standard practice in engineering disciplines. Consequently, when we compare architectures like the ones in Fig. 3.1, we ignore irrelevant issues that have to do with arbitrary visualisation. We therefore distinguish between the *content* and the *visualisation* of a model or view, where the first refers to the concepts involved, and the second refers to the form in which these are presented.

For example, in one visualisation of an architecture a process may be visualised as a circle, and in another one by a square. Moreover, the content may express that one concept is more important than another one, which is visualised by drawing the first concept above the second one. The same relation of importance can also be visualised by the intensity of the colour which is used to visualise the concepts. The architect is motivated to make explicit whether visual information like 'above' or 'red' has a meaning in the model, or is incidental. When something is incidental the architect is motivated to remove it from the picture, as it only distracts from the message of the picture. When it is meaningful, its meaning has to be made explicit. When a new viewpoint is defined, the content and its visualisation can be defined in two separate phases.

The 'content' and 'visualisation' should be interpreted here in a loose way. For example, the visualisation may also include input devices such as menus or buttons, and the content may also include actions that change the model by for example adding or deleting concepts. Actions in models are used here to deal with interaction with the user.

Our motivation to stress the importance of modelling is that there is something about architecture independent of visualisation. Two distinct views, which are based on viewpoints from stakeholders with distinct concerns, still have something in common. This is called the *semantics* of the architecture. Semantics does not have to be explicitly given, it can also be an unspoken common understanding among the users of the architecture. It does not have to be one unified semantics, as there can also be several semantics for different purposes and uses of the architecture. But in the latter case, these semantics again have something in common. Perhaps they just have to be consistent.

The importance of semantics has been emphasised in several other areas too, with a related motivation. In some parts of computer science, the term 'semantics' of something in a model is used to refer to the 'effect' of that something in the model, referring to the dynamics within that model. In linguistics there is a much older distinction between syntax, semantics, and pragmatics. Another example is in the meaning of information on the Web: Web pages have traditionally been used to describe all kinds of issues, but they often refer to the same objects using distinct terminology. This led Tim Berners-Lee to the invention of the semantic Web, in which ontologies play a crucial role.

3.3.1   Symbolic and Semantic Models

To make the notion of semantics explicit, we distinguish between a symbolic model and a semantic model (Arbab et al. 2007). A *symbolic model* expresses properties of architectures of systems. It therefore contains symbols that refer to reality, which explains the name of this type of model.

> A **symbolic model** expresses properties of architectures of systems by means of symbols that refer to reality.

The role of symbols is crucial, as we do not talk about systems without using symbols. The reason is that systems are parts of reality, and we can only talk about reality by using some symbolic form of communication.

When stakeholders refer to architectures and systems, they can do so only by interpreting the symbols in the symbolic models. We call such an interpretation of a symbolic model a *semantic model*.

> A **semantic model** is an interpretation of a symbolic model, expressing the meaning of the symbols in that model.

A semantic model does not have a symbolic relation to architecture, as it does not contain symbolic references to reality.

However, there is a relation between semantic model and reality, because a semantic model is an abstraction of the architecture. To understand this relation between semantic model and architectures, one should realise that an important goal of modelling is to predict reality. When a symbolic model makes a prediction, we have to interpret this prediction and test it in reality. The relevant issue in the relation between a system and semantic models of it is how we can translate results such that we can make test cases for the symbolic model.

There are various ways in which we can visualise the relation between the four central concepts of enterprise, architecture, symbolic model, and semantic model. We put the concept of architecture central, as is illustrated in Fig. 3.3.

There are three important observations we have to make here. First, the above four concepts and their relations are used in engineering both for informal as well as

Fig. 3.3 The enterprise, its architecture, symbolic and semantic models

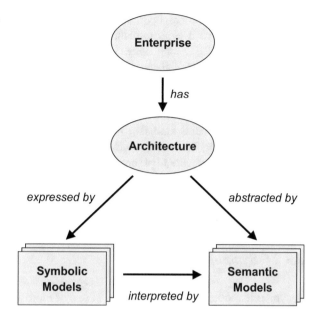

formal models. The relevant distinction we emphasise between symbolic and semantic models is the distinction between using symbols to refer to reality, and abstractions of reality that only refer to reality by interpreting the symbols of the symbolic model. Note that this is not the same distinction as that between informal and formal models: within the class of informal models, expressed for example in natural language, both kinds exist, as well as within the class of formal models, expressed for example in first-order logic.

Second, an architecture may be expressed by multiple symbolic models, and one symbolic model may in turn be interpreted by several semantic models. For example, we might define separate semantic models for performance and for cost of a system that is expressed by one symbolic model, e.g., in UML.

Third, in architecture often a distinction is made between the *architectural semantics* and the *formal semantics* of a modelling language. As explained in Sect. 3.2.1, the enterprise under consideration is thought of in terms of architecture concepts, which exist in the minds of, for instance, the enterprise architect. These concepts can be represented in models, which are expressed in a modelling language. Architectural semantics is defined as the relationship between architectural concepts and their possible representations in a modelling language (Turner 1987). To understand this distinction, consider Venn diagrams. They are useful structures for the visualisation of the language of Boolean logic, but they are not a model themselves. Their semantic model is given by the set-theoretical explanation of their meaning. The formal semantics of a model or language, on the other hand, is a mathematical representation of specific formal properties of that model or language. The formal semantics of a computer program, for example, expresses the possible computations of that program. Different branches of formal semantics exist, such as denotational, operational, axiomatic, and action semantics. Harel and Rumpe (2004) give a clear explanation of the need for rigorously defining the semantics of modelling languages.

There are two kinds of abstraction we use in creating a model of reality. The first is abstracting from (properties of) the precise entity in reality to which a concept refers. This occurs for example when we make a model of the static structure of an application in terms of its components, leaving out (i.e., abstracting from) their behaviour. The second kind is abstraction from differences between entities in reality by grouping them into a single concept. This is sometimes referred to as generalisation, and occurs for example when we use the concept 'employee', which groups the individuals in a company. This is related to the notion of 'sorts' discussed below.

3.3.2   Symbolic Models

A symbolic model is the formalisation of one or more aspects of the architecture of a concrete system. It comprises those parts of an architecture that can be modelled mathematically, as opposed to the more pragmatic aspects of an architecture that are concerned with characteristic notions like rationale, goals, and plans.

A symbolic model is expressed using a description language, a representation of the model that is often confused with its interpretation. For example, the expression $3 + 5$ may be intended to mean a particular natural number, but here is just notation for the syntactic model of the natural numbers. Strictly speaking, a description language describes both the *syntactic structure* of the model and its *notation*, i.e., the words or symbols used for the concepts in the language. As we explained in Sect. 3.3.1, we make a strict separation between structure and the notation, and we will use the term 'model' to refer to the structure.

The core of every symbolic model is its *signature*. It categorises the entities of the symbolic model according to some names that are related, linguistically or by convention, to the things they represent. These names are called *sorts*. Relations between entities of some sorts and operations on them are also declared as relation symbols in the signature. After the relations have been specified, they can be used in languages for constraining further or analysing the nature of the symbolic model. An example is in order here, before we go any further.

Fig. 3.4 exhibits a structural description of the employees of a company.

We need to recall that the above is a syntactic structure; that is, a description of a symbolic model with a signature whose sorts are *Employee* and *Director*, and with respective entities related by a relation named *Responsible_for*. As yet we have

Fig. 3.4 Symbolic model of the director–employee relationship

Fig. 3.5 Extended
symbolic model

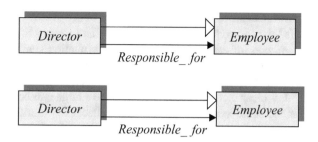

assigned no meaning to it; we have only categorised the entities of the symbolic model into two categories and named a relation between the entities belonging to two sorts. The syntactic names used for the sorts and relations push our intuition some steps ahead: we know what an employee is, what a director is, and what responsible for means. However, while these syntactic names help us in our understanding, they are also the main source of confusion in the communication and analysis of an architecture. We could have named the above sorts X and Y better to retain the meaningless quality of the syntax, and avoid confusion with semantics.

A signature thus provides a conceptual glossary in whose terms everything else in the symbolic model must be described, similar to an English dictionary for the English language. Additionally, a signature comprises information to capture certain aspects of the ontology of an architecture. For example, it may include hierarchical information between sorts in terms of an 'is-a' relationship, or containment information in terms of an 'includes' relationship, or dependency information in terms of a 'requires' relationship. Signatures that contain this additional information are more general than a glossary. They provide a conceptual schema, similar to the schema provided to biologists by the species classification.

For example, Fig. 3.5 extends the previous signature with an 'is-a' relationship between the sorts *Director* and *Employee* (denoted by a UML inheritance relation), intuitively suggesting that every director is also an employee.

Moreover, the symbolic model may also contain a set of actions, and the signature a set of action symbols, the meaning of which we discuss below.

3.3.3 Semantic Models

The formalised meaning of a symbolic model is given by a semantic model, an interpretation of the symbolic model. A semantic model usually assumes the existence of some mathematical objects (sets, for example), used to represent the basic elements of a symbolic model. Operations and relations of a symbolic model are mapped to usually better understood operations and relations amongst the mathematical objects.

As an example, the formal semantics of a signature is provided by a collection of sets (one for each sort of the signature), and a set of relations and functions among them, one for each relation symbol and function symbol in the signature. Hierarchical information between sorts is captured by the ordinary subset inclusion, whereas containment information is denoted by the usual element-of relation.

It is clear that, in general, there can be a large number of different interpretations for the same symbolic model. This reflects the intuition that there can be many architectures that fit a specific architecture description. In fact, the signature of a symbolic model of an architecture specifies only some basic building blocks by means of which the architecture is described.

In other words, we see the formal semantics of a symbolic model as a concrete collection of mathematical objects interpreting a system according to a specific architecture description. As such, it involves concrete components and their concrete relationships which may change in time because of the dynamic behaviour of a system. Concrete situations of a system are described by means of variables typed according to the sort of the individuals they are referring to. More concretely, for a symbolic model, we will denote by $x{:}T$ a variable x which ranges over individuals of sort T. For example, we could use the logical sentence

$$\exists\, x : Director.\, \forall y : Employee.\, Responsible\_for(x, y)$$

to constraint the interpretation of the sort *Director* to be a non-empty set. Note that since *Director is_a Employee*, also the interpretation of the latter sort will be non-empty.

The actions occurring in a symbolic model are interpreted as changes of the model based on interaction with the user. To define actions, we have to define the input variables of the action, and how we can retrieve these input variables from the user. In Chap. 8 we discuss the use of actions in models in viewpoints and visualisation, and in Chap. 11 we describe some technical aspects of implementing these actions in models.

Finally, in our approach described more explicitly in Chap. 9, the formal semantics is rich enough to capture the dynamics of a system by interpreting the symbolic (and often pictorial) information available for describing business and software processes in the ArchiMate language discussed in Chap. 5.

In the remainder of the book, whenever we use the unqualified terms 'model' or 'semantics' of an architecture, we refer to its *symbolic* model and *formal* semantics, which is the common interpretation of these terms in the architecture discipline.

3.3.4 Semantics in ArchiMate Versus UML

The ArchiMate approach can be contrasted with the original approach in UML, which we described in Chap. 2. In this approach, semantics was explicitly left out of the program. People who used the models could develop semantics for them, but a general semantics was not supplied. This approach also stemmed from the origins of UML as a combination of three existing notations that did not have formal semantics. Hence, the focus of UML was and is on notation, i.e., syntax, and not on semantics. Although some of the diagrams of the more recent versions of UML have a formal semantics (see, e.g., the token-based Petrinet-like semantics of activity diagrams in UML 2), there is no overall semantics for the entire language.

We have taken the opposite approach. We do not put the notation of the ArchiMate language central, but rather focus on the meaning of the language concepts and their relations. Of course, any modelling language needs a notation and we do supply a standard way of depicting the ArchiMate concepts, but this is subordinate to the architectural semantics of the language.

3.4 Summary

An integrated architectural approach is indispensable to control today's complex organisations and information systems. It is widely recognised that a company needs to 'do architecture'; the legacy spaghetti of the past has shown us that business and ICT development without an architectural vision leads to uncontrollable systems that can only be adapted with great difficulty. However, architectures are seldom defined on a single level. Within an enterprise, many different but related issues need to be addressed. Business processes should contribute to an organisation's products and services, applications should support these processes, systems and networks should be designed to handle the applications, and all of these should be in line with the overall goals of the organisation. Many of these domains have their own architecture practice, and hence different aspects of the enterprise will be described in different architectures. These architectures cannot be viewed in isolation.

For example, architectural domains are related, and structural and behavioural viewpoints are related. The integration has to deal with the fact that the various viewpoints are defined by stakeholders with their own concerns.

The core of our approach to enterprise architecture is therefore that multiple domains should be viewed in a coherent, integrated way. We provide support for architects and other stakeholders in the design and use of such integrated architectures. To this end, we have to provide adequate concepts for specifying architectures on the one hand, and on the other hand support the architect with visualisation and analysis techniques that create insight into their structure and relations. In this approach, relations with existing standards and tools are to be emphasised; we aim to integrate what is already available and useful. The approach that we follow is very generic and systematically covers both the necessary architectural concepts and the supporting techniques for visualisation, analysis, and use of architectures.

We adopt a framework around a stakeholder, enterprise, architecture, and architecture description as a viewer with universe, conception, and representation. The view and viewpoint of the stakeholder are the result of modelling, an act of purposely abstracting a model from reality, i.e., from a domain that is conceived to be a part of the universe. These views consist of a set of enterprise architecture models.

Within this framework, a distinction is made between the content of a view and its visualisation, and a distinction is also made between a symbolic model, which refers to the enterprise architecture, and a semantic model as an abstraction from the architecture and which interprets the symbolic model. The core of every symbolic model is its signature, which categorises the entities of the symbolic model.

Chapter 4
Communication of Enterprise Architectures

H.A. (Erik) Proper, Stijn J.B.A. Hoppenbrouwers, and Gert E. Veldhuijzen van Zanten

4.1 Introduction

Describing architectures is all about communication. If some architecture description is not used as a means of communication in some shape or form, then this description should not have been created in the first place. Whatever the role of an *architecture description* is, it always involves some communicative aspect. Consider, as an illustration, the potential *uses* of architecture descriptions as identified in the IEEE 1471 standard (IEEE Computer Society 2000):

- Expression of the system and its (potential) evolution.
- Analysis of alternative architectures.
- Business planning for transition from a legacy architecture to a new architecture.
- Communications among organisations involved in the development, production, fielding, operation, and maintenance of a system.
- Communications between acquirers and developers as a part of contract negotiations.
- Criteria for certifying conformance of implementations to the architecture.
- Development and maintenance documentation, including material for reuse repositories and training material.
- Input to subsequent system design and development activities.
- Input to system generation and analysis tools.

H.A. Proper (✉)
Luxembourg Institute of Science and Technology, Luxembourg, Luxembourg

S.J.B.A. Hoppenbrouwers
Radboud University Nijmegen, Nijmegen, The Netherlands

G.E. Veldhuijzen van Zanten
Dutch Tax and Customs Administration, Apeldoorn, The Netherlands

© Springer-Verlag Berlin Heidelberg 2017
M. Lankhorst et al., *Enterprise Architecture at Work*, The Enterprise Engineering Series, DOI 10.1007/978-3-662-53933-0_4

- Operational and infrastructure support; configuration management and repair; redesign and maintenance of systems, subsystems, and components.
- Planning and budget support.
- Preparation of acquisition documents (e.g., requests for proposal and statements of work).
- Review, analysis, and evaluation of the system across the life cycle.
- Specification for a group of systems sharing a common set of features, (e.g., product lines).

Each of these uses of architecture involves forms of communication. In this vein, in this chapter we present a 'communication-aware' perspective of enterprise architectures. In doing so, we provide both a theoretical and a practical perspective of the issues involved in the communication of enterprise architectures. The theoretical perspective will focus on communication during system development in general, where the word system should be interpreted as any open and active system, consisting of both human and computerised actors, that is purposely designed. The practical perspective will take shape as a set of practical guidelines that should aid architects in the selection (and definition) of architecture description languages and approaches that are apt for a specific (communication) situation.

Architecture descriptions are used to communicate the architecture of a planned or pre-existing system. This could be a system that is part of an enterprise, an organisation, a business, an information system, a software system, or the hardware infrastructure. The communication about the system and its architecture is likely to take place between different stakeholders of that system.

In this book, the primary focus is on architectural models of a graphical (as opposed to a textual or verbal) nature. One may refer to these as architectural models 'in the narrow sense'. In this chapter, however, we are concerned with architecture descriptions in 'the broader sense'. In other words, textual, verbal, or any other types of architecture descriptions are included.

At present, many description languages are already available to architects, while many more are being created by both academia and industry. Why all these languages? How does one select the language that is most apt in a given situation? Such questions beg for a well-conceived answer. In line with the old adage 'practice what you preach', we argue that just as proper requirements engineering is needed for the development of systems, proper requirements should also be formulated for languages and approaches that are to be used as vehicles for communication during system development. In formulating these requirements, several factors should be taken into account, such as the development goals, the communication goals, the concerns, personal goals, abilities, and attitudes of the actors involved, etc.

We set out to provide a theoretical underpinning of the issues involved, as well as practical guidelines that will aid architects in selecting the best approach for their architectural communicative needs. We will therefore start out with a theoretical exploration of the issues involved in communication during system development (Sects. 4.2 and 4.3), followed by the application of this exploration to the field of enterprise architecture (Sect. 4.4).

4.2 System Development as a Knowledge Transformation Process

In essence, we regard system development as a knowledge transformation process whereby conversations are used to share and create knowledge pertaining to both the system being developed, as well as the development process itself. The notion of 'conversation' should be interpreted here in the broadest sense, ranging from a single person producing an (architectural) description, via a one-on-one design or elicitation session, to a workshop with several stakeholders, and even the widespread dissemination of definitive architectures. This way of thinking provides a frame of thought with which one can better understand the (communicative) requirements posed on architecture description languages.

4.2.1 System Development Community

Given our focus on communication, it is important to identify the actors that can play a role in the communication that takes place during the system development process. These actors are likely to have some stake with regards to the system being developed. Examples of such actors are problem owners, prospective actors in the future system (such as the future 'users' of the system), domain experts, sponsors, architects, engineers, business analysts, etc.

These actors, however, are not the only 'objects' playing an important role in system development. Another important class of objects are the many different documents, models, forms, etc., that represent bits and pieces of knowledge pertaining to the system that is being developed. This entire group of objects, and the different roles they can play, is what we shall refer to as a system development community.

> **System development community**: a group of objects, such as actors and representations, which are involved in the development of a system.

(We will clarify below why we regard documents as being part of the community.)

The actors in a system development community will (typically as a consequence of their stakes) have some specific interests with regards to the system being developed. This interest implies a sub-interest with regard to (the contents of) the system descriptions that are communicated within the community. This interest, in line with the ISO/IEC/IEEE 42010:2011 standard (ISO/IEC/IEEE 2011), is referred to as the *concern* of stakeholders.

> **Concern**: an interest of a stakeholder with regards to the architecture description of some system, resulting from the stakeholder's goals, and the present or future role(s) played by the system in relation to these goals.

Some examples of concerns are:

- The current situation with regards to the computerised support of a business process.
- The requirements of a specific stakeholder with regards to the desired situation.
- The improvements, which a new system may bring, to a pre-existing situation in relation to the costs of acquiring the system.
- The potential impact of a new system on the activities of a prospective user.
- The potential impact of a new system on the work of the system administrators that are to maintain the new system.

4.2.2   System Development Knowledge

The system development community harbours knowledge about the system being developed. The communication occurring within a system development community essentially is aimed at creating, furthering, and disseminating this knowledge. Depending on their concerns, stakeholders will be interested in different knowledge topics pertaining to the system being developed.

We will now briefly explore the kinds of knowledge that are relevant to a system and its development; in other words, the knowledge topics that can be distinguished. In the next subsections, we will discuss in more detail in what ways this knowledge can be made (more) explicit.

During system development, members of the system development community will create and exchange knowledge pertaining to different topics. We can make a first distinction between the target domain pertaining to the system being developed and the project domain, about the development process itself. We have borrowed these terms from the Information Services Procurement Library (ISPL) (Franckson and Verhoef 1999). For both of these knowledge domains, further refinements can be made with regards to the possible topics. We identify the following additional characterisations:

- **Perspective**: Artefacts, such as systems, can be considered from different perspectives. Some examples are:
  - business, application, and technology aspects of a (computerised) information system;

- social, symbolical, and physical aspects of a system;
- process, information, actors, and technology featuring in a system.

In Chap. 8, the notion of 'viewpoint' will be discussed in depth. A viewpoint takes a specific perspective of a system. The concept of viewpoint is, however, not synonymous with perspective as the former includes some additional items, such as the modelling language that is to be used to describe the system from the given perspective. In contrast, a perspective is purely 'topical'.

- **Scope**: Given a domain, such as a system or a development project, we can identify several scopes when approaching the domain: enterprise-wide, department-specific, task-specific, etc.
- **Design chain**: When considering the design of some artefact, a distinction can be made between:

  - *Purpose*: to what purpose the artefact is needed.
  - *Functionality*: what functionality the artefact should provide to its environment.
  - *Design*: how it should realise this functionality.
  - *Quality*: how well it should do so.
  - *Costs*: at what cost it may do so, and may be constructed.

  This distinction applies to the target domain as well as the project domain. In the latter case, the project's execution plan/strategy is the designed artefact.
  Based on the above distinction, knowledge topics can be characterised in terms of their focus on, for example, functionality or quality in isolation, or their focus on bridging the gaps between purpose, functionality, and design in terms of design rationale.
- **Historical perspective**: Given an artefact with a design, one may consider different versions of this artefact's design over time.
  In the case of a system, one may consider the current version, the version that will be in existence after the development project has finished, and the (sketchy) version of the 'future' system that serves as a navigational beacon in a sea of possibilities to guide future development. In the case of a development process, one may consider the execution plan/strategy that is being used at the moment, or the plan/strategy that was used before.
- **Abstraction level**: When considering a domain, one may do so at several levels of abstraction. Various forms of abstraction can be distinguished: for example, type-instance, generalisation/is-a, encapsulation, and hiding of implementation details.

As mentioned before, depending on their concerns, stakeholders may be interested in different knowledge topics. For example, a financial controller will be interested in an investment perspective of the overall scope of a future system, a designer will be interested in all aspects of the design chain from different perspectives, etc.

4.2.3 Explicitness of Knowledge

The actors in a system development community have a need to communicate system development knowledge among each other. In the field of knowledge management, a key distinction is made between *explicit* and *tacit* knowledge (Nonaka and Takeuchi 1991). *Explicit knowledge* refers to knowledge that can be externalised in terms of some representation. With representation of knowledge, we refer to the process of encoding knowledge in terms of some language on some medium, e.g., creating an architecture model.

However, not all forms of knowledge lend themselves well to explicit representation. For example, the ability to maintain one's balance on a bicycle is learned by (painful) trial and error rather than reading instructions. This knowledge is actively and personally passed on from generation to generation: parents assist their children in this process by encouraging them and by protecting them from serious injury during the trial-and-error process. In Nonaka and Takeuchi (1991), this is referred to as *socialising* as a means to transfer knowledge that cannot be made explicit. The type of knowledge concerned, which cannot easily be represented on a medium, is referred to as *tacit knowledge*.

Our focus is on the communication of system development knowledge by way of explicit representations, in other words *explicit knowledge*. In the context of this book, these representations mainly take the form of architecture descriptions. As discussed in Sect. 4.1, our initial theoretical considerations cover development of systems in general. In accordance with this generalisation we will, for now, use the terms *systems description* and *system description language* rather than the terms *architecture description* and *architecture description language*.

System descriptions are essentially forms of explicit knowledge pertaining to an existing/future system: its design, the development process by which it was/is to be created, the underlying considerations, etc. Given this focus, we can make a more precise classification with regards to what we mean by 'explicitness'. Based on Franckson and Verhoef (1999) and Proper (2001), we identify the following dimensions of explicitness for representations of system development knowledge:

– **Formality**: The degree of formality indicates the type of language used to represent the knowledge. Such a language could be formal, in other words a language with an underlying well-defined semantics in some mathematical domain, or it could be informal—not mathematically underpinned, typically natural language, graphical illustrations, animations, etc.
– **Quantifiability**: Different aspects of the designed artefact, be it (part of) the target or the project domain, may be quantified. Quantification may be expressed in terms of volume, capacity, workload, effort, resource, usage, time, duration, frequency, etc.
– **Executability**: The represented knowledge may, where it concerns artefacts with operational behaviour, be explicit enough so as to allow for execution. This execution may take the form of a simulation, a prototype, generated animations, or even fully operational behaviour based on executable specifications.

- **Comprehensibility**: The knowledge representation may not be comprehensible to the indented audience. Tuning the required level of comprehensibility of the representation, in particular the representation language used, is crucial for effective communication. The representation language may offer special constructs to increase comprehension, such as stepwise refinements, grouping/clustering of topically related items/statements, etc.
- **Completeness**: The knowledge representation may be complete, incomplete, or overcomplete with regards to the knowledge topic (see previous subsection) it intends to cover.

4.2.4 Transformations of Knowledge

During the development of a system, the knowledge about the system and its development will evolve. New insights emerge, designs are created, views are shared, opinions are formed, design decisions made, etc. These all lead to transformations of the 'knowledge state' of the development community as a whole. The transformations of this 'knowledge state' are brought about by conversations. This immediately raises the question: what are these 'knowledge states'?

The discussion above already provides us with some insight into the answer to this question. The representations and the actors in a development community can both be seen as *harbouring* certain *knowledge topics*. As such, both representations and actors are (potential) *knowledge carriers*. Knowledge topics refer to some subdomain of the system being developed and/or its development process. The knowledge topics can therefore be classified further in terms of their focus, scope, etc., as discussed in Sect. 4.2.2.

The actual knowledge that is harboured by a knowledge carrier is not explicitly taken into account. The knowledge that is available from/on/in a knowledge carrier is a subjective notion. An aspect of this knowledge that we can reason about more objectively is its level of explicitness, as we have seen in Sect. 4.2.3.

The knowledge as it is present in a development community can be seen to evolve through a number of states. Knowledge first needs to be introduced into the community, either by creating the knowledge internally or importing it from outside the community. Once the knowledge has been introduced into a community, it can be shared among members of that community. Sharing knowledge between different actors may progress through a number of stages. We distinguish three major stages:

- **Aware**: An actor may become aware of (possible) knowledge by way of the sharing by another actor.
- **Agreed**: Once knowledge is shared, an actor can make up his or her own mind about it, and decide whether or not to *agree* to the knowledge shared.
- **Committed**: Actors who agree to a specific knowledge topic may decide actually to commit to this knowledge. In other words, they may decide to adapt their future behaviour in accordance with this knowledge.

There is no way to determine objectively and absolutely the level of awareness, agreement, or commitment of a given set of actors. It is in the eyes of the beholder. Since these 'beholders' are actors in the system development community, we can safely assume that some of them will be able to (and have a reason to) judge the level of sharing of knowledge between sets of actors, and communicate about this.

4.3 Conversation Strategies

The knowledge transformations as discussed in the previous section are brought about by conversations. These conversations may range from 'atomic' actions involving a small number of actors, via discussions and workgroups, to the development process as a whole. This has been illustrated informally in Fig. 4.1.

Each conversation is presumed to have some *knowledge goal*: a knowledge state which the conversation aims to achieve (or to maintain). In achieving this goal, a conversation will follow a *conversation strategy*. Such a strategy is needed to achieve the goal of the conversation, starting out from the current state.

Conversations take place in some situation that may limit the execution of the conversation. We may characterise such a situation further in terms of situational factors:

- **Availability of resources**: Refers to the availability of resources that can be used in a conversation. The availability of resources can be refined to more specific factors such as time for execution, actors, intellectual capacities needed from the actors, or financial means.
- **Complexity**: The resources needed for the conversation, the knowledge being conversed about, etc., will exhibit a certain level of complexity. This complexity also influences the conversation strategy to be followed. Examples of such complexity factors, inspired by Franckson and Verhoef (1999), are the heterogeneity of the actors involved, the quantity of actors, complexity of the technology used, the complexity of the knowledge being conversed about, and the size of the gap between the initial knowledge state and the desired knowledge state.
- **Uncertainty**: If you want to determine a conversation strategy fit for a given situation, you have to make assumptions about the knowledge goal, the initial

Fig. 4.1 Example sequence
of conversations

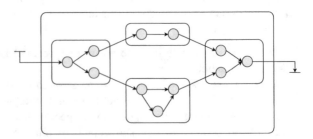

state, the availability of resources, as well as the complexities of these factors. During the execution of a conversation, some of these assumptions may prove to be wrong. For example, the commitment of certain actors involved may be lower than anticipated (initial state); materials needed for a workshop may not be available on time (resources); during a requirements elicitation session it may come to the fore that the actors involved do not (yet) have enough knowledge about the future system and its impact to formulate/reflect on the requirements of the future system (initial state).

Note that it may actually be part of a conversation strategy to first initiate conversations that aim to reduce these uncertainties, in order to reduce potential adverse consequences.

If you formulate a conversation strategy, you should take all of the above-mentioned factors into account. A conversation strategy should typically cover at least the following elements:

- **Execution plan**: As we said before, a conversation can be composed of subconversations. Each of these subconversations focuses on a sub-goal, but they all contribute towards the goal of the conversation as a whole. The execution plan of a (composed!) conversation consists of a set of subconversations, together with a planned execution order.
- **Description languages**: The description languages to be used in the conversation(s).
- **Media**: The kind of media to be used during the conversation(s).
- **Cognitive mode**: The cognitive mode refers to the way in which knowledge is gathered or processed by the actors involved in a conversation. We distinguish two options:

  - *Analytical approach*: When information is processed analytically, the available information is simplified through abstraction in order to reach a deeper and more invariant understanding. An analytical approach is typically used to handle complexity.
  - *Experimental approach*: When using an experimental approach, the project actors learn from doing experiments. The purpose is to reduce uncertainties by generating more information. Experiments can, for example, be based on prototypes, mock-ups, benchmark tests of migrated components, or other kinds of techniques which make the results of migration scenarios visible.

You may need to combine the two cognitive modes in specific situations, in particular in the case of conversations that are composed of several smaller subconversations.

- **Social mode**: The social mode is the way in which the actors executing the system development process collaborate with the actors from the business domain. We distinguish two options:

  - *Expert-driven*: In an expert-driven approach, project actors (the experts) will produce descriptions on the basis of their own expertise, and interviews and observations of business actors. The descriptions can then be delivered to the business actors for remarks or approval.

- *Participatory*: In a participatory approach, the project actors produce the descriptions in close cooperation with some or all the business actors, e.g., in workshops with presentations, discussions and design decisions. A participatory approach may allow the acquisition of knowledge, the refinement of requirements and the facilitation of organisational change.

– **Communication mode**: We can distinguish a small number of basic patterns of communication here, as covered by combinations of the following five factors:

- *Speaker–hearer ratio*: Most typically many to one, one to many, one to one, many to many.
- *Response*: Simply whether or not an answer is expected from the hearer; if a response is indeed expected, one response may lead to a further response, leading to dialogue and turn taking.
- *Time lag*: Whether or not communication takes some time between 'speaking' and 'hearing'. Consider the difference between a telephone call and an e-mail message.
- *Locality*: Whether or not there is a perceived distance between participants. Note that this is a relative notion; two people communicating via videophone between Tokyo and Amsterdam may feel 'close', while two people from different departments housed in the same building may feel 'distant'. Distance can be not only physical, but also cultural.
- *Persistency*: Whether or not a message can be kept after communication, i.e., can be 'reread'. This is of course closely linked to the medium used, but it may also be related to the status of a document: persistency of a 'temporary document' or intermediary version may actually be counterproductive.

We can use combinations of these factors to typify many different modes of communication, which can have a major impact on the resources required for communication and the likelihood that a knowledge goal is reached. For example, one-to-many communication is relatively efficient and effective, assuming that no immediate (n:1) response is given; however, if a time lag is added, n:1 responses become possible but the one participant will have to invest much time to digest all these responses. Also, if n:1 responses are given rapidly, but the communication is persistent (e.g., people respond through altered copies of a file), then these responses are no problem except for the load on the recipient. And if many relatively distant people participate, in-depth and context-dependent communication will be difficult.

In a modelling context, not all combinations (communication modes) will be relevant, but it is still vital to consider things like 'Do I expect anyone to respond to this model?'; 'How many people will have to respond?'; 'How distant are they?'; 'How quick will the response (have to) be?'; 'How long will it take me to process responses?', etc.

Fig. 4.2 From knowledge
goal to conversation
strategy

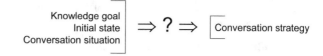

A summary of this discussion is provided in Fig. 4.2. Given a *knowledge goal*, an *initial state*, and *conversation situation*, a *conversation strategy* can be determined, which should lead us from the *initial state* to the *knowledge state* as desired by the *knowledge goal*, taking into account the *conversation situation* at hand.

4.4   Architectural Conversations

After the theoretical discussions of the previous sections, we now return to the practice of communicating enterprise architectures. The situation as depicted in Sect. 4.2 may indeed portray the underlying mechanics in theory, but it still leaves practitioners with the question of how actually to produce such a conversation strategy. In all fairness, current research into these matters is still in its initial stages. The theoretical model as discussed above will have to be scientifically validated and refined. In addition, practical heuristics should be formulated, matching elements from conversation strategies to conversation situations and thus addressing the gap between the knowledge goal and the initial state.

Even so, we can already provide practitioners with some guidance in selecting conversation strategies to communicate about enterprise architectures, by reducing the discussion of selecting a conversation strategy to the selection of a class of architectural conversation in conjunction with an appropriate architectural viewpoint. To direct this selection, we will define a number of classes of architectural knowledge goals. The selected viewpoints identify *what* shall be conversed about, and what *language* (and language conventions) shall be used to do so, while the selected *conversation technique* identifies the style of conversation that is to be used.

So this section provides a discussion of the classes of architectural knowledge goals and conversation techniques that we distinguish within the context of enterprise architecture, as well as their relationship. In Chap. 8, the notion of viewpoint will be discussed in more detail, and additional heuristics on the selection of viewpoints and conversation types will be given.

4.4.1   Knowledge Goals

In Sect. 4.2.4, we identified three major stages in communicating knowledge: awareness, agreement, and commitment. Based on these and on the levels of sharing of knowledge and explicitness of knowledge as identified in Sect. 4.2.3, we can identify the following classes of knowledge goals that you may want to achieve in a conversation:

- **Introduction of knowledge**: This refers to situations where there is a need to introduce into or create new knowledge in a (part of a) development community. These kinds of knowledge goals typically lead to training or awareness sessions.
- **Agreement to knowledge**: With this class of knowledge goals, we refer to situations in which the mutual agreement of different stakeholders (with their own specific stakes and concerns!) needs to be improved or validated.
- **Commitment to knowledge**: In these cases, the knowledge goal goes beyond that of achieving agreement. Stakeholders should be willing to act upon the knowledge they agree to.

Note that the introduction of knowledge, as described above, may pertain to a subset of the development community. At the start of a system development project, the development team may not (yet!) have knowledge pertaining to the specific application domain. Domain experts and other informants, by nature of their roles, do have this knowledge. The development community as a whole comprises at least both the development team and the domain experts. A domain analysis session involving, for example, a business analyst and a domain expert *introduces* (part of) the domain knowledge of the domain expert into the development team.

4.4.2   Conversation Techniques

In architecture development, we find a number of common conversation techniques where it concerns the communication of architectural models:

- **Brown-paper session**: Structured brainstorm-like group session (up to about 15 people) in which items (keywords or short phrases) are elicited from the individuals in the group in answer to a question such as: 'What are the key functionality issues in our current IT architecture?' Typically, every individual item is written on a small adhesive note ('PostIt'). The items are then collected on a sheet of paper (traditionally of the cheap *brown* kind) and, by means of an open and creative group process, structured and categorised. This may involve adding, deleting, merging, or changing items. Usually, a mediator or facilitator is involved.
- **Elicitation interview**: An interview where an analyst puts informative questions to the informants. The aim is to gather knowledge from the informants. Interviews can be more or less 'open': they can be strictly focused or guided, but the conversation can also be left open to go where the interest of the interviewer or informants leads it.
- **Workshop**: Involves one to, say, 15 people, working on a model or view interactively, mediated by an architect or analyst. This class also encompasses so-called joint modelling sessions. A popular, effective, and realistic technique

is to project a view or model and have a facilitator adapt it in full view of the participants, thus generating immediate feedback. With a few participants, a workshop can of course simply take place behind a screen and keyboard.

- **Validation interview:** An interview where an analyst will aim to find out if the view or model matches the views and expectations of an informant. This could be a view or model that has been communicated to the informants beforehand, or during the interview. A validation interview will typically be much more 'closed' than an elicitation interview: there will have to be some systematic approach by which validity of the view or model is checked.
- **Committing review**: A group of stakeholders are presented with a number of alternative models or views and their impact. They are requested to select one alternative and commit to this alternative based on their insights into the potential impact. This typically involves a formal decision-making processes (Franckson and Verhoef 1999).
- **Presentation**: Involves one to three people presenting a model or view to a group of, say, up to a hundred people. One may decide to elicit feedback, but this is usually gathered afterwards, in a more personal way, or at least 1:1 (e.g. through a round of feedback).
- **Mailing**: A form of 'mass' communication, where a model or view is presented or handed over to a large number of people. Feedback may or may not be encouraged.

Even though we have not yet discussed viewpoints, we can already relate the identified knowledge goals to the conversation techniques. This is shown in Table 4.1, which is based on interviews and discussions with many architects from industry.

Table 4.1 Knowledge goals and conversation techniques

	Knowledge Goal		
Conversation Technique	Introduce	Agree	Commit
Brown-paper session	++	+	−
Elicitation interview	++	+	−
Workshop	+	++	+
Validation interview	−	++	+
Committing review	−	−	++
Presentation	++	−	−
Mailing	+	−	−

A + indicates that a certain conversation class is well suited for the selected technique of knowledge goals, while ++ indicates that it is particularly well suited. On the other hand, a − indicates that a certain conversation technique is ill-suited for the selected class of knowledge goals

This table can fruitfully be used in practice to choose the conversation technique for the task and knowledge goal at hand. In Chap. 8, we will have a more in-depth look at the use of viewpoints to assist communication between the different stakeholders.

4.5 Summary

In the previous sections, we have presented both a theoretical and a practical perspective of the issues involved in the communication of enterprise architectures. The theoretical perspective described the communication during system development in general. Based on the one hand on this theoretical view and on the other hand on the experiences of architects, the practical perspective presented a number of practical guidelines and conversation techniques that should aid architects in the selection and definition of architecture description approaches that are fit for a specific communication situation.

Chapter 5
A Language for Enterprise Modelling

Henk Jonkers, Luuk Groenewegen, Marcello Bonsangue, René van Buuren, Dick A.C. Quartel, Marc M. Lankhorst, and Adina Aldea

Architecture provides a means to handle the complexity of modern information-intensive enterprises. To this end, architects need ways to express architectures as clearly as possible: both for their own understanding and for communication with other stakeholders, such as system developers, end users, and managers. Unfortunately, the current situation is that architects in different domains, even within the same organisation, often use their own description techniques and conventions. To date, there is no standard language for describing enterprise architectures in a precise way across domain borders. They are often described either in informal pictures that lack a well-defined meaning, or in detailed design languages (such as UML) that are difficult to understand for non-experts. This frequently leads to misunderstandings that hinder the collaboration of architects and other stakeholders. Also, it makes it very difficult to provide tools for visualisation and analysis of these architectures.

The description of the ArchiMate language in this section is based on the official ArchiMate 3.0 Specification as published by The Open Group (2016a), which describes ArchiMate in much more detail and precision. The ideas behind of ArchiMate's construction are further elaborated by Lankhorst et al. (2010). We refer the interested reader to these publications for more information and background on the language and its construction.

H. Jonkers • D.A.C. Quartel • A. Aldea
BiZZdesign, Enschede, The Netherlands

L. Groenewegen • M. Bonsangue
University of Leiden, Leiden, The Netherlands

R. van Buuren
Thales, Huizen, The Netherlands

M.M. Lankhorst (✉)
BiZZdesign, Capitool 15, 7521 PL Enschede, The Netherlands
e-mail: m.lankhorst@bizzdesign.com

© Springer-Verlag Berlin Heidelberg 2017   73
M. Lankhorst et al., *Enterprise Architecture at Work*, The Enterprise Engineering
Series, DOI 10.1007/978-3-662-53933-0_5

5.1 Describing Coherence

In information and ICT-intensive organisations, several types of architects and architectural practice can be found, ranging from product and process architectures to the more technically oriented application and infrastructure architectures.

The ICT-related disciplines already have a somewhat longer architectural tradition, although there the distinction between architecture and design is not always sharp. Application architects, for example, describe the relations between the many software applications used within the enterprise, as well as the global internal structure of these applications. Presently, UML is usually the language of choice for this purpose, although there are still organisations using their own proprietary notation. The architecture of the technical infrastructure, describing, among others, the layout of the computer hardware and networks hardware in the company, is generally captured in informal drawings of 'clouds' and 'boxes', if at all.

In the more business-oriented disciplines, 'working under architecture' is a more recent development. Since the advent of process orientation in the 1990s [e.g., Business Process Redesign (Davenport and Short 1990)], more and more organisations have started to document their business processes in a more or less formal way. However, these descriptions do not focus on the architectural aspects, i.e., they do not provide an overview of the global structure within processes and the relationships between them. Some organisations have a description of their product portfolio, which is generally text based, however.

Thus, we can say that within many of the different domains of expertise that are present in an enterprise, some sort of architectural practice exists, with varying degrees of maturity. However, due to the heterogeneity of the methods and techniques used to document the architectures, it is very difficult to determine how the different domains are interrelated. Still, it is clear that there are strong dependencies between the domains. For example, the goal of the (primary) business processes of an organisation is to realise their products; software applications support business processes, while the technical infrastructure is needed to run the applications; information is used in the business processes and processed by the applications. For optimal communication between domain architects, needed to align designs in the different domains, a clear picture of the domain interdependencies is indispensable.

With these observations in mind, we conclude that a language for modelling *enterprise architectures* should focus on inter-domain relations. With such a language, we should be able to model:

- Any global structure *within* each domain, showing the main elements and their dependencies, in a way that is easy to understand for non-experts of the domain.
- The relevant relations *between* the domains.

Another important property of an enterprise modelling language—and of any modelling language—is a formal foundation, which ensures that models can be interpreted in an unambiguous way and that they are amenable to automated

High-level modelling
within a domain

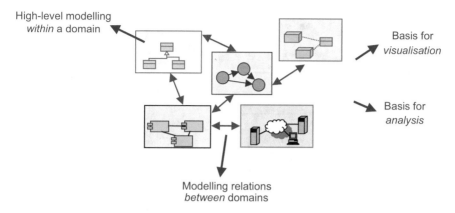

Basis for
visualisation

Basis for
analysis

Modelling relations
between domains

Fig. 5.1 The role of the ArchiMate language

analysis. Also, it should be possible to visualise the same model in different ways, tailored towards specific stakeholders with specific information requirements.

In this chapter, we present the enterprise modelling language that we use throughout this book. Although, in principle, the concepts of this language are sufficiently generic and expressive to model many of the aspects within specific domains, it is clearly *not* our intention to introduce a language that can replace all the domain-specific languages that exist. For specific (detailed) designs of, for example, business processes or applications, the existing languages are likely to be more suitable. We do, however, conform as much as possible to the modelling standards that exist in the different domains.

In Fig. 5.1, the role that the enterprise architecture modelling language plays in our approach is summarised. It provides a means for *integration*, by allowing the creation of models that show high-level structures *within* domains and the relations *between* domains. Also, it occupies a central spot in the approach in that it provides the basis for the *visualisation* and *analysis* techniques described elsewhere in this book.

5.2   Service Orientation and Layering

In the enterprise modelling language that we propose, the service concept plays a central role. A *service* is defined as a unit of functionality that some entity (e.g., a system, organisation, or department) makes available to its environment, and which has some value for certain entities in the environment (typically the 'service users'). Service orientation supports current trends ranging from the service-based network economy to ICT integration with Web services. These examples already show that services of a very different nature and granularity can be discerned: they can be

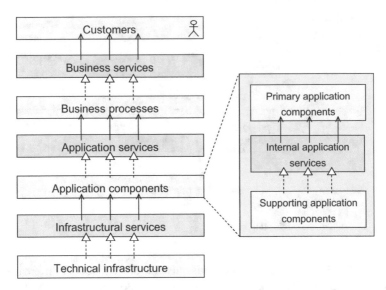

Fig. 5.2 Layered view

provided by organisations to their customers, by applications to business processes, or by technological facilities (e.g., communication networks) to applications.

Service orientation may typically lead to a layered view of enterprise architecture models, where the service concept is one of the main linking pins between the different layers. *Service layers* with services made available to higher layers are interleaved with *implementation layers* that realise the services. Within a layer, there may also be *internal* services, e.g., services of supporting applications that are used by the end-user applications. How this leads to a stack of service layers and implementation layers is shown in Fig. 5.2. These are linked by *serving* relations, showing how the implementation layers make use of the services of other layers, and *realisation* relations, showing how services are realised in an implementation layer.

Although, at an abstract level, the concepts that are used within each layer are similar, we define more concrete concepts that are specific for a certain layer. In this context, we distinguish three main layers:

1. The *business layer* offers products and services to external customers, which are realised in the organisation by business processes (performed by business actors or roles).
2. The *application layer* supports the business layer with application services which are realised by (software) application components.
3. The *technology layer* offers infrastructural services (e.g., processing, storage, and communication services) needed to run applications, realised by computer and communication devices and system software.

5.3   Three Dimensions of Modelling

A premise of the ArchiMate language is that the general structure of models within the different layers is similar. The same types of concepts and relations are used, although their exact nature and granularity differ. As a result of this uniformity, models created for the different layers can quite easily be aligned with each other. To identify the concepts that make up this general structure, we start from the three dimensions shown in Fig. 5.3.

The core concepts that are found in each layer of the language are depicted in Fig. 5.4. First, we distinguish the *structural* or *static* aspect (right side of Fig. 5.4) and the *behavioural* or *dynamic* aspect (centre of Fig. 5.4). Behavioural concepts are *assigned* to structural concepts, to show who or what displays the behaviour.

In addition to *active* structural elements (the business actors, application components and devices that display actual behaviour, i.e. the 'subjects' of activity), we also recognise *passive* structural elements (left side of Fig. 5.4), i.e. the *objects* on which behaviour is performed. In the domain of information-intensive organisations, which is the intended application area of our language, these are usually information objects, but physical objects can be modelled in the same way.

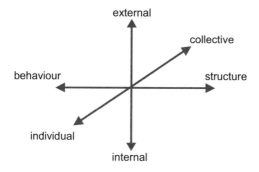

Fig. 5.3   Three dimensions of architectural concepts

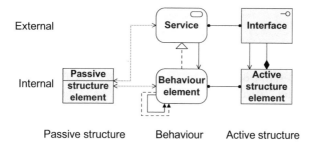

Fig. 5.4   The core concepts of the ArchiMate language

These three aspects—active structure, behaviour, and passive structure—are derived from natural language: they correspond to the subject-verb-object elements that all human languages exhibit (Crystal 1997) (although their grammatical order may vary between different languages). Thus, these aspects are fundamental to the way in which we describe the world. Having a similar structure in the modelling language therefore enhances its ease of use.

Next, we make a distinction between an *external view* (top layer of Fig. 5.4) and an *internal* view of systems (bottom layer). When looking at the behavioural aspect, these views reflect the principles of service orientation as introduced in the previous section. The *service* concept represents a unit of essential functionality that a system exposes to its environment. For the external users, only this external functionality, together with non-functional aspects such as the quality of service, costs, etc., are relevant. If required, these can be specified in a contract or service-level agreement. Services are accessible through *interfaces*, which constitute the external view of the structural aspect.

Third, for the internal realisation of services and interfaces, we distinguish between behaviour that is performed by an *individual* structural element (e.g., actor, role component, etc.), and *collective* behaviour (interaction) that is performed by a collaboration of multiple structural elements. An interaction can be treated as a specialisation of a behaviour element: it can trigger or be triggered by other behaviour elements (including other interactions), and it can be part of a process. Similarly, a collaboration can be treated as a specialisation of a structure element. This introduces the possibility of recurrence: next to individual structure elements, a collaboration may also aggregate other, more fine-grained collaborations.

The core of the ArchiMate language consists of these concepts, specialised for the three layers identified in the previous section. For example, at the business layer, we have business services, business processes and business functions as speciali-sations of behaviour element; actors and roles as business-specific active structure elements; and business objects as passive structure elements. Although these layer-specific concepts follow the general structure shown in this section, they differ with respect to, for example, their granularity. Also, some of the layers have a number of additional concepts.

5.4   Full Framework

The modelling concepts of the core language as introduced in the previous section can be used to describe or design actual architectures. The full ArchiMate language (The Open Group 2016a) adds a number of concepts to this core to provide more complete support for the architecture development process:

– Motivation concepts, to model the reasons behind the choices made in the architecture. It corresponds to the 'Why' column of the Zachman framework

(Zachman 1987; Sowa and Zachman 1992). This includes modelling of stake-holders, drivers for change, business goals, principles, requirements and outcomes.

– Strategy concepts, for modelling the enterprise at a strategic level with its capabilities, resources and the courses of action (strategies, tactics) it may take.
– Physical concepts, to describe the physical world of equipment, materials and transport.
– Implementation and migration concepts, to support project portfolio management, gap analysis and transition and migration planning. This includes modelling of work packages (e.g. projects), deliverables, plateaus and gaps.

The structure of the language and the most important concepts are summarised in Fig. 5.5. A full overview of the language meta-model can be found in the official specification document (The Open Group 2016a) and the notation is given in Appendix A.

In the following sections, we discuss the concepts within the three layers of the ArchiMate core language, as described in the previous sections, followed by a description of the additional concepts mentioned above. We use simple example models to illustrate the use of the concepts. More elaborate examples can be found in Sect. 5.15 and in some of the other chapters of this book.

	Passive structure	Behavior	Active structure	Motivation
Strategy	resources	courses of action, capabilities	resources	
Business	business objects	business services, functions and processes	business actors and roles	
Application	data objects	application services, functions and processes	application components and interfaces	stakeholders, drivers, goals, principles and requirements
Technology	artifacts	technology services, functions and processes	devices, system software, communication networks	
Physical	material		facilities, equipment, distribution networks	
Implementation & migration	deliverables	work packages	plateaus	

Fig. 5.5 Main concepts of the ArchiMate language

5.5   Composite Concepts

Before we address the concepts in the different layers and aspects, we first need to discuss a number of generic, composite elements that are not layer-specific. The grouping element is used to aggregate or compose an arbitrary group of concepts, which can be elements and relationships of the same or of different types.

> **Grouping**: aggregates or composes concepts that belong together based on some common characteristic.

The grouping element is used to aggregate or compose an arbitrary group of concepts, which can be elements and/or relationships of the same or of different types. Concepts may be aggregated by multiple (overlapping) groups. One useful way of using grouping is for modelling Architecture and Solution Building Blocks (ABBs and SBBs), as described in the TOGAF framework (The Open Group 2011). Another type of use is for modelling various kinds of architecture or business domains.

In some cases, it is relevant to model the (logical or physical) distribution of structural elements such as business actors, application components or nodes in the technology layer. For this purpose, the *location* concept can be used, which may be assigned to these structural elements.

> **Location**: a place or position where structure elements can be located or behaviour can be performed.

The location element is used to model the places where structure elements such as business actors, application components and devices are located and where, for example, business processes or application functions are performed. This element corresponds to the "Where" column of the Zachman framework (Zachman 1987). An example is shown in Fig. 5.10 later in this chapter.

5.6   Motivation Concepts

Motivation concepts are used to model the motivations, or reasons, that underlie the design or change of an enterprise architecture. They influence, guide and constrain the design. These concepts were partly inspired on previous work on goal-oriented requirements engineering (Yu 1997; Lamsweerde 2004) and architecture principles (Greefhorst and Proper 2011).

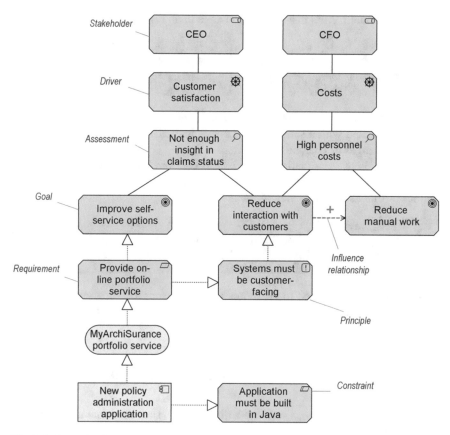

Fig. 5.6 Example of a motivation model

An example of a motivation model is shown in Fig. 5.6. The example illustrates the use of the central concepts and relations. In the following subsections, we will explain the motivation concepts in more detail.

5.6.1   Stakeholder, Driver and Assessment

A *stakeholder* has one or more interests in, or concerns about, the organisation and its enterprise architecture. In order to direct efforts to these interests, stakeholders change, set and emphasise goals.

Stakeholder: the role of an individual, team or organisation (or classes thereof) that represents their interest in the outcome of the architecture.

Drivers model factors that drive the change in an organisation.

> **Driver**: an external or internal condition that motivates an organisation to define its goals and implement the changes necessary to achieve them.

These may be internal drivers (also called 'concerns'), in which case they are usually associated with a stakeholder. Drivers may also be external, for example, economic changes or changing legislation.

The analysis of the situation in the enterprise from the perspective of a driver results in an *assessment*. An assessment may reveal strengths, weaknesses, opportunities or threats for some area of interest.

> **Assessment**: the result of an analysis of the state of affairs of the enterprise with respect to some driver.

These assessments need to be addressed by adjusting existing goals or setting new ones, which may trigger changes to the enterprise architecture.

5.6.2 Goal, Requirement, Constraint and Principle

A *goal* represents anything a stakeholder may desire, such as a state of affairs, or a produced value.

> **Goal**: a high-level statement of intent, direction or desired end state for an organisation and its stakeholders.

Goals are generally expressed using qualitative words, for example, 'increase', 'improve' or 'easier'. However, it is also very common to associate concrete, quantifiable objectives with goals. In the end, a goal must be realised by a plan or concrete change goal, which may or may not require a new system or changes to existing systems. *Requirements* model the properties of the elements in the architecture that are needed to achieve the 'ends' that are modelled by the goals.

> **Requirement**: a statement of need that must be met by the architecture.

A requirement can be realised by any applicable core element of the language.

In contrast to a requirement, a *constraint* does not prescribe some intended functionality of the system to be realised, but imposes a restriction on the way in which the system may be realised.

> **Constraint**: a factor that prevents or obstructs the realisation of goals.

This may be a restriction on the implementation of the system (e.g. specific technology that is to be used) or a restriction on the implementation process (e.g. time or budget constraints).

Principles are strongly related to goals and requirements. Similar to requirements, principles define intended properties of the architecture. However, in contrast to requirements, principles are broader in scope and more abstract. While a requirement relates to a specific need that the architecture must address, a principle refers to the general intent (of some stakeholder) that the architecture should meet.

> **Principle**: a qualitative statement of intent that should be met by the architecture.

A principle must be made specific for a given solution by means of one or more requirements or constraints, in order to enforce that the solution conforms to the principle.

The results achieved by the architecture are modelled as *outcomes*.

> **Outcome**: an end result that has been achieved.

Note that not all outcomes have to be intended, i.e. be tied to some goal. Unexpected and undesired outcomes may also be relevant in an architecture model.

5.6.3 Value and Meaning

The *value* of an element of the core architecture is that which makes some party appreciate it.

> **Value**: the relative worth, utility or importance of a core element or an outcome.

Value can go two ways: it may apply to what a party gets by selling or making available some product or service or to what a party gets by buying or obtaining access to it. Value is often expressed in terms of money, but it has long been recognised that nonmonetary value also is essential to business: for example, practical/functional value (including the *right* to use a service) and the value of information or knowledge. Although value can be internally relevant for some system or organisational unit, it is most typically applied to *external* appreciation of goods, services, information, knowledge or money, normally as part of some sort of customer–provider relationship. Although the name of a value can be expressed in many different ways (including amounts, objects), when the 'functional' value of a service is concerned, it is recommended to try and express it as an action or state that can be performed or reached as a result of the corresponding service being available.

Similar to the way in which we associate a value with a product, we can associate a *meaning* with a business object or its representation.

Meaning: the knowledge or expertise present in a business object or its representation, given a particular context.

In other words, meaning represents the informative value of a business object for a user of such an object. It is through a certain interpretation of a representation of the object that meaning is being offered to a certain user or to a certain category of users. The name of a meaning should preferably be a noun or noun phrase expressing this and distinguishing it from the business object or representation being interpreted.

5.7   Strategy Concepts

Next to the motivation concepts described in Sect. 5.6, which focus on what the enterprise wants to achieve, the language includes a number of strategy concepts, used to express the high-level direction setting of the enterprise, for example, in approaches such as capability-based planning.

A *course of action* represents what an enterprise has decided to do to realise its goals. It can be used to model a high-level strategic plan or direction, or more concrete lower-level tactics. Courses of action are typically realised by capabilities and resources, as shown in Fig. 5.7.

Course of action: an approach or plan for configuring some capabilities and resources of the enterprise, undertaken to achieve a goal.

This concept corresponds directly with the course of action element in the Business Motivation Model (BMM) (Object Management Group 2015b).

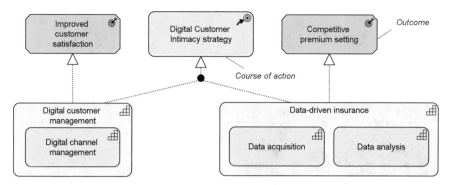

Fig. 5.7 Course of action and outcomes realised by capabilities

Capabilities define what an organisation needs to be able to do, in order to successfully achieve the outcomes that are defined as part of the corporate strategy. They are the key building blocks of the business, unique and independent from each other, and tend to be stable over time.

> **Capability**: an ability that an active structure element, such as an organisation, person or system, possesses.

A capability defines *what* the business does or can do, not *how* it does that or who is doing it. They are different from business processes, functions, services, organisation units or IT systems, although these may all contribute to a capability. The same capability may be implemented in different ways, e.g. manually, IT-supported or fully automated. Capabilities are typically aimed at achieving some goal or delivering value by realising an outcome and are themselves realised by core elements of ArchiMate.

Resources are structure elements that are assigned to capabilities (Fig. 5.8), which in turn are realised by the active and passive structure elements from the other layers of the architecture. These may include, for example, business actors, application components, devices, equipment, data objects or material, defined in other sections in this chapter.

> **Resource:** an asset owned or controlled by an individual or organisation.

Capabilities and resources are often considered to be sources of competitive advantage for organisations. They are analysed in terms of strengths and weaknesses, and they are considered when implementing strategies. Since resources are limited, they can often be a deciding factor in choosing which strategy, goal and project to implement and in which order.

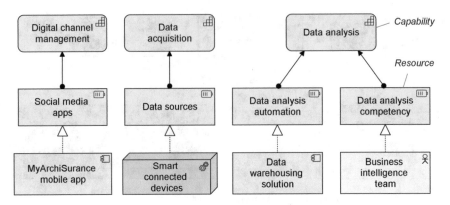

Fig. 5.8 Resources assigned to capabilities and realised by structure elements

By putting it all together, this provides a line of sight from the different assets of the enterprise upwards to the capabilities they support and to the strategies, goals and outcomes that the enterprise aims to achieve. This way, you can gain insights into the effects of strategic decisions and, vice versa, uncover new options and innovations provided by the capabilities you possess and the resources you employ.

5.7.1 Defining Capabilities

To help you define capabilities, the following guidelines may be helpful:

- A capability defines what the business does or can do, not how it does that or who is doing it. They are different from business processes, functions, services, organisation units or IT systems, although these may all contribute to a capability. The same capability may be implemented in different ways, e.g. manually, IT-supported or fully automated.
- Capabilities are owned by the business and named and defined in business terms. Their definition should be readily understandable by all business professionals involved. Their names are nouns (e.g. 'Product innovation') as opposed to business processes, which are named with verbs (e.g. 'Purchase materials').
- Capabilities are unique and stable. They are defined only once for the whole enterprise and they rarely change, unless, for example, the enterprise undertakes a completely new line of business or divests part of its current business.
- Capabilities may be composite, consisting of sub-capabilities. A capability may also use other capabilities.
- Capabilities can be organised in a capability map that provides an overview of the entire enterprise.

– A capability's maturity can be assessed across different dimensions, such as people, process, technology, assets or information. These are the basis for capability-based planning.

Capabilities can also be classified further, for example, in:

– Core vs. non-core
– Strategic vs. operational vs. supporting
– Customer-facing vs. internal
– Innovating vs. differentiating vs. commodity

Such a classification scheme helps in investment and sourcing decisions, for example, by distinguishing between:

– Differentiating, customer-facing capabilities, which are core and are seldom outsourced
– Strategic, innovating capabilities, which are important for the long-term future of an enterprise and are often assigned a separate budget, to avoid the 'innovation squeeze' where the core, operational capabilities eat up all budget
– Non-core, commodity or supporting capabilities, which are good candidates for outsourcing to partners that have these as their core, differentiating capabilities

Capabilities are distinct from business functions (Sect. 5.8.2). Capabilities represent the current or desired abilities of an enterprise, realised by its people, processes, information and technology, but defined independently from the structure of the organisation. They are focused on specific business outcomes, are used for strategic planning purposes and may include abilities that the enterprise does not recognise or use yet. In contrast, business functions describe the work actually done by the organisation, and they are more closely aligned with the organisation structure. Each capability occurs only once in a capability map, whereas in a functional decomposition of the enterprise the same sub-function can occur multiple times.

In describing the current-state business architecture, the value of capabilities mostly lies in the analysis of the current versus desired levels of capability and in uncovering capabilities that the organisation already possesses but does not recognise or manage explicitly. Capabilities and capability levels in a target business architecture give high-level direction for change. This is the core of capability-based planning.

Of course, when you draw a map of the current capabilities of the organisation, its current business functions will often figure prominently, since what you actually do today must by nature be something you are able to do as well. And multiple business functions may (together with other behaviour elements) contribute to the realisation of a capability.

More extensive guidance on capability-based planning and capability mapping is provided by the BIZBOK® Guide (Business Architecture Guild 2016) and the Open Group Business Capabilities Guide (The Open Group 2016b).

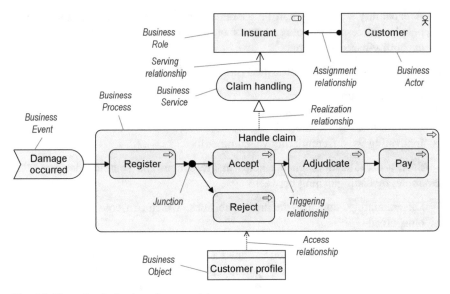

Fig. 5.9 Example of a business layer model

5.8   Business Layer Concepts

An example of a business layer model is shown in Fig. 5.9, illustrating the use of the central concepts and relations. In the following subsections, we will explain the business layer concepts in more detail.

5.8.1   Business Structure Concepts

The structure aspect at the business layer refers to the organisation structure, in terms of the actors that make up the organisation and their relationships. The central structural concept is the *business actor*.

> **Business actor**: a business entity that is capable of performing behaviour.

A business actor may be an individual *person* (e.g., a customer or an employee), but also a group of people and resources that have a permanent (or at least long-term) status within the organisation. Typical examples of the latter are a *department* and a *business unit*. Two different specialisations may be defined to distinguish the two cases. This is illustrated in Fig. 5.24. The name of a business actor should preferably be a noun.

> **Business role**: the responsibility for performing specific behaviour, to which an actor can be assigned, or the part an actor plays in a particular action or event.

The idea is that the work that an actor performs within an organisation is always based on a certain role that the actor fulfils. The set of roles in an organisation can be expected to be much more stable than the specific actors fulfilling these roles. Multiple actors can fulfil the same role, and, conversely, a single actor can fulfil multiple roles. The name of a business role should preferably be a noun.

A business process or function may be interpreted as the internal behaviour assigned to a single business role. In some cases, behaviour is the collective effort of more than one business role: in fact, a collaboration of two or more business roles results in collective behaviour which may be more than simply the sum of the behaviour of the separate roles.

> **Business collaboration**: an aggregate of two or more business internal active structure elements that work together to perform collective behaviour.

Unlike a department, which may also group roles, a business collaboration does not need to have an official (permanent) status within the organisation: it is aimed at a specific interaction or set of interactions between roles. The name of a business collaboration should preferably be a noun. It is also rather common to leave a business collaboration unnamed.

The same service may be offered on a number of different interfaces, e.g., by mail, by telephone or through the Internet. This example suggests that different 'channels' for offering products or services are typically modelled as business interfaces.

> **Business interface**: a point of access where a business service is made available to the environment.

The name of a business interface should preferably be a noun.

Business objects represent the important 'informational' or 'conceptual' elements in which the business thinks about a domain. Generally, a business object is used to model an object type (cf. a UML class), of which several instances may exist within the organisation. A wide variety of business objects can be defined.

> **Business object**: a concept used within a particular business domain.

Business objects are passive in the sense that they do not trigger or perform processes. A business object may be accessed (e.g., created, read, written) by a business process, function, interaction, event, or service. The name of a business object should preferably be a noun.

Useful specialisations (see Sect. 5.14.2) of the business object concept are *Message*, i.e., an object intended to exchange information between parties, and *Administration*, i.e., a coherent collection of information used internally.

> **Representation**: the perceptible form of the information carried by a business object.

If relevant, representations can be classified in various ways: for example, in terms of medium (e.g., electronic, paper, audio) or format (e.g., HTML, PDF, plain text, bar chart). A single business object can have a number of different representations, but a representation always belongs to one specific business object.

5.8.2   Business Behaviour Concepts

Business services are used to expose business functionality to the environment.

> **Business service**: an explicitly defined exposed business behaviour.

The name of a business service should preferably be or contain a verb ending with '-ing', e.g. 'Transaction processing', or explicitly contain the word 'service', as in 'Claims registration service'.

A distinction can be made between 'external' business services, offered to external customers, and 'internal' business services, offering supporting functionality to processes or functions within the organisation. (The term *business service* is sometimes also used to refer to application services used by 'the business', which may be somewhat confusing).

Internally to the organisation, business services are realised by *business behaviour*, for which we have a number of concepts: *business process*, *business function*, *business activity*, or *business interaction*. For the 'consumers' of a business service the internal behaviour of an organisation is usually irrelevant: they are only interested in the (functional and non-functional) results of the behaviour that are advertised by the business service. Internal business behaviour, in turn, may use other services (internal to the organisation, but external to a smaller entity within the organisation). Note that in some organisations, the term *(business) function* is used to designate an external, implementation-independent unit of behaviour, which is very similar to our *service* concept.

Although the distinction between the two is not always sharp, it is often useful to distinguish a *process view* from a *function view* of behaviour. Both concepts can be used to group activities, but based on different grouping criteria.

> **Business process**: a sequence of business behaviours that achieves a specific outcome such as a defined set of products and services.

The is sometimes described as a 'customer-to-customer' process, where 'customer' may also be an 'internal customer', in the case of sub-processes within an organisation. The name of a business process should preferably be or contain a verb in the simple present tense, e.g. 'Receive request'.

> **Business function**: a collection of business behaviour based on a chosen set of criteria (typically required business resources and/or competences), closely aligned to an organisation, but not necessarily explicitly governed by the organisation.

A *business function* groups behaviour based on, for example, required skills, capabilities, resources, or (application) support. The name of a business function should preferably be or contain a verb ending with '-ing', e.g. 'Claims processing' (Fig. 5.10).

Typically, the business processes of an organisation are defined based on the *products* and *services* that the organisation offers, while the business functions are the basis for the assignment of resources to tasks and for the application support.

The example of Fig. 5.11 illustrates the process view and function view in one picture. As the figure suggests, there is a potential many-to-many relation between functions and processes.

A *business interaction* is a unit of behaviour similar to a business process or function, but which is performed in by two or more collaborating roles within the organisation.

> **Business interaction**: a unit of collective business behaviour performed by (a collaboration of) two or more business roles.

Although interactions are external behaviour from the perspective of the roles participating in the collaboration, the behaviour is internal to the collaboration as a whole. Similar to processes or functions, the result of a business interaction can be made available to the environment through a business service. As in the case of a business process, the name of a business interaction should preferably be a verb in the simple present tense.

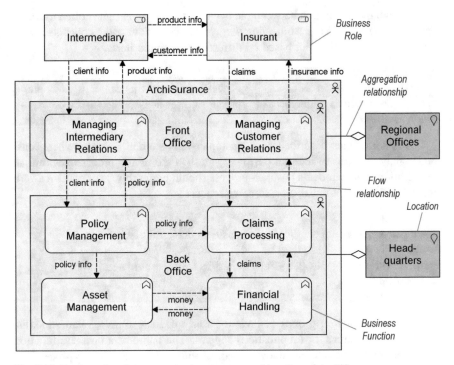

Fig. 5.10 Business functions, organisation structure and location of ArchiSurance

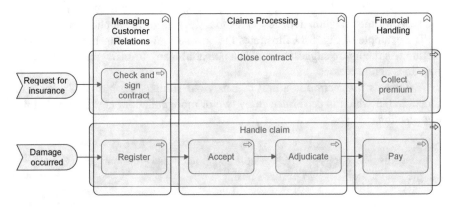

Fig. 5.11 Business processes versus business functions

The example of Fig. 5.12 illustrates how an interaction and collaboration can be used to model a business transaction and how the same situation can be modelled with the service and interface concepts. These two alternatives can be seen as two views, a symmetrical ('peer-to-peer') view and an asymmetrical ('client–server') view, of the same process. In the former view, the buyer and seller perform

Fig. 5.12 Interaction
versus service use

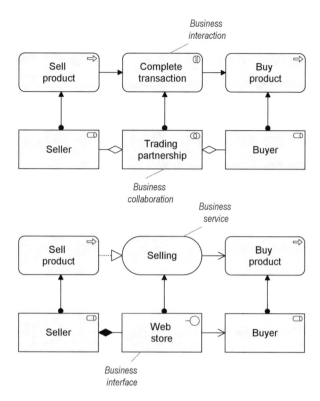

collaborative behaviour to settle a transaction, while in the latter view the selling of
a product is considered to be a service that the seller offers to the buyer.

> **Business event**: a business behaviour element that denotes an organisational
> state change. It may originate from and be resolved inside or outside the
> organisation.

A business event is most commonly used to model something that *triggers*
behaviour, but other types of events are also conceivable, e.g., an event that
interrupts a process. A business event should ideally have a name containing verb
in the past or present perfect tense, e.g. 'claim received' or 'claim has arrived'.

Unlike other business behaviour, a business event is instantaneous: it does not
have duration. Events may originate from the environment of the organisation (e.g.,
from a customer), but also internal events may occur, generated by other processes
within the organisation.

The example of Fig. 5.13 shows how an event can be used to decouple processes.
The 'Adjudicate' and 'Pay' processes can be modelled separately, with their own
incoming and possibly outgoing events. The 'Payment request sent' event, a result

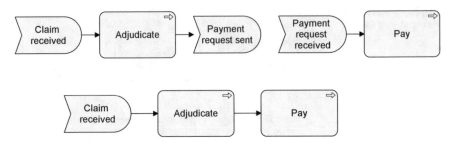

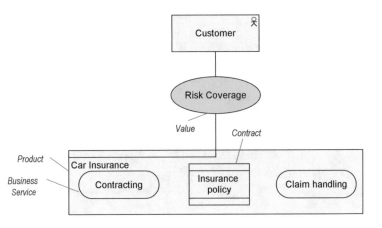

Fig. 5.13 Events to decouple processes

Fig. 5.14 Services grouped into a product

of the 'Adjudicate' process, is a trigger for the 'Pay' process to start (here called 'Payment request received'). When composing these two models into one new model, the linking event can be omitted; it is then replaced by the triggering relationship between the two processes.

5.8.3 Higher-Level Business Concepts

The higher-level business concepts provide a way to link the operational side of an organisation to its business goals. These concepts are also concerned with the products or services that an organisation offers to its customers.

We define a *product* as a collection of services and/or passive structure elements (e.g. business objects, data objects or material), together with the rules for their use (see Fig. 5.14).

> **Product**: a coherent collection of services and/or passive structure elements, accompanied by a *contract*/set of agreements, which is offered as a whole to (internal or external) customers.

Informally speaking, the collection of services and passive structure elements constitutes the actual product. These services are often business services, but application or technology services may also be part of a product. This 'package' is offered as a whole to (internal or external) customers. 'Buying' a product gives the customer the right to use the associated services. Generally, the product concept is used to specify a product *type*. The number of product types in an organisation is typically relatively stable compared to, for example, the processes that realise or support the products. 'Buying' is usually one of the services associated with a product, which results in a new instance of that product (belonging to a specific customer). Similarly, there may be services to modify or discontinue a product. The name of a product is usually the name which is used in the communication with customers, or possibly a more generic noun (e.g., 'travel insurance').

The *contract* concept may be used to model a contract in the legal sense, but also a more informal agreement associated with a product. It may also be, or include, a Service Level Agreement (SLA), describing an agreement about the functionality and quality of the services that are part of a product. A contract is a specialisation of a business object. The name of a contract is preferably a noun.

> **Contract**: a formal or informal specification of an agreement between a provider and a consumer that specifies the rights and obligations associated with a product and establishes functional and non-functional parameters for interaction.

5.9 Application Layer Concepts

A typical example of an application layer model is shown in Fig. 5.15, illustrating the use of the central concepts. In the following subsections, we explain the application layer concepts in more detail. Also, we show how the relations between the application layer and the business layer can be modelled.

5.9.1 Application Structure Concepts

The main structural concept for the application layer is the *application component*.

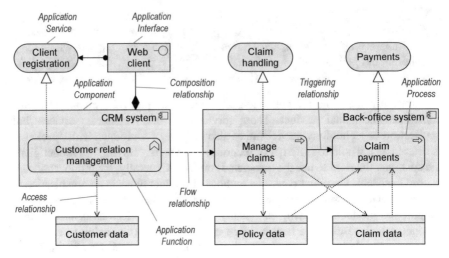

Fig. 5.15 Example of an application layer model

> **Application component**: an encapsulation of application functionality aligned to implementation structure, which is modular and replaceable. It encapsulates its behaviour and data, exposes services and makes them available through interfaces.

This concept is used to model any structural entity in the application layer: not just (reusable) software components that can be part of one or more applications but also complete software applications, sub-applications or information systems. This concept is very similar to the UML component. The name of an application component should preferably be a noun.

The interrelationships of components are also an essential ingredient in application architecture. Therefore, we also introduce the concept of *application collaboration*.

> **Application collaboration**: an aggregate of two or more application components that work together to perform collective application behaviour.

The concept is very similar to the collaboration as defined in the UML standard (Object Management Group 2015a). The name of an application collaboration should preferably be a noun.

In the purely structural sense, an *application interface* is the (logical) location where the services of a component can be accessed. In a broader sense (as used in, among others, the UML definition), an application interface also defines some elementary behavioural characteristics: it defines the set of operations and events that are provided by the component, or those that are required from the environment.

> **Application interface**: a point of access where an application service is made available to a user, another application component or a node.

Thus, it is used to access the functionality of a component. The application interface concept can be used to model both *application-to-application* interfaces, offering internal application services, and *application-to-business* interfaces (or *user interfaces*), offering external application services. The name of an application interface should preferably be a noun.

Also at the application layer, we distinguish the passive counterpart of the component, which we call a *data object*.

> **Data object**: data structured for automated processing.

This concept is similar to data objects (in fact, object *types* or *classes*) in well-known data modelling approaches. The name of a data object should preferably be a noun.

5.9.2 Application Behaviour Concepts

Behaviour in the application layer can be described in a way that is very similar to business layer behaviour. We make a distinction between the external behaviour of application components in terms of *application services*, and the internal behaviour of these components to realise these services.

> **Application service**: an explicitly defined exposed application behaviour.

The service concept provides a way to describe explicitly the functionality that components share with each other and the functionality that they make available to the environment. The concept fits well within the current developments in the area of, for example, Web services. The term 'business service' is sometimes used for an external application service, i.e., application functionality that is used to directly support the work performed in a business process or function, exposed by an application-to-business interface. However, we reserve the term 'business service' for services provided by the business layer to the environment. Internal application services are exposed through an application-to-application interface. The name of an application service should preferably be a verb ending with '-ing' or explicitly contain the word 'service'. Application services expose *application functions* and *application processes* to the environment.

Application function: automated behaviour that can be performed by an application component.

The name of an application function should preferably be a verb ending with '-ing', e.g., 'accounting'.

Application process: a sequence of application behaviours that achieves a specific outcome.

Application processes are used to model the time-ordering of behaviour, for example, to describe the orchestration between applications.

Application processes and functions model the internal behaviour of a single application component; for the collaborative behaviour of application components, we use *application interactions*.

Application interaction: a unit of collective application behaviour performed by (a collaboration of) two or more application components.

The UML standard (Object Management Group 2015a) also includes the interaction concept. An application interaction is external behaviour from the perspective of each of the participating components, but the behaviour is internal to the collaboration as a whole. The name of an application interaction should preferably be or contain a verb in the present tense.

Finally, we can use *application events* to model state changes in the application layer, which may, for example, trigger application processes.

Application event: an application behaviour element that denotes a state change.

5.9.3   Business–Application Alignment

The application layer and the business layer can be easily linked in ArchiMate (Fig. 5.16). Two types of relations provide this link:

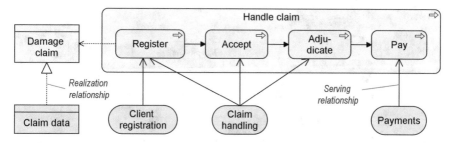

Fig. 5.16 Example of a business–application alignment model

1. Application services can *serve* business behaviour and application interfaces *serve* business actors and roles, i.e. there is a *support* relation between the application and business layers. Less common, but also possible, is the reverse relationship, i.e. the business layer providing services to the application layer.
2. Data objects can *realise* business objects; this means that a data object is an electronic *representation* of the business object, i.e., there is an *implementation* relation between the application and business layers.

5.10   Technology Layer Concepts

A typical example of a technology layer model is shown in Fig. 5.17, illustrating the use of the central concepts. In the following subsections, we explain the technology layer concepts in more detail. Also, we show how the relations between the technology layer and the application layer can be modelled.

5.10.1   Technology Structure Concepts

The main structural concept for the application layer is the *node*.

> **Node**: a computational or physical resource that hosts, manipulates or interacts with other computational or physical resources.

It is identical to the node concept of UML 2. It strictly models the structural aspect of an application; its behaviour is modelled by an explicit relationship to the behavioural concepts.

Similar to the business and application layers, the collaboration between different structure elements is described by a *technology collaboration*.

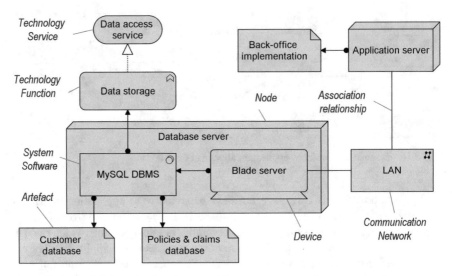

Fig. 5.17 Example of a technology layer model

Technology collaboration: an aggregate of two or more nodes that work together to perform collective technology behaviour.

A *technology interface* (not shown in Fig. 5.17) specifies how the *technology* services of a node can be accessed by other nodes (provided interface) or which functionality the node requires from its environment (required interface). A technology interface exposes a technology service to the environment. The same service may be exposed through different interfaces.

Technology interface: a point of access where technology services offered by a node can be accessed.

A *device* is a specialisation of a node that represents a physical resource with processing capability. It is typically used to model hardware systems such as mainframes, PCs, or routers. It can be part of a node together with system software. Devices may be composite, i.e. consist of sub-devices.

Device: a physical IT resource upon which system software and artefacts may be deployed for execution.

System software is a specialisation of a node that is used to model the software environment in which artefacts are stored or run. This can be, for example, an operating system, a JEE application server, a database system, a workflow engine or COTS software such as ERP or CRM packages. Also, system software can be used to represent, for example, communication middleware. Usually, system software is combined with a device representing the hardware environment to form a general node.

> **System software**: software that provides or contributes to an environment for storing, executing and using software or data deployed within it.

Typically, a node will consist of a number of sub-nodes, for example, a device such as a server and system software to model the operating system.

The interrelationships of components in the technology layer are mainly formed by communication infrastructure.

> **Path**: a link between two or more nodes, through which these nodes can exchange data or material.
>
> **Communication network**: a set of structures that connects computer systems or other electronic devices for transmission, routing and reception of data or data-based communications such as voice and video.

Artefacts are used to model the representation, in the form of, for example, a file, a data object or an application component, and can be assigned to (i.e. deployed on) a node.

> **Artefact**: a piece of data that is used or produced in a software development process or by deployment and operation of a system.

The artefact concept has been borrowed from UML.

Names for technology structure elements are usually taken directly from the corresponding product or technical designations.

5.10.2   Technology Behaviour Concepts

The technology layer provides *technology services* to be used by applications.

> **Technology service**: externally visible unit of functionality, provided by one or more nodes, exposed through well-defined interfaces, and meaningful to the environment.

Like the other service types, the name of a technology service either contains a verb in the '-ing' form or the word 'service' itself. Technology services are realised by *technology functions* and *technology processes*.

Technology function: a behaviour element that groups infrastructural behaviour that can be performed by a node.
Technology process: a sequence of technology behaviours that achieves a specific outcome.

A technology function or process describes the internal behaviour of a node; for the user of a node, this function or process is invisible. If its behaviour is exposed externally, this is done through one or more technology services. A technology function abstracts from the way it is implemented. Only the necessary behaviour is specified.

For the collaborative behaviour in the technology layer, we use *technology interactions*.

Technology interaction: a unit of collective technology behaviour performed by (a collaboration of) two or more nodes.

Finally, state changes in the technology layer are described with *technology events*.

Technology event: a technology behaviour element that denotes a state change.

5.10.3   Application–Technology Alignment

The technology layer and the application layer can also be linked very easily. Similar to business–application alignment, two types of relations provide this link:

1. Technology services can *serve* application functions and technology interfaces *serve* application components, i.e. there is a support relation between the technology and application layers (Fig. 5.18).
2. Artefacts can *realise* data objects and application components, i.e. there is an implementation relation between the technology and application layers (Fig. 5.18).

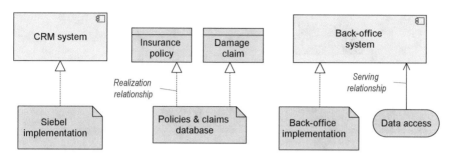

Fig. 5.18 Example of applications and data supported by technology

Artefacts play a central role in showing how 'logical' application components are realised by 'physical' components (modelled as artefacts). A single physical component may realise multiple logical components and, conversely, multiple physical components may be used to realise a single logical component.

The technology layer may also use the services from the other layers, although this is less common in practice.

5.11   Physical Concepts

The ArchiMate language was initially aimed at modelling the world of information technology since it was developed by and for typical IT-intensive administrative organisations in government and finance. However, enterprise architecture is also used increasingly in other types of organisations, for example, in healthcare, manufacturing or logistics. Moreover, technology innovations such as the Internet of Things have become increasingly important. Modelling the physical world and its interplay with IT is therefore an important addition to the language in ArchiMate version 3.0 (The Open Group 2016a). An example of these concepts is shown in Fig. 5.19.

The *equipment* element is the main active structure element within the set of physical concepts.

> **Equipment**: one or more physical machines, tools or instruments that can create, use, store, move or transform materials.

Equipment comprises all active structure elements that carry out physical processes in which materials are used or transformed. It is a specialisation of the node element from the technology layer. Thus, nodes can be modelled that combine IT technology (devices, system software) and physical technology (equipment), for example, computer-controlled production machinery, a fitness tracker monitoring

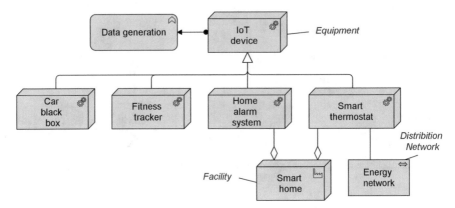

Fig. 5.19 Example of physical concepts

your movements or a smart thermostat measuring and controlling the temperature in your home.

A *facility* represents a physical resource that has the capability of facilitating (e.g. housing) the use of equipment. It is typically used to model factories, buildings or outdoor constructions that have an important role in production or distribution processes. In an ICT context, a data centre would typically be modelled as a facility.

Facility: a physical structure or environment.

Facilities can be interconnected by *distribution networks*. These represent the physical distribution or transportation infrastructure and embody the physical realisation of the logical paths between nodes.

Distribution network: a physical network used to transport materials or energy.

Material can be accessed (e.g. created, used, stored, moved or transformed) by equipment. It is typically used to model raw materials and physical products, and also energy sources such as fuel, and it can be transported via distribution networks.

Material: tangible physical matter or physical elements.

There are no separate physical behaviour elements. Rather, the behaviour elements from the technology layer (Sect. 5.10) are used to model the behaviour of all nodes, including physical equipment. Since equipment will very often be computer-controlled or in other ways have a close relationship to IT, this lets you describe their behaviour in an integral way.

5.12   Implementation and Migration Concepts

The implementation and migration concepts are used to describe how an architecture is going to be realised. In the following subsections, we will explain the implementation and migration concepts in more detail.

5.12.1   Implementation-Related Concepts

An example of a model using the implementation-related concepts is shown in Fig. 5.20, illustrating the use of the central concepts and relations for expressing the work that needs to be done to realise an architecture.

Conceptually, a *work package* is similar to a business process, in that it consists of a set of causally related tasks, aimed at producing a well-defined result. However, a work package is a unique, 'one-off' process.

> **Work package**: a series of actions identified and designed to achieve specific results within specified time and resource constraints.

A work package has a clearly defined beginning and end date, and a well-defined set of goals or results. The work package concept can be used to model projects, but also subprojects or tasks within a project, programs, or project portfolios. A work package can be assigned to a business role that carries out the work.

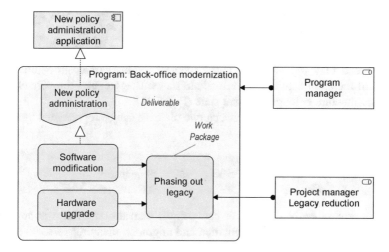

Fig. 5.20 Example of an implementation model

Work packages may be triggered or interrupted by *implementation events*. Also, work packages may raise events that trigger other behaviour. Unlike a work package, an event is instantaneous: it does not have duration.

> **Implementation event**: a behaviour element that denotes a state change related to implementation or migration.

An implementation event may have a time attribute that denotes the moment or moments at which the event happens. For example, this can be used to model project schedules and milestones such as the completion of *deliverables* produced by a work package. These may be results of any kind, including reports, services, software, physical products and intangible results such as organisational change. A deliverable may also be the implementation of (a part of) an architecture.

> **Deliverable**: a precisely defined outcome of a work package.

5.12.2   Migration Planning Concepts

In order to model the change of an architecture over time, the *plateau* concept is introduced.

> **Plateau**: a relatively stable state of the architecture that exists during a limited period of time.

A plateau may represent the current state (baseline) or desired future state (target) of the architecture, or intermediate states. It aggregates the core elements of the architecture belonging to that state (Fig. 5.21).

The result of a gap analysis between two plateaus can be represented by the *gap* concept.

> **Gap**: a statement of difference between two plateaus.

A gap represents the differences between the plateaus, and forms an important input for the subsequent implementation and migration planning.

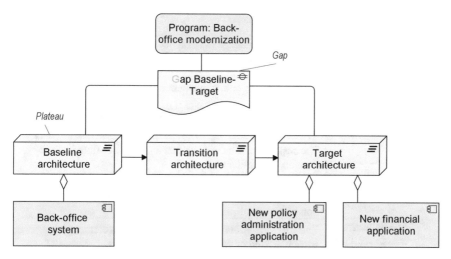

Fig. 5.21 Example of a migration model

5.13   Relations

As we argued before, enterprise architecture is, above all, about the description of *coherence*: coherence within different domains but also the coherence among domains. Therefore, in contrast to many other modelling languages, a fairly extensive set of clearly defined *relationship concepts* has been defined. In the examples throughout this chapter, most of the relations have already been used. In this section, we summarise them and show some of their properties. As we did for the concepts used to describe the different conceptual domains, we adopt corresponding relationship concepts from existing standards as much as possible. For instance, relationship concepts such as composition, association and specialisation are taken from UML, while triggering is used in most business process modelling languages, for example, in BPMN.

The structural and dependency relations, summarised in Table 5.1, form an important category of relations to describe coherence. The relations are listed in ascending order by 'strength': association is the weakest structural relation; composition is the strongest structural relation.

Any concept may be used in a *nested* way: that is, a concept may consist of 'smaller' concepts of the same type, e.g. a business actor may consist of sub-actors, a service may consist of subservices, an application component may consist of subcomponents, etc. Depending on the context (and possibly the chosen view), nesting formally denotes an *aggregation* or a *composition* relation (i.e. the concept aggregates or is composed of sub-concepts of the same type). See, for example, the model of Fig. 5.9, in which the Handle Claim process is composed of several sub-processes.

Table 5.1 Structural and dependency relations

Association	*Association* models a relation between objects that is not covered by another, more specific relationship
Influence +/- --------->	The *influence* relation models that an element affects the implementation or achievement of some motivation element
Access ....>	The *access* relation models that behavioural elements can observe or act upon passive structure elements
Serving ———————>	The *serving* relation models that an element offers its functionality to another element
Realisation ------▷	The *realisation* relation indicates that an entity plays a critical role in the creation, achievement, sustenance, or operation of a more abstract entity
Specialisation ———————▷	The *specialisation* relation indicates that an element is a particular kind of another element
Assignment ●——————▶	The *assignment* relation expresses the allocation of responsibility, performance of behaviour or execution
Aggregation ◇———	The *aggregation* relation indicates that an element groups a number of other elements
Composition ◆———	The *composition* relation indicates that an element consists of a number of other elements

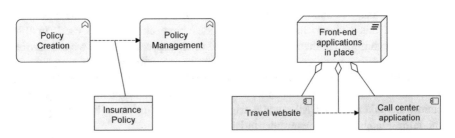

Fig. 5.22 Relationships to relationships

Nesting of concepts of different types usually denotes an *assignment* relation, e.g. the functions assigned to an application component are drawn inside that component, or the artefacts assigned to (deployed on) a node are drawn inside the node.

In a number of specific cases, relationships to relationships are also allowed. This can be used, for example, to show that a business object is flowing between two business processes, as depicted in Fig. 5.22. On the left, we see the business object Insurance Policy related to flow relation between Policy Creation and Policy

Management; on the right, the flow relation between the two application components is aggregated in the plateau Front-end applications in place.

The ArchiMate language contains an abstraction rule that states that a 'chain' of
structural relations (with intermediate model elements) can be replaced by the
weakest structural relation. For a more precise description and derivation of the
original definition of this rule, we refer to Buuren et al. (2004). With this rule, it is
possible to determine the indirect, derived relations that exist between model
elements without a direct relation, which may be useful for, among others, impact
analysis. An example is shown in Fig. 5.23: assume that we would like to know
what the impact on the business is if the Financial application fails? In this case, an
indirect 'serving' relation (the thick arrow on the left) can be derived from this
system to the 'Invoicing and Collections' business process (from the chain 'assignment—composition—realisation—serving').

All these derived relations are also valid in the ArchiMate language. The full set
of possible relations between elements of the language is listed in the standard (The
Open Group 2016a).

For behaviour modelling, in addition to the structural relations, we may also use
dynamic relations, summarised in Table 5.2. The *triggering* relation models the
'control flow' in a process, while the *flow* relation, inspired by Steen et al. (2002),
models the flow of information, data, goods or value, typically between functions. It
is also allowed to abstract from behaviour elements and use the flow relation
between structural elements. As there may be information associated with a triggering relation, triggering can be considered a stronger form of the flow relation,
i.e. a flow that is intended to trigger behaviour.

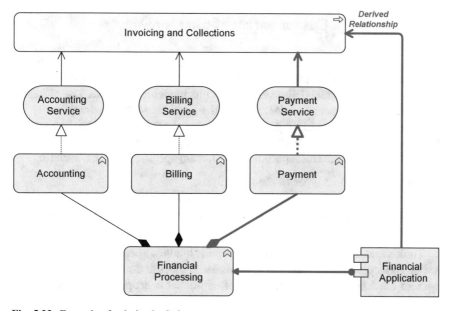

Fig. 5.23 Example of a derived relation

Table 5.2 Dynamic relations

Triggering	The triggering relation describes a temporal or causal relationship between elements
Flow	The flow relation represents transfer from one element to another
Junction	A junction is used to connect relations of the same type. Regular (or and-) junctions signify a combination; or-junctions denote alternatives

For the two dynamic relationships, another set of derivation rules apply:

- A flow relation between elements may be transferred 'upstream' following any structural relationship. For example, a flow between two services may be transferred to the processes that realise these services.
- A triggering relation may be transferred 'upstream' following assignment relationships. For example, a triggering between two processes may be transferred to the actors assigned to these processes.
- Triggering relationships are transitive: if a triggers b and b triggers c, we may derive that a indirectly triggers c.

These derived relations are also valid in the ArchiMate language. See also the description of this derivation property and the list of permitted relations in the standard (The Open Group 2016a).

5.14   Language Customisation Mechanisms

Every specific purpose and usage of an architecture modelling language brings about its own specific demands on the language. Yet, it should be possible to use a language for only a limited, though non-specific, modelling purpose. Therefore, the ArchiMate core language as described in the previous sections contains only the basic concepts and relationships that serve general enterprise architecture modelling purposes. However, the language should also be able to facilitate, through customisation mechanisms, specialised or domain-specific purposes, such as:

- Supporting specific types of model analysis;
- Supporting the communication of architectures;
- Capturing the specifics of a certain application domain (e.g., the financial sector).

To this end, the language provides a means to allow specialisations of the core set of concepts that are tailored towards such specific domains or applications, without burdening the core with a lot of additional concepts and notation which most people would barely use.

5.14.1   Adding Attributes to ArchiMate Concepts and Relations

As said before, the core of ArchiMate contains only the concepts and relationships that are necessary for general architecture modelling. However, users might want to be able to, for example, perform model-based performance or cost calculations, or to attach supplementary information (textual, numerical, etc.) to the model elements. A simple way to enrich ArchiMate concepts and relationships in a generic way is to add supplementary information by means of a 'profiling' specialisation mechanism (see also Eertink et al. 1999). A profile is a data structure which can be defined separately from the ArchiMate language, but can be coupled dynamically with concepts or relationships, i.e. the user of the language is free to decide whether and when the assignment of a profile to a model element is necessary. Profiles can be specified as sets of typed attributes, by means of a profile definition language. Each of these attributes may have a default value that can be changed by the user.

We distinguish two types of profiles:

– Pre-defined profiles: These are profiles that have a predefined attribute structure and can be implemented beforehand in any tool supporting the ArchiMate language. Examples of such profiles are sets of attributes for ArchiMate concepts and relationships that have to be specified in order to execute common types of analysis.
– User-defined profiles: Through a profile definition language, the user is able to define new profiles, thus extending the definition of ArchiMate concepts or relationships with supplementary attribute sets.

In Chap. 9, we use this mechanism to add profiles for quantitative analysis to model elements.

5.14.2   Specialisation of Concepts

Specialisation is a simple and powerful way to define new concepts based on the existing ones. Specialised concepts inherit the properties of their 'parent' concepts, but additional restrictions with respect to their use may apply. For example, some of the relationships that apply for the 'parent' concept may not be allowed for the specialisation. A specialised concept strongly resembles a stereotype as it is used in UML, and its default notation is the UML's guillemet notation ("specialisation name").

Specialisation of concepts provides extra flexibility, as it allows organisations or individual users to customise the language to their own preferences and needs, while the underlying precise definition of the concepts is conserved. This also implies that analysis and visualisation techniques developed for the ArchiMate language still apply when the specialised concepts are used.

Figure 5.24 shows a number of examples of concept specialisations that have proven to be useful in several practical cases. As the examples indicate, we may

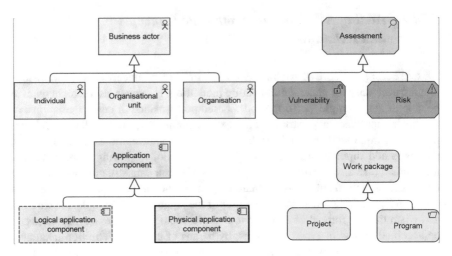

Fig. 5.24 Examples of specialisation

introduce a new graphical notation for a specialised concept, but usually with a resemblance to the notation of the parent concept, e.g., by adding or changing the icon or changing the line style. Finally, for a specialised concept, certain attributes may be predefined, as described in Sect. 5.14.1.

5.15 Modelling Example

To illustrate the use of the ArchiMate language, we introduce the fictitious (though realistic) insurance company ArchiSurance. ArchiSurance originally provided home and travel insurance, but merged recently with two other insurance companies, PRO-FIT (car insurance) and LegallyYours (legal aid insurance). By streamlining their operations and removing duplication, substantial synergy is expected from this merger.

ArchiSurance's management is now wrestling with the intricacies of integrating these three companies, and has decided to take an enterprise architecture approach to create more insight into this complexity.

5.16 Capabilities, Business Functions and Organisation Structure

As a first description of what the company needs to be able to do, the enterprise architects of ArchiSurance, together with a group of its business managers, have created a capability map, inspired by the Panorama 360 reference model for the

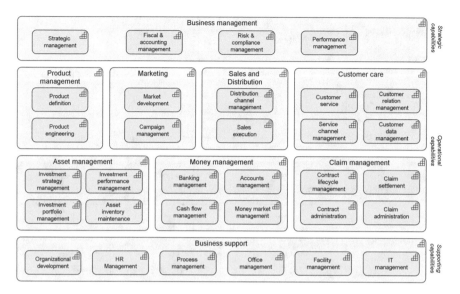

Fig. 5.25 Capability map of ArchiSurance

insurance industry (Insurance Frameworks 2013). These capabilities are very similar for many insurance companies and represent what is most stable about this type of enterprise (Fig. 5.25).

To provide a high-level overview of ArchiSurance's primary operations that realise its operational capabilities, the company is described in terms of its main business functions:

– Maintaining Customer Relations and Intermediary Relations: these business functions are responsible for the contacts of ArchiSurance with its customers and the intermediaries that sell its products. This function handles customer questions and incoming claims, and performs marketing and sales.
– Contracting: this function does the 'back-office' processing of contracts. It performs risk analysis and ensures legally and financially correct contracts.
– Claims Processing: this function is responsible for processing insurance claims, judging their validity and valuation, and deciding the further course of action.
– Financial Handling: this function performs the regular premium collection, according to the insurance policies with customers as produced by Contracting, handles payment of insurance claims and manages other money flows.
– Asset Management: this function manages the financial assets of ArchiSurance, e.g., by investing in stocks and bonds.

The relationship between capabilities and business functions is not one to one: some functions contribute to the realisation of multiple capabilities, and some capabilities require multiple functions. This is shown in Fig. 5.26. Its business

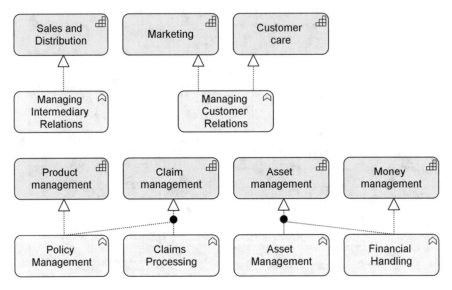

Fig. 5.26 Capabilities realised by business functions

functions are closely aligned with the organisation structure of ArchiSurance (Fig. 5.28), whereas its capabilities are defined in an organisation-independent way.

These business functions are shown in Fig. 5.27, connected by the flows associated with claims handling.

Post-merger integration is in full swing. The first step in the integration process has been the creation of a unified front office, comprising departments for managing relations with customers on the one hand, and intermediaries on the other hand. However, behind this front office are still three separate back offices:

– Home & Away: this department was the original pre-merger ArchiSurance, responsible for home and travel insurance.
– Legal Aid: this is the old LegallyYours, responsible for legal aid and liability insurance.
– Car: this department is the core of the old PRO-FIT and handles car insurance, including some legal expense insurance.

Furthermore, ArchiSurance is in the process of setting up a Shared Service Centre for document processing, which will handle all document streams and performs scanning, printing and archiving jobs. The company's structure is shown in Fig. 5.28. ArchiSurance's front-office departments are located in regional branch offices; its back office is centralised at the company's headquarters.

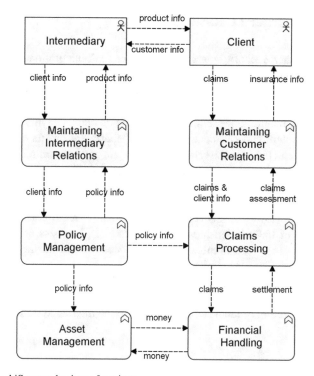

Fig. 5.27 ArchiSurance business functions

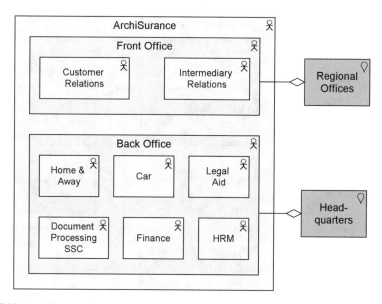

Fig. 5.28 ArchiSurance departments

5.17   Post-Merger IT Rationalisation

As in many other recently merged companies, IT integration is a problem. ArchiSurance wants to move to a single CRM system, separate back-office systems for policy administration and finance, and a single document management system. However, Home & Away still has separate systems for the policy administration and the financial handling of premium collection and claims payment, and uses the central CRM system and call centre. The Car department has its own monolithic back-office system, but uses the central CRM system and call centre. The Legal Aid department has its own back- and front-office systems (Fig. 5.29).

An important prerequisite for the changes in ArchiSurance's IT is that the IT integration should be 'invisible' to ArchiSurance's clients: products and services remain the same. However, this is not a straightforward requirement. To illustrate the complexity of the relationships between products, business processes and IT support, Fig. 5.30 shows a number of core services and the business process that provide these, and Fig. 5.31 shows the relations between this business process and its supporting IT applications. Note that this only shows these relations for a *single* business process. In general, many different business processes within the back office link the external products and services with the internal systems. This web of

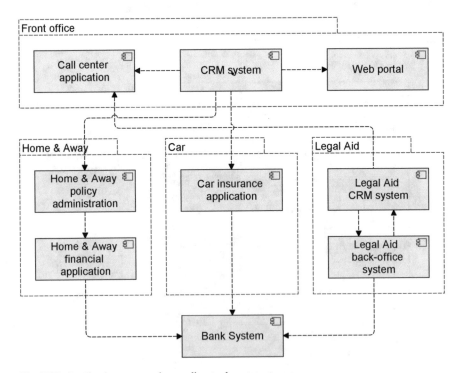

Fig. 5.29 Applications grouped according to departments

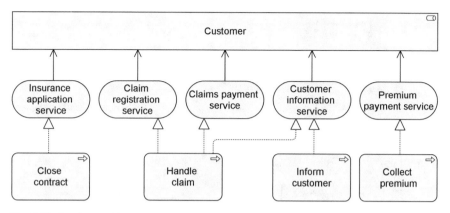

Fig. 5.30 Services and business processes

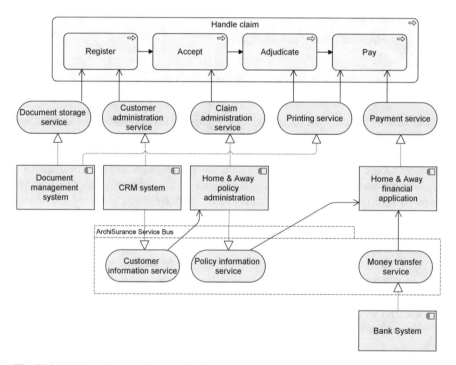

Fig. 5.31 Relations between the Handle Claim business process and its IT support

relations creates a major problem if we want to create insight into the IT support of ArchiSurance.

To improve this application landscape, ArchiSurance has defined a number of projects and programs, for example, to replace the separate policy administrations for its lines of business by a single integrated one. This is shown in Fig. 5.32.

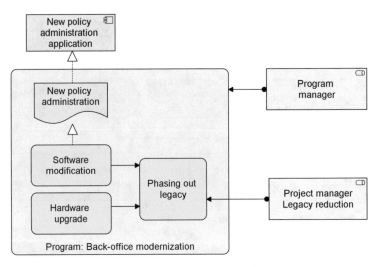

Fig. 5.32 Projects and programs realise change

5.17.1 New Digital Customer Intimacy Strategy

ArchiSurance not only has to deal with the complexities of post-merger integration. Insurance companies operate under challenging circumstances. The low interest rates in financial markets make it difficult for them to fulfil their financial obligations, and digital disruption threatens their business models and market share.

ArchiSurance has made a strategic analysis of the main ways in which it can improve returns. To sustain profitability, the company needs to increase revenue, which requires a higher customer retention and/or increasing market share. To this end, it wants to achieve an improved customer satisfaction and a more competitive premium setting.

ArchiSurance sees the rapid pace of technology innovation as both a challenge and an opportunity. This has led it to define a new strategy based on 'digital customer intimacy', which employs a combination of social media, big data and the Internet of Things (IoT). According to this strategy, they intend to use more detailed customer data to improve customer interaction and satisfaction and to determine customised insurance premiums. This is depicted in Fig. 5.33.

In its digital customer intimacy strategy, ArchiSurance takes a two-pronged approach. First, it wants to engage with its customers more intimately through various social media channels. Second, it aims to use various kinds of external data. For insurance products sold in the consumer market, this entails data from smart, connected devices such as fitness trackers, black boxes in vehicles or home automation gateways; in various b2b markets it wants to use data from sources such as fleet management, energy networks, in-store RFID devices or smart building sensors. Ultimately, this may result in real-time insurance products where

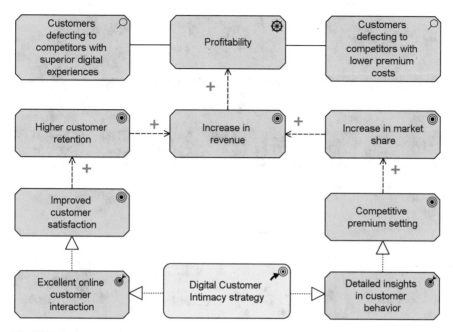

Fig. 5.33 Strategic analysis of ArchiSurance

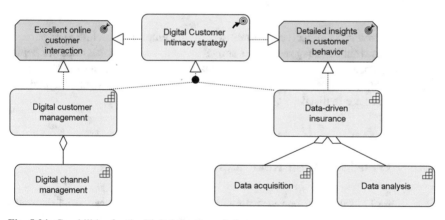

Fig. 5.34 Capabilities for the Digital Customer Intimacy strategy

customers receive direct feedback on the financial consequences of their behaviour and advice on adjusting this behaviour to lower their insurance premium.

In Fig. 5.34, we see the main new capabilities needed to realise this strategy and how these contribute to the business outcomes ArchiSurance wants to achieve.

These capabilities need to be supported by the right resources including personnel with the right knowledge and skills for the digital age, smart devices for data acquisition and the customer data itself. This is shown in Fig. 5.35.

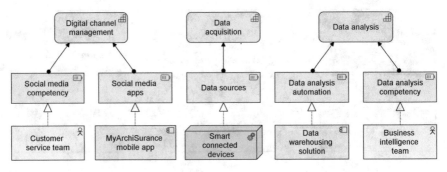

Fig. 5.35 Resources supporting capabilities

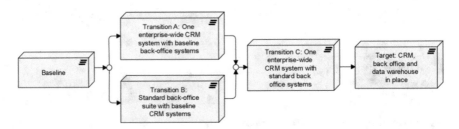

Fig. 5.36 Application architecture roadmap

These resources themselves are realised by the enterprise architecture core. A small part of what this may result in is shown as well. Note that this does not depict all elements needed to realise these resources, but only a representative sample. In practice, separate views will often be created to show how individual capabilities and resources are realised.

5.18   Transformation Roadmap

Combining both the post-merger rationalisation of its IT landscape and the realisation of its new strategy, ArchiSurance has drawn up a roadmap showing the architecture plateaus that step by step move it into the future (Fig. 5.36) and two alternative transition scenarios.

Each plateau aggregates the elements of the architecture that are valid during this specific period, as exemplified in Fig. 5.37.

By putting all of this information together, you obtain a line of sight between your different assets and the projects and programs working on these, upwards to the business functions, processes and capabilities they support and finally to the strategies, goals and outcomes. Thus, ArchiMate models support the full trajectory of strategy implementation.

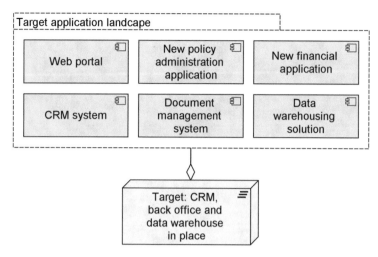

Fig. 5.37 Contents of target plateau

5.19 Summary

A well-defined language for enterprise architecture modelling helps to reach a common understanding between different architects and other stakeholders in an enterprise. It allows for the integration of architectural models and detailed designs within specific domains, which is a prerequisite for the integration of domain-specific modelling tools. In this way, enterprise architecture models may serve as a starting point for model-driven system development. They also provide the basis for visualisation and analysis of architectures.

Service orientation plays a central role in the enterprise modelling language we presented in this chapter, where the service concept is applicable at several layers: business services made available to internal or external customers, application services made available to 'the business' or to other applications, and infrastructure technology services made available to applications. Services provide a way to show the alignment between the different modelling layers.

This emphasis on service orientation is but one aspect of the strong focus we put on the relations between the different domains and aspects of the enterprise. Integrating these is essential for providing coherent descriptions of enterprise architectures.

In this chapter, we have only described the essentials of the language. A more extensive description of its background and details can be found in Jonkers et al. (2004) and in The Open Group's ArchiMate 3.0 specification document (The Open Group 2016a).

Chapter 6
Combining ArchiMate with Other Standards and Approaches

Marc M. Lankhorst, Adina Aldea, and Joost Niehof

The ArchiMate language is not intended to replace other standards and modelling approaches. Rather, it is meant to function together with these other techniques and function as a kind of 'umbrella', binding them together to create an integrated set of models of an enterprise architecture.

6.1 Introduction

For many domains, there are languages and techniques available to provide more detailed descriptions than ArchiMate offers. Those languages, such as UML, BPMN and others, have a narrower scope (e.g. UML for specifying software, BPMN for business processes) than ArchiMate, but they lack concepts for relating these to other domains.

The uniqueness of ArchiMate does not lie in the individual concepts, but rather the opposite: many concepts in the language are designed to have a direct correspondence with similar concepts in other techniques, in which you can zoom in in more detail for specific parts of your architecture. As Fig. 6.1 shows, there is some overlap between ArchiMate and these other techniques. For example, the ArchiMate concept of Application Component is largely identical to UML's Component concept. This allows you to connect ArchiMate models to models for these individual domains, so you can zoom in on specific parts of the enterprise architecture by drilling down into these other models.

M.M. Lankhorst (✉)
BiZZdesign, Capitool 15, 7521 PL Enschede, The Netherlands
e-mail: m.lankhorst@bizzdesign.com

A. Aldea • J. Niehof
BiZZdesign, Enschede, The Netherlands

© Springer-Verlag Berlin Heidelberg 2017
M. Lankhorst et al., *Enterprise Architecture at Work*, The Enterprise Engineering Series, DOI 10.1007/978-3-662-53933-0_6

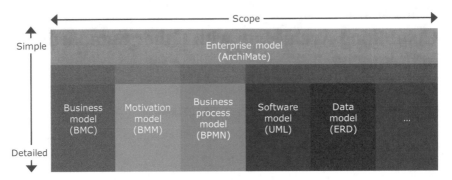

Fig. 6.1 Enterprise architecture model connecting other models

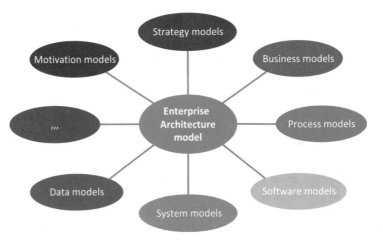

Fig. 6.2 Enterprise architecture model as hub between other models

This is where ArchiMate adds value. You need such a less detailed but broader description to have a general overview of your enterprise, in order to see the dependencies between different aspects and areas, but at the same time avoid drowning in details.

Moreover, ArchiMate provides you with an integrated description of the enterprise that relates (sub)models from formerly separate domains in a meaningful manner. This way, you can analyse and define the dependencies between desired business outcomes, products and processes, IT systems, data, projects and programs and other aspects of your enterprise, all within one environment. This is very important in realising your business strategy: a clear line-of-sight between all the elements of your enterprise, with a single source of truth instead of disparate modelling silos, efficient analysis of the impact of management decisions and easy collaboration between the different experts that work on designing and changing your enterprise.

Existing languages focus on detailed descriptions of individual domains, but lack concepts for relating these to others. The ArchiMate language acts as a hub between models for these domains (Fig. 6.2). These models can be seen as more detailed views on specific parts of the enterprise architecture. If they are tied in to an overall enterprise architecture model in ArchiMate, an integrated model of the enterprise can be constructed that relates (sub)models from formerly separate domains in a meaningful way.

To help you relate ArchiMate models to a number of those other techniques, the following sections provide an approximate mapping between ArchiMate concepts and concepts from those techniques, illustrated with examples.

6.2   Business Motivation Model

The Business Motivation Model (BMM) (Object Management Group 2015b) has been one of the inspirations behind ArchiMate's motivation concepts (Sect. 5.6). BMM distinguishes between means, ends, and influencers and assessments and provides a more detailed, fine-grained description of business motivation that ArchiMate's motivation concepts (Table 6.1).

In Fig. 6.3, we see how ArchiMate concepts are used to model concepts from the Business Motivation Model. Between the stereotype notations with guillemets ("«...»"), we show the name of the ArchiMate type (AM) and the Business Motivation Model type (BMM).

6.3   Balanced Scorecard

As discussed in Sect. 2.1.1, the Balanced Scorecard (Kaplan and Norton 1992) is a widely used high-level technique for strategic performance management of organisations. It provides four perspectives on this performance and addresses these in a layered structure using mission, objectives, measures, targets and initiatives to express the strategic direction. Figure 6.4 shows these concepts can be mapped onto ArchiMate (Table 6.2).

An example of the Balanced Scorecard modelled with ArchiMate is shown in Fig. 6.4.

Table 6.1 ArchiMate and BMM

BMM	ArchiMate
Vision, Desired Result (Goal, Objective)	Goal
Mission, Course of Action (Strategy, Tactic)	Course of Action
Directive (Business Policy, Business Rule)	Principle, Requirement, Constraint
Assessment	Assessment
Influencer	Driver
Potential Impact	Outcome

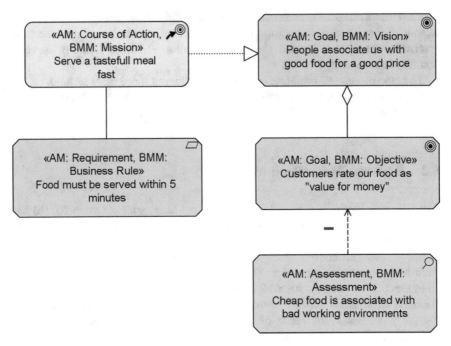

Fig. 6.3 BMM concepts expressed in ArchiMate

6.4 Business Model Canvas

The Business Model Canvas (Osterwalder and Pigneur 2010), as described in Sect. 2.1.2, provides you with a high-level overview of the structure of the current or envisaged business models of an organisation. Its concepts can be mapped onto ArchiMate in a straightforward way, as shown in Table 6.3. This provides a useful starting point for further definition of the business architecture.

An example of an automatically generated mapping from the Business Model Canvas to ArchiMate concepts is shown in Fig. 6.5.

6.5 Value Map

Value mapping is a useful technique in business architecture. It provides insight into the value produced by the various activities of the organisation, how this contributes to its overall value proposition and how this value is exchanged with other parties in a value network.

The classical example of this is the Value Chain defined by Porter (1985), which divides the activities of an enterprise in value-creating and supporting and subdivides the former in the typical stages of a production process, with inbound

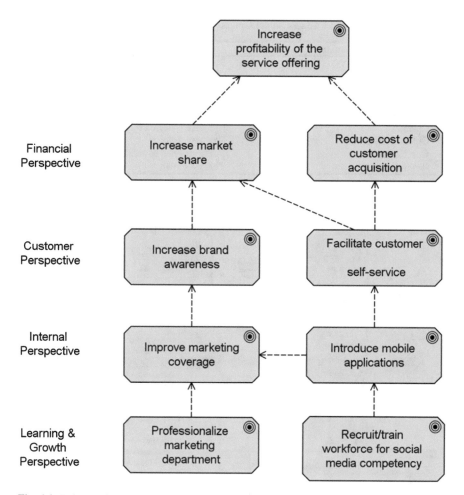

Fig. 6.4   Balanced Scorecard concepts expressed in ArchiMate

Table 6.2   ArchiMate and Balanced Scorecard

Balanced Scorecard	ArchiMate
Mission, Objective	Goal
Measure	Metric (specialisation of Driver)
Target	Outcome, Value
Initiative	Course of Action (high-level)
	Work Package (detailed)

Table 6.3 ArchiMate and Business Model Canvas

Business Model Canvas	ArchiMate
Key Partner	Business Actor (or Role)
Key Activity	Capability
Key Resource	Resource
Value Proposition	Product + Value
Customer Relationship	Business Collaboration
Channel	Resource (realised by Interface)
Customer Segment	Business Actor
Cost Structure	Value attached to architecture elements
Revenue Stream	Value + Flow

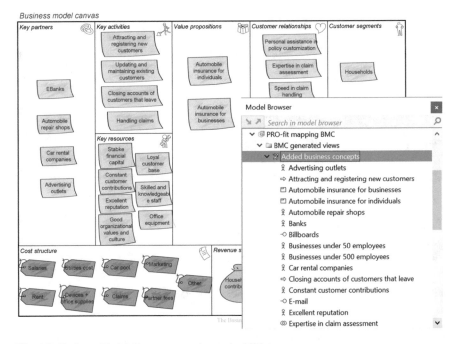

Fig. 6.5 Business Model Canvas mapped onto ArchiMate

logistics, operations, outbound logistics, marketing and sales and service. More recent approaches such as e^{3}value (Gordijn 2002), the Value Delivery Metamodel (VDML) (Object Management Group 2015f) and the BIZBOK® Guide (Business Architecture Guild 2016) take a more general stance and also look at value exchange in the broader ecosystem. Table 6.4 provides a general mapping aimed at supporting most of these approaches. For more on value modelling and ArchiMate, see, for example, De Kinderen et al. (2012).

The mapping shown in Table 6.4 mainly uses ArchiMate's business layer concepts to express value maps. Remember that ArchiMate uses the same concept

Table 6.4 ArchiMate and Value Maps

Value Map	ArchiMate
Value Proposition	Product + Value
Value Item	Value
Value Stream	Business Process (highest-level)
Value Stage, Activity	Business Process or Function
Value Exchange	Flow + associated Value
Actor, Organisation Unit	Business Actor
Role	Business Role
Collaboration	Business Collaboration
Capability	Capability

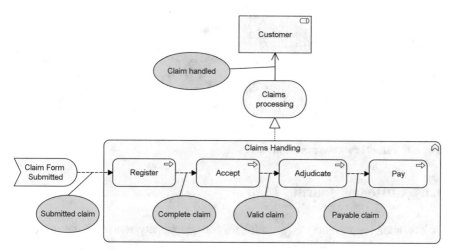

Fig. 6.6 Value Stream expressed in ArchiMate

for all levels of granularity, i.e. a business process can express an entire value stream, a value stage in that stream or activities within such a stage, down to the smallest individual task. Furthermore, this mapping uses value elements associated with products and with flow relationships to model the value propositions and exchange of value along the value chain, stream or network. This maps well onto typical Porter Value Chain models. Alternatively, for a somewhat more abstract view, we may map a value stage to a (named) grouping of capabilities in ArchiMate and relate these groupings via flow relationships with associated value elements.

An example of a Value Map with a Value Stream and Value Exchanges between its different stages is shown in Fig. 6.6.

A partial Value Network containing several Actors Value Exchanges and Value Items can be seen in Fig. 6.7.

Using ArchiMate helps you express and analyse the business model of your organisation and how it produces stakeholder value, and lets you focus on the important value-producing activities in strategic planning and change.

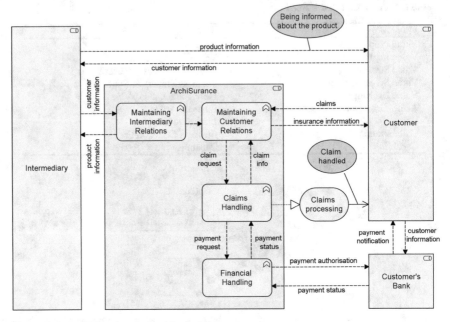

Fig. 6.7 Value Network expressed in ArchiMate

6.6   Customer Journey Map

A customer journey map is a useful way to graphically represent the customer experience of an organisation. It focuses on the touchpoints that characterise the customers' interaction with the services of the organisation and helps you optimise this experience.

ArchiMate concepts can easily be used in such a customer journey map. The backbone of a customer journey map is course the business process, with the stages therein modelled as subprocesses. The touchpoints with the customer are modelled as business services plus business interfaces, to model both the behaviour of the organisation and the channels it uses in the customer contact. Different customer journey maps for the same process could be specified for various personas, who are typically modelled as business roles.

Information from customer surveys and other measurements of the customer experience (e.g. data from the website or call centre, net promoter score) is added to the steps in the process, using the profile mechanism (Sect. 5.14.1) to specify relevant attributes. Alternatively, you can define Metric as a specialisation of the Driver concept, in the way described in Sect. 9.6. Different metrics for different aspects of the customer journey can be associated with the steps in the journey. This information has to be evaluated, which can be modelled with the Assessment concept, and appropriate improvements to the customer experience may be specified as Requirements.

Table 6.5 ArchiMate and Customer Journey Maps

Customer Journey Map	ArchiMate
Persona	Business Role
Customer Journey, Process, Scenario	Business Process
Stage	Business Process
Touchpoint	Business Service
Channel	Business Interface
Experience, Feeling	Metric (specialisation of Driver), or profile attribute
Evaluation	Assessment
Opportunity, Improvement	Requirement

There is no fixed, standardised vocabulary in customer journey maps. Table 6.5 shows a number of common terms and their mapping onto appropriate ArchiMate concepts.

Customer journey maps are typically depicted using a graph that shows the touchpoints in the process on the horizontal axis and the quality of the experience from the customers' point of view (e.g. in terms of meeting or exceeding their expectations) on the vertical axis. Around this, various other kinds of information can be shown in various ways, for example, using swimlanes to depict the channels used and smiley faces to show the feeling of your customers with certain touchpoints, as shown in Fig. 6.8. This is of course not expressed in the standard ArchiMate notation, but it is based on an underlying ArchiMate model.

6.7 Service Blueprint

Another technique for service innovation is the service blueprint (Shostack 1984). It is related to customer journey maps (Sect. 6.6) in its emphasis of customer touchpoints but focuses more on the realisation of services by underlying activities and less on the quality of the customer's experience. A service blueprint provides a layered depiction of a service, showing from top to bottom:

- Physical evidence: the tangibles obtained by the customer as a result of the service delivery process
- Customer actions: the steps taken by customers in the service delivery
- Onstage/visible actions: the activities performed by the organisation in direct, face-to-face contact with the customer
- Backstage/invisible actions: the activities by the customer contact employees in the service delivery process that are invisible to the customer
- Support processes: the activities performed by others than customer contact employees that are needed to deliver a service

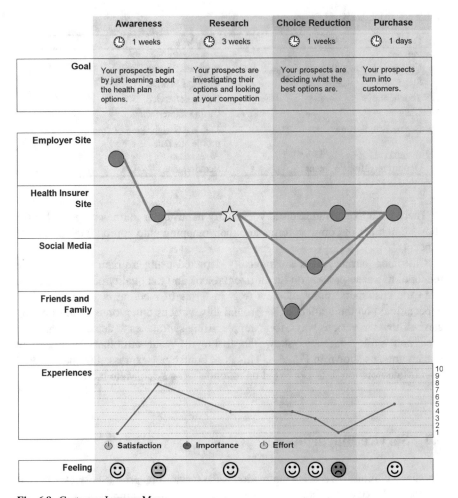

Fig. 6.8 Customer Journey Map

The user and on-stage actions are separated by the so-called line of interaction, the on- and backstage actions by the 'line of visibility' and the backstage actions and support processes by the 'line of internal interaction'.

Nowadays, given the importance of online experiences, the 'physical' evidence and face-to-face nature of visible customer interactions as defined in the original service blueprint are often interpreted more liberally, to include electronic means as well (e.g. email, webpage, social media, etc.). A straightforward mapping on ArchiMate concepts is listed in Table 6.6.

A Service Blueprint modelled with ArchiMate is shown in Fig. 6.9.

Table 6.6 ArchiMate and Service Blueprints

Service Blueprint	ArchiMate
Physical Evidence	Business Object, Data Object, Representation, Artefact, Material
Customer Action	Business Process
Onstage Action	Business Interaction
Backstage Action	Business Process
Support Process	Business Process

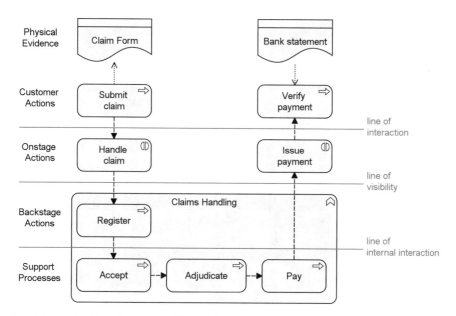

Fig. 6.9 Service Blueprint expressed in ArchiMate

6.8 BPMN

The main standard for modelling business processes is BPMN (Sect. 2.3.2). ArchiMate is typically used for high-level processes and their relations to the enterprise context, but it is not intended for detailed workflow modelling. BPMN supports detailed subprocess and task modelling down to the level of executable specifications but lacks the broader enterprise context, for example, to model the application services that support a process or the goals and requirements it has to fulfil. To this end, BPMN has a more fine-grained set of elements, with various types of events, tasks and gateways. Both languages can be used quite easily in combination. Mapping from ArchiMate down to BPMN is fairly straightforward, as is shown in Table 6.7.

Table 6.7 ArchiMate and BPMN

BPMN	ArchiMate
Participant/Pool, Lane	Business Actor, Role, Application Component
Collaboration	Business/Application Collaboration
Process	Business/Application Process
Sequence flow	Triggering
Data association	Access
Inclusive and parallel gateways	Junction
Exclusive and event-based gateways	Or-junction

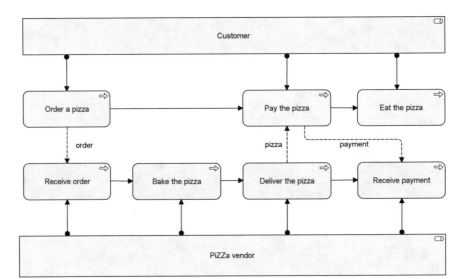

Fig. 6.10 High-level ArchiMate model of pizza ordering process

The most common use of such a mapping is to utilise ArchiMate to make a high-level process view and draw a corresponding, more detailed BPMN model based on the mapping in the Table 6.7 (see Figs. 6.10 and 6.11). The relations between the individual concepts in both languages are shown in Fig. 6.12. Here you can see that a single ArchiMate concept (e.g. 'Order a pizza') may expand into multiple BPMN concepts.

6.9   Business Logic

Explicit definitions of business logic are increasingly used to separate the 'know' from the 'flow' in business process models. The two main open standards in this domain are SBVR (Semantics of Business Vocabulary and Rules) (Object Management Group 2015g) and DMN (Decision Model and Notation) (Object

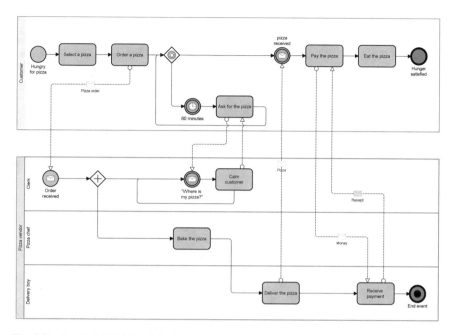

Fig. 6.11 Detailed BPMN model of pizza ordering process

Management Group 2016a). Often, business logic models will be used in conjunction with process models expressed in BPMN (Sect. 6.8) which has an explicit business rule task type.

In Table 6.8, an approximate mapping of SBVR and DMN concepts onto ArchiMate is shown. A small example is shown in Fig. 6.13. In this example, we use the stereotype notation for expressing language customisations, as explained in Sect. 5.14.2.

6.10 UML

The Unified Modeling Language (UML) (Sect. 2.3.3) is the de facto standard for software modelling. Several concepts in ArchiMate were strongly inspired by UML. The most obvious is the application component concepts, which corresponds to the UML component. The node, artefact, device, system software and path elements have also been taken more or less directly from UML (where system software is called execution environment). This close linkage facilitates a continuous development chain between higher-level enterprise architecture models

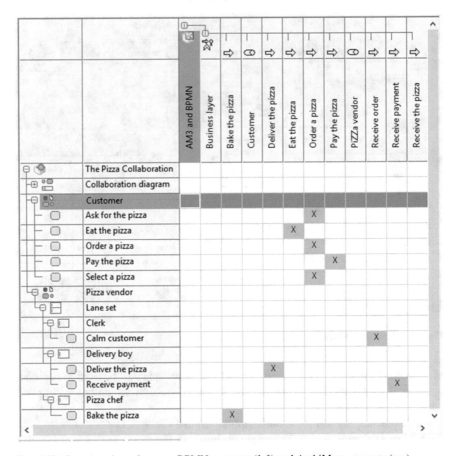

Fig. 6.12 Correspondence between BPMN concepts (*left*) and ArchiMate concepts (*top*)

Table 6.8 ArchiMate, SBVR and DMN

SBVR	ArchiMate
Fact, Rule, Proposition, Concept, Meaning	Meaning
Community	Stakeholder
DMN	
Business Knowledge Model, Decision Table, Rule Set	Data Object, Business Object
Decision	Application Service, Business Service
Input Data	Data Object
Knowledge Source	Requirement

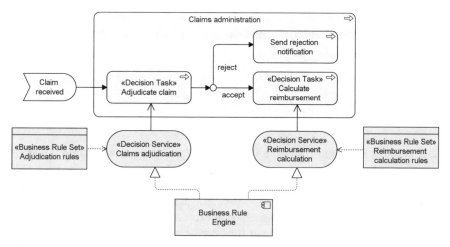

Fig. 6.13 Expressing business rules and decisions in ArchiMate using stereotypes

Table 6.9 ArchiMate and UML

UML	ArchiMate
Actor	Business Actor, Role
Use Case	Requirement + Service
Component	Application Component
Class	Business Object, Data Object
Collaboration	Application Collaboration
Node, Device, Execution Environment	Node, Device, System Software
Artefact	Artefact
Interface	Application Interface + Service
Aggregation, Composition, Generalisation	Aggregation, Composition, Specialisation

described in ArchiMate notation and lower-level solution architecture and implementation models in UML (Table 6.9).

There are also some important differences between the two. The ArchiMate serving relationship, although superficially similar in notation, is semantically different from UML's dependency and often points in the opposite direction. A UML dependency is used to model, for example, function calls in software programs. At the architectural level at which the ArchiMate language is aimed, run-time operational details of such call graphs are less important than the more stable and generic notion of service provision. In ArchiMate, the direction of the serving relationship therefore denotes the direction of service *delivery*, independent of whether this service is called by the user or offered pro-actively by the provider.

This also points to another important difference: UML does not have a separate service concept, since in its object-oriented paradigm the behaviour expressed by a service is encapsulated via (the operations of) an interface. The ArchiMate language differentiates between interfaces and the services they provide, in order to specify that the same service is offered through multiple interfaces. Hence, UML interface corresponds with the combination of an ArchiMate application interface and service.

6.11   SysML

The Systems Modeling Language (SysML) (Object Management Group 2015e) is an offshoot from UML for systems engineering and offers concepts for specification, analysis, design, verification and validation of a broad range of systems and systems-of-systems. It is less software-centric than UML and a lot smaller and simpler to learn (although its diagrams can become quite complicated).

When designing physical systems (or systems with physical parts), SysML may be suited as a language for the more detailed design, while ArchiMate is used for the architecture level of abstraction. Table 6.10 shows the correspondence between ArchiMate and SysML concepts in such a context.

6.12   Entity-Relationship Model

One of the older type of modelling techniques in ICT is the entity-relationship (ER) model (Chen 1976). An ER model comprises entity types, which classify the things of interest and specific relationships between the instances of these types. There are various techniques to depict ER models in ER diagrams, one of the most popular being the Crow's Foot notation.

ER models are often used in data modelling, in particular in the design of relational databases. As such, they map most naturally on ArchiMate's passive structure concepts, as shown in the Table 6.11. Attributes, keys or instances of entities would typically not be modelled in ArchiMate, as these are usually too detailed for the enterprise architecture level of abstraction. For the same reason, ArchiMate does not support cardinalities of relationships.

Table 6.10   ArchiMate and SysML

SysML	ArchiMate
Block	Active Structure Element, e.g. Application Component, Business Actor, Device, Equipment, Facility
Requirement	Requirement, Constraint
Port	Service+Interface
Activity	Function, Process

Table 6.11 ArchiMate and ER models

ER model	ArchiMate
Entity (conceptual)	Business Object, Meaning
Entity (logical)	Data Object
Entity (physical)	Artefact
Relationship	Association (with label)

6.13 TOGAF

The structure of the ArchiMate core language neatly corresponds with the three main architectural domains of TOGAF's Architecture Development Method (ADM) (see also Sect. 2.2.3). Therefore, the core of ArchiMate primarily supports the creation of architectural views in Phases B, C and D of the ADM (Business, Information Systems and Technology Architectures), as is illustrated in Fig. 6.14. The Strategy and the Motivation concepts can be used to capture the strategy of the enterprise, its architecture vision, stakeholders, drivers, business goals and principles in the Preliminary Phase and Phase A and to capture and manage business requirements throughout the ADM cycle (with a focus on Phase H, Change Management and the central Requirements Management process). The Implementation and Migration concepts offer support for implementation and migration planning in Phases E, F and G of the ADM.

Thus, TOGAF and ArchiMate can easily be used in conjunction, and they cover much of the same ground. TOGAF itself provides some guidance on creating a consistent overall model of the architecture, but mostly refers to tools that should provide this support (The Open Group 2011, Sect. 35.3.1):

> In order to achieve the goals of completeness and integrity in an architecture, architecture views are usually developed, visualized, communicated, and managed using a tool.
>
> In the current state of the market, different tools normally have to be used to develop and analyze different views of the architecture. It is highly desirable that an architecture description be encoded in a standard language, to enable a standard approach to the description of architecture semantics and their re-use among different tools.

This is where ArchiMate nicely complements TOGAF: it provides a vendor-independent, standardised set of concepts that helps to create a consistent, integrated model 'below the waterline', which can be depicted in the form of TOGAF's views (see also Sect. 8.10).

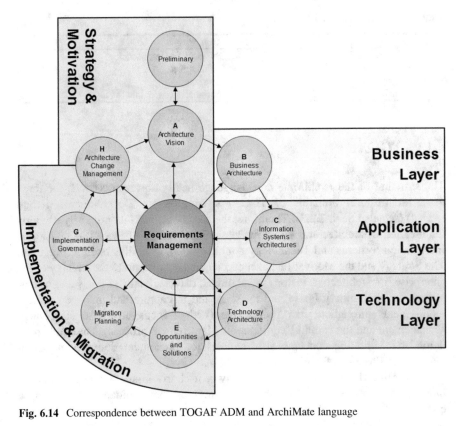

Fig. 6.14 Correspondence between TOGAF ADM and ArchiMate language

6.14 Summary

In designing your enterprise, no single modelling technique will ever be sufficient. Combining different models covering different parts of the overall enterprise scope is therefore essential. The ArchiMate language provides an excellent instrument to bring those models together and create an integrated view of the enterprise.

As we have demonstrated in this chapter, the ArchiMate language works very well in conjunction with various other techniques, ranging from strategic planning and analysis such as the Balanced Scorecard to more detailed design languages like UML and BPMN. It also provides a good fit with the TOGAF framework for enterprise architecture, which is of course not surprising given that they are both Open Group standards.

Chapter 7
Guidelines for Modelling

Robert J. Slagter, Stijn J.B.A. Hoppenbrouwers, Marc M. Lankhorst, and Jan Campschroer

7.1 Introduction

Two architects, without a common method, tend to develop different models of the same real world. How should we decide what is a good architecture? Pioneers in the design of complex systems (Dijkstra 1968; Brooks 1975) have described design principles to ensure the *conceptual integrity* of a model: 'It is not enough to learn the elements and rules of combination; one must also learn idiomatic usage, a whole lore of how the elements are combined in practice. Simplicity and straightforwardness proceed from conceptual integrity. Every part must reflect the same philosophies and the same balancing of desiderata. [. . .] Ease of use, then, dictates unity of design, conceptual integrity' (Brooks 1975).

Conceptual integrity is the degree to which a model can be understood by a single human mind, despite its complexity. The core idea of conceptual integrity is that any good design exhibits a single, coherent vision, which is easy to understand by others. This allows someone with a limited knowledge and understanding of a model to understand easily yet unknown parts of the model. In emphasising the role of the 'single mind', this design principle clearly advocates the important role of an architect in any larger design project.

R.J. Slagter
GriDD Consultancy, Enschede, The Netherlands

S.J.B.A. Hoppenbrouwers
Radboud University Nijmegen, Nijmegen, The Netherlands

M.M. Lankhorst (✉)
BiZZdesign, Capitool 15, 7521 PL Enschede, The Netherlands
e-mail: m.lankhorst@bizzdesign.com

J. Campschroer
Ordina, Nieuwegein, The Netherlands

© Springer-Verlag Berlin Heidelberg 2017
M. Lankhorst et al., *Enterprise Architecture at Work*, The Enterprise Engineering Series, DOI 10.1007/978-3-662-53933-0_7

To ensure conceptual integrity, one can use subordinate design principles such as: do not link what is independent (orthogonality), do not introduce multiple functions that are slightly divergent (generality), do not introduce what is irrelevant (economy; sometimes denoted as parsimony), and do not restrict what is inherent (propriety). The literature on quality requirements for models shows a broad consensus about the general applicability of these heuristics (Krogstie et al. 1995; Lindland et al. 1994; Teeuw and Berg 1997). Applying these design principles increases the *internal quality* of a model (Teeuw and Berg 1997).

Additionally, the quality of an architecture is also determined by its stakeholders: we state that an enterprise architecture that is a 'correct' and 'complete' representation of the real-life enterprise that is being modelled, given the objectives of stakeholders, has a high *external quality*. In short, external quality refers to the fitness for use of a model (Biemans et al. 2001).

Notwithstanding this, the quality of many architectures is often also determined by less rational choices. As Rechtin and Maier state about the political process (1997, p. 206): 'The best engineering solutions are not necessarily the best political ones'.

In enterprise architecture, as in other design ventures, these general principles are of course very valuable. However, the broad scope, and wide-ranging nature of enterprise architecture make the ideal of conceptual integrity particularly difficult to achieve.

There is no such thing as an inherently good – or inherently bad – model. To assess the quality of an architecture model, you have to take into account for what purpose the model is created and who the target audience is. Different purposes and different target audiences may require fundamentally different models: while an IT manager may wish to have an overview of the system software, the devices it runs on, and the communication paths between these devices, the manager of a company may wish to have an overview of the products the company produces and the services they depend on. Nevertheless, it is possible to formulate generic guidelines that help to make clear and useful models, comparable to the guidelines that the TOGAF Architecture Development Method (The Open Group 2011) formulates (see also Chap. 2).

This chapter provides such guidelines for our approach, founded on a basic theoretical view of enterprise architecture modelling. After introducing this view and its implications, the chapter continues with a discussion of general aspects of readability and usability of models. The last part of this chapter provides guidelines for creating models in the ArchiMate language that was introduced in Chap. 5, and discusses issues such as what to capture in an ArchiMate model, how to structure such models, and how to present them.

7.2   The Modelling Process

A model, in the context of this book, is an unambiguous, abstract conception of some parts or aspects of the real world (see Sect. 3.2.3). Models focus on specific aspects of the real world, based on the purpose for which the model is created.

Hence, modelling is part of a goal-driven communication process, as discussed in Chap. 4.

In enterprise architecture, modelling typically involves creating abstract representations of enterprises: the business processes involved, the IT-infrastructure, as well as the relations between them. Given a specific goal and focus, an enterprise architect decides which aspects of an enterprise are relevant and should be represented in the model. Examples of aspects that are frequently included in enterprise architecture models are: products, business processes, applications and IT-infrastructure elements, as well as their relations. As such, an enterprise architect gathers relevant information and transforms this into a model; the aim of this chapter is to provide you with design guidelines for this process.

7.2.1 Modelling as a Transformation Process

First, we go back to some fundamental issues discussed in Chap. 4 and link these up with a view of the modelling process.

Architecture models are created in order to communicate something, either to the people *reading* the model or between people *making* the model. But communication also has its underlying goal: the participants are to introduce, agree on, and commit to some *knowledge representation*. This means that the model that is the result of a modelling process is not the ultimate goal, and not even the only product of that process. Transformations in the knowledge, agreements, and commitments in the minds of the people involved are as important, if not more important, than the representations (models). So the goals underlying the modelling process are essentially *knowledge goals*, and (the creation of) models should be directly aimed at fulfilling those knowledge goals. From this point of view, then, the modelling process concerns a *transformation* of knowledge, agreements, and commitments (the *knowledge state* of the participants) and of the central *representations* used as a tool in this transformation: the models. This is depicted graphically in Fig. 7.1. The input of the process consists of the knowledge state of participants involved in the modelling process and possibly of one or more existing models (or related descriptions, e.g. texts).

Fig. 7.1 Knowledge goals and modelling guidelines steer the modelling process

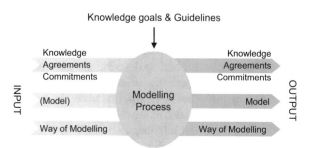

Note, however, that a third sort of input/output is included in Fig. 7.1: the 'Way of Modelling' (WoM). As we described in Sect. 3.2.5, the WoM refers to the meta-model and the concepts that the modellers work with. As modelling progresses, the participants may or may not decide that more, or different, meta-concepts are needed to answer the questions that are asked. For example, they may decide to start using the concept 'service', or a specialisation of that concept fit for their specific modelling context. Such changes in the WoM are commonplace during modelling and are, in most cases, not an undesirable action due to bad WoM choices earlier on. It cannot easily be foreseen what precise WoM will be needed. In fact, finding out the best WoM for a model is an inherent part of the process as such.

The knowledge goals steer the modelling process, or should do so. Of course, these goals depend on the modelling context. However, there are also a number of principles that hold more generally. They can be boiled down to *modelling guidelines*. The combined knowledge goals and modelling guidelines are what should guide each and every step of the transformational process.

7.2.2 Basic Modelling Activities

In a modelling process, you carry out different types of activities. This section describes these activities and a logical order to perform them in. However, real-life modelling processes are not linear, but iterative and highly interactive: an architect will discuss design decisions and intermediate versions of the model with various stakeholders and, as a result, repeat some activities, perform activities in a different order, combine or even skip activities. We distinguish the following activities in a modelling process:

– **Establishing the purpose, scope and focus**. Modelling is a goal-driven activity. So initially, an architect should determine who the stakeholders and are what the purpose of the model is, in relation to these stakeholders. As described in Sect. 1.3, a business strategy often forms the starting point to establish the modelling purpose. Typical purposes of enterprise architecture models are to provide (1) insight into processes, IT infrastructure, and their alignment, (2) a basis for business process redesign, (3) a basis for application (re)design, (4) a basis for infrastructure (re)design, and (5) a basis for business–IT alignment. Related to the purpose, you have to decide on the *scope* and *focus* of the model: (1) what part of reality will be described in the model (e.g., only the primary processes), (2) what aspects will be described, and (3) with what level of detail? Note that models can be applied to describe the current situation 'as is' as well as the situation 'to be', possibly including the required transition.
– **Selecting one or more viewpoints** to create the model. Architects create models using viewpoints, such as the ones described in Chap. 8. These viewpoints give a set of concepts and relations to be used during the modelling process. As such, they guide you in determining what information should be included in the model, given the stakeholder, the purpose for which the model is created and the focus.

In our approach, we typically use the *design viewpoints* described in Chap. 8 to create a model, but this can also be done using the other types of viewpoints.

– **Creating and structuring the model**: In this stage you gather the required information, and create, structure, and visualise the enterprise architecture model. The actions of creating and structuring a model are strongly related and should not be performed in isolation.

  • Enterprise architecture is hardly ever performed in a green field situation: typically, business process models, information models, or infrastructure models about (parts of) the enterprise already exist. A main objective of enterprise architecture is to reveal the relations between the different domains, and to provide a high-level overview. As such, you should always check the validity of any existing models, and incorporate their information on an appropriate level of abstraction; domain-specific models provide more details about parts of the enterprise than an enterprise architecture model. As such, an enterprise architecture model should, for example, not be considered a replacement for the existing information models or business process models.

  • You can elicit the additional information you need for example by using interviews or by discussing scenarios of the situation 'to be' with stakeholders.

  • Based on this information, you create and structure a model. Creating a model is done via the modelling actions, described in the following section. The purpose of structuring the model is to reduce its (visual) complexity, which makes it easier to recognise and understand. Structuring a model also helps to discover recurring patterns as well as inconsistencies. There are many ways to structure models. One type of structuring that is frequently applied in enterprise modelling is to structure the model around one key concept: structuring your model around *services* is for instance practical if the model should reveal the links between business processes and application components that are in use. Another type of structuring frequently used in business process descriptions reveals the flow of processes that are triggered by an event or an activity. More examples of this are given in Sect. 7.3.4.

  • In our approach, you create a model via one or more (visual) representations, in accordance with a selected viewpoint. You have to decide, depending on the modelling purpose and the stakeholders, what (visual) representations to apply for the various concepts and relations, how to structure the visualisation, and, for instance, what colours to use. While in some exceptional cases a textual representation of a model may be preferred, our approach focuses on visual representations of enterprise architecture models.

– **Visualising the model**: Depending on the types of stakeholders and their needs, you select one or more appropriate ways to visualise the model. The enterprise architecture approach presented in this book advocates one central model, which is visualised in different ways, for different purposes. Graphical viewpoints, like those described in Chap. 8, form a useful starting point to visualise models, although other representations, such as text and tables, are also possible.

– **Using the model**: At this stage, you use the representation of the model to communicate with the stakeholders. Independent of whether the model is meant as a basis for designing, deciding, or just to inform stakeholders, you have to assess whether the model and the selected visualisation achieve the intended result. Section 7.3.5 describes which breakdowns can occur in this process, and how to handle them. The typical steps in using visual representations are:

- *Validation.* You can validate a model indirectly, by checking whether the stakeholders agree that the views created from this model are correct representations of the actual or intended situation.
- *Obtaining commitment* from the key stakeholders. After reaching agreement, the key stakeholders have to commit themselves to the (potential) impact of what is described.
- *Informing* the other stakeholders.

These steps will be described in more detail Sect. 8.4.2.

– **Maintaining the model**: A modelling process is iterative. In the early stages of modelling, you discuss intermediate, but stable, versions of the model with stakeholders. These iterations help in getting a clear understanding of the purpose of the modelling process, the concerns of the individual stakeholders, and the degree to which the model helps in achieving this purpose. Such discussions may for instance reveal places in the model that have to be updated, and places where the model includes too much or too little detail. Also in later stages of the modelling process iterations remain crucial: if the enterprise architecture model is not kept up to date it loses its value for the stakeholders. As such, the model should be maintained to reflect, for instance, changes in the infrastructure, the business processes, or the enterprise's products. Consequently, maintaining an existing model may also be the *purpose* of an enterprise architecture process.

After providing some more theory about modelling and the types of modelling actions, we continue the chapter with a discussion of the most relevant principles guiding the design choices in a modelling process.

7.2.3 Types of Modelling Actions

There are a virtually endless number of ways in which an enterprise architect can go about creating or changing the contents of a model. Even so, there are a limited number of basic, general types of modelling actions that can be distinguished with respect to the detailed actions we perform while modelling. This section describes these types of modelling actions, thereby providing a vocabulary for talking and reasoning about *how concepts and relations are handled during modelling*. This is of course closely related to *modelling decisions* that are taken. Without wanting to prescribe specific causes of action during modelling, we believe it is useful to introduce terms that enable us to discuss the basic actions of modelling, but also – and even more importantly – help architects to think in these terms, and to *externalise* some of the intuitive decision making and acting they have always been doing as they were modelling. In other words, this can help you to become more aware of what you are doing, and think about it more explicitly and rationally.

The basic types of modelling actions that we distinguish are listed below; some modelling actions are sub-classified. In this overview, modelling actions are operations on concrete concepts and relations from the domain that is being modelled; as such, these concepts and relations can be considered *instances* of the concepts and relations that are defined in the ArchiMate language.

We also provide some typical questions that you could reflect on as you make your modelling decisions. These questions should be seen as 'guidelines for reflection'; they provide concrete examples of what aspects of your modelling actions you might need to reflect on.

- **Introduce** a candidate element in the model.
  By this we mean simply the act of placing a fresh term for a concept or relation within the model. It may not even be linked (related) to anything, it just seems 'somehow relevant'. It may be changed or even deleted later on. Note that such an element may at this point be just some unclassified item with a name on it. It may be *refined* later on. The main questions one might ask here is: why this element, why not another one, or perhaps not do it at all? Why is it relevant? Why give it this particular name?

- **Refine** an element in the model.
  This corresponds to adding detail to the element. Note that a *model* can of course also be refined by *introducing* elements. Refining an element can take two main forms:

  - *Classify* the newly introduced (candidate) element. You classify a yet unclassified element, or may have thought of a more specific classification, or simply a better one. Classifications are of course selected from the meta-concepts used, so that depends on the modelling context. You may even decide to select a classification not used so far, which amounts to extending the WoM used. Why this classification? For reclassification: what was wrong with the old classification?

  - Provide a *description* of the element in another way than adding more elements, for instance by:

    - *Adding internal detail* to an element: for example, add attributes to a business object, or cardinality to a 'serving' relation. Why this instead of introducing a new element?

    - *Writing a definition* or gloss kept outside the model: for example, in a dictionary. Why this instead of expressing the definition by modelling it? Why define at all? Will anyone (including you!) ever read the definition?

- *Nesting* models: elaborate on an element by introducing another model – 'zooming in'. (This action is related to *abstraction* as described below, but concerns adding detail instead of hiding it.) Why not include those details in the actual model; what is the reason for using multiple levels in your model?

– **Abandon** a model element.
This is an action that is harder and more complex than it may look. Of course, concepts and relations (or internal details, for that matter) can be simply scrapped and deleted if they turn out to be 'wrong'. However, especially if a model has been around for a while, it may be a good idea to make an *explicit* (even communal) decision to abandon a concept or relation, in order to avoid the concept 'lingering around'. There is a difference between just throwing away a model element and saying a proper and noted 'goodbye' to it. A record of this potential but rejected element might be kept somewhere, as a 'lesson learned'. Why is this element no good? Do we want to abandon it or *abstract* from it?

– **Abstract** from a concept or relation.
Importantly, this action is quite different from *abandoning* a concept, or scrapping some detail. Abstraction rather is the opposite of *refinement*.
Abstraction can take place at two levels: abstract the *whole concept or relation* or some *internal detail*. In either case, you decide that some information that is available to you is to be left out of the model. You may want to keep the information (because it is not 'wrong' as such), but 'hide' it (perhaps describing it somewhere else). The trick here is to 'show information on demand'. Why do you not want to show this particular information? Hide this detail (keeping the information somewhere) or throw it away entirely?

So far we have introduced some helpful terms for describing the basic actions involving model elements. However, enterprise architecture modelling typically involves a larger context: relations with other models, other domains, other concerns, etc. You may need to make relations with other contexts explicit, or even to rephrase some model within some other context. This is why we also distinguish the following modelling action:

– **Translate** an element.
Translation may of course simply mean finding a fitting alternative for an interesting element in another model. If so, there is no crucial difference with *introduction* or *refinement* (perhaps combined with *abandonment*). However, an act of translation has its own special rationale behind it. More importantly, it may need to be documented in order to keep track of the existing relationship between models/contexts. Also, a future translation may have to be kept in line with previous translations. This is why we distinguish the following subtypes:

- *Create or replace* an element so it matches the meaning of a concept from another language or context. Why use a translation? Why this translation? Why from that particular source model, context, or language?

- *Link* an element to an element in the other model or modelling language. Keep some record of this particular link, and the particular contexts and/or languages it concerns (see also *documentation* below).
- Link an element to some *intermediary language*. This is an old trick in translation. If a model needs to be translated to more than one language or context, it may be a problem to find translators with expertise in all combinations of contexts or languages. Instead, you could first translate to a language or context that is understood by everyone, and then take the next step. In this case, you may want to keep records of both the translations to the intermediary language and to the final target language.
- A *translation rule* may be specified that enables standardised, coherent translation between some contexts or languages. If translation is structural, this may be a good thing to do. However, a note of caution is in order here: translation is a heavily contextualised and subtle business. If translation rules are too generically applied, gross mistranslations may occur. To keep on the safe side, translation rules should preferably be seen as guidelines (time-saving suggestions) rather than strict and generic rules.
- Based on experiences in previous translations, or in confusion between contexts/languages, sources of confusion may be listed explicitly, for example homonyms and synonyms. These may be part of the translation rules, but even if no such rules are formulated, particularly notorious risks may be noted and communicated.

- **Document modelling actions**. While this will often be too much of a burden (automation may help here, of course), documentation and administration of all or some modelling actions may be useful. Why should you document a modelling action, if at all, and what aspects of it? There are several reasons to do so:

  - To be able to 'undo': you may simply regret a decision and backtrack to a previous state. Of course, many modelling tools have this option.
  - To revisit rejected alternatives.
  - To record modelling rationales related to traceability, accountability, etc. of the modelling process.
  - To add conceptual meta-data. It may be interesting to keep track of who did what with a model element, and where it occurs:

    - In which language/context/model is the element used? Is it part of any standard?
    - Who first introduced the element?

  Translation records and rules may also be linked in here.

7.3 Guidelines for Modelling

The main guideline for modelling results from our notion of modelling as a goal-driven activity (Chap. 4) is the following:

A model has to provide answers to questions.

Modelling in itself is not an objective: a model serves a purpose to answer some particular questions. Making these questions explicit help you to find the appropriate scope and focus while creating a model.

Make a clear distinction between a model and its visualisations.

Architects have a tendency to consider a visualisation of a model as the model itself (see also the remarks in Chap. 3). You should be aware of this difference and not use visual terms while describing a model. For example, avoid using terms such as 'above' to denote that some concept is more important than another one.

The processes that underlie the functioning of enterprises are complex activities that, by definition, contain a large amount of detail. When you model such activities, you leave out information you feel is unimportant and emphasise information you feel is essential, given the modelling goal and target audience. This economy of communication is an example of obeying Grice's Maxims (Grice 1975). These maxims have been formulated as heuristics for optimising communication. Since the visualisation of an enterprise architecture model is a means to communicate information about an enterprise, these maxims are relevant for us as well. Applying Grice's Maxims to enterprise architecture, we interpret them as follows:

Maxim of quantity:
– Make your model as informative as necessary.
– Do not make your model more informative than necessary.
Maxim of quality:
– Do not model what you believe to be false.
– Do not model that for which you lack adequate evidence.
Maxim of relevance:
– Be relevant (i.e. model things related to the modelling goal).
Maxim of manner:
– Avoid obscurity of expression.
– Avoid ambiguity.
– Be brief (avoid unnecessary concepts and relations).
– Be orderly.

If you apply these maxims, they will help you to create models that include appropriate details, given the modelling goal and the target stakeholders.

There are typically multiple stakeholders involved in an enterprise architecture and its model. Apart from the enterprise architect, possible stakeholders include managers, CIOs, CEOs, software developers, and business process designers. In such settings, the types of stakeholders and the purpose for which the model is created determine what makes an appropriate model. Always remember that, while the architect determines the internal quality of a model (e.g., its conceptual integrity), the external quality of a model is largely determined by the stakeholders, not the architect.

We have obtained a series of such guidelines based on interviews with enterprise architects, combined with our own experience and information from the literature. These guidelines are listed below.

> **Model iteratively.**

When modelling an enterprise architecture, use several iterations to discuss intermediate, stable models with the stakeholders. Use their feedback to improve the model and to determine parts of the model that do not yet have the appropriate level of detail.

> **Model for dynamics.**

Models often include real-life aspects that are likely to change over time, such as a company's product portfolio. As such, models are dynamic. If certain changes can be foreseen, architects should add a description of how the model can change.

> **Be economical in models.**

Model only those concepts and relations that are relevant given the purpose of the model and the type of stakeholders it is intended for.

> **Be economical in views.**

When communicating with a specific stakeholder, use a view of the model that only includes the concepts and relations that are relevant for that stakeholder.

> **Make concepts recognisable.**

Indicate concepts in a model by the same names the stakeholders apply to those concepts.

> **Make structures recognisable.**

Use the same type of structuring that the stakeholders apply: if the stakeholders for instance describe their business in terms of a process with various steps, make sure this process and the individual steps are clearly present in the model.

Make a model consistent.

In a model, apply the same type of concepts to denote the same type of elements from the real world. Model similar relations in a similar manner. Use the same terms to denote the same concepts, *also in related models*.

Keep related models consistent.

In many cases, architects will create a series of related models to model different aspects of the same enterprise. Coherence between these models is very important: you should try to avoid conflicts between related models and use uniform terminology.

Make models as correct and complete as needed.

A model should be a correct representation of something from the real world, focusing on specific aspects. While models abstract from certain aspects, the aspects they focus on should be modelled in a correct and complete manner. In many cases you do not want to create 100% complete or correct models. Models do not always have to be complete, because people can easily fill in the gaps. Main structures must be clear, but details and exceptions are left for the implementation phase. Although not a complete or 100% correct representation of reality, models must be unambiguous.

Treat different concerns orthogonally.

Different concerns should be addressed in different parts of the model, or in different, related models.

7.3.1   *Before You Start*

When you are about to start creating models, i.e., you are about to model an enterprise architecture, you should ask yourself the following questions:

– Is there a clear stakeholder?
– Is the objective explicit?
– Will creating an enterprise architecture model help to reach this objective?
– Are the boundaries clear of what you should model?
– Is it clear whether the situation 'as is' or the situation 'to be' should be modelled?
– Can you obtain the information needed to create the model?
– Are there realistic expectations regarding your role as an enterprise architect in the process?

Only if all these questions can be answered positively should you start the modelling process. Now the next question is; what to capture in the model?

7.3.2   What to Capture in a Model?

The contents to capture in a model primarily depend on the purpose of the model and the intended target audience: the stakeholders for which the model is created. Based on this purpose and target audience, you decide on a scope and focus: which aspects of the enterprise to include in the model and what abstraction levels to use?

In deciding the scope of the model, you should focus only on those aspects that contribute to the modelling objective. In order to model appropriate aspects, the following guidelines can be applied:

Select the design viewpoints that match your objective.

Choose design viewpoints that include all concepts and relations that are of primary importance to the purpose of the model. If you need to communicate how various business roles contribute to the realisation of one specific business process, make sure you select a design viewpoint that includes these concepts. The selected design viewpoints determine which types of concepts and relations to include in the model.

Focus.

Only include those elements in the model that directly contribute to the realisation of the modelling objective.

Neglect matters of secondary importance and exceptions.

Initially, assume that no errors occur in the processes you model and that all processes complete successfully.

Do not be afraid to abandon model elements.

Some aspects or relations that may seem important when you start modelling may later on prove to be of secondary importance. For this reason, models tend to include too much detail and too many aspects after a while. Do not be afraid to abandon those elements that clutter the model with less relevant details: even though the resulting model will contain less information, it will be more valuable for the stakeholders.

Discuss stable, intermediate versions of the model with the stakeholders.

As discussed in Sect. 7.2, what to include in a model is determined by its purpose and stakeholders. As a result, an architect should discuss intermediate, but stable, versions of the model with the various stakeholders to get feedback on the selected concepts and relations, the level of detail, and the representation applied. Involving stakeholders throughout an enterprise architecture process not only increases their commitment, but also contributes to a higher quality of the resulting models.

Start modelling from a single element.

Depending on the selected design viewpoint, one element (for instance, a specific role, a service, a process, or a product) is of prime importance. Form your model around this central element. For instance, in the Application Behaviour Viewpoint (Sect. 8.5.12) the provided *Application service* is the central concept. Start modelling by systematically investigating one concrete application service that is most relevant given your modelling objective. Investigate all *Application functions* that contribute to realising this *Application service* and all *Data objects* that are used.

Starting from a single element, you can use the following four metaphorical directions (inspired by Veryard 2004) to find other relevant model elements:

1. **Inwards**: towards the internal composition of the element.
2. **Upwards**: towards the elements that are supported by it.
3. **Downwards**: towards its realisation by other elements.
4. **Sideways**: towards peer elements with which it cooperates.

This is illustrated in Fig. 7.2. Of course, this approach can be iterated over multiple elements in your model.

Fig. 7.2 Metaphorical
directions for viewpoints

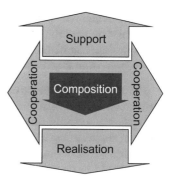

7.3.3   *Modelling and Abstraction*

The iterative modelling approach, as described in the previous section, helps you to handle the complexity of enterprise architecture modelling by allowing you to use different levels of abstraction. Through the use of abstraction levels, you can first capture the key concepts and key relations in an enterprise architecture model, before providing more details.

> First capture key concepts and key relations at a high level of abstraction.

A high-level enterprise architecture model that only includes key concepts and key relations forms an appropriate means of communication with the stakeholders in the early stages of the modelling process: not only does it show the key concepts and relation, but also it forms a basis to discuss the purpose and scope of the modelling process. It is of the utmost importance to agree with the stakeholders on the key concepts and key relations, as these make up the framework on which the rest of the enterprise architecture model is based.

After reaching an agreement on this high level of abstraction, you can use various other levels of abstraction to specify the enterprise architecture model. Each of these levels zooms in on a specific part of the higher-level model and allows you to add detail. To benefit from the use of different levels of abstraction, you have (formally) to identify the levels, each with a well-defined scope, and maintain consistency among the levels (Biemans et al. 2001).

> Use a limited number of predefined abstraction levels.
> Define abstraction levels based on the modelling goals.

Abstraction levels can abstract from aspects, such as physical distribution, or abstract from details, such as the internal structure of a system. As a result, refinements of a model can for instance provide more details regarding:

- Implementation: adding details about how behaviour is realised. In the ArchiMate notation the 'realises' arrow indicates this relation.
- Extension: augmenting a model with new elements, such as exceptions.
- Decomposition: adding the internal structure of parts of the model.

In correspondence to the enterprise modelling language chapter, typical levels of abstraction are the *business level* (focusing, for example, on business objectives, products, and organisational structures), the *application level* (focusing, for example, on applications and the services they provide), and the *technology level* (focusing, for example, on computer systems and networks). However, abstraction levels should be chosen depending on the modelling objective and the concerns of the stakeholders.

Maintaining consistency among abstraction levels is a necessary, but complex, task. Tool support can help an architect in this task, for instance by checking whether a detailed description of a part of the model conforms to a higher-level description.

Keep abstraction levels consistent.

So, in creating an enterprise architecture model, we suggest an iterative approach, using multiple abstraction levels, where the first iteration is performed in a top-down manner. This top-down first iteration stimulates you to capture, on a high level, the key concepts and key relations of the model in relation to the modelling purpose, before looking at lower-level details.

7.3.4   *Structuring Models and Visualisations*

When a model consists of many concepts and relations, structuring a model helps to reduce the visual complexity of the model, which makes it easier for your stakeholders to recognise and understand your model. Structuring a model may also help to discover recurring structures, patterns, or inconsistencies.

Especially in an enterprise architecture, which integrates many different domains, several of these structures will be apparent at the same time. However, different structures will be dominant in different parts of the enterprise architecture. For example, in business processes a temporal structure will be dominant, whereas functional decomposition is more prominent in the application architecture.

Architecture models may contain different types of structure. Commonly used structural dimensions include:

- Functionality: functional decomposition
- Time: temporal structure, data flow, control flow
- Usage: dependencies, call graphs

- Location: physical distribution
- Data structure: type/class hierarchies
- Work: units of implementation, module structure

In structuring any model, the modelling objective is of prime importance: different types of structure help you to make different aspects of the enterprise architecture explicit. If you, for instance, would like to reveal how various applications contribute to the realisation of the products of an enterprise, a grouping based on products may be the most suitable structure.

Below, we give some of the most important and widely used structuring principles.

Make a model as self-explanatory as possible.

Any part of the model should be specified in such a way that (potential) users require a minimum amount of additional information about both its context and its contents to understand what its role in the architecture is. To achieve this, you should use existing shared understanding: apply the user's terminology and build on their existing knowledge.

Separate internal and external behaviour.

This principle is a further elaboration of the previous one. In describing the behaviour of any system element, you should clearly separate what its environment perceives and how it operates internally. Thus, the user of that system element does not need to be concerned with its inner working and only has to understand what it shows to the outside world. A prime example of this principle is the use of the service concept. Following its definition in Chap. 5, a service should only describe the externally observable behaviour of a system, not how that behaviour is realised. Such encapsulation has long been a guiding principle in software development (e.g., see Dijkstra 1968). It provides a mechanism for being truly platform independent, for substituting different implementations with the same external behaviour, or interchanging different suppliers of services.

Use layers.

Structure the elements in the model in terms of layers, for instance the business, application, and technology layers as applied in the ArchiMate language. The link between layers in an enterprise architecture is typically made explicit via the services one layer provides to the other. An example is given in Fig. 7.3, which shows the business and application layers joined by a layer of application services.

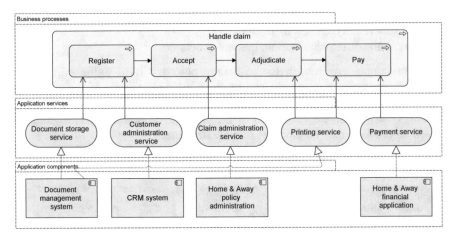

Fig. 7.3 Layered model

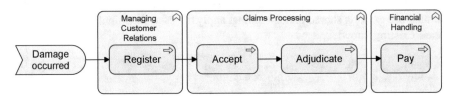

Fig. 7.4 Business functions grouped by phase

Group by phase.

Structure the elements in the model in terms of the time at which they take place. If the organisation, for instance, distinguishes different phases in a production process, arranging the enterprise architecture model in terms of these phases may help your stakeholders to recognise and understand the model. In Fig. 7.4, for instance, the business functions that come into play after damage occurs are grouped by the phases in the process.

Group by product or service.

Group elements in the model (such as business processes, information, and actors) that contribute to the realisation of a specific product or service.

Group by information used.

Structure the elements in the model according to the information they have or need. This can be applied on a technical level, e.g., in a data warehouse architecture, but also on a business level, as in a business model for an electronic marketplace or a broker.

Group by physical distribution.

Group elements in the model based on their physical (geographical) location, for instance as specific activities take place in a specific region.

Separate independent parts.

Split the model into smaller sub-models of (largely) independent parts of the enterprise.

While structuring an enterprise architecture may help your stakeholders to recognise and understand the model, it is also a powerful means to make the *coherence* in an enterprise explicit. For instance, the relations that cross the boundaries in a layered structuring indicate dependencies where one layer uses information or services provided by another layer. Revealing coherence, for instance between business roles, business processes, and the resulting products, is a main objective of many enterprise architecting processes.

Linked to the different dimensions of structure, a number of elementary structuring operations can be discerned (Bass et al. 1998), including abstraction and separation (e.g., part–whole decomposition, 'is-a' decomposition, and replication).

Applying these operations to an architecture has an impact on its quality attributes, such as performance, scalability, or modifiability. By transforming an architecture using these operations, the qualities of that architecture can be influenced. However, since these quality attributes are interrelated, the end result will always be a compromise between different requirements. It is the task of the enterprise architect to ensure a workable outcome, both in balancing the needs of the different stakeholders within the architecture itself and in guiding the process of communication and negotiation with all these stakeholders.

7.3.5 Constructive Use of Modelling Breakdowns

In communication, a failure to communicate effectively is typically denoted as a *breakdown*. In a modelling process, breakdowns become evident when – for some reason – a stakeholder does not properly understand the model. As such, breakdowns should be avoided. Nevertheless, if they do occur you can use them in a constructive manner. Most importantly, you should check for readability and effect.

Check for Readability

Readability breakdowns occur when communicating models that are visualised in an inappropriate manner given your stakeholders and the modelling goals. Having your stakeholders understand the model is of the utmost importance, independent of whether your model is meant for designing, deciding, or informing. This section describes typical breakdowns related to the readability of models: it states the symptoms (how can you determine that such a breakdown is occurring?) and possible solutions to repair the breakdown. We distinguish the following readability breakdowns:

- The model is **not understood**: Unknown terms and concepts are used.
  Symptoms: If asked, the stakeholder cannot explain the model. Furthermore the stakeholder will not show any enthusiasm. A cooperative receiver will ask questions such as: 'What do you mean by that? Can you give an example? What does this term mean?'. In the worst case the receiver will say the model is useless and ignore it.
  Solution: Analyse the stakeholder and use his or her language, terms, and concepts. It can be useful to build a model using the terms of the stakeholder or to explain new introduced vocabulary.
- The model is **understood in the wrong way**.
  Symptoms: When asked the stakeholder turns out to have his or her own conflicting interpretation of the model. The stakeholder will draw strange conclusions and take initiatives you do not expect.
  Solution: Analyse the stakeholder and use his or her language, terms and concepts. It can be useful to build a model in terms of the receiver or to explain newly introduced vocabulary.
- The model has **no intuitive structure** for the receiver.
  Symptoms: The receiver finds it difficult to recall all of the elements of the model and thinks of it as a bag full of propositions. It is hard to keep him interested. If the receiver refers to the model, he or she always uses another representation, e.g., another diagram or another sequence, to explain the content.
  Solution: Copy the structure used by the stakeholder or analyse it to find out about its underlying logic. Use this logic in the new model.
- The model has an **unclear** structure or notation.
  Symptoms: The structure of the model or the language or diagrams used causes questions. The receiver will reject the model, although he or she agrees with its contents. The remarks made only concern the structure of the model.
  Solution: Explain the structure of the model or use structures the receiver is used to. Introduce new kinds of diagrams describing a well-known situation to explain the diagram constructs.
- The **visualisation** of the model **distracts** from the original message.
  Symptoms: Diagrams and colours are so awful or beautiful that nobody takes any notice of the contents. The form of the model is the only thing that people remember, not its contents.

Solution: Adjust the visualisation of the model: first give the message as text, or as a story. Apologise for ugly models.

Check for Effect

Even with a properly readable model, the communication with the stakeholder may not result in the intended effect. We can identify several typical breakdowns related to the inability of models to achieve the intended effect:

- The model or architect **lacks status**.
  Symptoms: The receiver is not willing to listen. He or she is always busy and cannot make time for you.
  Solution: This is a relational breakdown, which needs to be solved before continuing the process. It is outside the scope of this book to describe solutions for such organisational issues.
- The model has a true but **unwanted message**.
  Symptoms: There is no room to negotiate. The model is forgotten or deliberately misunderstood. Some sort of delaying tactics are used.
  Solution: This too is a relational breakdown, which needs to be solved before continuing the process.
- The model is **irrelevant**: The model is true, it is a good representation of the modelled situation, but it has no relation with the problem.
  Symptoms: The stakeholder will ask: 'Why do you tell me this?' to which you have no good reply.
  Solution: See 'the model contains superfluous elements'.
- The model contains **superfluous elements**: The model is true, it is a good representation of the modelled situation, and there is a relation with the problem, but not everything is relevant. The real message is hidden somewhere in the larger message.
  Symptoms: The architect has too much to say, but does not always have an answer to the question: 'Why do you tell me this?'.
  Solution: Construct and get commitment for a problem description. For every line and every drawing, you should ask yourself: 'Do I miss something if I leave this thing out?' If you are convinced that the model should include some elements that should be left out considering the problem description, re-evaluate the problem description together with the stakeholders.
- The model is **too complex**. The model may contain relevant information, but there is just too much of it.
  Symptoms: The stakeholder appears to be puzzled by the model or spends a lot of time looking at the model.
  Solution: Use abstraction levels to allow the stakeholder to zoom in on or out of parts of the model.
- The model is **too vague**. The model is true but not very specific. It does not provide the stakeholder with the desired knowledge.
  Symptoms: The stakeholder will not be interested.

Solution: Iterate and create a more concrete model, focusing on the objective of the stakeholder.

– The model is **not sufficiently complete**. Not all required information is included in the model. If the model is part of a sequence, this might not be a problem.
Symptoms: The model does not provide the stakeholder with all the desired knowledge. The stakeholder will be dissatisfied, as you are not fully addressing the problem.
Solution: Iterate and create a more complete model, focusing on the objective of the stakeholder. An architect always has to find a balance in order to create models that are sufficiently complete, while not being too complex.

– The model is **not true**. The model contains incorrect arguments, or inaccurate or untrue reasoning.
Symptoms: The stakeholder does not agree with the arguments and reasoning used. The stakeholder will dispute the content.
Solution: Gather the required information and check it for correctness.

7.4   Readability and Usability of Models

The prime purpose of enterprise architecture models is to capture and communicate key functions and key relations of different domains relevant for enterprises. As such, these models have to be readable and usable, given their particular purpose and given the stakeholders for which they are intended. The readability and usability is, to a large extent, determined by the complexity of the model. While creating models, you should aim for models with a limited complexity, by reducing:

– The number of elements in the model
– The number of types of elements in the model
– The number of relations depicted in the model

Nevertheless, complex designs and complex relations from the real world cannot always be captured in models with a limited complexity. In that case, the use of *viewpoints* can help to reduce the complexity for stakeholders. Such viewpoints focus on specific aspects of the model, reducing the number of elements that are visible, as well as the number of element types and the number of visible relations. Viewpoints are discussed in detail in Chap. 8.

In order to promote readability and usability of models, visualisations of models should *link the visualisations of model elements with the elements themselves*. This principle is especially important for enterprise architecture models, since these typically integrate different architectural models.

When creating a visualisation of an enterprise architecture model, there are two conflicting forces. First, the visualisation should state as much information as possible, given the purpose of the visualisation and the intended stakeholders of the visualisation. Second, the stakeholders of the visualisation can only handle a limited *visual complexity* of a presented model. Balancing these two conflicting forces is an important challenge when creating a model.

The level of detail must be attuned to the purpose of the model and the intended stakeholder. A new user's initial focus may be the system as a whole, with few details. When the user focuses on a specific part of the model, more detail should be added. When users can zoom in on parts of a model, navigational information becomes important: users should be provided with awareness information regarding the current level of abstraction and switching between levels of abstraction should be supported. Additionally, the meaning of the symbols at the given level of abstraction should be stated.

7.4.1 Reducing the Visual Complexity of Models

Reducing the visual complexity of models is primarily achieved by limiting the number of concepts and relations that are visible in a model. Related to this, the number of types of concepts and relations should also be limited. Having different views of models is one means to reduce the visual and conceptual complexity: given a specific objective and a specific type of stakeholder, a view only includes those aspects of the model that are relevant for that situation. Chapter 8 elaborates on the notion of viewpoints for design and visualisation, and provides examples of various viewpoints.

Another solution is the use of abstraction (see Sect. 7.3.3). Humans are only good at working with models that do not include more than 30 elements (Horton 1991). Even more restricting is the rule by Miller (1956), based on the capacity of our short-term memory, which states that humans are only good at processing seven plus or minus two elements at a time. If the number of elements in a model exceeds this limit, elements should be grouped and substituted with an aggregate, abstract object. Based on this principle, one can create models with different levels of abstraction: on the highest level, only the key concepts and key relations are shown. Such high-level models show the essentials of the enterprise architecture and abstract from details, for instance regarding implementation of processes or distribution aspects. Each concept and relation on this highest level may be an abstraction for a more complex set of concepts and relations. In a model with different layers of abstraction, the more detailed concepts and relations can be reached by zooming in on the composite object. This process is iterative: in each layer, concepts and relations may in turn be compositions of more detailed concepts and relations. However, to maintain an overview of the model, enterprise architecture models should not apply more than three layers of abstraction (Koning 2002).

Within one view and given an abstraction level, the visual complexity of a model depends for a significant part on how well humans perceive the relations between concepts. To create appropriate visualisations of complex models a number of generic organising principles can be identified. These principles, derived from the Gestalt theory of human perception, are particularly useful for assisting in the

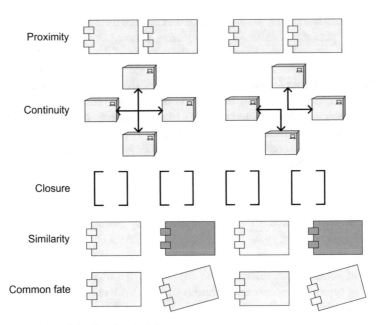

Fig. 7.5 Examples of the Gestalt principles

representation of relationships that exist between different entities in architectural models. They are illustrated in Fig. 7.5 and explained below:

- **Proximity**: People have a tendency to relate objects that are near to each other. Therefore, related objects should be placed near to each other in a model. The proximity rule also applies for colours. Therefore, the colour of objects in a model can be applied to indicate relations between objects.
- **Continuity**: People have a tendency to perceive a line as continuing its established direction. For example, a cross is perceived as two straight lines bisecting each other rather than two (or even four) right angles positioned next to each other. Therefore, right angles should not be positioned next to each other in a model.
- **Closure**: People have a tendency to perceive incomplete objects as complete and to close or fill gaps and to perceive asymmetric objects as symmetric. In general, symmetry and regularity of models increases the readability of models and reduces the perceived complexity.
- **Similarity**: People have a tendency to perceive objects that are similar to each other as belonging together as a unit. As a specialisation of this principle, people have a tendency to perceive objects with similar size as being of equal importance: when shown a larger object and a smaller object, people have a tendency to perceive the larger object as being more important.
- **Common fate**: People have a tendency to perceive different objects that move or function in a similar manner as a unit. Consider a group of four similar objects

that are perceived as a group: if two objects are rotated, the group of objects is no longer perceived as one group, but rather as two pairs.

In the next subsections, we have translated these general principles into a number of practical requirements, illustrated with some examples.

7.4.2 Representation Conventions

Representation conventions can be applied to increase the ease of understanding models. Especially for the experienced user, they may provide useful clues for the meaning of a model. Using conventions does not influence the formal meaning of the model. Typical conventions encountered in textual programming are naming conventions and indentation conventions for clarifying the nesting structure of the code.

Use of Layout
The layout is one of the most important visual attributes of a model. A good layout is perceived instantly and almost unconsciously. An unclear, cluttered layout is distracting and hinders perception of more detailed information. Putting the objects in a diagram in a pattern that is easily recognisable and fitting to the underlying message is a great aid to the viewer of the diagram. It very much helps in discerning and remembering which objects there are and which relationships are relevant. Layout aspects of a diagram include: basic pattern, horizontal and vertical alignment, above/before positioning, symmetry, distance of objects from the centre and from other objects, distribution of white space, distribution of connectors, density of objects and connectors. A basic pattern makes clear to the viewer what strategy is being followed in positioning objects and what meaning can be derived from the position of an object. For instance, in a workflow diagram the activities might be positioned from left to right in the order of execution and having the same vertical position can mean being executed in the same stage of the process.

Use white space.

Providing enough, but not too much, white space makes diagrams elegant. White space gives room to envision alterations or additions, and in that way (again) supports reasoning about the diagram.

Distinguish between normal and exceptional cases.

In order to reduce the complexity of a model, it is useful to make a clear distinction between the normal proceedings and exceptions. This can for instance be realised by presenting the normal activities within a process at the same horizontal level, while placing the exceptional activities above or below that level.

Use symmetry to stress similarities.

Symmetry can be used to suggest or stress similarities between parts of the model. This is used in Fig. 7.6 to suggest, for example, the similarities between the two front-office departments and also between the three back-office departments.

Model time dependence from left to right.

By letting triggering relations point from left to right, the time dimension in behaviour models matches the natural reading direction in Western cultures. An example is the process model of Fig. 7.7.

Avoid crossing lines.

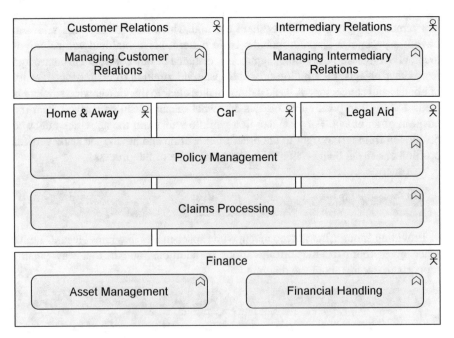

Fig. 7.6 Symmetry and similarity

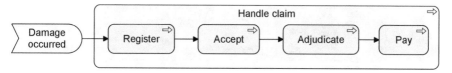

Fig. 7.7 Time dependence from left to right

Avoiding crossing lines can increase the readability of a model. In case of a crossing line, the user may have to spend extra time finding out in what direction each of the lines continues.

Use of Symbols
The shapes of objects usually match the intrinsic properties of the objects (e.g., the cylinder shape for a data store, an actor represented by a stick figure, etc.). There is a tendency to use realistic, possibly three-dimensional symbols for concrete and tangible objects (e.g., cylinder, human figure, factory symbol, graphics of computers) and to use simple, geometric shapes for abstract concepts (e.g., process, function, component, etc.).

> Use similar shapes for similar concepts.

Similar concepts should be represented by similar shapes. In the ArchiMate language, for example, all behavioural concepts such as business process, service, and function, have rounded corners, whereas the structural concepts such as actor, component, and object have sharp corners.

> Use line width to stress important relations.

In order to differentiate several types of relationships (for instance, flow of goods, flow of money, and flow of information), different line styles and arrows are used in the ArchiMate language. To differentiate relations of the same type, line widths (e.g., thicker lines) can be used to stress the most important ones, e.g., the main flow of information. This is used in Fig. 7.8 to emphasise the flow associated with the Handle Claim business process.

Use of Colour
Colour is a very strong visual signal. It is a visual attribute that is strongly influenced by 'prior knowledge', like cultural values, fashion colours, or company colours. Additional meanings can be easily (temporarily) attached to a certain colour. Using a distinct colour for an object with a particular attribute can program the meaning of that colour for the rest of the models describing a particular architecture. It is important to keep in mind that colours can enlarge the appeal of

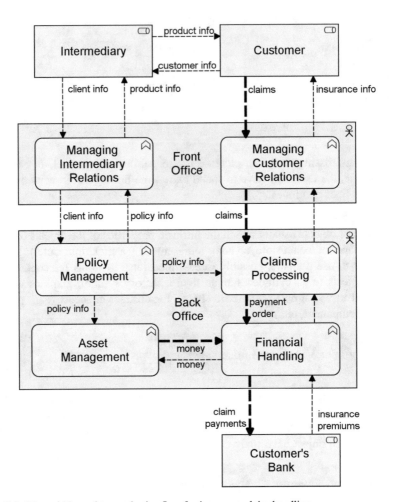

Fig. 7.8 Line width used to emphasise flow for insurance claim handling

the diagram, but can also lead to contrary effects by abusive usage of them (such as confusion, distraction, eye fatigue, difficulties in following the diagram).

Use colour for emphasis.

There is a perceptual order to colour that follows the spectrum of red, yellow, green, and blue. When viewing these colours, red tends to focus in the foreground, yellow and green focus in the middle, and blue focuses in the background. Consequently, red is usually used to emphasise a feature, while blue is used for backgrounds.

Use colour for similarity.

One way of indicating that certain elements have something in common is to use the same colour. For instance, processes performed by the same actors can be given the same colour as the representation of the actor. Different objects or concepts are usually represented by different colours. For example, in many of the examples throughout the book, colour is used to distinguish between business, application, and technology layer concepts.

Use colour to convey emotions.

There is a language to colour, based on the culture, education, and experience of people. Colours can be very symbolic. This fact should be kept in mind when designing graphic representations of models. Some obvious examples of this are: the colour red implies importance or danger; yellow refers to caution; in mapping, green often represents vegetation. Colour also has physical and emotional effects on the viewer. For example, red may be perceived as exciting, green as restful, and blue as cheerful.

Limit the number of colours.

For aesthetic reasons, too gaudy visualisations should be avoided, since this will annoy the users of the model. Another reason for this constraint is that too many different colours in a graphic hinder the viewer from developing an effective mental model of the meaningful relationships between objects and their colours.

Use of Text

Most modelling languages combine the power of text and graphics. Text can be very strong in suggesting the proper interpretations and associations and in stimulating thinking. The guidelines on the use of text try to stimulate you to be diligent in adding proper titles, subscripts, and annotations. They do matter. Text is important to speed up the creation of the proper mental model and to create a good starting point for a line of reasoning.

Use domain-specific terminology.

Using the terminology of the stakeholders facilitates communication with them and helps to make a recognisable model (Biemans et al. 2001).

Use naming conventions.

Naming conventions can be used for indicating the kind of element, such as verbs for actions and nouns for resources. Use short names (if possible consisting of one word) that are clear and unique. These will allow quick identification of an object throughout the whole architecture.

In the ArchiMate example models throughout the book, we use nouns for structural elements such as actors, roles, and components (e.g., 'insurer' and 'policy administration'), first-person-singular verbs for business processes (e.g., 'handle claim'), and gerunds for functions (e.g., 'contracting').

7.5 Summary

As described in this chapter, modelling is a goal-driven process in which an enterprise architect, in cooperation with the stakeholders, creates and structures a model via one or more viewpoints. As described in Chap. 4, enterprise architecture models are created for many reasons: they may for instance form a basis for design, for deciding, or for informing stakeholders. Depending on the purpose and the stakeholders, an enterprise architect can choose from a wide range of tools and techniques to create an appropriate model. In this chapter the stages in a modelling process have been described, as well as important principles influencing the modelling process. These principles concern the choice of modelling concepts, the use of abstraction, the structuring of models, as well as the visual representation of models. We have formulated concrete guidelines to describe good practices and illustrate principles, with the intention of helping an enterprise architect to create models that suit their purpose and cover the concerns of the various stakeholders.

Chapter 8
Viewpoints and Visualisation

Marc M. Lankhorst, Leon van der Torre, H.A. (Erik) Proper,
Farhad Arbab, Stijn J.B.A. Hoppenbrouwers, and Maarten W.A. Steen

Establishing and maintaining a coherent enterprise architecture is clearly a complex task, because it involves many different people with differing backgrounds using various notations. In order to get to grips with this complexity, researchers have initially focused on the definition of architectural frameworks for classifying and positioning the various architecture descriptions with respect to each other. A problem with looking at enterprise architecture through the lens of an architectural framework is that it categorises and divides architecture descriptions rather than providing insight into their coherence.

To integrate the diverse architecture descriptions, we advocate an approach in which architects and other stakeholders can define their own views of the enterprise architecture. In this approach views are specified by viewpoints. *Viewpoints* define abstractions on the set of models representing the enterprise architecture, each aimed at a particular type of stakeholder and addressing a particular set of concerns. Viewpoints can be used both to view certain aspects in isolation, and for relating two or more aspects.

M.M. Lankhorst (✉)
BiZZdesign, Capitool 15, 7521 PL Enschede, The Netherlands
e-mail: m.lankhorst@bizzdesign.com

L. van der Torre
University of Luxembourg, Luxembourg, Luxembourg

H.A. Proper
Luxembourg Institute of Science and Technology, Luxembourg, Luxembourg

F. Arbab
University of Leiden, Leiden, The Netherlands

S.J.B.A. Hoppenbrouwers
Radboud University Nijmegen, Nijmegen, The Netherlands

M.W.A. Steen
BiZZdesign, Enschede, The Netherlands

© Springer-Verlag Berlin Heidelberg 2017
M. Lankhorst et al., *Enterprise Architecture at Work*, The Enterprise Engineering
Series, DOI 10.1007/978-3-662-53933-0_8

8.1 Architecture Viewpoints

In this section we discuss the notion of views and viewpoints as basic tools in communicating about architectures. In the context of enterprise architectures, a viewpoint is typically used for activities like design, analysis, obtaining commitment, formal decision making, etc. As we argued in Chap. 4, we regard all of these activities to be communicative in nature.

As defined in Sect. 3.2.4, a *viewpoint* essentially prescribes the concepts, models, analysis techniques, and visualisations that are to be used in the construction of different views of an architecture description. A *view* is typically geared towards a set of stakeholders and their concerns. Simply put, a view is what you see, and a viewpoint describes from where you are looking.

In discussing the notion of viewpoint, we will first provide a brief overview of the origin of viewpoints. This is followed by a more precise definition of viewpoints, and the concept of viewpoint *frameworks*.

8.1.1 Origin of Viewpoints

The concept of viewpoint is not new. For example, in the mid 1980s, Multiview (Wood-Harper et al. 1985) already introduced the notion of views. In fact, Multiview identified five viewpoints for the development of (computerised) information systems: Human Activity System, Information Modelling, Socio-Technical System, Human–Computer Interface, and the Technical System. During the same period in which Multiview was developed, the so-called CRIS Task Group of IFIP Working Group 8.1 developed similar notions, where stakeholder views were reconciled via appropriate 'representations'. Special attention was paid to disagreement about which aspect (or *perspective*) was to dominate the system design (namely, 'process', 'data', or 'behaviour'). As a precursor to the notion of *concern*, the CRIS Task Group identified several *human roles* involved in information system development, such as executive responsible, development coordinator, business analyst, business designer (Olle et al. 1988).

The use of viewpoints is not limited to the information systems community; it was also introduced by the software engineering community. In the 1990s, a substantial number of software engineering researchers worked on what was phrased as 'the multiple perspectives problem' (Finkelstein et al. 1992; Kotonya and Sommerville 1992; Nuseibeh 1994; Reeves et al. 1995). By this term, the authors referred to the problem of how to organise and guide (software) development in a setting with many actors, using diverse representation schemes, having diverse domain knowledge, and using different development strategies. A general framework has been developed in order to address the diverse issues related to this problem (Finkelstein et al. 1992; Kotonya and Sommerville 1992; Nuseibeh 1994). In this framework, a viewpoint combines the notion of *actor*, *role*, or *agent* in the development process with the idea of a *perspective* or *view* which an actor maintains. A viewpoint is more than a partial specification; in addition, it contains partial knowledge of how further to develop that partial specification. These early ideas on viewpoint-oriented software engineering have found their way into the IEEE 1471 standard for architecture description (IEEE Computer Society 2000) and the subsequent ISO/IEC/IEEE 42010:2011 standard (ISO/IEC/IEEE 2011), on which we have based our definitions below.

8.1.2 Architecture Viewpoints

In the context of architecture, viewpoints provide a means to focus on particular aspects of an architecture description. These aspects are determined by the concerns of the stakeholders with whom communication takes place. What should and should not be visible from a specific viewpoint is therefore entirely dependent on argumentation with respect to a stakeholder's concerns. Viewpoints are designed for the purpose of serving as a means of communication in a conversation about certain aspects of an architecture. Though viewpoints can be used in strictly uni-directional, informative conversations, they can in general also be used in bi-directional classes of conversations: the architect informs stakeholders, and stakeholders give their feedback (critique or consent) on the presented aspects. What is and what is not shown in a view depends on the scope of the viewpoint and on what is relevant to the concerns of the stakeholders. Ideally, these are the same, i.e., the viewpoint is designed with the specific concerns of a stakeholder in mind. Relevance to a stakeholder's concern, therefore, is the selection criterion that is used to determine which objects and relations are to appear in a view.

Below we list some examples of stakeholders and their concerns, which could typically serve as the basis for the definition/selection of viewpoints:

- Upper-level management: How can we ensure our policies are followed in the development and operation of processes and systems? What is the impact of decisions (on personnel, finance, ICT, etc.)? Which improvements can a new system bring to a pre-existing situation in relation to the costs of acquiring that system?
- Middle-level management: What is the current situation with regards to the computerised support of a business process?
- End user: What is the potential impact of a new system on the activities of a prospective user?
- Architect: What are the consequences for the maintainability of a system with respect to corrective, preventive, and adaptive maintenance?
- Operational manager: What new technologies do we need to prepare for? Is there a need to adapt maintenance processes? What is the impact of changes to existing applications? How secure are the systems?
- Project manager (of system development project): What are the relevant domains and their relations? What is the dependence of business processes on the applications to be built? What is their expected performance?

- System developer: What are the modifications with respect to the current situation that need to be performed?
- System administrators: What is the potential impact of a new system on the work of the system administrators that are to maintain the new system?

In line with the ISO/IEC/IEEE 42010:2011 standard, and based on the detailed definition given in Proper (2004), we define a viewpoint as follows:

> **Viewpoint**: a specification of the conventions for constructing and using views.

This should also involve the various 'ways of . . .' that we outlined in Sect. 3.2.5, but in this chapter we will focus on the selection of the content of views, the visual representation of this content, and the typical use of these viewpoints, i.e., on the ways of modelling, communicating, and using. The 'way of supporting', i.e., tool support for views, will be addressed in Chap. 11, and the 'way of working' has already been addressed in Chap. 7.

8.1.3 Viewpoint Frameworks

In the context of architecture descriptions, a score of viewpoint frameworks exists, leaving designers and architects with the burden of selecting the viewpoints to be used in a specific situation. Some of these frameworks of viewpoints are: the Zachman framework (Zachman 1987), Kruchten's 4+1 view model (Kruchten 1995), RM-ODP (ITU 1996), and TOGAF (The Open Group 2011). These frameworks have usually been constructed by their authors in an attempt to cover all relevant aspects/concerns of the architecture of some class of systems. In practice, numerous large organisations have defined their own frameworks of viewpoints by which they describe their architectures. We shall discuss two of these framework in more detail below.

The '4+1' View Model
Kruchten (1995) introduced a framework of viewpoints (a view model) comprising five viewpoints. The use of multiple viewpoints is motivated by the observation that it 'allows to address separately the concerns of the various stakeholders of the architecture: end-user, developers, systems engineers, project managers, etc., and to handle separately the functional and non-functional requirements'.

The goals, stakeholders, concerns and meta-model of the 4+1 framework can be presented, in brief, as in Table 8.1. Note that in Kruchten (2000), the viewpoints have been renamed; physical viewpoint → deployment viewpoint, development viewpoint → implementation viewpoint, and scenario viewpoint → use-case viewpoint, better to match the terminology of UML.

The framework proposes modelling concepts (the meta-model) for each of the specific viewpoints. It does so, however, without explicitly discussing how these

Table 8.1 Kruchten's '4+1' view model.

Viewpoint	Logical	Process	Development	Physical	Scenarios
Goal	Capture the services which the system should provide	Capture concurrency and synchronisation aspects of the design	Describe static organisation of the software and its development	Describe mapping of software onto hardware, and its distribution	Provide a driver to discover key elements in design Validation and illustration
Stake-holders	Architect End users	Architect System designer Integrator	Architect Developer Manager	Architect System designer	Architect End users Developer
Concerns	Functionality	Performance Availability Fault tolerance ...	Organisation Reuse Portability ...	Scalability Performance Availability ...	Understand-ability
Meta-model	Object classes Associations Inheritance ...	Event Message Broadcast ...	Module Subsystem Layer ...	Processor Device Bandwidth ...	Objects Events Steps ...

modelling concepts contribute to the goals of the specific viewpoints. One might, for example, wonder whether object classes, associations, etc., are the right concepts for communication with end users about the services they require from the system. The 4 +1 framework is based on experiences in practical settings by its author.

RM-ODP

The Reference Model for Open Distributed Processing (RM-ODP) (ITU 1996) was produced in a joint effort by the international standard bodies ISO and ITU in order to develop a coordinating framework for the standardisation of open distributed processing. The resulting framework defines five viewpoints: *enterprise, information, computation, engineering* and *technology.* The modelling concepts used in each of these views are based on the object-oriented paradigm.

The goals, concerns and associated meta-models of the viewpoints identified by the RM-ODP can be presented, in brief, as in Table 8.2.

RM-ODP provides a modelling language for each of the viewpoints identified. It furthermore states: 'Each language [for creating views/models conforming to a viewpoint] has sufficient expressive power to specify an ODP function, application or policy from the corresponding viewpoint.' RM-ODP does not explicitly associate viewpoints to a specific class of stakeholders. This is left implicit in the concerns which the viewpoints aim to address.

Table 8.2 The RM-ODP viewpoints

Viewpoint	Enterprise	Information	Computational	Engineering	Technology
Goal	Capture purpose, scope, and policies of the system	Capture semantics of information and processing performed by the system	Express distribution of the system in interacting objects	Describe design of distribution-oriented aspects of the system	Describe choice of technology used in the system
Concerns	Organisational requirements and structure	Information and processing required	Distribution of system Functional decomposition	Distribution of the system, and mechanisms and functions needed	Hardware and software choices Compliancy to other views
Meta-model	Objects Communities Permissions Obligations Contract ...	Object classes Associations Process ...	Objects Interfaces Interaction Activities ...	Objects Channels Node Capsule Cluster ...	Not stated explicitly

8.2 Models, Views, and Visualisations

An important principle in our approach is the separation of the content and the presentation or visualisation of a view. This separation is not explicitly made in the IEEE standard, but it has important advantages. It facilitates the use of different visualisation techniques on the same modelling concepts, and vice versa. Operations on the visualisation of a view, e.g., changing its layout, need not change its content.

The view content, referred to as the 'view' in the remainder of this chapter, is a selection or derivation from a (symbolic) model of the architecture, and is expressed in terms of the same modelling concepts. The presentation or notation of this view, referred to as 'visualisation' in the remainder, can take many forms, from standard diagrams to tables, cartoons, or even dynamic visualisations like movies. Editing operations on this visualisation can lead to updates of the view and of the underlying model. The creation and update of both the view and the visualisation are governed by a viewpoint. This viewpoint is jointly defined and/or selected in an iterative process by architect and stakeholder together. This is illustrated in Fig. 8.1.

The separation between view and visualisation is based on the notion of 'meaning'. In Chap. 3 we introduced the concept of the signature of an architecture as its alphabet: that is, the set of symbols used to describe the concepts of the architecture and the relations among these concepts. This idea can also be used to clarify the distinction between view and its visualisation. A further discussion of these formal foundations can be found in Chap. 9.

A view stripped from its visual properties can be formalised just like any other model, e.g., by defining its signature, as outlined in Chap. 3. By formalising its relation with an underlying model, a view's quality and consistency can be greatly

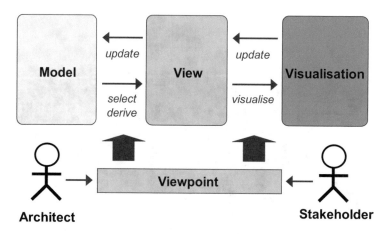

Fig. 8.1 Separation of concerns: model, view, visualisation, and viewpoint

enhanced and new opportunities for its use may arise, e.g., in changing the underlying models by interacting with such a view.

8.2.1   Example: Process Illustrations

To illustrate the difference between a view and its visualisation, we introduce the *process illustration* viewpoint. This viewpoint illustrates a process model in an informal way for employees and managers. A process illustration is derived from a model of the architecture using a set of translation and abstraction rules. As process illustrations are meant for communicating the coherence between business processes, they typically abstract from details regarding the applications and technology involved. Moreover, process illustrations do not apply abstract concepts and notations, but rather use recognisable terms and intuitive notations.

A process illustration of the Car Tax Collection process is depicted in Fig. 8.2. The figure shows the various sub-processes involved and the information flows between them. The figure is derived from an ArchiMate model via a series of translation and abstraction rules, for instance to replace abstract shapes with meaningful symbols, abstract from complex relations, and visually group all objects and relations that belong to or happen within a certain actor.

In Fig. 8.3 you can see a number of presentation rules that can be applied in the 'model-to-illustration' derivation. The basic idea behind these rules is to find suitable and intuitive graphic symbols that will replace ArchiMate shapes. These rules apply to ArchiMate concepts for which there is an immediate correspondent in the process illustration notation (i.e., actor, role, device, service, business object, etc.).

Of course, many other rules can be added here. For instance, rules referring to a specific layout of the final drawing or to the more extensive usage of 3D graphic symbols can increase the readability and usability of the final drawing.

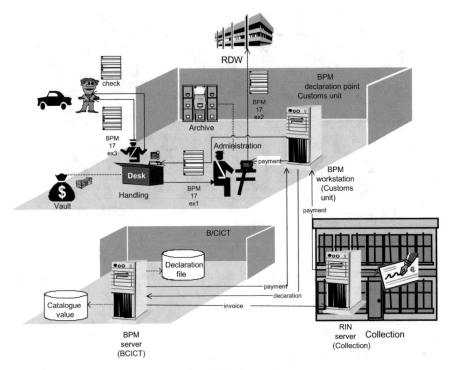

Fig. 8.2   Process illustration of the Car Tax Collection process

8.2.2   Example: Landscape Maps

A more complex example to illustrate the differences between a model, a view, and its visualisation, is the *landscape map* viewpoint. Landscape maps, as defined in Sanden and Sturm (1997), are a technique for visualising enterprise architectures. They present architectural elements in the form of an easy-to-understand 2D 'map'. A landscape map view of architectures provides non-technical stakeholders, such as managers, with a high-level overview, without burdening them with the technical-ities of architectural drawings.

Many systems used by many processes realising various products and services comprise too much detail to display in a single figure. This is a typical example of where landscape maps can help. In Fig. 8.4, a landscape map is depicted that shows which information systems support the operations of our fictitious insurance com-pany ArchiSurance. The vertical axis represents the company's business functions; the horizontal axis shows its insurance products. An application rectangle covering one or more cells means that this particular function/product pair is supported by the application, e.g., contracting of a legal aid insurance is supported by the legal aid back-office system. The visualisation chosen makes it immediately obvious to the viewer that there is (possibly unwanted) overlap between applications, as is the case in the Car insurance application and the Legal Aid CRM system. Clearly,

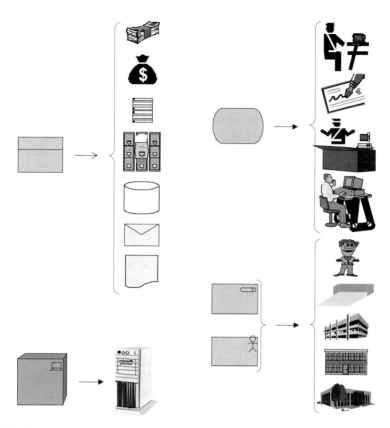

Fig. 8.3 Translation rules

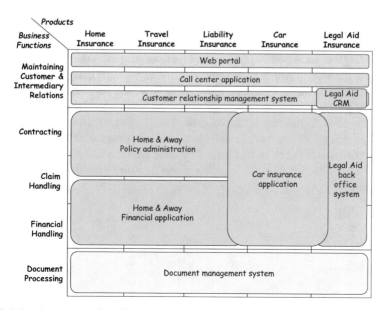

Fig. 8.4 Landscape map of ArchiSurance

landscape maps are a richer representation than cross-reference tables, which cover only two dimensions. In order to obtain the same expressive power of a landscape map two cross-reference tables would be necessary; but even then, you would get a presentation that is not as insightful and informative as a landscape map.

The dimensions of the landscape maps can be freely chosen from the architecture that is being modelled. In practice, dimensions are often chosen from different architectural domains, for instance business functions, products and applications, etc. In most cases, the vertical axis represents behaviour such as business processes or functions; the horizontal axis represents 'cases' for which those functions or processes must be executed. These 'cases' can be different products, services, market segments, or scenarios. The third dimension represented by the cells of the matrix is used for assigning resources like information systems, infrastructure, or human resources.

The visualisation of architecture models as landscape maps is based on architecture relations. The dimensions that are used in the landscape maps determine which relations are used. For instance, the landscape map in Fig. 8.4 relates business functions (contracting, claim handling, etc.) to products (home insurance, travel insurance, etc.) to applications (Web portal, car insurance application, etc.). The relation between business functions, products, and applications is not directly supported by relations in the underlying model. Rather, this needs to be inferred indirectly: a product comprises a number of business services, which are realised by business processes and functions, which use (the application services of) application components. For this inference, the formalisation of the underlying symbolic models and the rules for the composition of relations described in Chaps. 3 and 4 are indispensable.

For landscape maps to be of practical use, the visualisation must be intuitive and easy to understand. To a large extent, the choice of the axes and the ordering of the rows and columns determine the layout of a landscape map. If adjacent cells in the plane have the same value assigned, they can be merged to form a single shape. If there are no other criteria for ordering the axes such as time or priority, changes to the ordering can be used to optimise the layout of shapes in the plane, and also to limit their number. Various layout optimisation algorithms can be employed, and user manipulation of, for example, the order of rows and columns may also help in creating a pleasing visualisation.

Summarising, in developing the landscape map viewpoint, it has been fruitful to distinguish the operation on the model from the visualisation of the view, because they are completely different concerns. The same holds for the other viewpoints we have defined. To separate these concerns, views have to be distinguished from their visualisation.

8.3 Visualisation and Interaction

The distinction we make between a model and its visualisation naturally leads to the concept of interactive visualisation; that is, visualisation which can change the model due to interaction with a stakeholder. Interaction has traditionally been considered as something completely outside the model and the view. Interaction is at least partly a visualisation issue: for example, when a user draws an object on the canvas of some tool. However, it can also partly be defined as part of the model and view, since the object the user draws may be put in the underlying model or view as well.

These two considerations have led to a new visualisation and interaction model for enterprise architectures in ArchiMate. Its goal is that interaction is separated from updating the model, or from its visualisation.

8.3.1 Actions in Views

The effect of a user interacting with the visualisation can be an update of the view. But where will this be defined? Clearly, the visualisation itself is 'dumb' and does not know about the semantics of the view. Hence, rules for changing the view cannot be tied to the visualisation and must be defined in the view itself. This is why we introduce the notion of *actions in views*. Consider for example a landscape map view, and a user who interacts with this view by moving an application to another business function. Does the relation between the interaction with the landscape map and the update of the model *mean* something? Obviously the relation between the move in the landscape map leads to an update of the underlying model or view, and thus means something.

In Sect. 7.2.3 we have identified a number of basic modelling actions, such as introducing, refining, abandoning, abstracting, and translating a concept in a model. These actions operate on the architecture model or view, not on its visualisation. However, most changes to a model will be conducted by a user who changes a visualisation of that model. Hence, we need to define the ways in which a user can manipulate these visualisations and the effects on the underlying model in terms of these basic modelling actions. We can then relate these actions to the manipulations of the visualisation by making the actions part of the view being visualised.

Thus, a clear separation of model and visualisation leads to a separation of concerns in tool building. An extremely generic visualisation engine can be constructed that does not need to know about the semantics of the models it displays. If we define the possible actions together with the views, a generic editor can be configured by this set of actions.

The actions in views should be defined in terms of the effects they have on elements of the underlying model. For example, consider a view of a business process model, and an action that merges two processes into a single process. Issues that are relevant for the action of merging processes are the effects of the merger: for example, the removal of processes, addition of a new process, transferring some relations from an old, removed process to a new process.

For each viewpoint, we define a set of actions. For example, for the landscape map viewpoint we define the move of an application to another cell, we define changing the columns and rows of the matrix, and we define the addition and deletion of applications. Moreover, we must determine for each action which parameters it needs as input, and define the consequences of executing the action.

When actions for each view have been defined, we can go one step further and define the relation between actions. One important relation is that one action may consist of a set of simpler actions. For example, consider an architect or stakeholder that wishes to change an existing landscape map. First the effects of this change on the underlying model need to be assessed. Some changes may be purely 'cosmetic' in nature, e.g., changing the colour of an object. Other changes need to be propagated to the underlying model by invoking one of the basic modelling actions of Sect. 7.2.3, e.g., if an object is added or deleted.

Mapping a seemingly simple change to the map onto the necessary modifications of the model may become quite complicated. Since a landscape map abstracts from many aspects of the underlying model, such a mapping might be ambiguous: many different modifications to the model might correspond to the same change of the landscape map. Human intervention is required to solve this, but a landscape map tool might suggest where the impact of the change is located.

In the example of Fig. 8.4, you may, for instance, want to remove the seemingly redundant Legal Aid CRM system by invoking a 'remove overlap' operation on this object. This operation influences both the visualisation and the architectural model. The effects of the operation on the underlying model are shown in Fig. 8.5. First, you select the object to be removed, in this case the Legal Aid CRM system. The envisaged tool colours this object and maps it back onto the underlying object in the architecture. Next, the relations connecting this object to its environment are computed, possibly using the impact-of-change analysis techniques described in Chap. 9 (the second part of Fig. 8.5). Here, this concerns the relations of Legal Aid CRM to the Call centre application and the Legal Aid back-office system. These relations will have to be connected to one or more objects that replace the objects that are to be removed. Since we have chosen a 'remove overlap' operation, the landscape tool computes with which other objects Legal Aid CRM overlaps, in this case the CRM system. The relations formerly connecting Legal Aid CRM are then moved to the other CRM system, unless these already exist (e.g. the relation with the Call centre application).

Naturally, this scenario presents an ideal situation with minimal user intervention. In reality, a tool cannot always decide how a proposed change is to be mapped back onto the model, and may only present the user with a number of options. For example, if the functionality of the Legal Aid CRM system overlaps with more than one other system, remapping its relations requires knowledge about the correspondence between these relations and the functions realised by these other systems.

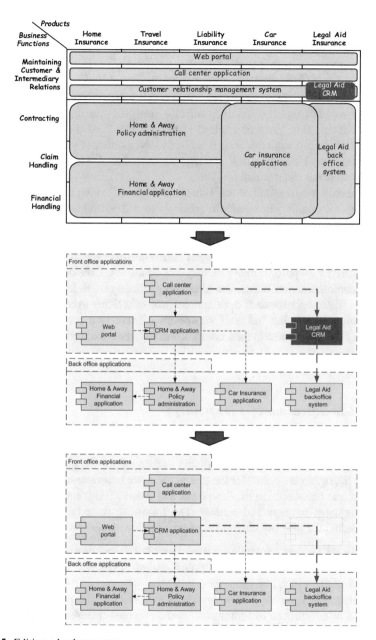

Fig. 8.5   Editing a landscape map

Implementing a tool that realises this 'actions in views' concept is not a trivial task. In Chap. 11, we will describe the design of a software tool that provides a proof of concept of these ideas.

8.4   Creating, Selecting, and Using Viewpoints

It is interesting to note that both of the discussed frameworks of viewpoints (Sect. 8.1.3) do not provide an explicit motivation for their choice regarding the modelling concepts used in specific viewpoints. When using one of the two frameworks, architects will not find it difficult to select a viewpoint for the modelling task at hand. However, this 'ease of choice' is more a result of the limitation of the selections of options available (one is limited to the number of viewpoints provided by the framework) than the result of a well-motivated choice about the viewpoint's utility towards the tasks at hand.

One should realise that a well-integrated set of viewpoints (such as the ArchiMate viewpoints) brings more (utility!) to a development project than the sum of its parts! Among other things, it allows views to be more easily related and integrated into a consistent whole. However, defining such an integrated viewpoint framework is an expensive undertaking. This means that even though a pre-existing (off-the-shelf) viewpoint framework may not be the ideal answer to an architect's specific communication needs, the alternative strategy of defining a tailor-made viewpoint framework for each development project is likely to be too costly. Hence our attention to defining 'ad hoc' viewpoints relative to a predefined modelling language (i.e., meta-model) as a compromise between fixed viewpoints and free viewpoints.

8.4.1   Classification of Viewpoints

As we can see from the list of stakeholders in Sect. 8.1.2, an architect is confronted with many different types of stakeholders and concerns. To help the architect in selecting the right viewpoints for the task at hand, we introduce a framework for the definition and classification of viewpoints and views. The framework is based on two dimensions, *purpose* and *content*. The following three types of architecture support define the purpose dimension of architecture views (Steen et al. 2004):

– **Designing**: Design viewpoints support architects and designers in the design process from initial sketch to detailed design. Typically, design viewpoints consist of diagrams, like those used in UML.
– **Deciding**: Decision support views assist managers in the process of decision making by offering an insight into cross-domain architecture relations, typically through projections and intersections of underlying models, but also by means of analytical techniques. Typical examples are cross-reference tables, landscape maps, lists, and reports.
– **Informing**: These viewpoints help to inform any stakeholder about the enterprise architecture, in order to achieve understanding, obtain commitment, and convince adversaries. Typical examples are illustrations, animations, cartoons, flyers, etc.

The goal of this classification is to assist architects and others to find suitable viewpoints given their task at hand, i.e., the purpose that a view must serve and the content it should display. With the help of this framework, it is easier to find typical viewpoints that might be useful in a given situation. This implies that we do not provide an orthogonal categorisation of each viewpoint into one of three classes; these categories are not exclusive in the sense that a viewpoint in one category cannot be applied to achieve another type of support. For instance, some decision support viewpoints may be used to communicate to any other stakeholders as well.

For characterising the content of a view we define the following abstraction levels:

- **Details:** Views of the detailed level typically consider one layer and one aspect from the framework that was introduced in Chap. 5. Typical stakeholders are a software engineer responsible for the design and implementation of a software component or a process owner responsible for effective and efficient process execution. Examples of views are a BPMN process diagram and a UML class diagram.
- **Coherence:** At the coherence abstraction level, multiple layers or multiple aspects are spanned. Extending the view to more than one layer or aspect enables the stakeholder to focus on architecture relations like process–use–system (multiple layer) or application–uses–object (multiple aspect). Typical stakeholders are operational managers responsible for a collection of IT services or business processes.
- **Overview:** The overview abstraction level addresses both multiple layers and multiple aspects. Typically, such overviews are addressed to enterprise architects and decision makers such as CEOs and CIOs.

In Fig. 8.6, the dimensions of purpose and abstraction level are visualised in a single picture, together with examples of stakeholders. Tables 8.3 and 8.4 summarise the different purposes and abstraction levels.

The landscape map viewpoint described in Sect. 8.2.1 is a typical example of a decision support view, which give a high-level overview and can, for example, be used to identify redundancies or gaps in the application landscape of an enterprise.

The process illustration viewpoint described in Sect. 8.2.1 is an example of a viewpoint intended for 'informing' others. It depicts workflows in a cartoon-like fashion, easily readable for employees and managers. Process illustrations can be on the detailed, coherence, or overview abstraction level.

To assist the architect in designing an enterprise architecture, we present a set of basic design viewpoints in the next sections. These viewpoints are all diagrams for designing architectures. Some viewpoints are multiple-aspect and multiple-layer overviews at the 'coherence' level of abstraction, while others are at the 'details' level.

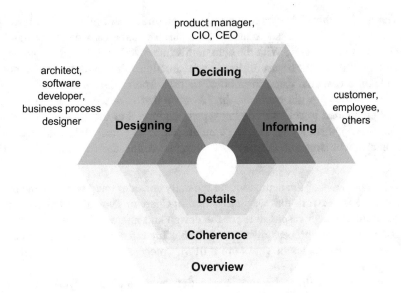

Fig. 8.6 Classification of enterprise architecture viewpoints

Table 8.3 Viewpoint purpose

	Typical stakeholders	Purpose	Examples
Designing	Architect, software developer, business process designer	Navigate, design, support design decisions, compare alternatives	UML diagram, BPMN diagram, flowchart, ER diagram
Deciding	Manager, CIO, CEO	Decision making	Cross-reference table, landscape map, list, report
Informing	Employee, customer, others	Explain, convince, obtain commitment	Animation, cartoon, process illustration, chart

Table 8.4 Viewpoint abstraction levels

	Typical stakeholders	Purpose	Examples
Details	Software engineer, process owner	Design, manage	UML class diagram, Testbed process diagram
Coherence	Operational managers	Analyse dependencies, impact of change	Views expressing relations like 'use', 'realise', and 'assign'
Overview	Enterprise architect, CIO, CEO	Change management	Landscape map

8.4.2   Guidelines for Using Viewpoints

To help you in selecting and using viewpoints for tasks at hand, we present a number of guidelines, based on our own experience and interviews with architects from practice.

In general, the use of an architectural viewpoint will pass through a number of phases. These phases roughly are:

1. **Scoping**: Select one or more appropriate viewpoints, select the (sub)domain that needs to be represented or modelled, and determine the constraints that apply to the domain being modelled.
2. **Creation of views**: Create or select the actual content of the viewpoint, i.e., create or select a view conforming to the viewpoint used. This can pertain to the selection of a part of the larger (pre-existing) architecture model, or the creation or refinement of a part of the architecture model (in terms of a view).
3. **Validation**: Validate the resulting view. Do the stakeholders agree that the view is a correct representation of the actual or intended situation?
4. **Obtaining commitment**: If *agreement* has been reached among the key stakeholders involved, the next step will be to create *commitment* for the results. In other words, do the stakeholders commit themselves to the (potential) impact of what is described by the view?
5. **Informing**: Inform other stakeholders of the results. These stakeholders will be those members of the development community, whose explicit commitment has, in a *conscious* decision, been considered not to be crucial.

Note that these phases will not necessarily be executed in a linear order. Practical circumstances usually dictate a more evolutionary approach. The viewpoints to be used for architectural communication will have to support the activities of each of the phases. The guidelines resulting from the interviews are divided over them. They are discussed in the next sections.

8.4.3   Scoping

The importance of focusing on the concerns of stakeholders, and the extent to which a specific view(point) addresses these concerns, was confirmed by the outcomes of the interviews. When you communicate with business managers, you only need those views or models that enable a discussion of factors deserving special attention. Typically, these are factors that have a high impact if they fail and also have a high risk of indeed failing. For communication with the actual software developers, on the other hand, more detailed models are crucial.

The selection of viewpoints should be done consciously and based on rational considerations. Furthermore, architects state that this decision, and its rationalisation, must be readily available. It is quite possible that a stakeholder (usually a technology-oriented one) will ask for more detail in a model than you can give, or want to give, in that particular phase of the project. An architect should be prepared to clarify better the goals of the particular model and phase, and why the requested details are not yet relevant (or even harmful).

Determining the constraints that should guide the ensuing creation phase is also considered to be important. Numerous IT projects suffer from the problem that designers have too much 'design freedom' when producing a model of a desired future system. This increases the risk of ending up with lengthy design processes. Limiting design freedom by means of architecture principles, a higher-level architecture, or any other means, reduces this risk considerably.

8.4.4 Creation of Views

During the creation of a view, in particular when it involves actual modelling, you should try to put a limit on the number of participants in a conversation. Graphical models may or may not be used in communication with stakeholders, but most actual modelling is done by individuals (or two people at most). Genuine group modelling sessions are very rare.

During the early stages of system design, it is often considered bad to 'think' in terms of 'solutions'. However, when detailed modelling takes place in a cooperative setting, give informants some room to think in terms of 'solutions' even if pure requirements thinking (what, not how) does not officially allow for this. Most people just think better in terms of concrete solutions; it is a vital part of their creativity. Just be sure that requirements thinking is returned to in due course. In general, when you discuss models with stakeholders and informants, in particular when you try to establish a common understanding, you should discuss different scenarios and alternatives to the model being considered. Doing so leads to an exploration of the meaning and impact of the model taking shape, and also leads to improved mutual understanding.

The graphical notation that is part of a viewpoint should be approached flexibly when it comes to communicating with non-technical stakeholders. If people are not used to or prepared to deal with abstract graphical models, do not use them. Use other forms of visualisation, text, or tables. Iconised diagrams work particularly well. However, be prepared to point out the relation between the alternative visualisation and your abstract models if asked to.

Even if graphical models play a big role in architecture, text is the chief form in which (written) communication takes place. Two main ways in which this occurs are:

– Graphical (partial!) models that are used to support textual descriptions ('illustration by diagram').
– Text explaining and elaborating on a graphical model ('textual modelling').

In fact, text is often better than a graphical model for conveying large amounts of detail.

Language studies have indeed shown how the specific form of a language does have an impact on what is expressed by means of the language (Cruse 2000). In the case of modelling languages, the modelling concepts offered by the language will, in general, influence the level of detail or abstraction that the resulting models will exhibit.

Finally, during a modelling session, several things may come to the fore that will influence the further process. External events may occur that are a threat to the process as a whole. Be prepared to stop modelling if executive commitment is withdrawn. It may be frustrating, but from a business perspective it may also be crucial. It is simply part of a flexible project setup. If the informants turn out to be less informed than expected, it is better to stop than to try and 'make the best of it' and produce an ill-conceived model.

In the field of agile development (Martin 2002; Rueping 2003; Ambler 2002), a refreshing perspective can be found on such considerations.

8.4.5   Validation

In validation of an architecture with stakeholders, a clear difference should be made between validation of content (qualitative validation, by modellers and experts) and validation in terms of commitment (by executives). Both are crucial, but very different. Obtaining (and validating) commitment is discussed in the next subsection.

Whether good mutual communication and understanding about a model is being reached is often a matter of intuition. If the people involved have a mutual feeling that 'their thoughts are well in sync', then dare to trust that feeling. However, if the opposite is the case, be prepared to invest in substantial discussion of concrete examples, or face the dire consequences of poor validation. If the required 'level of agreement' between participants is high, an atmosphere of mutual trust and cooperation between these participants is crucial.

Validation is an activity that should be conducted in limited groups. 'Feedback rounds' involving a larger number of people, by e-mail or printed documentation, do not really work. If you want feedback that is worth something, find key people and discuss the models/views, preferably face to face. Make sure the 'opinion leaders' in an organisation agree to the model.

Also, you should take care that the languages used to express a view do not have a wrong connotation that may result in incorrect impressions about the scope and status of models. A language like UML cannot be used in a discussion with business people. Even though the language is suitable to express the models, the notation has an implementation-oriented connotation to this audience.

Furthermore, do not show a concrete view of the desired system too early on in the development process. The concreteness of the diagram may give the stakeholders a feeling that important decisions have already been made.

With regards to the last observation, an interesting statement on this issue can also be found in Weinberg (1988). He argues that when the design of a system, or a model in general, is still in its early stages, and different aspects are not yet clear and definite, the graphical notation used should also reflect this. He suggests using squiggly lines rather than firm lines, so as to communicate to the reader of a view that specific parts of the view are still open to debate. We use this principle in the Introductory viewpoint discussed in Sect. 8.5.2.

8.4.6 Obtaining Commitment

Obtaining commitment for a specific architectural design involves obtaining commitment for the *impact* of this design on the future system and its evolution, as well as the *costs/resources* needed to arrive at this future system. This means that the message that one needs to get across to the stakeholders involves:

– What are the major problems in the current situation?
– How bad are these problems (to the concerns and objectives of the stakeholders)?
– How will this improve in the new situation? (Benefits!)
– At what costs will these improvements come?

When discussing costs and benefits with stakeholders, make these costs and benefits as SMART (Specific, Measurable, Attainable, Realisable, and Timebound) as possible. Make sure that the stakeholders agree, up front, with the criteria that are used to express/determine costs and benefits. It is their commitment that is needed. They will be the judge. Let them also decide what they want to base their judgement on! Create shared responsibility towards the outcomes.

Selecting the stakeholders that should be involved when obtaining commitment is also of key importance. Involving the wrong stakeholders, or leaving out important ones, will have obvious repercussions. At the same time, selecting a too large a group of stakeholders may bog down the process. Too much communication may be a bad thing: it may create unnoticed and uncontrolled discussion outside the main discussion, leading to twisted conceptualisations and expectations.

Though ideally 'everyone' should be heard, this is generally a practical impossibility. Therefore, choose your experts carefully. Aim for the opinion leaders, and also accept that you cannot please everyone. Realise that some people will not be perfectly satisfied, prepare for it, and deal with it.

People who actually make the decisions are usually those who are just outside the group of people who really know what is going on. Make sure that the former people are *also* involved and aware of what is happening.

Getting executive commitment may actually be dictated technologically. If their business is highly technological, business people do not see technology as secondary, and will only commit to something if they are assured that 'their organisation will be able to run it'.

Sharing design decisions and their underlying considerations at a late stage has a negative impact on the commitment of stakeholders. Start building commitment early on in the process. This implies that the linear ordering of the 'viewpoint use phases' as provided at the start of this section should not be applied strictly.

Once agreement has been reached, you should document this explicitly. Models are never accepted as sufficient statements to base agreements and commitment on. Commitments and agreements also need to be spelled out separately, in text.

8.4.7   Informing Stakeholders

Once commitment from the opinion leaders has been obtained, other stakeholders may be informed about the future plans and their impact. In doing so, it still makes sense to concentrate on cost/benefit considerations when trying to 'sell' the new system. Below, we have gathered some observations that apply to the informing phase. However, due to their general communicative nature, some of these observations are also applicable to the creation, validation, and commitment phases.

Do not impose presumed architectural terminology on true business people. Use *their* terminology. Even a concept like 'service' is suspect because it is relatively technology oriented and often unknown by stakeholders that are strictly on the business side.

Models are particularly important in giving stakeholders a feeling that they are 'part of the larger whole'. Often, just knowing where in the model 'they can be found' is important to stakeholders, even if they do not understand the fine points of the model.

Communication is the crucial factor in enterprise architecture. It will even pay off actually to employ some communication experts (think marketing, PR, even entertainment!) in larger projects. As a result, you will end up with stakeholders who are genuinely prepared to change the way they and their business work, not just with some interesting looking plans and models. Crucially, communication can be quite different for various stages of system development. Therefore, it is important to have a good communication strategy and a framework guiding you in this.

Even if people are willing to and able to read models thoroughly, text (spoken or written) needs to be added. Models alone never suffice.

8.5   Basic Design Viewpoints

The most basic type of viewpoint is the selection of a relevant subset of the ArchiMate concepts and the representation of that part of an architecture that is expressed in the concepts in this selection. This is sometimes called a 'diagram', akin to, for instance, the UML diagrams.

In Sect. 7.3.2, we introduced the following four metaphorical directions from which we can identify relevant model elements:

1. 'Inwards', towards the internal composition of the element
2. 'Upwards', towards the elements that are supported by it
3. 'Downwards', towards its realisation by other elements
4. 'Sideways', towards peer elements with which it cooperates

We also use these directions to identify possibly useful viewpoints.

For the 'composition' viewpoints, we start from the basic structure of our modelling language. In its elementary form, the generic meta-model that is behind the language consists of active structural elements such as actors, behavioural elements such as functions and processes and passive informational elements such as business and data objects, which are processed by the active elements in the course of their behaviour.

From this basic structure, we can deduce a first set of viewpoint types, containing three viewpoints that are centred around one specific type of concept:

1. Active elements, e.g. the composition of a business actor from sub-actors, i.e. an organisation structure
2. Behaviour elements, e.g. the structure of a business process in terms of sub-processes
3. Passive elements, e.g. the information structure in terms of data objects

Although these viewpoints take a specific type of concept and its structure as their focus, they are not limited to these concepts, and closely related concepts are also included.

For the 'upwards' support of elements in their environment, the active elements offer interfaces through which their services can be used. 'Downwards' services are realised by processes and functions, and application components are deployed on infrastructure elements. 'Sideways' cooperation is achieved through collaborations between active elements and their behaviour in the form of interactions, and flows of information and value that relate the elements. Passive elements often play a role in these relations, e.g., by being passed from one element to another, but are not the focus. Hence we concentrate on the relations between the active and behaviour elements.

Next to the design viewpoints resulting from these metaphorical directions, which focus on a limited part of an enterprise architecture, we also need to represent the whole architecture, but in a simplified form. Especially early in the design process, when we do not yet know all the details that are added later on, we want to

Table 8.5 Design viewpoints

Early design	*Cooperation*
Introductory, p. 210	Actor Cooperation, p. 212
	Business Process Cooperation, p. 216
	Application Cooperation, p. 219
Composition	*Realisation*
Organisation, p. 212	Service Realisation, p. 216
Business Function, p. 214	Implementation & Deployment, p. 224
Business Process, p. 217	
Information Structure, p. 218	*Support*
Application Behaviour, p. 222	Product, p. 215
Application Structure, p. 222	Application Usage, p. 221
Infrastructure, p. 223	Infrastructure Usage, p. 224

express an architecture using a subset of the ArchiMate language denoted in an informal, simplified form. This helps to avoid the impression that the design is already fixed and immutable, which may easily arise from a more formal diagram. Furthermore, such a high-level overview is very useful in obtaining commitment from stakeholders at an early stage of the design (see also Sect. 8.4.6). To this end, we introduce the Simplified viewpoint.

In each of the viewpoint types, concepts from the three layers of business, application, and technology may be used. However, not every combination of these would give meaningful results; in some cases, for example, separate viewpoints for the different layers are advisable. Based on common architectural practice, our experiences with the use of ArchiMate models in practical cases and the diagrams used in other languages like UML, we have selected the most useful combinations in the form of a 'standard' set of basic viewpoints to be used with the ArchiMate concepts (Table 8.5).

Some of these viewpoints have a scope that is limited to a single layer or aspect: the Business Function and Business Process viewpoints show the two main perspectives on the business behaviour; the Organisation viewpoint depicts the structure of the enterprise in terms of its departments, roles, etc.; the Information Structure viewpoint describes the information and data used; the Application Structure, Behaviour, and Cooperation viewpoints contain the applications and components and their mutual relations; and the Infrastructure viewpoint shows the infrastructure and platforms underlying the enterprise's information systems in terms of networks, devices, and system software. Other viewpoints link multiple layers and/or aspects: The Actor Cooperation and Product viewpoints relate the enterprise to its environment; the Application Usage viewpoint relates applications to their use in, for example, business processes; and the Deployment viewpoint shows how applications are mapped onto the underlying infrastructure.

In the next subsections, we will explain these design viewpoints in more detail and provide examples of each one. In these examples, we have made extensive use of the abstraction rule that can be applied on chains of structural relations in ArchiMate, which was explained in Sect. 5.11. Note that it is explicitly *not* the intention to limit the user of the ArchiMate language to these viewpoints; neither do we expect an architect to draw all these diagrams in a given situation! They are meant to assist the modeller in choosing the contents of a view, but combinations or subsets of these viewpoints could well be useful in specific situations.

It is important in the examples that these views exhibit considerable overlap. Different aspects of the Handle Claim business process are shown, for example, in Fig. 8.15 (its use of information), Fig. 8.13 (realisation of services by business processes) and Fig. 8.14 (its relations with other business processes), and there are many more of these overlaps between views. This shows that underlying these different views there is a single model, and each view is a projection of the relevant elements in that model. We will use two examples throughout the description of the basic design viewpoints to illustrate this coherence:

– The handling of insurance claims
– The policy administration systems and infrastructure

8.5.1   Introductory Viewpoint

The Introductory viewpoint forms a subset of the full ArchiMate language using a simplified notation. It is typically used at the start of a design trajectory, when not everything needs to be detailed, or to explain the essence of an architecture model to non-architects who require a simpler notation. Another use of this basic, less formal viewpoint is that it tries to avoid the impression that the architectural design is already fixed, an impression that may easily arise when using a more formal, highly structured, or detailed visualisation.

We use a simplified notation for the concepts and for the relations. All relations except 'triggering' and 'realisation' are denoted by simple lines; 'realisation' has an arrow in the direction of the realised service; 'triggering' is also represented by an arrow. The concepts are denoted with slightly thicker lines and rounded corners, which give a less formal impression. The example in Fig. 8.7 illustrates this notation.

On purpose, the layout of this example is not as 'straight' as an ordinary architecture diagram; this serves to avoid the idea that the design is already fixed and immutable. This conforms to the suggestion made in Weinberg (1988) to use squiggly lines rather than firm lines, to show to the reader of a view that specific parts of the view are still open to debate.

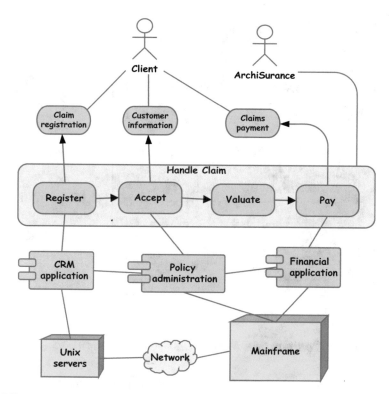

Fig. 8.7 Example of an Introductory view

8.5.2   *Organisation Viewpoint*

The Organisation viewpoint shows the structure of an internal organisation of the enterprise, department, or other organisational entity. It can be represented in the form of a nested block diagram, but also in more traditional ways like the organigram. An Organisation view is typically used to identify authority, competencies, and responsibilities within an organisation.

In Fig. 8.8, we see the high-level subdivision of ArchiSurance into a front and back office and a finance department. Within the back office, there are three departments responsible for specific products, e.g., car, travel, or legal aid insurance, and the shared service centre for document processing. The front office comprises two departments that handle the relations with customers and intermediaries, respectively.

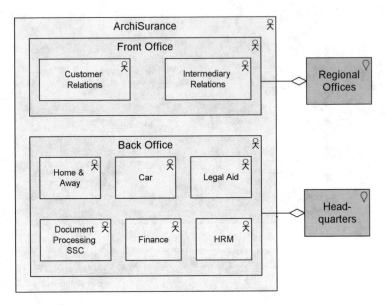

Fig. 8.8 ArchiSurance organisation structure

8.5.3 Actor Cooperation Viewpoint

The Actor Cooperation viewpoint focuses on the relations of actors with each other and their environment. A common example of this is what is sometimes called a 'context diagram', which puts an organisation into its environment, consisting of external parties such as customers, suppliers, and other business partners. It is useful in determining external dependencies and collaborations and shows the value chain or network in which the organisation operates. Another important use of this viewpoint is in showing how a number of cooperating (business and/or application) actors together realise a business process, by showing the flows between them.

The main roles involved in the insurance business are the insurant, the insurer, the intermediary and the customer's bank. These cooperate in different settings. For example, closing an insurance contract involves the customer, insurer and intermediary, whereas premium collection involves the insurer, the customer and the customer's bank. The main collaborations of ArchiSurance, which fulfils the role of the insurer, are shown in Fig. 8.9 and the information flows in Fig. 8.10.

8.5.4 Business Function Viewpoint

The Business Function viewpoint shows the main business functions of an organisation and their relations in terms of the flows of information, value, or goods

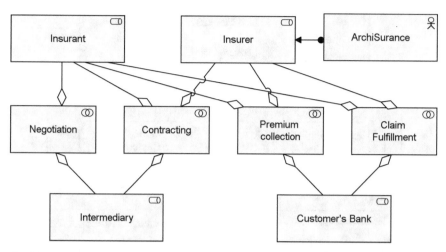

Fig. 8.9 Collaborations of ArchiSurance and its partners

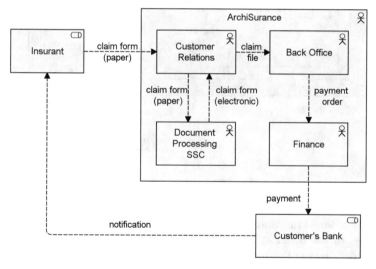

Fig. 8.10 Information flows between ArchiSurance's departments and partners in handling insurance claims

between them. Business functions are used to represent what is most stable about a company in terms of the primary activities it performs, regardless of organisational changes or technological developments. Business function architectures of companies that operate in the same market therefore often exhibit many similarities. The Business Function viewpoint thus provides high-level insight into the general operations of the company, and can be used to identify necessary competencies, or to structure an organisation according to its main activities.

In the example of Fig. 8.11, we can see the information flow associated with the handling of insurance claims. Claims are submitted to the Maintaining Customer

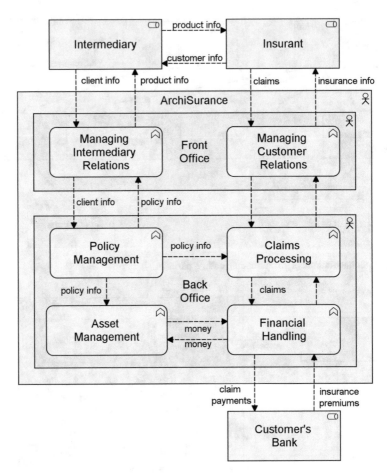

Fig. 8.11 Business functions and flows of information and money

Relations business function, processed by Claim Handling, and paid by Financial Handling. In the Business Process viewpoint (Sect. 8.5.6), we will see a more detailed depiction of this process.

8.5.5 Product Viewpoint

The Product viewpoint depicts the value this product offers to the customers or other external parties involved and shows the composition of one or more products in terms of the constituting (business or application) services, and the associated contract(s) or other agreements. It may also be used to show the interfaces (channels) through which this product is offered, and the events associated with the product.

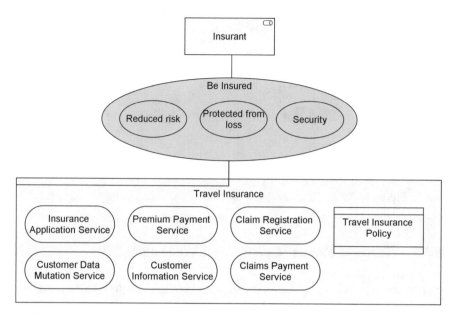

Fig. 8.12 The travel insurance product

A Product view is typically used in designing a product by composing existing services or by identifying which new services have to be created for this product, given the value a customer expects from it. It may then serve as input for business process architects and others that need to design the processes and IT systems that realise this product.

A typical insurance product of ArchiSurance is depicted in Fig. 8.12. The value to the customer of an insurance is typically the added security it provides, the protection from loss and the reduced risk. The services mentioned here are realised by various business processes, an example of which is given in Sect. 8.5.7.

8.5.6 Service Realisation Viewpoint

The Service Realisation viewpoint is used to show how one or more business services are realised by the underlying processes (and sometimes by application components). Thus, it forms the bridge between the Product viewpoint and the Business Process viewpoint. It provides a 'view from the outside' of one or more business processes.

Business services are realised by business processes. In Fig. 8.12, we saw the services that constitute the travel insurance product. The business processes that realise these services are shown in Fig. 8.13. For example, the Claim registration service is realised by the Handle Claim business process that we use as an example throughout this chapter.

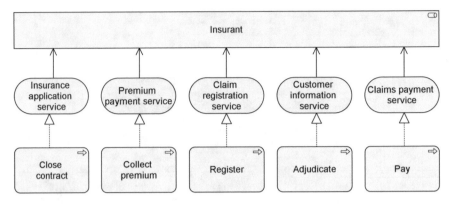

Fig. 8.13 Realisation of business services by ArchiSurance business processes

8.5.7 Business Process Cooperation Viewpoint

The Business Process Cooperation viewpoint is used to show the relations of one or more business processes with each other and/or their surroundings. It can be used both to create a high-level design of business processes within their context and to provide an operational manager responsible for one or more such processes with insight into their dependencies. Important aspects of coordination are:

– Causal relations between the main business processes of the enterprise
– The mapping of business processes onto business functions
– Realisation of services by business processes
– The use of shared data
– The execution of a business process by the same roles or actors

Each of these can be regarded as a 'sub-viewpoint' of the Business Process Cooperation viewpoint. Below, we give examples of some of the resulting views.

In Fig. 8.14, the most important business processes of ArchiSurance are depicted. It also shows their causal dependencies, e.g. the Collect premium process needs to be preceded by the Close Contract process, since of course no premium can be collected before the insurance policy has been issued. This figure also shows the Handle Claim process that occurs in many of the other viewpoints.

8.5.8 Business Process Viewpoint

The Business Process viewpoint is used to show the high-level structure and composition of one or more business processes. Next to the processes themselves, this viewpoint contains other directly related concepts such as:

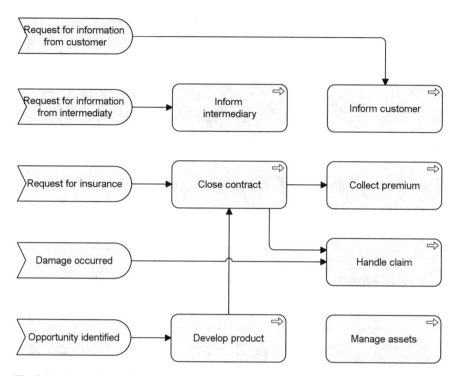

Fig. 8.14 Some of the main business processes, triggers, and relations of ArchiSurance

- The services a business process offers to the outside world, showing how a process contributes to the realisation of the company's products
- The assignment of business processes to roles, which gives insight into the responsibilities of the associated actors
- The information used by the business process

Each of these can be regarded as a 'sub-viewpoint' of the Business Process viewpoint.

In Fig. 8.15, the Handle Claim business process is shown with the sub-processes that are carried out in handling insurance claims.

8.5.9   Information Structure Viewpoint

The Information Structure viewpoint is basically identical to the traditional information models created in the development of almost any information system. It shows the structure of the information used in the enterprise or in a specific business process or application, in terms of data types or (object-oriented) class structures. Furthermore, it may show how the information at the business level is represented

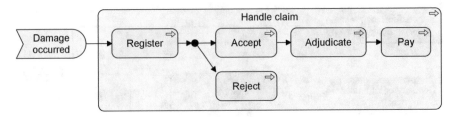

Fig. 8.15 The Handle Claim business process and its use of information

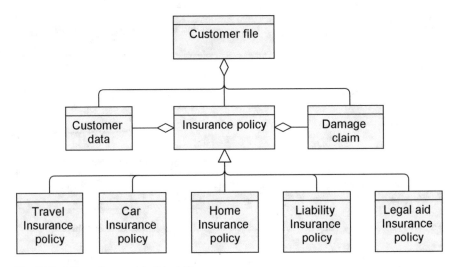

Fig. 8.16 Information model of ArchiSurance

at the application level in the form of the data structures used there, and how these are then mapped onto the underlying infrastructure, e.g., by means of a database schema.

In Fig. 8.16, the most important business objects of ArchiSurance are shown. Some of these are used in the Handle Claim business process, as depicted in Fig. 8.15.

8.5.10 Application Cooperation Viewpoint

The Application Cooperation viewpoint shows the relations of a number of applications or components. It describes the dependencies in terms of the information flows between them, or the services they offer and use. This viewpoint is typically used to create an overview of the application landscape of an organisation.

This viewpoint is also used to express the coordination or orchestration (i.e., internal coordination) of services that together support the execution of a business

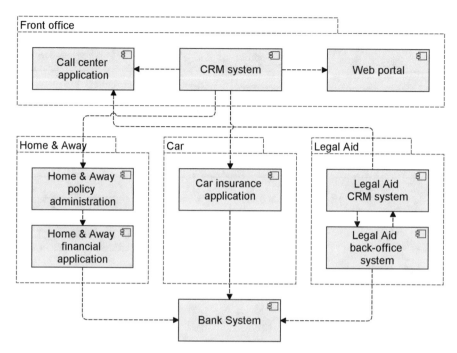

Fig. 8.17 Applications and information flow of ArchiSurance

process. By modelling the interdependencies between services, the coordination of the underlying applications is established in a more independent way. If this coordination is centralised and internal to the enterprise, we speak of 'orchestration'; in the case of coordination between independent entities, the term 'choreography' is often used.

The front- and back-office applications of ArchiSurance are shown in Fig. 8.17. It is clear that the back office is structured according to the different types of products, whereas the front office is already more integrated. One of the applications shown is the Home & Away policy administration used in several other viewpoints as well.

Some of the connections between the ArchiSurance applications are shown in Fig. 8.18, which shows that ArchiSurance uses the Enterprise Service Bus concept to link its applications.

In Fig. 8.19, we see in more detail how the Policy information service from the Home & Away Policy administration is used by the department's Financial application, through an interface in which the message queuing service from the lower-level infrastructure is used (see also Fig. 8.24).

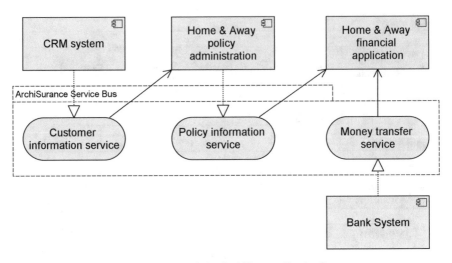

Fig. 8.18 Applications connected through the ArchiSurance Service Bus

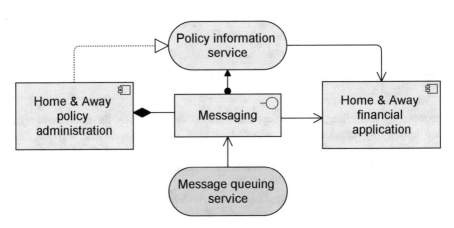

Fig. 8.19 Details of the connection between the Home & Away Policy administration and Financial application

8.5.11   Application Usage Viewpoint

The Application Usage viewpoint describes how applications are used to support one or more business processes, and how they are used by other applications. It can be used in designing an application by identifying the services needed by business processes and other applications, or in designing business processes by describing the services that are available. Furthermore, since it identifies the dependencies of business processes upon applications, it may be useful to operational managers responsible for these processes.

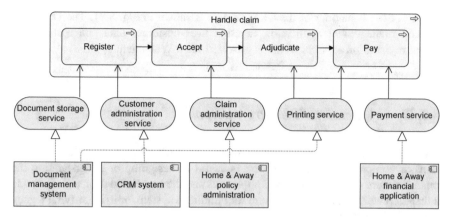

Fig. 8.20 Application usage by the Handle Claim business process

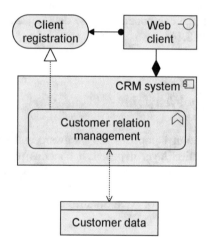

Fig. 8.21 Behaviour of the CRM system

Figure 8.20 shows how the Handle Claim business process uses the application services offered by several applications. Each of these services is realised by the behaviour of an application, an example of which is given in Fig. 8.21.

8.5.12 Application Behaviour Viewpoint

The Application Behaviour viewpoint describes the internal behaviour of an application or component, for example, as it realises one or more application services. This viewpoint is useful in designing the main behaviour of applications or components, or in identifying functional overlap between different applications.

Part of the behaviour of the CRM system is shown in Fig. 8.21. The Customer relation management application function uses customer data and realises the Client registration service, which is provided via a Web client.

8.5.13   Application Structure Viewpoint

The Application Structure viewpoint shows the structure of one or more applications or components. This viewpoint is useful in designing or understanding the main structure of applications or components and the associated data, e.g., to create a first-step work breakdown structure for building a system, or in identifying legacy parts suitable for migration.

Figure 8.22 shows the main components that constitute the policy administration of ArchiSurance's Home & Away department. It also depicts some of the important data objects used by these components. These data objects are realisations of the business objects of Fig. 8.16.

8.5.14   Technology Viewpoint

The Technology viewpoint comprises the hardware and software infrastructure upon which the application layer depends. It contains physical devices and networks, and supporting system software such as operating systems, databases, and middleware.

Part of the IT infrastructure of ArchiSurance and its intermediaries is shown in Fig. 8.23.

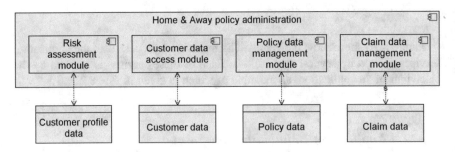

Fig. 8.22 Main structure of the Home & Away Policy administration

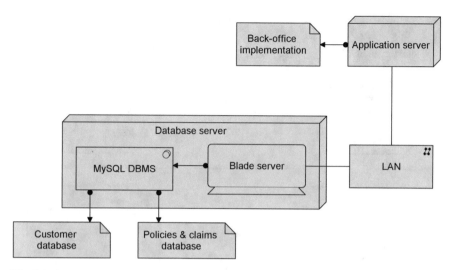

Fig. 8.23 Infrastructure of ArchiSurance

8.5.15   Technology Usage Viewpoint

The Technology Usage viewpoint shows how applications are supported by the software and hardware infrastructure: technology services delivered by the devices, system software and networks are provided to the applications. An example of this viewpoint is given in Fig. 8.24, which shows the use, by a number of back-office applications, of the messaging and data access services offered by ArchiSurance's technical infrastructure.

This viewpoint plays an important role in the analysis of performance and scalability, since it relates the technical infrastructure to the world of applications. It is very useful in determining the performance and quality requirements of the infrastructure based on the demands of the various applications that use it. In Chap. 9, we will describe a quantitative analysis technique that can be used to determine, for example, the load on the infrastructure, based on its use by applications (and their use by business processes).

8.5.16   Implementation & Deployment Viewpoint

The Implementation & Deployment viewpoint shows how one or more applications are deployed on the technical infrastructure. This comprises the mapping of (logical) applications and components onto (physical) artefacts, for instance, Enterprise Java Beans, and the mapping of the information used by these applications and components onto the underlying storage infrastructure, e.g. database tables or other

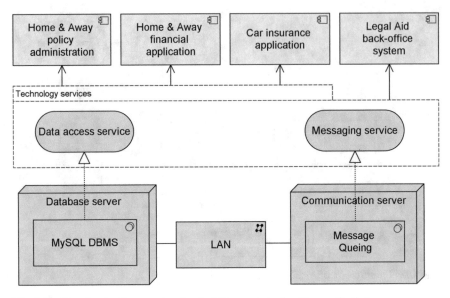

Fig. 8.24 Use of technology services by ArchiSurance's back-office applications

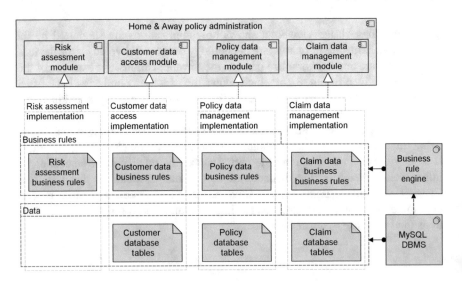

Fig. 8.25 Implementation of the Home & Away Policy administration

files. In security and risk analysis, Deployment views are used to identify critical dependencies and risks.

Figure 8.25 shows the mapping of logical application components of the Home & Away Policy administration (see Fig. 8.22) used in several of the other examples onto physical artefacts such as database tables. This figure also shows that the artefacts are part of multiple groupings and that a grouping as a whole is related to

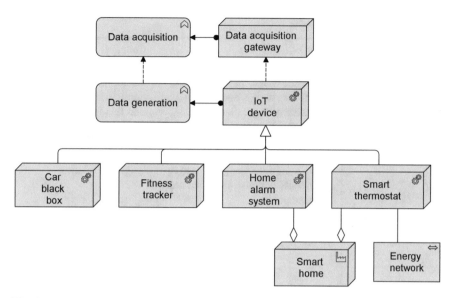

Fig. 8.26 Physical devices used by ArchiSurance to acquire data

the system software on which it is deployed. This saves you from having to draw all the individual relations with the elements in a group.

8.5.17 Physical Viewpoint

The Physical viewpoint contains equipment such as physical machines, tools or instruments that can create, use, store, move or transform materials and shows how this equipment is connected via the distribution network, on which facilities it is deployed and what other active elements are assigned to the equipment (Fig. 8.26).

8.6 Motivation Viewpoints

For the Motivation concepts, we have also defined a number of example viewpoints. Table 8.6 summarises these viewpoints.

8.7 Strategy Viewpoints

The next table summarises the viewpoints for the Strategy concepts (Table 8.7).

Table 8.6 Motivation viewpoints

Viewpoint	Description	Concepts and relations
Stakeholder viewpoint	Allows the analyst to model the stakeholders, internal or external drivers for change, and the assessments of these drivers	Stakeholder, Driver, Assessment, Goal, Association relation, Aggregation relation
Goal realisation viewpoint	Allows the designer to model the refinement of high-level goals into more concrete goals, and the refinement of concrete goals into requirements or constraints that realise these goals	Goal, Requirement, Constraint, Principle, Realisation relation, Aggregation relation
Goal contribution viewpoint	Allows a designer or analyst to model the influence relationships between goals and requirements	Goal, Requirement, Constraint, Principle, Realisation relation, Aggregation relation, Influence relation
Principles viewpoint	Allows the analyst or designer to model the principles that are relevant to the design problem at hand, including the goals that motivate those principles.	Goal, Principle, Realisation relation, Aggregation relation, Influence relation
Requirements realisation viewpoint	Allows the designer to model the realisation of requirements by core elements.	Goal, Requirement, Constraint, all Core elements, Realisation relation, Aggregation relation
Motivation viewpoint	Allows the designer or analyst to model the motivation aspect, without focusing on certain elements within this aspect	All Motivation elements and relations

8.7.1 Capability Map Viewpoint

One often used strategy viewpoint that we want to highlight explicitly is the capability map. This is a map of the enterprise that visualises its capabilities in some state, for example, current capabilities and their current maturity level, or required capabilities in a future state. Each key capability can be made more specific by showing its sub-capabilities.

From a top-down perspective, capabilities are derived from the strategic direction of the organisation. From a bottom-up perspective, resources (e.g. people, information, technology and other assets) can be linked to the capabilities they support, providing a link between these and the strategic direction of the enterprise.

Table 8.7 Strategy viewpoints

Viewpoint	Description	Concepts and relations
Strategy viewpoint	A high-level, strategic overview of the strategies (courses of action) of the enterprise, the capabilities and resources supporting those and the envisaged outcomes	Course of action, Capability, Resource, Outcome
Capability Map viewpoint	A structured overview of the capabilities of the enterprise. A capability map typically shows two or three levels of capabilities across the entire enterprise	Capability, Resource, Outcome
Resource Map viewpoint	A structured overview of the resources of the enterprise, how these support its capabilities and how they are realised by projects and programs	Capability, Resource, Work package
Outcome Realisation viewpoint	Is used to show how the highest-level, business-oriented results are produced by the capabilities and underlying core elements	Capability, Resource, Outcome, Value, Meaning, Core element

This way, capabilities can be used as a starting point for the definition of asset portfolios.

As an example, a typical capability map is shown in Fig. 8.27.

Because the capabilities of an enterprise are relatively stable and easily recognisable by its stakeholders, capability maps are very useful as a canvas onto which other information can be projected. You can create various kinds of heat maps and colour maps that all exhibit the same familiar structure. For example, you might show benchmark data on the efficiency of capability implementations, highlighting those capabilities that need to be improved. Or you can display the organisation's departments involved in capabilities using different colours or plot the applications supporting capabilities on such a map.

8.8 Implementation and Migration Viewpoints

Table 8.8 summarises the viewpoints for the Implementation and Migration concepts.

For more details on all of these viewpoints, please consult the ArchiMate standard (The Open Group 2016a).

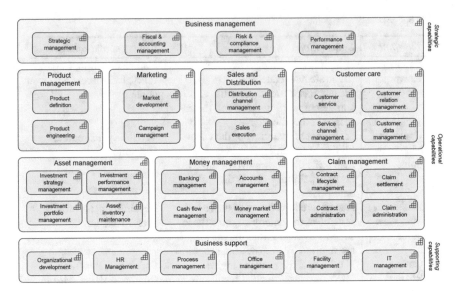

Fig. 8.27 Example of a capability map

Table 8.8 Implementation and Migration viewpoints

Viewpoint	Description	Concepts and relations
Project viewpoint	Is used to model the management of architecture change.	Work package Deliverable, Goal, Business Role, Business Actor, Realisation relation, Aggregation relation, Triggering relation, Flow relation, Assignment relation
Migration viewpoint	Entails models and concepts that can be used for specifying the transition from an existing architecture to a desired architecture.	Plateau, Gap, Association relation, Aggregation relation, Triggering relation
Implementation and Migration viewpoint	Is used to relate programs and projects to the parts of the architecture that they implement.	All Implementation and Migration concepts, all Core concepts, Requirement, Constraint, Goal, all relations

8.9   Combined Viewpoints

Next to the viewpoints for specific parts of the ArchiMate language, we can of course also combine elements from different parts of the language to create composite viewpoints. Moreover, we need not stick to the standard ArchiMate notation described in Chap. 5, but we can use other symbols if that is a better fit with the intended audience. This is also particularly useful if we want to use ArchiMate in combination with other techniques, such as those described in Chap. 6. Creating cross-cutting views that combine information from different but related models may create new insights that cannot be had from viewing these models in isolation.

8.10   ArchiMate and TOGAF Viewpoints

TOGAF (The Open Group 2011) identifies a large number of viewpoints as part of its content meta-model, subdivided in three main types of architectural artefact: matrices, catalogues and diagrams. As we have seen in Sect. 6.13, ArchiMate and TOGAF exhibit a very similar layered structure. This correspondence suggests a fairly easy mapping between TOGAF's views and the ArchiMate viewpoints. Although corresponding viewpoints from ArchiMate and TOGAF do not necessarily have identical coverage, we can see that many viewpoints from both methods address approximately the same issues.

Moreover, ArchiMate is not limited to a specific set of viewpoints and allows the definition of new viewpoints via the viewpoint mechanism described in the standard (The Open Group 2016a, Chap. 14). Most TOGAF views can easily be expressed in ArchiMate concepts.

The most important disparity we observe between TOGAF and ArchiMate is that the ArchiMate viewpoints that deal with the relationships between architectural layers, such as the product and application usage viewpoints, are difficult to map onto TOGAF's diagrams, which are largely confined to a single architectural layer. Although TOGAF does support several matrices that provide such a correspondence between layers, such as the 'Application/Organization Matrix' or the 'Data Entity/Business Function Matrix' it does not provide graphical representations of these.

The ArchiMate language and its analysis techniques support pretty much all of TOGAF's diagrammatic views. Using ArchiMate as a description language together with TOGAF as a method for developing architectures provides the architect with two nicely complementary, open and vendor-independent methods. Since both are administered by The Open Group, further integration of TOGAF and ArchiMate can be expected.

8.11 Summary

In the previous sections, we have advocated a viewpoint-oriented approach to enterprise architecture modelling, in which architects and other stakeholders can define their own views of the architecture. In this approach views are specified by viewpoints, which define abstractions on the set of models representing the enterprise architecture, each aimed at a particular type of stakeholder and addressing a particular set of concerns.

We have described the use of viewpoints in communication, and the distinction between an architecture model, a view of that model, and its visualisation and manipulation. We have presented guidelines for the selection and use of viewpoints, and outlined a number of viewpoints in the ArchiMate language that can be used by architects involved in the creation or change of enterprise architecture models. Finally, we have shown how TOGAF's views and ArchiMate's viewpoints match.

Chapter 9
Architecture Analysis

Maria-Eugenia Iacob, Henk Jonkers, Leon van der Torre, Frank S. de Boer,
Marcello Bonsangue, Andries W. Stam, Marc M. Lankhorst,
Dick A.C. Quartel, and Adina Aldea

As we have argued in previous chapters, organisational effectiveness cannot be achieved through local optimisations, but is realised by well-orchestrated interaction of organisational components (Nadler et al. 1992). To create such an integrated perspective of enterprise architecture, we need both a description technique for architectural models and model-based analysis techniques to realise this global optimisation in practice.

In Chap. 5, we have presented a description language that not only captures the complexity of architectural domains and their relations, but also enables the integration at the appropriate level of abstraction of already existing partial architecture models. However, the value of architecture models increases significantly if they can also be used to support the decision-making process. In this chapter we argue that whenever a change in the enterprise architecture is needed, model-based analysis plays a central role. Therefore, we present a number of techniques that help architects and stakeholders to compare alternative designs and, hence, take well-informed

---

M.-E. Iacob
University of Twente, Enschede, The Netherlands

H. Jonkers • D.A.C. Quartel • A. Aldea
BiZZdesign, Enschede, The Netherlands

L. van der Torre
University of Luxembourg, Luxembourg, Luxembourg

F.S. de Boer • M. Bonsangue
University of Leiden, Leiden, The Netherlands

A.W. Stam
Almende, Rotterdam, The Netherlands

M.M. Lankhorst (✉)
BiZZdesign, Capitool 15, 7521 PL Rotterdam, The Netherlands
e-mail: m.lankhorst@bizzdesign.com

© Springer-Verlag Berlin Heidelberg 2017
M. Lankhorst et al., *Enterprise Architecture at Work*, The Enterprise Engineering
Series, DOI 10.1007/978-3-662-53933-0_9

design decisions when making trade-offs between aspects like cost, quality, and performance and to be able to study the impact of a change to the design.

9.1 Analysis Techniques

One of the central motivations for enterprise architecture in general is getting to grips with *change*. Architects and stakeholders want to take well-informed design decisions. To that end, they need to compare alternative designs, make trade-offs between aspects like cost, quality, and performance, and know the impact of a change across all aspects of an architecture. Given the size and complexity of enterprise architectures, this is something that can no longer be done by hand and requires sophisticated analysis techniques. These analysis techniques do more than simply 'walk through a picture', but require well-defined semantic underpinnings and advanced analysis algorithms.

We can classify architecture analysis techniques according to different aspects (Fig. 9.1). First, we make a distinction based on the types of analysis inputs and results: functional (e.g., structural and dynamic properties) and quantitative (e.g., performance and costs).

Functional analysis is performed to gain insight into the functional aspects of an architecture. Among others, it is used to understand how a system that conforms to an architecture works, to find the impact of a change on an architecture, or to validate the correctness of an architecture.

Functional analysis techniques do not answer quantitative questions, like 'how quick' or 'how cheap'. These are typically questions addressed by the *quantitative* analysis techniques. Usually, architectural models do not provide sufficient information to perform detailed quantitative studies. In our view, an approach for quantitative analysis of enterprise architectures should make it possible to structure and relate quantitative results obtained with existing detailed analysis methods (e.g., queuing analysis or simulation).

Second, for both functional and quantitative analysis, we distinguish two main types of techniques: analytical techniques and simulation.

Basically, *simulation* can be seen as the 'execution' of a model. *Functional simulation* and *animation* are useful to illustrate the dynamic behaviour of a system. The aim of functional simulation is to *gain insight* into the properties and behaviour of an architecture. Architects can 'play' with the architecture and see how it works,

Fig. 9.1 Analysis dimensions

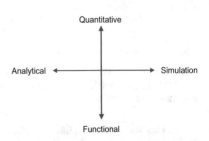

feels, looks, can be adapted to certain changes, etc. Moreover, functional simulation can also play an important role in the communication between stakeholders, by giving them a better common understanding of the architecture. Interpretation problems, often stemming from the high level of abstraction of architectures, may come to light when using functional simulation. *Quantitative simulation* is used to make statistical statements about the quantitative measures of a system based on multiple simulation runs. It can be seen as performing 'measurements' in a model. Thus, quantitative simulation allows for a thorough examination of the performance measures in a specific situation.

In this chapter, we mainly consider *formal* and *analytical* analysis techniques. In contrast to simulation, these are not of a statistical nature, but provide a unique, reproducible result. Analytical techniques for quantitative analysis are typically more efficient than quantitative simulation, and therefore more suitable for providing the architect with a first indication of performance measures and bottlenecks in an architecture model. They are also useful when a comparison of a (large) number of alternatives is needed in so-called 'what if' analysis.

Another issue to be addressed when using analysis techniques for enterprise architectures is whether to apply existing techniques, or to develop new ones. Buy or build? In the first case, two other questions are to be answered: which technique to choose from the available ones, and how to apply it? In the second case, the questions are for what problem a technique is developed, and how the development itself can be carried out.

This chapter illustrates both of the above-mentioned options. For quantitative analysis, described in Sect. 9.2, we have chosen to propose a new top-down bottom-up approach. Nevertheless, this approach also facilitates the integration with existent, domain-specific analysis techniques. For functional analysis, explained in Sect. 9.3, we have chosen the first approach, i.e., we show how existing techniques from formal methods can be used in analysing the functional properties of architectures.

9.2 Quantitative Analysis

As noted earlier, enterprise architecture is concerned with a description of how all the relevant elements that make up an enterprise interrelate. It covers aspects ranging from business processes and products, through software applications, to the technical infrastructure. The relations between these 'layers' play a central role. Also, from a quantitative perspective, these aspects are interrelated in several ways. For example, the business processes impose a workload on the software applications and infrastructure, while the performance characteristics of the lower layers directly influence the performance of the higher layers.

There is a common misconception that quantitative analysis is 'too detailed' to be performed at the architecture level. However, performance engineering practitioners argue that next to functional aspects, non-functional (quantitative) aspects of systems should also be taken into account at all stages of the design of a system, and not just as an afterthought (Smith 1990). This implies that these aspects are also relevant for enterprise architectures. In this case, however—as for enterprise architecture modelling—the quantitative aspects are considered at a relatively global level. Also, the emphasis is on *structure*: enterprise architectures can provide a useful instrument to structure quantitative properties of organisations and systems.

Quantitative analysis can serve several purposes. In the first place it is often used for the *optimisation* of, for example, processes or systems, by quantifying the effect of alternative design choices. Similarly, it can be used to obtain measures to support impact-of-change analysis: what is the quantitative effect of changes in a design? This shows that the distinction between functional and quantitative analysis is not always sharp. A third application of quantitative analysis is *capacity planning*, e.g., how many people should fulfil a certain role to finish the processes on time, or how should the infrastructure be dimensioned (processing, storage, and network capacity) given an expected workload?

Models of organisations and systems can be quantified in several ways. Measures of interest may include:

– *Performance* measures, i.e., time-related measures such as completion and response times, throughputs, resource utilisations.
– *Reliability* measures such as availability and dependability.
– *Cost* measures.

The techniques and examples presented in this section focus on performance measures.

9.2.1   Performance Views

As explained earlier, the different ways to structure an enterprise architecture model provide different *views* of the same model. These views are aimed at different stakeholders and their concerns. Also in the context of the performance of a system, a number of views can be discerned, each having their own performance measures, explained below:

– **User/customer view** (stakeholders: customer; user of an application or system): The *response time* is the time between issuing a request and receiving the result, e.g., the time between the moment that a customer arrives at a counter and the moment of completion of the service, or the time between sending a letter and receiving an answer. Also in the supporting IT applications the response time plays an important role; a well-known example is the (mean) time between a database query and the presentation of its results. Examples of ArchiMate concepts for which the calculation of the response time is suited are actors, roles, and services.
– **Process view** (stakeholders: process owner; operational manager): *Completion time* is the time required to complete one instance of a process (possibly involving multiple customers, orders, products, etc., as opposed to the response

time, which is defined as the time to complete *one* request). In batch processing by means of an information system the completion time can be defined as the time required to finish a batch.

– **Product view** (stakeholders: product manager; operational manager): *Processing time* is the amount of time that actual work is performed on the realisation of a certain product or result, i.e., the response time without waiting times. The processing time can be orders of magnitude lower than the response time. In a computer system, an example of the processing time is the actual time that the CPU is busy.

– **System view** (stakeholders: system owner/manager): *Throughput* is the number of transactions or requests that a system completes per time unit (e.g., the average number of customers served per hour). Related to this is the maximum attainable throughput (also called the *processing capacity*, or in a more technically oriented context such as communication networks, the *bandwidth*), which depends on the number of available resources and their capacity.

– **Resource view** (stakeholders: resource manager; capacity planner): *Utilisation* is the percentage of the operational time that a resource is busy. On the one hand, the utilisation is a measure of the effectiveness with which a resource is used. On the other hand, a high utilisation can be an indication of the fact that the resource is a potential *bottleneck*, and that increasing that resource's capacity (or adding an extra resource) can lead to a relatively high performance improvement. In the case of humans, the utilisation can be used as a more or less objective measure for work stress. In information systems architectures, a typical example of the utilisation is the network load. Examples of ArchiMate concepts for which the calculation of the utilisation is suited are the infrastructure concepts and the actor.

The different performance views are summarised in Fig. 9.2. Performance measures belonging to the different views are interrelated, and may be in

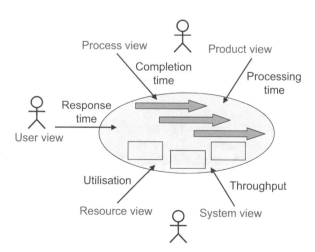

Fig. 9.2 Performance views

conflict when trying to optimise the performance of a system. For example, a higher throughput leads to a higher resource utilisation, which may be favourable from a resource manager's point of view; however, this generally leads to an increase in the response times, which is unfavourable from a user's point of view. Therefore, when aiming to optimise the performance of a system, it is important to have a clear picture of which performance measures should be optimised.

9.2.2 Performance Analysis Techniques for Architectures

Although several software tools exist to model enterprise architectures, hardly any attention has been paid to the analysis of their quantitative aspects. For detailed design models of (distributed) systems, such as computing and telecommunication systems, and manufacturing systems, a broad range of performance analysis techniques have been proposed. There are very efficient static techniques that offer relatively inaccurate first estimates or bounds for the performance. Analytical solutions of queuing models are more accurate but also more computation intensive, while they still impose certain restrictions on the models. With detailed quantitative simulations, any model can be analysed with arbitrary accuracy, although this presumes that accurate input parameters are available.

As mentioned above, enterprise architecture covers a broad range of aspects, from the technology layer (e.g. computer hardware and networks), through software applications running on top of the infrastructure, to business processes supported by these applications. Within each of these layers, quantitative analysis techniques can be applied, which often require detailed models as input. In this subsection, we will only be able to give a global impression of analysis approaches for each of these layers.

We also noted earlier that enterprise architecture is specifically concerned with the *relations* between the layers. Also from a quantitative perspective the layers are interrelated: higher layers impose a workload on lower layers, while the performance characteristics of the lower layers directly influence the performance of the higher layers. The service concept that is central to the ArchiMate language plays an important role in connecting these layers, also in a quantitative sense (Jonkers and Iacob 2009).

Technology Layer
Traditionally, approaches to performance evaluation of computer systems and communication systems (see Harrison and Patel 1992) have a strong focus on the technical infrastructure domain. Queuing models, for example, describe the characteristics of the (hardware) resources in a system, while an abstract stochastic arrival process captures the workload imposed by the applications. Also, a lot of literature exists on performance studies of specific hardware configurations, sometimes extended to the system software and middleware levels. Most of these approaches commonly are based on detailed models and require detailed input data.

Application Layer

Performance engineering of software applications (see Smith 1990) is a much newer discipline compared to the traditional techniques described above. A number of papers consider the performance of software architectures at a global level. Bosch and Grahn (1998) present some first observations about the performance characteristics of a number of often occurring architectural styles. Performance issues in the context of the SAAM method (see Kazman et al. 1994) for scenario-based analysis are considered in Lung et al. (1998).

Another direction of research addresses the approaches that have been proposed to derive queuing models from a software architecture described in an architecture description language (ADL). The method described by Spitznagel and Garlan (1998) is restricted to a number of popular architectural styles (e.g., the distributed message passing style but not the pipe and filter style). Other similar approaches are described in Aquilani et al. (2001) and Williams and Smith (1998). In Di Marco and Inverardi (2004) queuing models are derived from UML 2 specifications, which in most cases, however, do not have an analytical solution.

As we noted in Sect. 3.1.1, *compositionality* is an important issue in architecture. In the context of performance analysis, compositionality of analysis results may also be a useful property. This means that the performance of a system as a whole can be expressed in terms of the performance of its components. Stochastic extensions of process algebras (see Hermanns et al. 2002) are often advocated as a tool for compositional performance analysis. However, process-algebra-based approaches to performance analysis are still fairly computation intensive, because they still suffer from a state space explosion. Moreover, while they allow for a compositional *specification* of performance models, this does not necessarily mean that the *analysis results* are also compositional.

Business Layer

Several business process modelling tools provide some support for quantitative analysis through discrete-event simulation. Also, general-purpose simulation tool such as Arena[1] or ExSpect[2] (based on high-level Petri nets) are often used for this purpose. A drawback of simulation is that it requires detailed input data, and for inexperienced users it may be difficult to use and to interpret the results correctly. BiZZdesign Enterprise Studio[3] offers, in addition to simulation, a number of analytical methods. They include completion time and critical path analysis of business processes (see Jonkers et al. 1999) and queuing model analysis (see Jonkers and Swelm 1999). Petri nets (and several of its variations) are fairly popular in business process modelling, either to model processes directly or as an underlying formalism for other languages (e.g., see Schomig and Rau 1995). They offer possibilities for

---

[1]http://www.arenasimulation.com

[2]http://www.exspect.com

[3]http://www.bizzdesign.com

performance analysis based on simulation, as described above, but they also allow for analytical solutions (which are, however, fairly computation intensive).

9.2.3   Quantitative Modelling

In this section we present our approach for the quantitative modelling of service-oriented enterprise architectures expressed in the ArchiMate language. First we show that ArchiMate models follow a certain structure that is explained by means of an 'analysis meta-model'. Our technique focuses on a subset of the ArchiMate language, namely the modelling constructs encompassed by this simple meta-model. Then we clarify what the necessary quantitative input is for our analysis technique. We also introduce an example that shows how quantitative information can be attached to model elements and their relations and that will later also illustrate the application of the algorithms.

Model Structure

As shown in Sect. 5.2, many architecture models can be viewed as a hierarchy of layers. We use this layered view for performance analysis as well, because it makes the explanation of our approach easier. Furthermore, layering will help the modeller to formulate and describe clearly the problem being analysed.

For each meta-model layer, we can distinguish one or more model layers of two types: service layers and realisation layers. A service layer exposes functionality that can 'serve' the next higher layer, while a realisation layer model shows how the consecutive service layer is 'realised'. The number of these layers is not fixed, but a natural layering of an ArchiMate model will contain the succession of layers depicted in Fig. 9.4.

Looking at the horizontal structure of the meta-model, we can see that realisation layers typically contain three types of elements. They might model some pieces of internal behaviour (expressed as processes or functions). Further, each behaviour element can access one or more objects, and it is assigned to exactly one resource (e.g. actors, devices, application components, etc.).

Thus, we can summarise our findings in terms of the 'analysis meta-model' depicted in Fig. 9.3, where

- 'Object' can be a business object, a data object or an artefact.
- 'Resource' can be a business role, a business actor, an application component, a system software component, a node or a device.
- 'Internal behaviour' can be a business process, a business function, an application function or a technology function.
- 'Service' can be a business service, an application service or a technology service.

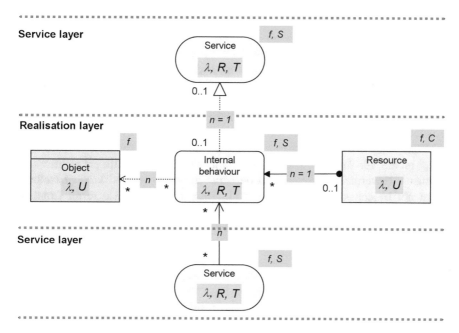

Fig. 9.3 Structural properties of ArchiMate models

Approach

Before we can analyse an ArchiMate model, we have to define clearly the quantities that can be assigned to the different ArchiMate concepts and relations. In Sect. 9.2.1 we have identified the relevant performance measures, independent of any modelling language. However, we have to make these measures specific for ArchiMate models. One may notice that not all the ArchiMate language elements are included in the model structure given in Fig. 9.3. Indeed, we consider some of them irrelevant for the current approach (e.g., the meaning concept, the aggregation and association relations, etc.) and, therefore, they will be ignored.

Iacob and Jonkers (2005) explore possible ways in which the concepts and relations that have been defined in the ArchiMate language can be quantified. An important observation made is that the richest ArchiMate relations in terms of quantification prospects are the 'triggering', 'access', 'realisation' and 'serving' relations. This is a good indication that any quantitative analysis method that might be used in the context of ArchiMate (sub)models must focus on this type of relation. The fact that 'triggering' relations are easily quantifiable does not come as a surprise. In fact, triggering relations are essential in revealing the behaviour of dynamic systems. Thus, we can draw the conclusion that any quantitative method that works for (business) process-oriented modelling formalisms can be applied (possibly after slight adaptations) as well for ArchiMate models. However, these types of methods have certain limitations from the ArchiMate point of view for at least two reasons. First, such methods are usually applied locally to partial architectural models that expose a mapping between a piece of behaviour and some resources (see Jonkers and Swelm 1999). Second, because only two types of elements, namely behaviour elements (e.g., processes, events, etc.), and resources (e.g., actors, devices, etc.) are concerned, such methods do not traverse all the architecture domains. They typically work within at most two layers of the architecture model (e.g. the application and the technology layer or within the business layer). We will refer to such analysis methods as being *horizontal methods*. We believe that apart from the classical horizontal methods we must expose *vertical methods* that work across multiple domains. We anticipate that such methods must focus on the 'serving' and 'realisation' relations bridging the different architectural domains. Nevertheless, the distinction between horizontal and vertical methods must not be considered restrictive at all, since (as it will also result from the example we are giving) the two types of methods can be combined, such that the output (i.e., calculated *performance measures*) of one type of method will provide the *input quantities* for another 'follow-up' analysis method.

Analysis across an architecture model is possible through the propagation of quantities through layers. A natural option for this is to consider workload measures (e.g., arrival frequencies) that are imposed as a 'demand' on the model elements by the users (located in the higher layers, e.g., customers). These quantities propagate towards the lower layers, eventually being translated in demands on each model element. Once workloads have been determined, we look at the effort these workloads require from the resources (modelled by structural elements) and from the behaviour elements (modelled by services, processes, and functions). This effort can be expressed in terms of performance measures (e.g., utilisations for resources, response and processing times for behaviour elements) and/or costs; it starts in the technical infrastructure and propagates back to the higher layers. In summary, our approach consists of the following two phases (see Fig. 9.4): a top-down calculation of the workloads imposed by the users; this provides input for a bottom-up calculation of performance measures.

Fig. 9.4 Layers of ArchiMate models

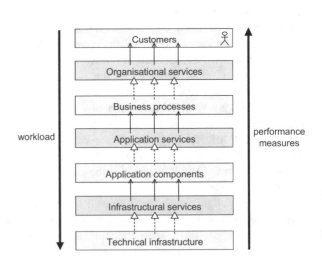

Quantitative Input Data

One of the most difficult tasks related to quantitative analysis is to obtain reliable input data. There are several possible sources for this data. For existing systems or organisations, measurement can be one of the most reliable methods, although it is not easy to do this in a correct way: among others, it should be clearly defined what exactly is to be measured, the number of measurements must be sufficient, and the measurements must be taken under various circumstances that can occur in practice.

In case the system or organisation is still to be developed, measurement is no option. Possible alternatives are then the use of documentation of components to be used, or to use estimates (e.g., based on comparable architectures). However, one should keep in mind that it is often very difficult to interpret correctly the available numerical data, and to evaluate the reliability of the available data.

We assume that the following quantitative input is provided for analysis (see Fig. 9.3):

- For any 'serving' and 'access' relation e, a weight n_e, representing the average number of uses and accesses
- For any behaviour element a, a service time S_a, representing the time spent internally for the realisation of a service (excluding the time spent waiting for supporting services). We assume that a service inherits the service time value of the element realising it.
- For any resource r, a capacity C_r.
- For any node a, an arrival frequency f_a. Typically, arrival frequencies are specified in the top layer of a model, although we do allow for the specification of arrival frequencies for any node in the model.

These quantitative attributes are attached to the corresponding model elements using the 'profile' mechanism described in Sect. 5.14.1.

Example

To show the practical use of this analysis technique, we illustrate our approach with the following simple example.

Suppose we want to analyse an insurance company that uses a document management system for the storage and retrieval of damage reports. We assume that the document management system is a centralised system, used by multiple offices throughout the country, which means that it is quite heavily used. A model of this system is depicted in Fig. 9.5. This model covers the whole stack from business processes and actors, through applications, to the technical infrastructure.

There are three applications offering services that are used directly by the business actors. The Administrator can search in the metadata database, resulting in short descriptions of the reports that meet the query and view reports that are returned by a search. The report scanning application is used to scan, digitise, and store damage reports (in PDF format). In addition to the two applications that are used directly by the end user, there are two supporting application components: a database access component, providing access to the metadata database, and a

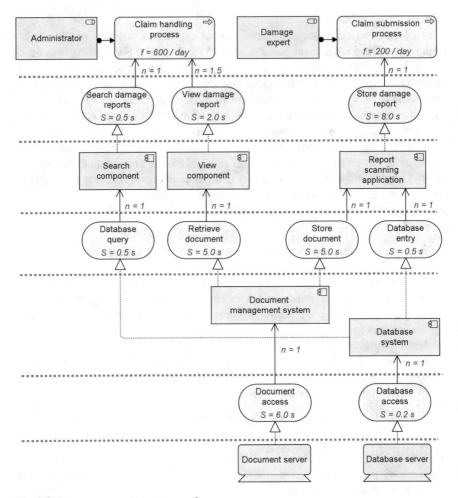

Fig. 9.5 Document management example

document management component, providing access to the document base. Finally, the model shows the physical devices of which the database access and document management components make use. They use file access services provided by these devices.

In the model we also specify the input quantities for the analysis. On the 'serving' relations, we specify workload values, in terms of the average number of uses n of the corresponding service by the layer above. For the business processes, an arrival frequency f is specified. In this example we assume that all resources have the default capacity 1. Finally, for service elements we may specify a service time S.

9.2.4 Quantitative Analysis Technique

The goal of our approach is to determine the following performance measures (see Fig. 9.3):

- the workload (arrival rate) λ_a for each node a (note that, provided that no resources are overloaded, the throughput for each node is equal to its arrival rate);
- the processing time T_a and the response time R_a, for each behaviour element or service;
- the utilisation U_r, for each resource r.

To derive the above-mentioned performance measures, given the input values, we proceed in three steps:

1. We will first 'normalise' any input model, using model transformations, in order to generate a model that is compliant with the structure presented in Fig. 9.3.
2. Top-down calculation of workloads (arrival rates) λ.
3. Bottom-up computation of performance measures T, U, and R.

Step 1: Model Normalisation
Typical ArchiMate models often do not fully conform to the ArchiMate meta-model. This is due to the fact that during the modelling process, abstraction rules are used to create simplified views of the architecture. These abstractions have, however, a formal basis in an operator that has been derived for the composition of relations. The derivation of this operator has been described in great detail in Buuren et al. (2004). It allows, for instance, the composition of a *realisation* relation with any consecutive *serving* relation, resulting in a new *serving* relation that short-circuits, in this case, a service.

Therefore, the first step in our approach addresses a model transformation procedure, which will derive from any input model a 'normalised' one, i.e. a model, which is fully compliant with the structure described in Fig. 9.3. Since some of the concepts and relations are not relevant for our approach, the normalisation procedure starts by eliminating them from the original model. The resulting model will then be subjected to a series of model transformations. One example of such a transformation rule is given in Fig. 9.6. The set of all possible transformation rules is finite, which makes the development of a normalisation algorithm based on these rules rather straightforward.

The application (if needed), following such an algorithm, of the proper rule for each edge in the input model will eventually lead to a normalised model.

Figure 9.7 shows the normalised version of the example model given in Fig. 9.5. The input parameters for the workload on the 'serving' relations are the same as in the original model. The service times are now transferred also to the inserted internal behaviour elements.

However, since model normalisation is not the primary focus of this approach we will not provide a formal description of the normalisation algorithm, although such an algorithm was implemented in the quantitative analysis prototype described in Sect. 11.5.

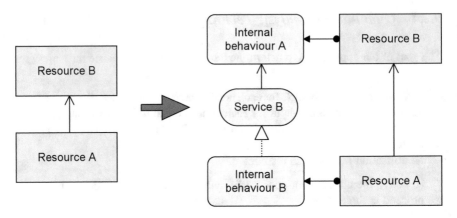

Fig. 9.6 Example of a normalisation step

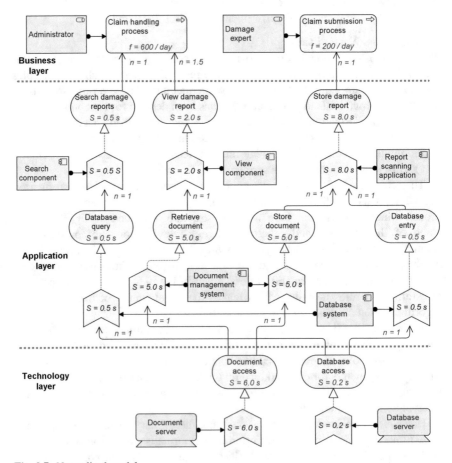

Fig. 9.7 Normalised model

Table 9.1 Workloads and performance results

Resource (r)	Service (s)	λ_s (s^{-1})	$T_s(s)$	$R_s(s)$	U_r
Doc. srv.	Doc. acc.	0.0382	6.0	7.8	0.229
DB srv.	Data acc.	0.0278	0.2	0.2	0.006
Doc.mgt.sys.	Retr. doc.	0.0313	12.8	25.0	0.488
Doc.mgt.sys.	Store doc.	0.0069	12.8	25.0	0.488
DB sys.	DB query	0.0278	0.7	0.7	0.019
DB sys.	DB entry	0.0069	0.7	0.7	0.019
Search comp.	Search rep.	0.0278	1.2	1.2	0.025
View comp.	View rep.	0.0313	27.0	174.0	0.843
Rep. scanning	Store rep.	0.0069	33.7	44.0	0.234

Step 2: Top-Down Workload Calculation

Given a normalised model, we can now calculate the workload (i.e., arrival rate) for any node a. The following recursive expression applies:

$$\lambda_a = f_a + \sum_{i=1}^{d_a^+} n_{a,k_i} \lambda_{k_i},$$

where d_a^+ denotes the out-degree of node a and k_i is a child node of a. In other words, the arrival rate for a node is determined by adding the requests from higher layers to the local arrival frequency f_a.

The results of this step in the 'document management system' example are given in Table 9.1, which shows the workload for the services s in the model, in terms of the arrival rates λ_s. The arrival rates depend on the frequencies of the customer input requests and the cardinalities n of the 'serving' relations. The table also shows the scaled arrival rates expressed in arrivals/second (assuming that systems are operational 8 h/day).

Step 3: Bottom-Up Performance Calculation

Once the workloads imposed on the various model components are calculated, we can proceed with the last analysis phase, the bottom-up calculation of the aforementioned set of performance measures. The approach we take is somewhat similar to the top-down one. In this step we focus on the bottom-up propagation of values corresponding to different time-related performance measures. The actual calculation can be done using the following recursive expressions:

– The utilisation of any resource r is

$$U_r = \frac{\sum_{i=1}^{d_r} \lambda_{k_i} T_{k_i}}{C_r},$$

where d_r is the number of internal behaviour elements k_i to which the resource is assigned.

- The processing time and response time of any service a coincide with the processing time and response time of the internal behaviour element realising it, i.e., $T_a = T_k$ and $R_a = R_k$, where (k, a) is the only realisation relation having a as end point.
- The processing time and response time of any internal behaviour element a can be computed using the following recursive equations:

$$T_a = S_a + \sum_{i=1}^{d_a^-} n_{k_i,a} R_{k_i} \quad \text{and} \quad R_a = F(a, r_a),$$

where d_a^- denotes the in-degree of node a, k_i is a parent of a, r_a is the resource assigned to a, and F is the response time expressed as a function of attributes of a and r_a.

For example, if we assume that the node can be modelled as an M/M/1 queue (Harrison and Patel 1992), this function is

$$F(a, r_a) = \frac{T_a}{1 - U_{r_a}} \tag{9.1}$$

We can replace this by another equation in case other assumptions apply, e.g., the Pollaczek–Khinchine formula for an M/G/1 if T_a has a non-exponential distribution, or the solution for an M/M/n queue based on the Erlang C formula for a structural element with a capacity greater than 1 (Iacob and Jonkers 2005). We might also consider more global solutions, e.g., operational performance bounds (Eager and Sevcik 1986). In case more precise results are required, instead of simple queuing formulae, more detailed techniques such as simulation can be applied in combination with our approach.

Table 9.1 also shows the performance results for the example model after the execution of step 3. We have calculated the processing and response times for the services and the utilisations for the resources at the application and infrastructure layers (in this example, the business layer is only relevant because it provides the input for the workloads). However, the performance results can easily be extended to the business layer as well.

For simplicity, we assume Poisson arrivals and exponentially distributed service times in this example, so that every structural element a can be modelled as an M/M/1 queue (Harrison and Patel 1992). Hence, the response time function is given by Eq. (9.1).

The results show that queuing times from the lower layers accumulate in the higher layers, which results in response times that are orders of magnitude greater than the local service times. For example, the 'view' component of the 'claim handling support' application has a utilisation of over 84%, which results in a response time of the 'view damage report' application service of almost 3 min.

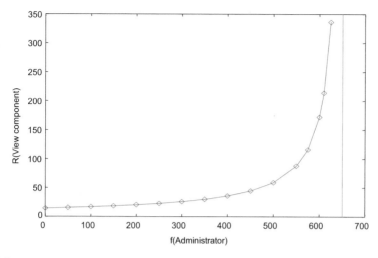

Fig. 9.8 Arrival rate vs. response time

Using our approach, it is easy to study the effect of input parameter changes on the performance. For example, Fig. 9.8 shows how the response time of the View component depends on the arrival frequency associated with the Administrator (assuming a fixed arrival frequency for the Damage expert). The maximum arrival frequency, which results in a utilisation of the View component of 100%, is 651 arrivals per day. In the design stage these results may help us to decide, for example, if an extra View component is needed.

9.3 Functional Analysis

In this section we illustrate how functional analysis techniques can be based on existing techniques in formal methods. Though these formal methods have been developed for systems and problems which have been defined in a mathematically precise way, and architecture descriptions in most cases have an informal character, we show that these formal methods can be used when we introduce a few basic definitions we briefly explained in Chap. 3, such as signature, symbolic model, and interpretation.

In functional analysis of architectures, we distinguish between static or structural and dynamic or behavioural aspects. For analysing the static structure of an architecture, its *signature* (see Sect. 3.3) forms the basis. This focuses on the symbolic representation of the structural elements of an architecture and their relationships, abstracting from other architectural aspects like rationale, pragmatics, and visualisation. It emphasises a separation of concerns which helps in mastering the complexity of the architecture. Notably, the signature of an architecture can be expressed in XML for storage and communication purposes, and can be integrated as an independent module with other tools including graphics for visualisation.

For the logical analysis of the dynamics of an architecture, the *formal semantics* (see also Sect. 3.3) of a symbolic model of that architecture provides a formal basis. A signature of an architecture only specifies the basic concepts with which the architecture is described, but an interpretation contains much more detail. In general, there can be a large number of different interpretations for a signature. This reflects the intuition that there are many possible architectures that fit a specific architecture description.

By applying the techniques for static and dynamic analysis discussed in the next subsections, we gain a better understanding of how enterprise architectures are to be interpreted and what is meant by the individual concepts and relationships. In other words, these techniques allow enterprise architects to validate the correctness of their architectures, to reduce the possibility of misinterpretations, and even to enrich their architecture descriptions with relevant information in a smooth and controllable way.

We do not detail the formal methods themselves, which would require at least a textbook for each method (and many good textbooks for these methods exist). Instead, we use small example architectures to illustrate the use of these methods for architectural analysis. More technical details can be found in Boer et al. (2004, 2005) and in Stam et al. (2004).

The structure of this section is as follows. In Sect. 9.3.1 we give an introduction to static analysis, in particular of impact-of-change analysis on an architecture, and we show how this can be applied to the ArchiSurance example case described earlier. In Sect. 9.3.2, we go deeper into dynamic analysis. Using another example architecture, we show how an ArchiMate description of an architecture can be translated into a signature, illustrate how this signature can be extended to a symbolic model, and how this symbolic model can be interpreted by a semantic model. We briefly describe two relevant formal methods, namely process algebras and data flow models. Finally, we show how we can interpret the example architecture as a process algebra and as a data flow network, respectively.

9.3.1 Static Analysis

For structural analysis of architectures, description logics are useful formalisms. Description logics are knowledge representation languages tailored to express knowledge about concepts and concept hierarchies. They are considered an important formalism unifying and giving a logical basis to the well-known traditions of frame-based systems, semantic networks, and KL-ONE-like languages (Woods and Schmolze 1992), object-oriented representations, semantic data models, and type systems. Description logic systems have been used for building a variety of applications including conceptual modelling, information integration, query mechanisms, view maintenance, software management systems, planning systems, configuration systems, and natural language understanding. In the case of enterprise architecture, the main application of description logics is in determining the impact of a change to an architecture: what elements of the model will be 'touched' by this change?

As an example of static analysis, we again consider our fictitious ArchiSurance company, which offers insurance to customers. ArchiSurance sells its products by means of *intermediaries*. Intermediaries investigate the concerns of customers, negotiate a policy contract and take care of the administrative work and the communication with ArchiSurance (see also Fig. 8.9, the Actor Cooperation view of ArchiSurance).

The role of the intermediary is purely commercial: he or she only sells products to customers and makes sure all paperwork is done correctly until the customer has signed a contract. After this, the intermediary is only involved in case of problems with the collection of premiums.

ArchiSurance architects want to investigate quickly if it would be possible to eliminate the entire idea of intermediaries. What would be the consequences of such a drastic change of the business model on the enterprise architecture of ArchiSurance?

The starting point of this analysis is the relationship between the various views and a logical theory. As we explained in Chap. 3, underlying these views is a single architecture model, which corresponds to a signature, which is used in the logical analysis.

In this signature there are sorts for roles, collaborations etc., and there are domain-dependent sorts, such as 'insurance company' and 'customer'. Performing such a structural analysis implies 'traversing' the architecture and taking into account each relation and its meaning to determine whether the proposed change might 'propagate' through this relation. If, for example, a service provided by an application changes, every user of that service may be affected.

To express this, every relation in the architecture model is translated into a relation in the logic. In the translation there are also some constraints between the sorts and the relations to make the correspondence precise. Examples of such constraints, expressed in first-order logic, are the following:

$$\forall x: Customer(x) \rightarrow Role(x)$$
$$\forall x,y: Participate(x,y) \rightarrow Role(x) \wedge Collaboration(y)$$

The first rule states that every *Customer* is also a *Role*; the second states that only *Roles* can participate in *Collaborations*, and, vice versa, that participants of *Collaborations* are *Roles*. Of course, much more complex rules are used to express the impact of a change of a model element on related elements. Such logic rules can be processed by a 'rules engine' that automates the impact analysis. A prototype of such an analysis tool is described in Sect. 11.6.

In our example, if ArchiSurance wants to change the role of the intermediary, this will have an impact on all collaborations in which this intermediary participates

(Fig. 9.9). Several business processes will be involved in this through interactions performed by these collaborations; one of these is the 'Close Contract' process, shown in Fig. 9.10. This uses a number of applications, some of which may also be influenced by the change (Fig. 9.11). Naturally, these examples show only a small part of the actual impact of the proposed change, but they serve to illustrate the general idea.

In these examples, we have not shown how an architecture description in the ArchiMate language can be translated into an underlying formalism that forms the basis of these analysis techniques. In the next subsection, on dynamic analysis, we will go deeper into this issue, and show how the signature of an architecture can be

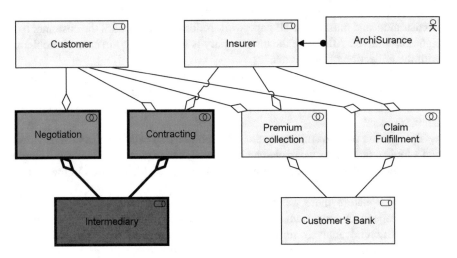

Fig. 9.9 Impact (in *red* and *pink*) on collaborations

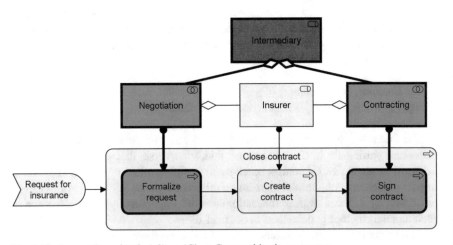

Fig. 9.10 Impact (in *red* and *pink*) on 'Close Contract' business process

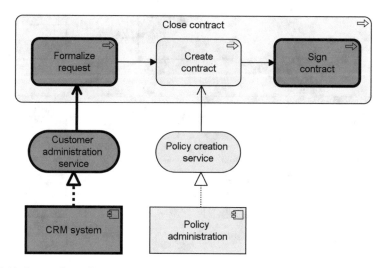

Fig. 9.11 Impact (in *pink*) on applications

defined, how this signature can be interpreted semantically, and how formal analysis techniques can be built upon that.

9.3.2 Dynamic Analysis

For dynamic analysis of architectures, functional analysis techniques based on formal approaches such as process algebras and data flow networks are useful. Issues like two roles acting at the same time, overwriting or destroying each other's work, can be identified and then a suitable protocol can be designed to prevent the problem. Thus, a functional behaviour analysis based on formal methods is primarily a qualitative analysis that can detect logical errors, leads to a better consistency, and focuses on the logic of models.

The dynamics of a concrete system with an architecture description given by its signature can be specified in different ways; we distinguish between specifications tailored towards control flow modelling and those tailored towards data flow modelling. For control flow modelling, we give a brief introduction to process algebra, while for data flow modelling, we introduce the reader to data flow networks.

To illustrate the use of these formal methods, we use the enterprise architecture of a small company, ArchiSell, modelled using the ArchiMate language. In ArchiSell, employees sell products to customers. Various suppliers deliver the products to ArchiSell. Employees of ArchiSell are responsible for ordering products and for selling them. Once products are delivered to ArchiSell, each product is assigned to an owner responsible for selling the product. More specifically, we look

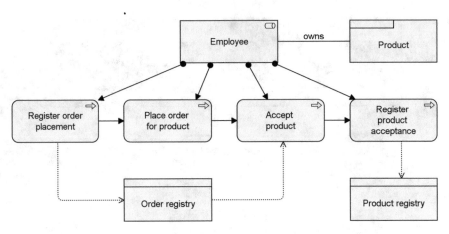

Fig. 9.12 ArchiSell: a business process architecture

at the business process architecture for ordering products, visualised in Fig. 9.12. To describe this enterprise, we use the ArchiMate modelling concepts and their relationships. In particular, we use structural concepts (*product, business role* and *business object*) and structural relationships (*association*), but also behavioural concepts (process) and behavioural relationships (*triggering*). Behavioural and structural concepts are connected by means of the *assignment* and *access* relations.

In order to fulfil the business process for ordering a product, the employee has to perform the following activities:

– Before placing an order, an employee must register the order within the Order Registry. This Order Registry is for administration purposes. It is used to check orders upon acceptance of goods later in the process. Orders contain a list of products to be ordered.
– After that, the employee places the order with the supplier. Based on the order, the supplier is supposed to collect the products and to deliver them as soon as possible.
– As soon as the supplier delivers the products, the employee first checks if there is an order that refers to this delivery. Then, the employee accepts the products.
– Next, the employee registers the acceptance of the products within the Product Registry and determines which employee will be the owner of the products.

Although the example is rather trivial, it serves to illustrate how an architecture description can be formalised and how it can be subjected to functional analysis.

Signature We first define the signature of the business process architecture described in Fig. 9.12. The sorts of the example are simply enumerated as follows:

Role
Object
Employee

Product
product
Order_Registry
Product_Registry

Note that we did not include processes as a sort, because processes are modelled below as functions.

Further information about the architecture is expressed symbolically in terms of suitable extensions of one of its signatures. Usually, a signature is extended with operations for constructing complex *types* from the primitive sorts. Examples are the standard type operations like the *product type* $T_1 \times T_2$ of the types T_1 and T_2, and the *function type* $T_1 \rightarrow T_2$ of all functions which require an argument of type T_1 and provide a result of type T_2. Given functional types, the name space of a signature can be extended with functions $F(T_1) : T_2$, where F specifies the name of a function of type $T_1 \rightarrow T_2$. Functions can be used to specify the *attributes* of a sort. For example, given the primitive sorts *Employee* and N, the function *Age* (*Employee*) : N is intended for specifying the age of each person. Examples of the sub-sort relation are the following:

Employee is_a *Role*
Product is_a *product*
Order_Registry is_a *Object*
Product_Registry is_a *Object*
Owns is_a *association*

Note that we have encoded meta-model information of an architecture description as part of the signature of the architecture itself. The relation between the meta-model sorts and relations and architecture sorts and relations is expressed by the respective partial orders between sorts and relations of the signature. For example, the sort *Product* in Fig. 9.12 is modelled as a sub-sort of the ArchiMate concept *product*. The 'owns' relation itself is specified by:

Employee owns *Product*

Also note that the triggering relation is not included in our concept of a signature. In our view such a relation specifies a temporal ordering between the processes, which are described in Sects. 10.1.3 and 10.1.4.

Interpretation

To obtain a formal model of a system as a semantic interpretation of the symbolic model of its architecture description, we start with an interpretation of the signature. An *interpretation I* of the types of a signature assigns to each primitive sort S a set I (S) of *individuals* of sort S which respects the sub-sort ordering: if S_1 is a sub-sort of S_2, then $I(S_1)$ is a subset of $I(S_2)$. Any primitive sort is interpreted by a subset of a universe which is given by the union of the interpretation of all primitive sorts. The subset relation expresses the hierarchy between primitive sorts. An interpretation I of the primitive sorts of a signature of an architecture can be inductively extended to an interpretation of more complex types. For example, an interpretation of the product type $T_1 \times T_2$ is given by the Cartesian product $I(T_1) \times I(T_2)$ of the sets $I(T_1)$ and $I(T_2)$. The function type $T_1 {\rightarrow} T_2$ thus denotes the set of all functions from the universe to itself such that the image of $I(T_1)$ is contained in $I(T_2)$. In general, there can be a large number of different interpretations for a signature. This reflects the intuition that there are many possible architectures that fit a specific architecture description.

The semantic model of a system involves its concrete components and their concrete relationships, which may change in time because of the dynamic behaviour of a system. To refer to the concrete situation of a system, we have to extend its signature with names for referring to the individuals of the types and relations. For a symbolic model, we denote by $n{:}T$ a name n, which ranges over individuals of type T.

As an example, we introduce the following semantic model. We define only two products: p_1 and p_2. In order to model the processing of orders and products, individuals of the sort *Employee* have a *product* attribute and an *order* attribute. These attributes indicate the order and product the employee is managing. In our model, individuals of the sort *Employee* are fully characterised by these attributes. Therefore, in our model the sort *Employee* contains four elements, namely:

e_1 *order* $= p_1$ *product* $= p_1$
e_2 *order* $= p_1$ *product* $= p_2$
e_3 *order* $= p_2$ *product* $= p_1$
e_4 *order* $= p_2$ *product* $= p_2$

Furthermore, we define the order and product registries as possibly infinite lists of products.

Finally, in order to refer to the elements of the different sorts we introduce individual names *emp*: *Employee*, *order-reg*: *Order_Registry*, and *product-reg*: *Product_Registry*. A semantic model assigns individuals to these names. For example:

emp $= e_1$ *order* $= p_1$ *product* $= p_1$
order-reg $= \{ p_1 \}$
product-reg $= \{ p_2 \}$

Note that this assignment describes an employee, who manages an order of product p_1 and a delivery of product p_1, an *Order_registry*, which registers an order of product p_1, and a *Product_registry*, which registers the acceptance of a product p_2.

Process Algebras

Process algebra (Baeten and Weijland 1990; Bergstra et al. 2001) is a formal description technique for specifying the control flow behaviour of complex systems. Starting from the language syntax, each statement of the language is supplied with some kind of behaviour, and a semantic equivalence says which behaviours are identical. Process algebras express such equivalences in *axioms* or *equational laws*. The axioms are to be *sound*, i.e., if two behaviours can be equated then they are semantically equivalent. The converse statement is optional, and is called *completeness*, i.e., if two behaviours are semantically equivalent then they can be equated.

The system is captured as a set of processes interacting with each other according to predefined rules. Starting from a set of *basic actions*, processes may be hierarchically composed by means of operators, e.g., sequential composition, choice, parallel composition.

We derive these basic actions from the functions of a symbolic model of an architecture. To this end, we define the *action of a function* $F(S) : T$ by an assignment of the form $n := F(m)$ where $n : T$ and $m : S$ are names ranging over the types T and S, respectively. The execution of such an action in a semantic model Σ *assigns* to the name n the return value of $\Sigma(F)(\Sigma(m))$ which denotes the result of applying the function $\Sigma(F) \in I(S{\rightarrow}T)$ to the element $\Sigma(m) \in I(S)$. Note that actions transform semantic models (i.e., the state of a system) but not the interpretation of a signature (i.e., the structural information of a system).

Given this concept of an action as a transformation of semantic models, we can define more complex *processes* by combining actions; that is, we can define operations on actions determining the order of their execution. For example, we can define the sequential composition $n := F(m); n' := G(m')$ of two actions $n := F(m)$ and $n' := G(m')$ as the composition of their transformation of semantic models.

Process algebras can be applied to model any business function and to prove its correctness. They enable properties of the business of an enterprise to be expressed in an abstract way and to deduce whether a specific process satisfies these properties.

Now let us consider the process steps within the ArchiSell example. Within the process algebra interpretation, processes are specified as functions. The types of the arguments and result values are determined as follows:

- A *role*, which is assigned to a process, specifies the type of both an argument and a result value of the corresponding function.
- An outgoing *access* relation from a process to a data object specifies the type of both an argument and a result value of the corresponding function.
- An incoming *access* relation from an object to a process only specifies the type of the corresponding argument (this captures the property of 'read-only').

This results in the following functions:

- *Register_order_placement*
  - domain name=*Employee*
  - domain name=*Order_Registry*
  - codomain name=*Employee*
  - codomain name=*Order_Registry*

– *Place_order_for_product*

  • domain name=*Employee*
  • codomain name=*Employee*

– *Accept_product*

  • domain name=*Employee*
  • domain name=*Order_Registry*
  • codomain name=*Employee*

– *Register_product_acceptance*

  • domain name=*Employee*
  • domain name=*Product_Registry*
  • codomain name=*Employee*
  • codomain name=*Product_Registry*

The interpretation of the processes can be specified in a pseudo-language. For more simple functions, matrices of input/output pairs can be given. For example, the interpretation of the *Register_order_placement* function can be as follows: add to the *Order_Registry* (which is a list, as defined in the signature) the product of the product attribute of the *Employee*. Other processes are formally described in a similar manner.

Within a process algebra, we can now concatenate the individual functions in order to model the transformation of an initial state of a concrete system to an eventual state. In this way, we can reason about the correctness of the transformation.

Data Flow Networks

A data flow network (Jagannathan 1995) is another formal description technique for the behavioural specifications of complex systems. Such a network consists of some *processes,* the functions of a symbolic model that communicate by passing data over *lines.* A process is a transformation of data within the system, whereas a line is a directed FIFO channel connecting at most two processes. Data passed over a line by a process will arrive in an unspecified but finite amount of time at the destination process in the same order as it was sent.

Data flow diagrams can be used to provide a clear representation of any business function. The technique starts with an overall picture of the business and continues by analysing each of the functional areas of interest. This analysis can be carried out to the level of detail required. The technique exploits a method called top-down expansion to conduct the analysis in a targeted way. The result is a series of diagrams that represent the business activities in a way that is precise, clear, and easy to communicate.

In a data flow interpretation of the ArchiSell process, we consider each individual process step as an independent data-consuming/data-producing entity. Such an entity has *input ports* and *output ports*. Within the data flow interpretation, we are interested in the data flow within the process, but not directly in the actors (or roles)

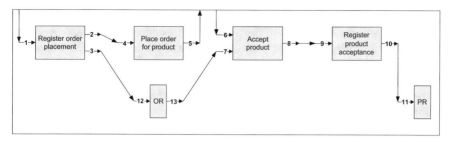

Fig. 9.13 ArchiSell as a data flow network

that perform the process. Therefore, this interpretation is specifically suited for situations in which many details are known about the data and less about the actors. However, as we will illustrate, a data flow interpretation can help us in the assignment of actors to process steps.

The way in which we can interpret the example as a data flow network is shown in Fig. 9.13. Note the following:

- We leave out any information about roles and individuals within the role sort. So, the data flow diagram does not contain information about which actor performs which process steps.
- We specify registries as stores, i.e., special functions, which resemble places in which information can be stored and from which the same information can be retrieved later.
- We explicitly identify which input/output ports receive/send which kind of values. A practical way is to begin with identifying the values on the input/output ports, and then to connect the output ports to other input ports.
  The following values are communicated:

1. list of products that have to be ordered;
2. list of products that have to be ordered;
3. order registry record;
4. list of products that have to be ordered;
5. supplier order;
6. list of products received;
7. order registry record;
8. list of products accepted;
9. list of products accepted;
10. product registry record;
11. product registry record;
12. order registry record;
13. order registry record.

With such a data flow diagram, we can define data flow for each individual process step. The functions transform certain inputs into a certain output. Such functions can be defined in, for example, a pseudo-language, but it is also possible to derive a working simulation of the process architecture in this way.

The data flow diagram also enables us to reason about the assignment of process steps to actors. For example, the process diagram, correct as it is, does not reveal if the step 'register order placement' should be fulfilled by the same actor as the step 'accept product'. The data flow diagram reveals what is needed in order to assign actors correctly to process steps.

An example of this is the following. Suppose that we would like to have the first two process steps to be performed by an actor different from the one that performs the last two process steps. The data flow diagram reveals that this is no problem, since no values are communicated directly between those two sets of process steps. In other words, the data flow diagram shows that, given this interpretation of the process architecture, it facilitates separation between order placement and product acceptance.

9.4 Risk Analysis

In recent years, organisations have started to realise that the IT security challenge cannot be solved in isolation by security specialists. Rather, it should be incorporated in an integral Enterprise Risk and Security Management (ERSM) approach. It is only natural to place ERSM in the context of enterprise architecture, for a holistic view that not only looks at IT-related risk and security but also at the social and business aspects. Therefore, it is not surprising that enterprise architecture frameworks such as TOGAF (The Open Group 2011) include chapters on risk and security, and a security framework such as SABSA (Sherwood et al. 2009) shows a remarkable similarity to the Zachman framework.

Seen in this light, it also makes sense to use the ArchiMate language to model risk and security aspects as an integral part of an enterprise architecture and use analysis techniques such as those outlined in Sect. 9.3 to assess vulnerabilities, threats and the ensuing risks. In a white paper published by The Open Group (Band et al. 2015), it is shown how concepts found in leading risk and security standards and frameworks can be mapped to ArchiMate concepts. Figure 9.14 summarises this risk and security 'overlay'. Specific icons, different from the standard ArchiMate icons, are used to denote risk and security-specific specialisations of concepts (in the white paper, a stereotype notation is used).

For the purpose of risk analysis, we can assign risk-related attributes to these concepts. The Factor Analysis of Information Risk (FAIR) taxonomy (The Open Group 2013) adopted by The Open Group provides a good starting point for this. If sufficiently accurate estimates of the input values are available, quantitative risk analysis provides the most reliable basis for risk-based decision-making. However, in practice, these estimates are often difficult to obtain. Therefore, FAIR proposes a risk assessment based on qualitative (ordinal) measures, e.g. threat capability ranging from very low to very high and risk ranging from low to critical. Figure 9.15

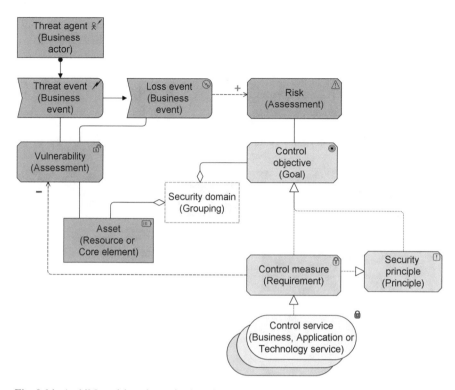

Fig. 9.14 ArchiMate risk and security 'overlay'

shows how these values can be linked to elements in an ArchiMate model, how they are related and how they can be visualised in heat maps:

- The *vulnerability level* (VL) depends on the *threat capability* (TC) and the *control strength* (CS) of the control measures applied. A high control strength reduces the vulnerability level. In case of multiple threats or multiple control measures, we assume that the maximum threat capability and maximum control strength determine the outcome, although more advanced ways to combine them are also conceivable.
- The *loss event frequency* (LEF) depends on both the *threat event frequency* (TEF) and the *vulnerability level* (VL). A higher vulnerability level increases the probability that a threat event will actually trigger a loss event.
- The *risk factor* (RF) is determined by the *loss event frequency* (LEF) and the *probable loss magnitude* (PLM). Informally, risk is the product of the 'likelihood' or frequency of a loss occurring and the 'impact' of the loss.

The example in Fig. 9.16 shows a simple application of a vulnerability and risk assessment. The 'traffic lights' show the ordinal values of the risk attributes as defined in the FAIR Body of Knowledge and summarised above.

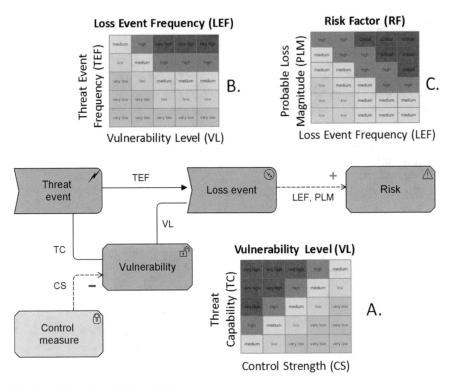

Fig. 9.15 Overview of risk analysis

A vulnerability scan of the transmission of payment data from a web shop to an online payment provider has shown that the encryption level of transmitted payment records is low (e.g. due to an outdated version of the used encryption protocol). This is classified as VL: 'high'. Also, the transmission channel using the public Internet is insecure, which is classified as a VL: 'medium'. These two vulnerabilities enable a man-in-the-middle attack, in which a cybercriminal may modify the data to make unauthorised payments, e.g. by changing the bank account number of the receiver. Assuming a cybercriminal with medium skills (TC: 'medium') and an average of multiple attempted attacks per week (TEF: 'high'), according to the loss event frequency matrix shown in Fig. 9.16, the expected value for LEF is 'high'. Finally, assuming that a potentially large sum of money may be lost (PLM: 'high'), the resulting risk factor RF is 'critical'.

Assuming that this risk is deemed unacceptable, a control objective can be defined to prevent unauthorised access to payment data. We can also attach a security profile to this control objective, specifying the security parameters that we require for payment data: confidentiality and integrity must be high (it should be prevented that unauthorised persons can view or modify the data), and the required level of availability is medium (payment data does not have to be available 24/7). This is illustrated in Fig. 9.17.

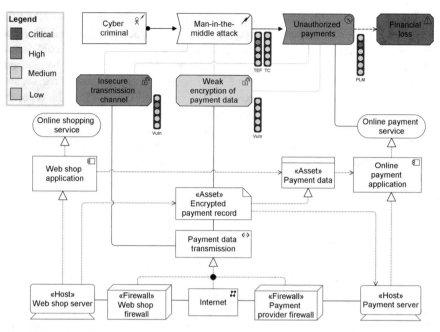

Fig. 9.16 Risk analysis example

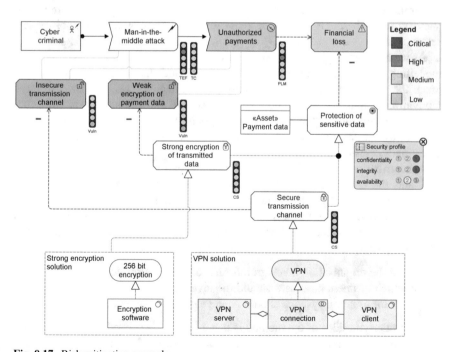

Fig. 9.17 Risk mitigation example

Based on the security profile of the control objective and the outcome of the risk analysis, specific requirements for control measures are elicitated. For example, as a preventive control measure that helps to achieve the required levels of confidentiality and integrity, a stronger encryption protocol is needed (which can be realised by e.g. 256-bit encryption instead of 128-bit encryption), as well as a secure transmission channel (which can be realised by using a VPN solution). Incorporating the control strengths of these measures in the risk analysis, an estimate can be made of the effect of the control strengths on the residual risk. Further reduction of this risk may also require other measures, e.g. a reduction of the probable loss magnitude by limiting the maximum amount of money that can be transferred using this payment provider.

9.5   Portfolio Analysis

Analysis of enterprise architecture models can provide important input for portfolio management, as is described by Quartel et al. (2010). A desired organisational or technical change requires the investigation of the stakeholders that are involved and their concerns regarding the change. New goals and requirements are identified, or existing ones are changed, to address these concerns. Analysis of these goals and requirements is needed to guarantee consistency and completeness and to propose one or more alternative architecture designs that realise the goals and requirements. Validation of these alternative designs aims at assessing their suitability and selecting the best alternative.

As we have outlined in Sect. 5.6, the ArchiMate Motivation concepts help you in modelling stakeholders, their goals and drivers and the resulting requirements. Since the various elements of the enterprise architecture can be related to these motivational elements, we are now able to assess in more detail how architectural decisions contribute to the organisation's goals. Quantifying such contributions helps in evaluating your project or application portfolio and in making the right investment decisions.

A contribution can be divided into two elements: its *importance* to a business goal and the quality or *effectiveness* in supporting that goal. The value of an organisation's service portfolio thus depends on the contribution that its constituent elements provide to the business. An interesting and useful way of computing a service portfolio's value based on these business contributions is Bedell's method (Schuurman et al. 2008). This method answers three questions:

1. Should the organisation invest in information systems/services?
2. On which business processes should the investment focus?
3. Which information systems should be developed or improved?

The underlying idea of the method is that a balance is needed between the level of effectiveness of the information systems and their level of strategic importance

Fig. 9.18 Investment decisions

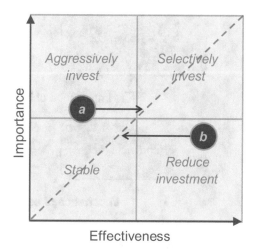

(the diagonal in Fig. 9.18). Investments are more crucial if the ratio between the effectiveness of an information system and its importance is worse. The example of Fig. 9.18 shows that application *a* is a candidate for aggressive investment, since its effectiveness is lower than its importance warrants; conversely, *b* can do with a lower investment level.

To calculate these values, Bedell's method uses:

- The importance of each business process to the organisation (IBO)
- The importance of each business activity to the business processes (IAB)
- The effectiveness of an information system (software application) in supporting business activities (ESA)

From these inputs, various other values can be calculated, starting with the effectiveness of an information system for a business process (ESB), computed as ESB = ESA × IAB; the effectiveness of all information systems for the business process EIB = $\sum_S$ ESB/$\sum_A$ IAB; and so on, until we know aggregate measures of the effectiveness and importance of each information system for the organisation. These can then provide input for investment decisions, as outlined above.

This type of calculations can easily be transferred to our architecture models, as shown in Fig. 9.19. However, Bedell's method was not designed for use in combination with architecture models, and it has two issues that we needed to address. First, it has a fixed level structure consisting of organisation, business processes, activities and information systems, whereas our models may have many more levels. Second, it assumes a one-to-one relationship between activities and information systems. In both areas, we have extended and generalised the method to fit with our models; for more detail, see Quartel et al. (2010).

Measuring importance requires insight in the ways in which an IT system, service or business process contributes to the business goals. This value can lie in

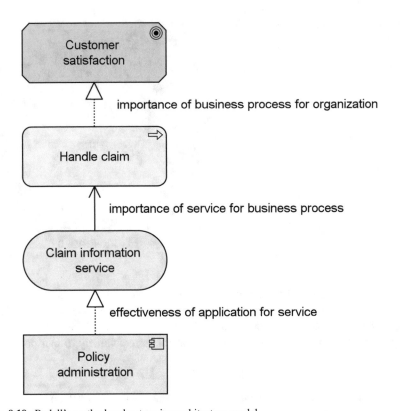

Fig. 9.19 Bedell's method and enterprise architecture model

many different aspects, such as the timely and accurate information that the system delivers as input for business decisions, the customer satisfaction and return business created through its user-friendly interface or the value of future opportunities opened up by IT.

Methods such as the Application Life Cycle Duration Measurement Method (ALMM) from the Application Services Library (ASL) methodology (Pols and Backer 2006) can provide relevant input for these calculations. The ALMM measures the life cycle of applications by determining their current Business Value (BV) and the Technical Value (TV) and then by estimating the development of the BV and TV in the future, assuming a continuation of the current IT policy. Business Value is very close to Bedell's definition of strategic importance, and Technical Value is close to Bedell's notion of effectiveness.

ALMM's main limitation is that it addresses only a single level of abstraction, that of applications. Complementing it with the calculations as outlined above provides us with a better foundation for assessing the contributions of architecture elements to business goals at different levels of our enterprise architecture.

9.6   Capability Analysis

ArchiMate can be a very useful instrument in the context of capability-based planning and analysis, as outlined by Aldea et al. (2015). Capability maps are an essential component of this and are used by organisations to perform high-level performance assessments. A very useful technique is capability heat mapping. It uses capability maps (Sect. 8.7.1) and projects various kinds of data on top of these using colours. An example is shown in Fig. 9.20. This depicts the capabilities of our ArchiSurance example company and shows in red which capabilities are less efficient than the benchmark and in green those which are more efficient.

The example below shows how you can use spider charts (which are not an ArchiMate notation) to visualise a capability analysis in more detail. The chart shows the current and desired performance of a capability along different axes. The example shows the notion of incremental development of a capability. For the 'Claim management' capability, six dimensions are defined. The baseline analysis for this capability results in values for the different dimensions, which are linked using the red line. The required maturity, broken down into values for the individual dimensions, is indicated with the green line (Fig. 9.21).

For the different dimensions of the capability analysis, we have defined a *metric* concept as a specialisation of Driver, using the language customisation mechanism described in Sect. 5.14.2.

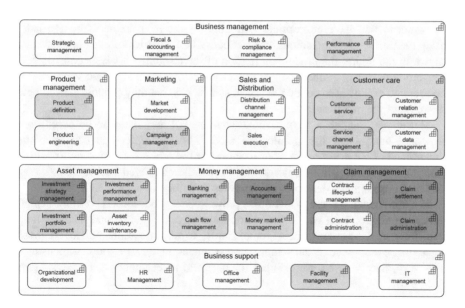

Fig. 9.20 Capability heat map

Capability analysis

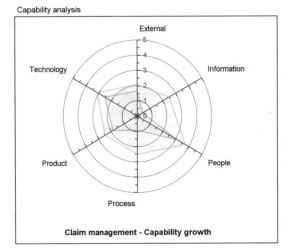

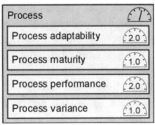

Fig. 9.21 Capability analysis

Metric: the extent, quantity, amount or degree of something, as determined by measurement or calculation.

A metric will have appropriate attributes for the measurements being made, using the profile mechanism outlined in Sect. 5.14.1. Metrics can be composite, as shown in the figure: the process dimension of the capability analysis consists of a weighted average of process adaptability, maturity, performance and variance. Of course, you will want to define metrics in such a way that they support the strategic direction of the organisation.

Metrics get their data from external sources, but they can also be based on a structural analysis of the architecture model. For example, you can trace the importance of applications for your strategy via the processes they support, which contribute to the capabilities needed to deliver the envisaged business outcomes. This is an example of the structural analyses described in Sect. 9.3.1.

In a more general sense, capabilities prove to be a good starting point for capital allocation aligned with your organisation's strategy. Capability analyses may help you draw up investment plans, for example, to allocate more budget to those capabilities that need a substantial improvement in one or more dimensions. This way, they may be useful input for portfolio management and analysis (see Sect. 9.5).

9.7 Summary

In this chapter we have considered the relation between enterprise architecture models and architecture analysis. We addressed two main classes of methods, quantitative analysis and functional analysis.

Although the importance of enterprise architecture modelling has been recognised, hardly any attention has been paid to the analysis of its *quantitative* properties. Most existing approaches to performance evaluation focus on detailed models within a specific domain. We demonstrated the applicability of quantitative modelling and analysis techniques for the effective evaluation of design choices at the enterprise architectures level, in the context of ArchiMate models. We discerned a number of architecture viewpoints with corresponding performance measures, which can be used as criteria for the optimisation or comparison of such designs. We introduced a new approach for the propagation of workload and performance measures through a layered enterprise architecture model. This can be used as an analysis framework where existing methods for detailed performance analysis, based on, for example, queuing models, Petri nets or simulation, can be plugged in. The presented example illustrates the use of our top-down and bottom-up technique to evaluate the performance of a document management system for the storage and retrieval of damage reports. Using a simple queuing formula for the response times, we showed that queuing times from the lower layers of the architecture accumulate in the higher layers, which may result in response times that are orders of magnitude greater than the local service times. In order further to illustrate and validate our approach, we have developed a prototype, which is outlined in Chap. 11. The practical use of these techniques is illustrated in a case study of the Dutch Tax and Customs Administration, which is described in Chap. 12.

By applying *functional* analysis techniques, we aim for a better understanding of how architectures are to be interpreted. These techniques allow enterprise architects to validate the correctness of their architectures, to reduce the possibility of misinterpretations, and to enrich their architecture descriptions with relevant information in a smooth and controllable way.

In functional analysis, we distinguished between static or structural and dynamic or behavioural aspects. Furthermore, our approach is based on the distinction between symbolic and semantic models of architectures. The core of a symbolic model consists of its signature that specifies symbolically its structural elements and their relationships. A semantic model is defined as a formal interpretation of the symbolic model. Semantic models are at the centre of our logical perspective of enterprise architectures, which integrates both static and dynamic aspects. This leads to more precise characterisation of the architecture concepts and provides a formal basis for functional analysis. The framework we have developed allows the integration of various techniques, ranging from static analysis to process algebras and data-flow networks. One important application of these techniques is impact-of-change analysis, a prototype of which will be described in Chap. 11.

As we have seen, both quantitative and functional analysis techniques help the architect in creating a better insight into the complexities of an enterprise architecture. For further integration into the architecture design process, combining quantitative and functional analysis (e.g., impact-of-change analysis based on quantitative results) could be fruitful.

Chapter 10
Architecture Alignment

Roel J. Wieringa, Pascal A.T. van Eck, and Dennis Krukkert

10.1 Introduction

The results presented in this chapter stem from the GRAAL project, a daughter project of ArchiMate. In this project, we investigate Guidelines Regarding Architecture ALignment. The Dutch word 'GRAAL' means 'grail', and sometimes during the project we felt like valiant knights in search of the holy grail of architecture alignment. This goal turned out to be very elusive indeed.

We have used case studies in large organisations in the public and finance sectors in the search for this grail. All organisations studied by us were actively seeking to align their IT (information technology and related technology) architecture with their business architecture. But the dynamics of current organisations are such that perfect alignment is never attained. There are too many changes in technology, business processes, organisation structure, and the business environment to make that happen. Alignment is thus a regulating idea, like a Kantian goal that is always hovering over the horizon wherever we are. It directs our decisions but it is never fully reached.

Our goal is to derive operational guidelines for aligning IT architecture with business architecture. At the time of writing, we have performed six case studies in various organisations. The idea at the start of the project was to derive guidelines in the form of patterns of well-aligned software applications that occur in different

R.J. Wieringa (✉)
University of Twente, Enschede, The Netherlands
e-mail: r.j.wieringa@utwente.nl

P.A.T. van Eck
Software Improvement Group, Amsterdam, The Netherlands

D. Krukkert
TNO, Soesterberg, The Netherlands

© Springer-Verlag Berlin Heidelberg 2017
M. Lankhorst et al., *Enterprise Architecture at Work*, The Enterprise Engineering
Series, DOI 10.1007/978-3-662-53933-0_10

organisations. It turned out that there are very few such patterns: we found exactly one. We did, however, learn many interesting and useful things about recurrent problems in achieving alignment, about ways to structure the problem, and about methods to achieve alignment (see also Eck et al. 2004). Our case studies also showed us that organisations are not so much in need of a library of patterns. The two major unsolved problems we encountered are how to govern the alignment process (the governance problem) and how to communicate architecture (the documentation problem). We return to these research questions at the end of this chapter.

The structure of this chapter is as follows. In Sect. 10.2, we discuss our architecture framework. In Sect. 10.3 we then summarise our observations and conclusions from six case studies about architecture alignment, and in Sect. 10.4 we present observations about the architecture process.

10.2   The GRAAL Alignment Framework

In order to be able to do a comparative analysis, we need a conceptual framework that allows us to describe in a uniform manner any alignment phenomena we find in different organisations. Our framework is based on an earlier analysis of similar frameworks in systems engineering (Hall 1962, 1969), industrial product engineering (Pahl and Beitz 1986; Roozenburg and Eekels 1995), and software engineering (Wieringa 1998b). The first version of our framework was published in 1996 (Wieringa 1996). It was further elaborated in later publications (Wieringa 1998a), and the current version was published as a result of the GRAAL project (Wieringa et al. 2003).

A conceptual framework is a collection of concepts and relations among them that can be used to describe phenomena. After almost 10 years of using the framework in describing IT architectures, the framework is now reduced to four simple dimensions.

- *System aspects*: externally observable properties.
- *System aggregation*: the composition of complex systems from simpler systems.
- *Systems process*: the life of a system from creation to disposal.
- Description levels: refinement.

The first three dimensions cover three possible ways of considering a system: by its externally observable properties, by its internal structure, and by the phases in its life. The fourth dimension concerns the level of detail we include in our system descriptions. In the next sections, we explain these dimensions and the way in which they can be combined.

10.2.1   *System Aspects*

The starting point for the GRAAL framework is that we consider systems, where a system is a coherent set of elements, whose coherence produces an added value for its environment (Blanchard and Fabrycky 1990; Hall 1962). Organisations are systems, houses are systems, and software programs are systems. We have borrowed the distinction made in general systems theory between aspect systems and subsystems. Given that each system consists of a set of elements, we can define two abstraction operations when we consider a system. An *aspect system* is the set of all of these elements, with only some of their properties, and a *subsystem* is a subset of these elements, but with all their properties. We can reduce the complexity of a system model by focusing on an aspect system or by ignoring subsystems. These are the first two dimensions of the GRAAL framework.

An analysis of a large number of software design techniques has resulted in a simple classification of relevant software aspects, shown in Fig. 10.1 (Wieringa 1998b). A system offers services to its environment; quality properties characterise the value that the system provides for stakeholders by the services it offers. For example, usability, efficiency, and security are aspects of the value that system services have for users of the system, and maintainability and portability are aspects of the value of the system for developers.

A system exists to deliver certain services to its environment. System services in turn are characterised by three functional properties. The behaviour aspect consists of the ordering over time of services and the functions that realise them. The communication aspect consists of the interactions with other entities (people, devices, businesses, software) during the delivery of the service, and the semantic aspect consists of the meaning of the symbols exchanged during the service. These aspects can all be described in the ArchiMate language, as we have outlined in Chap. 5.

The 'meaning' aspect is the only aspect typical of information systems. Other kinds of systems deliver services by means of physical processes such as the exchange of heat or electricity, which do not have a meaning. Software systems deliver services by exchanging symbols with their environment, and these have a meaning (usually documented in a dictionary).

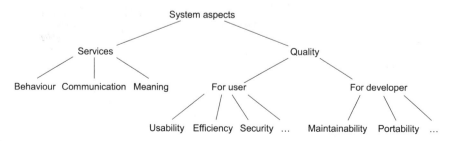

Fig. 10.1 System aspects

10.2.2   The Aggregation Hierarchy

Next to focusing on one system aspect, ignoring subsystems is a major abstraction operation. Every system can be placed in an aggregation hierarchy. In the GRAAL framework, the system aspects can be observed at each level of the aggregation hierarchy (Fig. 10.2).

When we study IT architecture alignment, this simple picture becomes more complicated because there are different kinds of aggregation. Information system architects must deal with three different aggregation hierarchies, namely the physical, social, and linguistic hierarchies. The physical world is the world of brick, mortar, plastic, metal, and other things that can drop on the ground. More in general, it consists of all entities and processes that can be described using the physical measures of metres, kilograms, amperes, and seconds. Relevant for the IT architect is that the physical world includes computers, printers, wires, glass fibre, wireless access points, radio waves, etc. The social world is the world of business processes, needs, added value, money, norms, laws, etc. Part of the social world is the linguistic world of symbol manipulation. We treat this separately because it is the world of software and documents. Note that software exists only in the linguistic world; computers exist only in the physical world; and people exist in all three worlds.

In the physical world, aggregation seems to be a relationship between smaller things that are contained in bigger things. In the three-dimensional world of physical things, this often amounts to a physical containment relationship. But what is aggregation in the social world? There are no big or small things in the social world, and physical containment does not exist in the social world. What does it mean to say that a department is part of an organisation? The department and the organisation have no physical place and size and if we say that one is contained

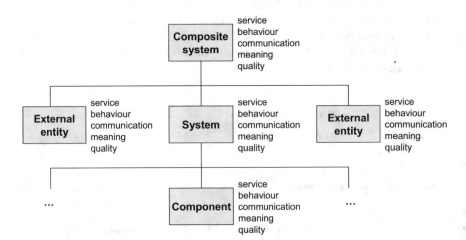

Fig. 10.2 Repetition of aspects at all levels of an aggregation hierarchy

in the other, then this is a metaphorical use of the verb 'to contain'. A similar problem exists in the world of software. What does it mean to say that a module is contained in a program, if this module may exist in several fragments in several physical places (on disk, in memory, in a cache) and may be used by several programs?

Rethinking the concept of aggregation, we identify the following two characteristic features (Wieringa 2003, p. 234). Consider a component C of an aggregate A. To say that C is a component of A means the following:

- **Service provisioning**: C provides a service to A. In other words, C plays a role in the realisation of the services of A itself.
- **Encapsulation**: An external entity, i.e., an entity that is not a component of A, can only interact with C through the interface of A. In the physical world, this means that A provides a protective cover for C. In the social world, this means that C is 'owned' by A, so that an interaction with C is always also an interaction with A. In the symbolic world of software, this means that an interaction with C requires interaction with the interface offered by A to its environment.

The aggregation hierarchies in these three worlds are independent. For example, if we observe that a software system is composed of subsystems, modules, components, etc., then this hierarchy can be mapped in any possible way to a physical hierarchy consisting of a computer network, computers and backup systems. The design problem is to find the most suitable way given some measure of suitability. This means that there are really three alignment problems, as suggested by Fig. 10.3.

Each of the three worlds in Fig. 10.3 has its own aggregation hierarchy, and each must be aligned to the other two.

- To align software (in the symbolic world) to people (in the social world), we must ensure that the meaning attached by people to the symbols at the software interface agree with the manipulations of these symbols by the software, and that these manipulations have value for the people. To align software (symbolic) to business processes (social), we must align the services offered by the software to the services needed by these processes.
- To align software to the physical world, we must allocate it to processing devices, which have a location in the physical world. In general, this is a many-to-many mapping.

Fig. 10.3 Three alignment problems

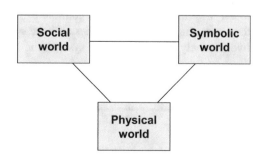

– To align the physical world to the social world, we must consider the physical
location where software is running, and align this with the physical location
where a business process service is needed.

None of these alignment problems is trivial.

10.2.3   The System Process

The third dimension of the GRAAL framework consists of the stages that a system
goes through in its life, from conception to creation, use and disposal (Fig. 10.4). We
can abstract from the complexity of real life by considering each system in its current
stage only. However, in all the cases we studied, an important part of the alignment
problem was the coordination of future development of IT systems. This problem is
sometimes complicated because, for every system, several versions may exist. Because
many systems are supplied by third parties, each with their own release frequency,
coordinating the successive versions that all systems go to is a major problem in
practice. The process dimension of the GRAAL framework draws attention to this.

10.2.4   Refinement Levels

The fourth and last dimension of the GRAAL framework is not a system dimension
but a description dimension. It classifies the level of detail at which we describe
systems. Some illustrative refinement levels in the three worlds are shown in
Fig. 10.5.

10.2.5   Comparison with Other Frameworks

Zachman distinguishes three kinds of descriptions, the data, process, and network
description (Sowa and Zachman 1992; Zachman 1987), which correspond, roughly,
to our meaning, behaviour, and communication aspects. These descriptions can be
used according to Zachman to describe the system from a great number of perspectives, namely the scope of the system, the business view, the system model, the

Fig. 10.4 Typical stages in the life of a system

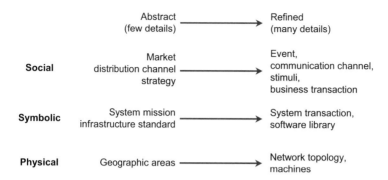

Fig. 10.5 Refinement relations

technology model, the component model, people, external business events, and business goals. This seemingly unrelated and arbitrary list of perspectives can be systematised by placing them at various levels in the service provision hierarchy and refinement hierarchy of the GRAAL framework figure. Details of this and other comparisons can be found elsewhere (Wieringa 1996, pp. 329–330; 1998b).

Our framework refines the alignment framework of Henderson and Venkatraman (Henderson and Venkatraman 1993; Eck et al. 2004), which is also described in Chap. 1. They distinguish two dimensions, the service provision dimension (IT infrastructure level and business level) and a refinement dimension (strategic and operational levels).

Most frameworks for software system development distinguish three views, namely the function view, the behavioural view, and the data view of the system (e.g., Olle et al. 1988). These views correspond to our service, behaviour, and meaning aspects. Harel and Pnueli (1985) add to this the aggregation dimension, which corresponds to our composition dimension.

Kruchten's 4+1 model (Kruchten 1995), described in Sect. 8.1.3, defines the logical and process views of a software system, which correspond roughly with our aggregation dimension and behaviour view, respectively. His physical and development view correspond roughly to the infrastructure layer (see our next section) and to our system process dimension, respectively.

The two basic abstraction operations of focusing on aspect systems and focusing on a subsystem correspond to the two semantic data modelling operations of generalisation (reducing the number of aspects considered) and aggregation (considering an overall system), introduced by Smith and Smith (1977). This seems to have been a case of reinvention, for Smith and Smith do not refer to the systems literature where this distinction originated.

10.3 Alignment Phenomena

In the various case studies we have carried out, we have attempted to identify general alignment phenomena. In the next subsections, we present our observations. We formulate a number of propositions that try to generalise from these observations.

10.3.1 Service Provisioning Layers

All cases studied by us use a layered architecture that distinguishes at least software applications from software infrastructure. Our generalisation of the many different examples that we saw is shown in Fig. 10.6. Each layer in this figure contains systems, represented by the rectangle at each layer, that are part of an aggregation hierarchy. Each of these systems has internal components and may be part of a bigger system. The physical layer contains buildings, computers, printers, wires, wireless access points, etc. The infrastructure layer contains operating systems, middleware, database management systems, etc. The business system layer contains applications and information systems dedicated to particular business processes. The business contains the people, departments, and processes that make up the business, and the business environment consists of suppliers, consumers, and other actors the business interacts with. These layers are a further refinement of the business, application, and technology layers of the ArchiMate language, as described in Chap. 5 and shown on the right of the figure.

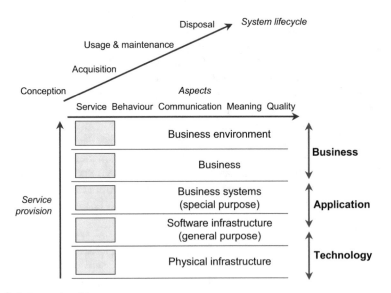

Fig. 10.6 Layered architectures

Systems at each layer provide services to systems at higher layers (see also Sect. 5.2, Fig. 5.2). They may directly interact with systems at any higher layer. The layering only represents one service provisioning relationship, which is primarily because the systems at each level exist in order to satisfy this relationship. There is also a secondary service provisioning relationship that implements system management. For example, some people in the business provide services to the infrastructure, because they keep this infrastructure running and repair it when it is broken. This secondary service provisioning relationship is not represented in the figure.

Layering is of course the basic architectural structuring technique (Dijkstra 1968; Buschmann et al. 1996). In Sect. 10.2.2 we saw that service provisioning is one of the two elements in the concept of aggregation. A component is encapsulated by its aggregate, and delivers a service to it. When we drop the concept of encapsulation from the concept of aggregation, we get the concept of layering. So if we allow a component to be used by several systems, none of which is a unique 'owner' of the component, then the component in effect moves to a lower layer in a layered architecture, and all systems that use it are located at some higher layer.

In Fig. 10.6, we see that at each layer, systems have the same aspects. Each system at any layer provides services, has behaviour, and, above the physical level, communicates with other systems by exchanging symbols with a meaning. And each system has certain quality properties.

Finally, each system at any layer has a life that starts with conception and ends with disposal. Some organisations studied by us maintained elaborate documentation of systems at different stages of their life. Often, organisations have difficulty managing this documentation and keeping it mutually consistent.

The fourth dimension of the GRAAL framework, the abstraction level of system descriptions, is not represented in Fig. 10.6. This figure gives a three-dimensional classification of system views, which we used in all our case studies. The success in using this framework to analyse IT architectures in different organisations leads us to our first proposition:

Proposition 1 All organisations exhibit the layered architecture of Fig. 10.6.

We now look closer at the infrastructure and business system layers.

10.3.2 Infrastructure Architecture

Infrastructure is the set of systems that should be available for use by all users whenever they need it. In GRAAL, we are interested in the software infrastructure of a business, but a large part of infrastructure is physical. It consists of the electricity network, telecommunication networks, the water provision network, the sewage disposal network, the central heating network, the network of roads, the rail network, broadcasting networks and other widely available service networks that provide services for the general public. Most of these networks were introduced in the twentieth century. Software infrastructures are just the latest addition to this set of infrastructures.

Because infrastructures provide services to a large heterogeneous set of user groups, they often have a network nature that allow users to use the services wherever they are in physical space. The software infrastructures that we found are no exception to this. They are usually partitioned into domains that have a rough layered structure, which partitions the infrastructure layer of Fig. 10.6; Fig. 10.7 shows a typical partitioning of the software infrastructure into domains. It also shows some physical infrastructure domains relevant for IT.

Each domain is a knowledge area; it is not a system, but a type of system. Experts in one domain are expert in this kind of system. They follow the trade press, follow trends in the technology market of that domain, and understand the offers made by technology vendors in that domain.

The hierarchy of domains in Fig. 10.7 represents a hierarchy of service provisioning levels to the user of the infrastructure. Software at higher levels uses services of software of lower levels, and so for higher-level software, the lower levels jointly form an implementation platform. At the same time, each higher level of software offers services with a semantics closer to the business concerns of the end user. At the highest level, personal productivity software (e.g., word processors, e-mail client) and business intelligence software (e.g., decision support tools) offer services that can be defined in terms of the concerns of the end user.

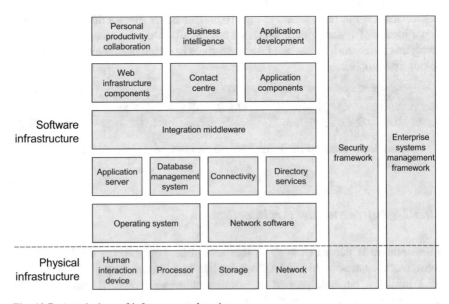

Fig. 10.7 A typical set of infrastructure domains

Infrastructure components can be classified according to the size of the set of processes that they support and the speed at which their services change.

Proposition 2 In general, the slower an infrastructure component's services change, the larger its set of users and vice versa.

The reason is that slow change allows a larger set of users to learn to use the infrastructure component, and the larger its user base, the more difficult it is to change anything in the component. Weill and Vitale (2002) classify infrastructure components according to scope and speed of change. At the lowest level of change, and the largest scope of users, we find commodities such as operating systems and certain user interface hardware such as credit card terminals. On top of that, we find stable services such as database management systems and workflow management systems. At the next higher level, we find standardised applications such as HRM applications, accounting applications and other components that might be included in an ERP system. We see this hierarchy roughly illustrated in the example infrastructure domains of Fig. 10.7.

An infrastructure architecture consists of a partitioning of the infrastructure into a set of domains, such as in Fig. 10.7, plus a set of company-wide standards for each infrastructure domain. A standard might be a *de jure* or *de facto* standard, or a selection of one or two vendors of software in one domain, company-specific agreements, branch-specific agreements, agreements with customers or suppliers, etc. In the companies we investigated, the infrastructure software is never built but bought.

Procurement decisions for infrastructure software are driven by four sources, as shown in Fig. 10.8. Business goals may lead to certain infrastructure decisions. For example, the business goal to facilitate location-independent work can be supported by the installation of wireless networks, groupware infrastructure, and standard browser interfaces accessible from anywhere. Business problems may lead to yet other decisions, such as the installation of more storage servers to solve performance problems, or the move to another network software supplier to solve problems with maintenance. Against these business drivers act forces coming from already existing software (legacy) and new software (technology trends). All organisations must deal with legacy systems. In fact, our six case studies lead us to formulate this tentative proposition:

Fig. 10.8 Infrastructure drivers

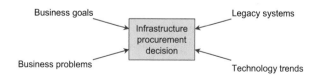

Proposition 3 New technology is added to old technology. It almost never fully replaces old technology.

Organisations differ widely in the relative priority given to these forces. We encountered organisations were the attention to business goals and business problems was merely symbolic and technology trends where the driving force. In other organisations, all four forces where given due weight in procurement decisions.

10.3.3   Business System Architecture

A business system is a software system used in some, but not all, business processes. It is developed or bought to provide certain services in certain business processes, and therefore has particular user groups. Infrastructure software can be found in all businesses, but business systems are often local to one business. A government organisation might have business systems to compute subsidies, income tax, or other legal obligations, and a financial organisation might have business systems to compute risk, mortgage interest, or an insurance premium.

It is customary to distinguish two types of business systems: information systems, which store data, and applications, which use data. Because of their close relationship with business processes, organisations can maintain a landscape map of business systems in tabular format such as shown in Fig. 10.9 (see Sect. 8.2.2 for more about landscape maps).

Each business process is represented by a column that contains the business systems used by that process. A system used in more than one process spans several columns. (If these columns are not adjacent, the business system must be represented by a rectangle fragmented over several columns.) If an application and an information system are in the same column, then the application has some interface to this information system. This interface can be made explicit in a CRUD table such as shown in Table 10.1, which gives more information about the interfaces between business systems in one column of the landscape map of Fig. 10.9. CRUD tables were introduced in the 1970s in information engineering and related methods (Martin 1982, 1989).

In terms of the GRAAL framework, landscape maps and CRUD tables are communication models. They represent communication interfaces among systems. These can be represented in yet another way, conveying other information, in a communication diagram. In Fig. 10.10, we see an ArchiMate diagram of the systems of Fig. 10.9 that shows the possible communication between business systems. It shows that information systems do not communicate directly but only through applications. This information is not visible in the landscape map or in the CRUD table. The communication diagram can be used to trace possible impacts of

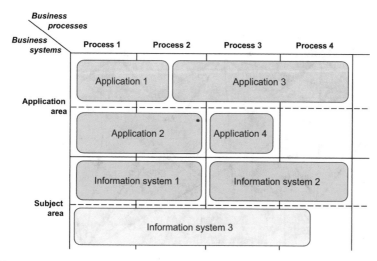

Fig. 10.9 Format of a landscape map of business systems

Table 10.1 Format of a CRUD table of business systems

	App. 1	App. 2	App. 3	App. 4
Information system 1	CR	UD		
Information system 2			U	
Information system 3	CD	RU	R	U

C create, *R* read, *U* update, *D* delete

changes. If a system is changed, then we must trace communication links to neighbouring systems to see if those systems are impacted by the change.

Applications can be grouped into application areas, which are coherent groups of business activities, that require the same business knowledge. For example, an insurance business might distinguish application areas such as claims handling, mortgages, life insurance, health insurance, etc. Each of these application areas requires certain expertise, and for each there are certain groups of applications that may be used in various business processes. In Fig. 10.9, two application areas are represented: the first area contains applications 1 and 3, and the second one contains applications 2 and 4.

Information systems can be grouped into subject areas, which are coherent parts of the world about which data is stored in information systems. Example subject areas in an insurance business are customers and insurance contracts. Two subject areas are shown in Fig. 10.9, one containing information systems 1, 2 and 4 and the other with information system 3.

If an information system is used by many different business processes, it spans many columns. This means that all these processes use the same data with the same definition, which is good for the coherence among these processes. On the other

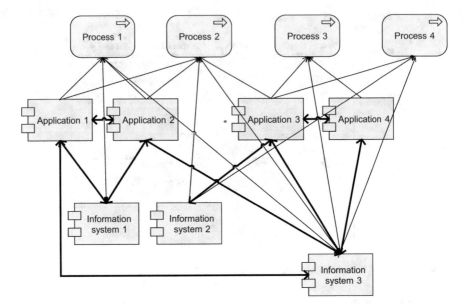

Fig. 10.10 Communication diagram of business systems. A bi-directional arrow represents the possibility of communication between the two systems

hand, the more business processes an information system spans, the more difficult the system is to manage. Different processes usually have different data needs and different data definitions, and the more processes a system is to support, the more complex requirements negotiations become and the more complex data definitions result. A similar observation can be made of applications spanning more than one column. This leads us to the following proposition.

Proposition 4 The manageability of a business system is inversely proportional to the number of business processes supported by the system.

The reason for this is that the semantics, behaviour, and interfaces needed to support different business processes are usually different.

Another generalisation we can make from our observations is the following:

Proposition 5 Business systems tend to gravitate to infrastructure.

As a business system becomes standardised, more users start using it until it is so generally available that it has become part of the infrastructure (Weill and Vitale 2002). Many components of ERP systems started out as special-purpose business systems and by the time they have become part of an ERP system, they are part of the infrastructure.

10.3.4   Strategic Misalignment

In a well-known paper, Henderson and Venkatraman identify different ways to align what they call IT infrastructure to the business (Henderson and Venkatraman 1993). We have also described their approach in Chap. 1. The GRAAL framework is a refinement of the Henderson–Venkatraman framework for strategic alignment because the GRAAL framework uses the same distinction between business systems and IT infrastructure. Three layers of our framework are shown in Fig. 10.11: infrastructure, business systems and business. It shows the framework along the refinement dimension, where on the left-hand side we have strategic, long-term descriptions and on the right-hand side we have operational descriptions of the IT infrastructure, business systems, and the business. The common way of working in the organisations we studied is that business operations, in particular business processes, drive the design decisions about business system architecture. Landscape maps in one form or another play a central role in this. Infrastructure decisions, on the other hand, are driven by various forces, one of which is business strategy. This leads to an infrastructure architecture that may not necessarily align very well with business system operations.

> **Proposition 6** Business system architecture is driven by business operations and infrastructure architecture is driven by the IT infrastructure strategy.

The result is a strategic misalignment that is hard to repair. This misalignment is aggravated because the business system development process is usually out of phase with the infrastructure development process. Business systems are (re)developed when the business calls for it; for example, because users ask for it. Infrastructure, by contrast, is (re)developed on a time-driven bases; for example, once a year. The two processes are usually out of step with each other. One solution to this problem is to (re)develop business systems in a time-driven manner too, and synchronise this with the infrastructure process. Although this solves the problem of synchronisation of the two processes, it introduces the problem that the response to business needs is slowed down. We have not seen this solution practised in the

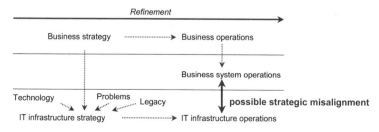

Fig. 10.11 Strategic misalignment

organisations we studied, so we cannot comment upon the effectiveness (or lack of it) of this solution.

10.3.5   Conway's Law

In a landmark article published in 1968, Conway claimed that the structure of a designed system will be isomorphic to the communication structure of the design-ing system (Conway 1968). This has become known as Conway's law. The reason is simple: if the system to be designed is too large to be understood by one person, then several persons will be involved in the design. But these must agree a work breakdown among themselves. This work breakdown will be reflected in the structure of the designed system, because each designer will work on his or her own part.

We see this law at work in the way infrastructure is managed. Infrastructure is partitioned into domains, and for each domain there are one or more infrastructure domain specialists who follow the technology market, translate business strategy into acquisition decisions for their infrastructure domain, and generally manage that domain. In all organisations studied, we found an isomorphism between the infra-structure domain architecture and the infrastructure management department, which was organised according to the same domains. This has an unexpected consequence for any reorganisation of the infrastructure architecture.

> **Proposition 7** A change in infrastructure architecture should be accompa-nied by a change in the infrastructure management structure.

This can be a hindrance to change, because infrastructure managers tend to derive their status, and also their salary, from the number of domains they manage.

In the business system architecture, Conway's law implies that the business system layer will be isomorphic to the business system design department (align-ment 1 in Fig. 10.12). This means that, say, different application areas and subject areas are designed by different design groups. But we have already seen that to align business systems to the business, there must be a structural similarity between the two (alignment 2 in Fig. 10.12) as represented by the landscape map. As a consequence, in order to achieve alignment, the business system department should

Fig. 10.12 Conway's law for the business system layer

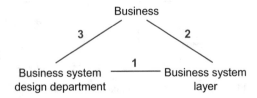

structure itself according to the business supported by the systems they design (alignment 3 in Fig. 10.12).

Proposition 8 Business system alignment is achieved by aligning the business system design department with the supported business operations.

For example, if the business is structured according to departments, where each department handles a set of business processes, then the business system design group should organise itself in the same way. This has the consequence that business system architects are in fact requirements engineers for particular business departments. They build a relationship with that department in which they build up implicit knowledge of user requirements, and develop an early warning system for impending changes in user requirements long before these changes are ratified officially.

The importance of such a relation was emphasised in one of the case studies we did. The organisation in question was divided into a number of departments, all of which served a specific part of the company's market. The IT department was organised according to the company's structure: for each department there was a business unit in the IT department that handled all IT-related work for the specific department. Each unit had its account managers, architects, software developers, and maintenance personnel. The advantage of structuring the IT department in such a way is that specific knowledge about a department is concentrated in one business unit.

At a certain point in time the IT department was reorganised according to the software development process. All account managers were put in their own business unit, as were all architects, software developers, and all maintenance personnel, respectively. The original idea was that each member of a business unit (e.g., an architect) could be assigned to projects of different departments, depending on availability of personnel within the business unit. Note that this is in contrast to Conway's law, and in practice meant that specific knowledge of a department's market was no longer available within projects. This problem was solved informally by forming teams within the business units, each of which (again) serving a specific department. When a project is started from a certain department, personnel from the related team are assigned to this project. Although the teams are informal units (and cannot be found on the organisation chart), the relation between the departments and people designing systems for these departments is restored, thereby confirming Conway's law.

10.3.6   The FMO Alignment Pattern

There are very few alignment patterns to be found at the business level. Nevertheless, one pattern can be widely observed, not because it is a fact of nature that will emerge in any case, but because it is a pattern consciously strived for by many businesses. This is the front-office/mid-office/back-office pattern, or the FMO pattern for short. An example of this pattern for the insurance business is given in Fig. 10.13. In the back office, operational excellence is obtained by managing large volumes of cases under white-label products that could be supplied as services to various insurance businesses. The front office, by contrast, presents branded products to its customers and focuses on customer intimacy (Treacy and Wiersema 1997). The mid office acts as an interface between the two and takes care of workflow, quality assurance, and other process-related matters.

10.4   The Architecture Process

Alignment is not just a matter of correctly coupling the diverse types of systems in the social, symbolic, and physical worlds of an enterprise, but also a matter of adjusting the development and management processes responsible for these systems.

10.4.1   Methods

The architecture design methods in the organisations studied by us were all based on information engineering, itself a method developed in the 1970s (Martin 1982,

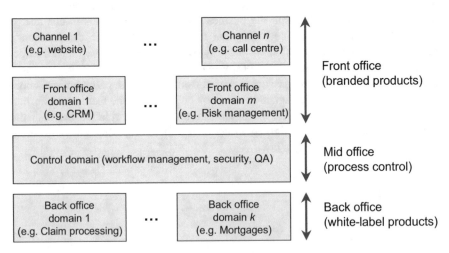

Fig. 10.13   The front/mid/back-office organisational pattern

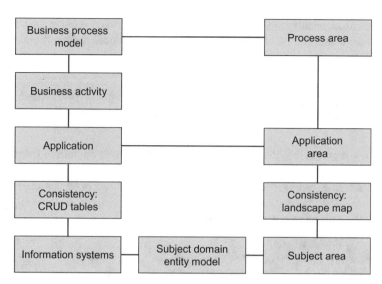

Fig. 10.14 Products delivered by an information-engineering-like method

1989; Sanden and Sturm 1997). The products delivered by an information-engineering-like method are shown in Fig. 10.14. In order to get a list of applications and information systems, a business process model is delivered. This may be represented by a simple bulleted list of activities, or it may be a complex UML diagram of activities and objects passed around among activities.

Our observation about business process modelling is this:

Proposition 9 The more complex a process modelling notation, the more decisions must be made to build the model, and the more errors are made in the model.

While some complex and mission-critical business processes may require a complex notation, we think that many business processes are not that complex and can do with a simpler notation. Process notations such as Testbed (Eertink et al. 1999) or the ones used in the area of process management may be suitable (Hardjono and Bakker 2001; Velzen et al. 2002).

Whatever the case, the business process model yields a list of business activities to be supported, and for each of these an application may be acquired to support executing the activity. Applications use data, and this is stored in information systems. In order to find the relevant information systems, the subject domain of the business processes is modelled, usually in an entity model. The subject domain of a business process is the part of the world about which the process needs data. Consistency between applications and information systems is maintained by means of CRUD tables or similar techniques. Because all of these models must show a lot of information, usually abstractions are made in the form of process area models, application area models, and subject area models. Our observation is that mutual consistency among all these models is never obtained.

> **Proposition 10** Consistency among process models, application models, and subject domain models is never achieved completely.

The reason for this is that these models represent a large amount of information that is managed and owned by different organisational actors who do not coordinate all their activities among each other. There are just too many organisational change processes going on concurrently to keep all models mutually consistent. In this context, the following observation is relevant:

> **Proposition 11** Current architecture methods and notations are too complex and inflexible to be used in the current dynamic business environment.

Notations like UML are at most used very fragmentarily, and architecture methods, if used at all, are used very opportunistically. There is a need for lightweight methods and techniques for architecture design. Furthermore, none of the organisations we studied incorporated techniques to deal with cross-organisational IT. Nevertheless, cross-organisational IT has been important since the rise of EDI in the early 1980s and the current trends in networked business, value networks, value chain automation, and outsourcing create an urgent need for incorporating network aspects in IT architecture alignment. Finally, the rapid rise of mobile and ubiquitous technology such as Radio Frequency Idenfication (RFID), cell phones, and wireless PDAs create an additional need to get to grips with the alignment between software infrastructure and physical infrastructure. With mobile technology, the physical location of software is important and this has consequences for the services offered by mobile technology, as well as for the management of this technology.

10.4.2   IT Governance

IT governance is the activity of controlling IT. It consists of making decisions about acquisition, change, and disposal of IT, as well as monitoring IT performance data in order to be able to control IT more effectively and efficiently. IT governance is part of corporate governance. As we discussed in Chap. 1, recent developments such as the Sarbanes–Oxley Act in the USA and the Basel II agreements in the financial sector have brought corporate governance, and in its wake IT governance, to the centre of attention of management of large corporations.

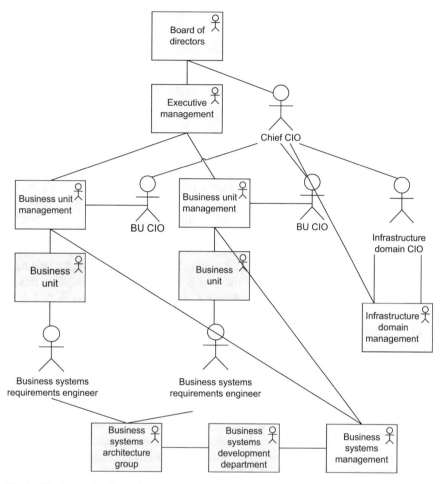

Fig. 10.15 A sample of coordination relations to manage. Each *line* represents one coordination relation

We view IT governance as a coordination problem. Some of the relationships to be coordinated in IT governance are shown in Fig. 10.15. In different companies, different organisational entities are involved, but usually there are executive management, CIOs, business units, and IT architects involved. Whatever the configuration of managers, committees, and other stakeholders, we can make one simple generalisation from our cases studies: architecture design is a top-down process that conflicts with the local interests. This tension occurred in all organisations studied by us as a tension between the architects of the business system layer and project managers who implement one particular business system.

Proposition 12 Architecture design of the business system layer uses global optimisation criteria. Architects of individual systems within the business system layer use optimisation criteria that are global for their project, but local for the business system layer.

The architecture of a business system layer is designed with global cost reduction in mind. This always requires reuse of components in different systems, or the imposition of standards that globally make sense but locally may seem awkward to follow. When an individual system is designed, the project manager or business unit manager responsible for the project will always find good reasons why this globally optimal design is not optimal for his or her system, and will try to get around the global architecture. The only way around this tension is to make the project manager directly accountable to someone responsible for maintaining the global architecture, such as the chief CIO in Fig. 10.15. In practice, the project manager often comes from a business unit and is accountable to a BU manager. This then leads to the conflict between local and global optimisation. In the USA, this is identified as a major concern. The Clinger–Cohen Act of 1996 (see Sect. 1.4.2), which aims to establish better IT governance in government agencies, tries to improve the situation somewhat by giving explicit responsibility for a coherent project portfolio to the CIO.

IT governance is currently for a large part addressed from the perspective of management science. This means that solutions for IT governance are sought solely in the business domain, e.g., by organisational change (as required by the Clinger–Cohen Act, for example), by control frameworks such as COBIT (see Sect. 2.1.5), but also by improving personal skills of CIOs and architects. It is doubtful whether this is sufficient. In addition to the management science approach, research is needed to develop an engineering approach that seeks to develop IT architectures with attention to governance at all stages of the system life cycle and for all layers, from IT infrastructure to the business layer.

10.5 Summary

We presented a framework for describing alignment phenomena consisting of three system dimensions: system aspects (services, behaviour, communication, semantics, and quality), system aggregation, and system life cycle states. The fourth dimension of our framework is not about systems, but about system descriptions, and concerns the abstraction level at which we describe systems. We have used this framework to analyse six cases of architecture alignment in large organisations in the government and finance sector. In all these organisations, IT architecture has a layered service provision structure. The infrastructure layer contains systems that must be available for all users; the business system layer contains systems available for particular business processes. Business systems have a tendency to gravitate towards the infrastructure layer. Because infrastructure is driven, among others, by the business strategy, and the business system layer is driven primarily by the actual business operations, there is usually a misalignment between these two layers. By Conway's law, this misalignment in the software architecture corresponds to a misalignment among system development departments. Most organisations structure their infrastructure layer into a number of technology domains, and structure their business system layer into a number of business domains. This roughly corresponds to a front/mid/back-office structure where the front office contains the business-specific systems and the back office contains generic, white-label systems.

Chapter 11
Tool Support

Hugo W.L. ter Doest, Diederik van Leeuwen, Peter Fennema, Leon van der Torre, Andries W. Stam, J. Jacob, and Farhad Arbab

11.1   Reasons for Enterprise Architecture Tooling

There are a number of reasons for dedicated tool support for enterprise architecture. First of all, tools help to standardise the semantics and notation of architecture models. If the use of tools is accompanied by proper training and education, a company-wide introduction of a tool (or set of tools) is a big step towards standardisation of the architecture languages and practice within the organisation. Second, tools can support the design of correct and consistent models through automated constraint checking and application of architecture principles. Third, tools can support the architect in the application of architecture patterns and reuse of components and solutions already in use in the organisation. Fourth, tools can support the comparison of alternatives, comparison of 'as is' and 'to be' situations, impact-of-change analysis and quantitative analysis of models. Moreover, tools can

H.W.L. ter Doest
Dimpact, Enschede, The Netherlands

D. van Leeuwen (✉)
BiZZdesign, Enschede, The Netherlands
e-mail: d.vanleeuwen@bizzdesign.com

P. Fennema
Freelance, Enschede, The Netherlands

L. van der Torre
University of Luxembourg, Luxembourg, Luxembourg

A.W. Stam
Almende, Rotterdam, The Netherlands

J. Jacob
Centrum Wiskunde & Informatica, Amsterdam, The Netherlands

F. Arbab
University of Leiden, Leiden, The Netherlands

© Springer-Verlag Berlin Heidelberg 2017
M. Lankhorst et al., *Enterprise Architecture at Work*, The Enterprise Engineering Series, DOI 10.1007/978-3-662-53933-0_11

support migration paths from the current situation to a newly designed 'to be' situation.

Modelling tools are of course an important category of tools for enterprise architecture, but not the only category. Architecture models need to be stored somehow for later reference, and it must be possible to publish architectures to other stakeholders. Support for enterprise architecture can therefore be subdivided into the following categories:

– Modelling and design: Tools that support modelling and design of architecture models.
– Reporting and publication: Tools that allow the design, either interactively or through configuration, of reports and viewpoints for specific stakeholders.
– Storage and retrieval: Metadata repositories that store meta-models, models, and viewpoint specifications.

11.2   The Architecture Tool Landscape

The market for enterprise architecture tools has matured over the last few years. However, the number of tools available is still fairly limited compared to e.g. software development tools, and those available often suffer from limited interoperability with other tools. Furthermore, tools presented as tools for enterprise architecture sometimes originated as domain-specific tools developed for purposes such as configuration management, software development or business process design. This origin is often reflected in their approach to enterprise architecture.

Weak interoperability between tools has both a technical and a conceptual aspect. Technically, tools are not designed with interoperability in mind. Of course, many tools have the ability to import or export XML Metadata Interchange (XMI) (Object Management Group 2015b) for UML, and some have features to import file formats of other tools. However, often these functionalities have the sole purpose of facilitating the migration from one modelling tool to another. Conceptually, tools are built for creating models in a specific modelling domain, and not for modelling relations to models or objects outside that domain. Depending on the starting point for setting up tool support for enterprise architecture, a number of tool categories are of interest (Fig. 11.1):

– Enterprise architecture modelling tools: Tools for enterprise architecture support the complete range of architecture domains, in most cases at a higher abstraction level than domain-specific tools.
– IT management tools: These tools are geared towards managing the IT assets of the enterprise, sometimes called portfolio management tools.
– Software design and development tools: These are software modelling tools that extend their scope to business process modelling and enterprise architecture modelling by adding concepts and diagram types.

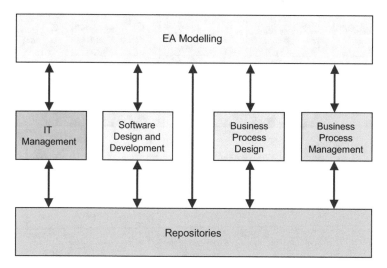

Fig. 11.1   Tool categories

- Business process design tools: Similar to the software modelling tools, business process modelling tools extend their scope with IT-related concepts and higher-level concepts for enterprise architecture modelling.
- Business process management tools: These are aimed at the operational management of business processes, e.g., by providing process measurements and other management data.
- Repositories: Metadata repositories and IT management tools that add modelling and analysis capabilities that partly cover the functionality expected from enterprise architecture modelling tools.

11.3   Tool Infrastructure

In order to make our vision tangible, we have defined a reference architecture that integrates both domain-specific tools and (new) tools for enterprise architecture. The foundation of the architecture is a repository for storage and retrieval of models, meta-models, viewpoint specifications and views. Another key element of the architecture, although not explicitly mentioned, is a language for describing enterprise architectures that enables integration of existing domain-specific architectures, architecture design and analysis, decision support and communication.

This tool infrastructure is depicted in Fig. 11.2. The Enterprise Architecture Service Layer in between the repository and the enterprise architecture tools at the top provides services for the manipulation of models and views:

- selection of content from domain-specific and enterprise architecture models;

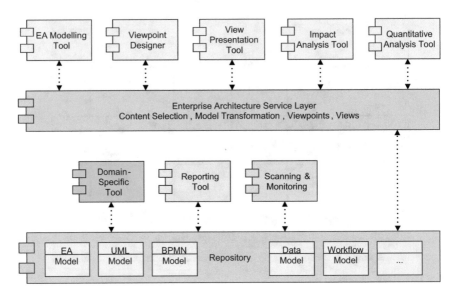

Fig. 11.2 Tool infrastructure for enterprise architecture

- transformation of domain-specific models to an enterprise architecture language and vice versa;
- creation and maintenance of views;
- specification and management of viewpoints.

The infrastructure outlined here requires the integration of existing tools with a repository, and the integration of enterprise architecture tools with the Enterprise Architecture Service Layer. Technically, the integration of tools can be characterised by the following aspects (Schefstroem and Broek 1993):

- Data integration addresses the issue of sharing data between tools and the storage of diagrams, models, views, and viewpoints.
- Control integration addresses the issue of communication and coordination between tools (and the integration framework, if existent).
- Presentation integration concerns the user interaction with the integrated set of tools. Some frameworks completely wrap the existing interfaces whereas others keep original interfaces intact and offer integration through a repository (model integration).

This is similar to the well-known 'model–view–controller' pattern. In our vision, a well-integrated suite of cooperating enterprise architecture tools should address all three integration aspects. Based on the reference architecture from Fig. 11.2, the ArchiMate project defined a tool architecture for the so-called ArchiMate workbench that does exactly that.

11.4 Workbench for Enterprise Architecture

This section presents the software architecture for the ArchiMate workbench. First, a number of design principles are identified that guided the design, then we present the workbench architecture.

The most essential design principle behind the ArchiMate workbench is that *the workbench integrates existing modelling languages*. The workbench does not integrate existing modelling languages one-to-one, but brings them to the abstraction level of enterprise architecture, by translating them to one general modelling language as advocated by Creasy and Ellis (1993).

A second important design principle is that *the workbench is viewpoint driven*. The workbench serves as an instrument to construct views of existing or future models and a modelling tool at the same time. The starting point of each workbench session is a *viewpoint definition* that specifies how to visualise and model a view. Furthermore, *the workbench is transparent and extensible*. The workbench can open architectural constructs in their native modelling tools. In addition, new modelling languages and associated modelling tools can easily be integrated with the workbench.

The following subsections zoom in on model integration, viewpoint definition, transparency and extensibility, the workbench architecture, and finally exchange formats. A more elaborate explanation is given in Leeuwen et al. (2004).

11.4.1 Model Integration

To integrate existing models expressed in heterogeneous modelling languages, the ArchiMate modelling language described in Chap. 5 is used. The ArchiMate modelling language is not 'just another modelling language', but integrates existing, more specific modelling languages, as we have outlined in Sect. 5.1. Here, we will describe in more detail how this language integration can be realised in a tool integration environment.

To integrate fully a specific modelling language with the workbench, both a bottom-up and a top-down transformation are required between that language and the ArchiMate language. Due to the potentially different abstraction levels between a specific language and the ArchiMate language, a bottom-up transformation is likely to lose details and a top-down transformation is likely to be incomplete. In extreme cases a top-down transformation may only produce a template.

To reduce the abstraction mismatch, ArchiMate constructs may be specialised by means of 'is-a' relations. The workbench may still treat these constructs as native ArchiMate constructs, while at the same time the transformations to and from these constructs can be made more exact. For example, the ArchiMate construct *application component* may be specialised to *UML application component* in order better to match the UML construct *component* (Fig. 11.3). Such a specialisation may add attributes or assign a more specific semantics to the concept of component.

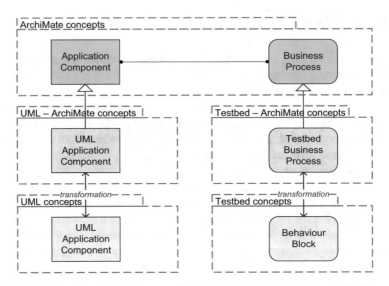

Fig. 11.3 Specialised ArchiMate constructs for UML and Testbed (Eertink et al. 1999)

11.4.2 Viewpoint Definition

As we have described in Chap. 8, a viewpoint is a pattern or template from which to construct individual views. A viewpoint establishes the purposes and audience for a view and the techniques or methods employed in constructing a view.

The ArchiMate workbench adopts an operational interpretation of viewpoints. A viewpoint consists of different types of rules governing the selection and presentation of view content, and controlling the interaction with, and interpreting changes to, the view presentation. Furthermore, a view might itself be based on another view, leading to a chain of views instead of a single step from a model to a view. Ultimately the distinction between model and view is rather arbitrary.

As the workbench aims to support the architecture design process, it focuses on the basic design viewpoints that are dedicated to the design process and were outlined in Sect. 8.5. These viewpoints consist of straightforward selection, presentation, interaction, and interpretation rules. In the context of the workbench, a design viewpoint simply defines which modelling constructs are allowed, with which symbols these constructs are presented, and which connections these constructs are allowed to have. Nevertheless the workbench may well serve as a starting point for more complex viewpoints that are based on more complex rules and designed to consult models rather than to manipulate models. In Sect. 11.5 we will focus in more detail on the design of such a more complex, interactive viewpoint infrastructure.

11.4.3   Transparency and Extensibility

To allow easy integration of new modelling tools, the workbench adopts an adapter pattern (Gamma et al. 1995) with the motivation that modelling tools should be made to integrate by means of 'plug and play'.

The workbench prescribes the tool adapter interfaces. The workbench trusts each adapter to be capable of bottom-up and top-down transformations, between the adapter's associated modelling language and the ArchiMate modelling language.

To obtain transparency, the workbench uses the tool-specific adapter associated with a modelling construct to open that modelling construct in its associated modelling tool.

11.4.4   Software Architecture

The workbench architecture consists of four tiers: a *tool tier*, an *integration tier*, a *view tier* and a *presentation tier* (Fig. 11.4). The main component in the workbench tier is the ArchiMate workbench: the workbench allows the manipulation of ArchiMate models. Each ArchiMate model conforms to an ArchiMate viewpoint that defines which modelling constructs are allowed, with which symbols these constructs are presented, and which connections these constructs are allowed to have. The *view presenter and interactor* is responsible for visualising the resulting view, and for interacting with the user. A specific implementation of the view manager and the view presenter and interactor is described in Sect. 11.5.

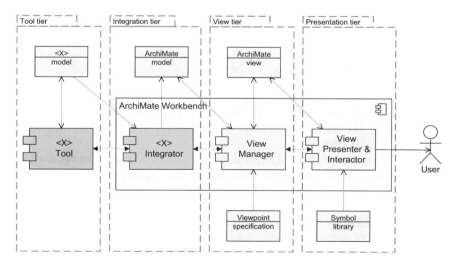

Fig. 11.4   The four-tier workbench architecture

In the tool tier, domain-specific modelling tools may be used to design tool-specific models according to a specific modelling language, such as UML or BPMN.

To allow ArchiMate models to elaborate upon or break down into tool-specific models, the integration tier links modelling tools and their languages to the ArchiMate workbench. The glue used is a tool adapter specific to each modelling tool: a *tool-specific integrator*. This integrator can perform transformations between tool-specific models and *ArchiMate models*. The ArchiMate workbench controls the integrator: the workbench dictates when to transform what models or what content and decides when to open a model in its native modelling tool.

11.4.5 Exchange Formats

ArchiMate models and integration content can be stored and exchanged using standard XML-based (W3C 2008) formats. These formats not only prescribe the way content should be formatted, but also provide a meta-language to express meta-information about the content, which helps to interpret that content. When a tool-specific integrator (see Fig. 11.4) provides integration content in XML, it uses this meta-language to express the integration schema, i.e. what modelling constructs that content uses. For example, a UML-specific integrator would use the meta-language to specify a schema with a UML-specific version of the ArchiMate concept *Application Component*.

Examples of XML-based exchange formats that come with meta-languages are XML itself, XMI (OMG 2015c) and OIFML (ODMG 2000). Corresponding meta-languages are XML Schema (W3C 2004) and ODL (ODMG 2000) respectively. For ArchiMate itself, The Open Group have published the XML-based ArchiMate Model Exchange File Format (The Open Group 2015).

11.4.6 Workbench at Work

To illustrate the value of the workbench, we present an example: an existing UML model and an existing Testbed model (Eertink et al. 1999) are integrated in an ArchiMate model (Fig. 11.5).

The UML model depicts a number of application components that are used by our imaginary insurance company ArchiSurance. The components are translated to ArchiMate components in a straightforward way. The Testbed model represents a number of process blocks that realise claim handling from registration to payment. This model is translated to ArchiMate concepts as well. Now, the workbench can be used to order the objects and define relations between them. In this case a layered architecture is created with services that are realised by components and provided to business processes. This results in a view relating business processes to IT

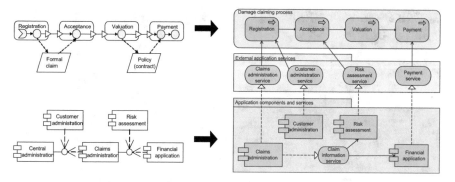

Fig. 11.5 An ArchiMate model (*right*) based on a Testbed model (*top left*) and a UML model (*bottom left*)

components by means of service concepts. The following operations are applied in the creation of the integrated model:

- **Translation**: The interface offered by the Claims administration component is translated to the Claim information service. UML dependency relations are translated to ArchiMate use relations.
- **Selection**: Mainly processes and components are selected. Several objects from the models on the left are not relevant in the ArchiMate model. For example, the Central administration component is left out because it is not used by the business process.
- **Extension**: Services offered by components to processes are added; concepts are grouped using ArchiMate grouping constructs.

The GUI of the workbench divides the application window into three frames (Fig. 11.6): a *content explorer*, a *canvas* for modelling and a *concept explorer*.

The canvas (centre) shows the currently opened ArchiMate model. Objects may be added to the model in two ways:

- Objects from the content explorer may be dragged and dropped onto the canvas. These objects are in fact references to objects in the underlying tool-specific models.
- Constructs from the concept explorer may be dragged and dropped onto the canvas. In this way, newly created instances of those constructs are added to the model.

The content explorer (left) shows hierarchical representations of the tool-specific models on which the currently open ArchiMate model is based. These tool-specific models have been translated into (possibly specialised) ArchiMate concepts, as was explained in Sect. 11.4.1. The concept explorer (right) shows only those concepts from the ArchiMate language that are relevant to the current viewpoint.

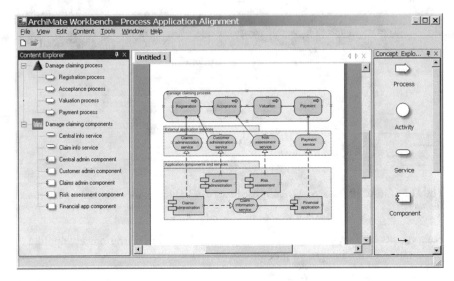

Fig. 11.6 Workbench user interface

11.5 View Designer Tool

The view designer tool supports the visualisation and editing of enterprise views
and forms a proof of concept of several key concepts introduced in this book, in
particular the separation of a model and its visualisation (Sects. 3.3 and 8.2) and
actions in models and views (Sect. 8.3). A viewpoint describes both model operations and visualisation issues. These two activities are strictly separated in the view
designer tool. It consists of two main interacting components, a *view manager* that
updates the views and models and a *view presenter and interactor* that visualises
the models and views and handles the interaction with the user (Fig. 11.7). These
components were also identified in the overall software architecture of the
ArchiMate workbench (Fig. 11.4).

A model or view contains not only concepts and relations, but also *actions* that
describe how the model or view can be changed. This includes a description of the
parameters needed to execute an action. The viewpoint specifies how these parameters can be collected, i.e., which input devices should be used and in which order
they should be invoked. Designing a viewpoint comes down to the following steps:

1. Define the static part of the viewpoint using viewpoint rules for the model and
   viewpoint rules for its visualisation.
2. For every model and view, define the actions that can change the model or view.
3. For every action, define which parameters it needs to have to be executed.
4. Define how these parameters can be collected.
5. Define the order of steps (protocol), including the use of virtual input devices
   (menus, text input, buttons, etc.), variables, and constants.

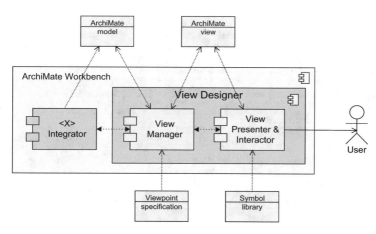

Fig. 11.7 High-level software architecture of the view designer

We illustrate the view designer by explaining how it has been used to develop the landscape map viewpoint introduced in Sect. 8.2.2. To understand how the view designer can be used, the user has to understand some technical details. For example, a model or view is represented in XML, and a viewpoint is based on XML transformations expressed as transformation rules (see also Sect. 11.4.2). We therefore also explain in this section how the designer realises the separation between model and its visualisation, and the use of actions in models and views. We do not discuss the reasons for a separation between a model and its visualisation, or the need for actions in models or views, as we have already explained these in Sects. 3.3, 8.2, and 8.3.

11.5.1 Viewpoint Rules for Creating Views and Visualisations

As outlined in the previous section, the first step we must take is to define the static part of a view and a viewpoint. When using the view designer, it is important to distinguish between the part of the viewpoint that is concerned with the models or views, and the part that is concerned with their visualisation. This is based on the distinction between the content of a model or view and its presentation or visualisation, as described in Sect. 8.2. When designing views and viewpoints, it is important to distinguish the two. Typically, first the models and views are defined, and only in a second phase their visualisation. Models and views should not contain visual references ('above'), but should be phrased in semantically meaningful terms ('more important'). Moreover, there are typically multiple visualisations of the same model, either to satisfy distinct stakeholders or to address distinct concerns.

In the landscape map viewpoint, the viewpoint rules for creating a view define a three-place relation from the relation available in the model. The three-place

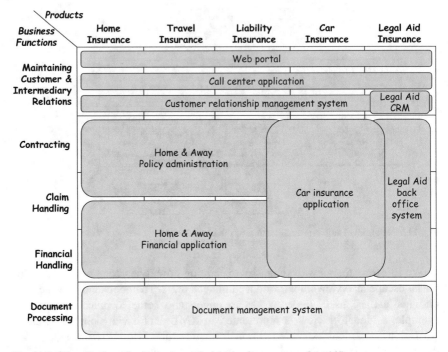

Fig. 11.8 Visualisation of a three-place relation: landscape map of ArchiSurance

relation details, for each pair of product and business function, which applications are used. The viewpoint rules for visualisation map this three-place relation to visual objects, like those depicted in Fig. 11.8.

In the software architecture of the view designer, the conceptual distinction between a model and its visualisation has led to a distinction between a view manager and a visualisation engine: the view manager updates the views and models, and the view presenter and interactor visualises the models and views and handles the interaction with the user.

11.5.2   Defining Actions in Models and Views

Having defined the static part of the viewpoint, we define the dynamic part. In Sect. 8.3 we introduced the concepts and the rationale behind embedding action in models and views. The basic idea is that enterprise models contain information about how the enterprise might change. For example, an organisation may specify what happens when two departments are merged. In the view designer, such changes to an enterprise can be mapped to meaningful actions in views, which are represented as action names with lists of parameters and their types. For example, a 'merge' action may exist with parameters to specify which departments should be merged. The viewpoint also contains a mapping from these parameters to (virtual) input devices. A department can be identified by entering its name, or by using the mouse to click on it. Finally, the viewpoint contains a routine name that should be executed (with the collected parameters as inputs) when the action is carried out. This routine defines the actual (XML) transformation of the view content. For example, when two departments are merged, the routine also specifies what happens with relations of the old department, which may or may not become relations of the newly created department.

It would not be feasible to construct all kinds of meaningful actions from scratch, therefore we first define atomic actions and thereafter composite actions. The basic atomic actions usually come down to adding and deleting concepts and relations. However, it is good practice to define the actions in model as meaningful operations from a business perspective: for example, as creating a new department, hiring a new employee, etc. Furthermore, we define a set of actions for each viewpoint. For example, for the landscape map viewpoint we define the move of an application to another cell, we define changing the columns and rows of the matrix, and we define the addition and deletion of applications. We determine for each action what kind of parameters it needs as input, and define the consequences of executing the action.

Next, larger actions can be defined as compositions of these atomic actions. For example, consider a view in which we define the action 'Decrease the average wage'. We can define this action in terms of actions on the underlying model containing the wages of the employees. For example, we can define this complex action as firing the boss, or decreasing everyone's wages by some percentage.

During this specification of the dynamic part of the model, in which we define the actions in models and views, we still have to respect the separation of the model or view from its visualisation as we already discussed for the static part. The actions should be defined in terms of concepts of the model, not in terms of interaction with the user—just like the static concepts and relations of a model should not be defined in terms of visual elements like boxes and lines. For example, the specification of an action should not deal with interaction issues such as the ordering of the values of the parameters of the action, how the values for the parameters are collected, when the action is evoked, why the action is evoked, etc.

For example, let us again consider an architect or stakeholder who wishes to change an existing landscape map. First, the effects of this change on the underlying model need to be assessed. Some changes may be purely 'cosmetic' in nature, e.g., changing the colour of an object. Other changes need to be propagated to the underlying model, e.g., if an object is added or deleted.

As a more complex example, consider a view of a business process model, and an action that merges two processes into a single process. Parameters of these action are two identifiers for the processes to be merged. Issues which are relevant for the action of merging processes are the effects of the merger: for example, the removal of processes, addition of a new process, transferring some relations from the old, removed process to the new process. Issues such as which processes are merged, when processes are merged, and why processes are merged, are not relevant for the specification of the action itself, but are part of the interaction with the user.

11.5.3   Interactive Visualisation

In the view designer, we have to bring the actions to life. Here, traditional
visualisation techniques are not sufficient. We need an interactive type of visualisation and we also need interactions with the user, for instance, to obtain values for
the parameters of the action. For example, when merging two business processes, it
is the user who decides which processes have to be merged, and when.

A crucial mechanism underlying the actions is the protocol for interaction
dialogues. For example, assume that the editor visualises the landscape map actions
as a set of buttons, and that pressing a button triggers the associated interaction
protocol. If the user presses the button for adding an object on the X-axis, the
system responds with a question for the name of the object, and asks the user where
the new column must be added. Clearly, there are also interactions that are not
visualised by buttons. For example, the action 'change columns' is typically
triggered by a user clicking on the column to be moved. If we look at the interaction
of the user with the landscape map editor in more detail, we can distinguish the
trigger, the atomic steps and the protocol:

1. Typically, the dialogues start with a trigger from the user, such as pressing a
   button on the screen.
2. The dialogue may contain several atomic interactions. For example, when an
   item is added to an architecture, there are atomic interactions of selecting the
   kind of item, typing in the name of the item, pointing at a place on the canvas
   where the item should appear, etc.
3. The protocol states in which order the atomic interactions should be done. We
   assume that the protocol consists of a complete ordering of atomic interactions,
   such that each new atomic interaction can be done only when the previous one
   has been finished.

For example, when a user presses a 'delete' button, the editor asks the user which
object is to be deleted (Fig. 11.9).

An example of interaction with a landscape map view that is concerned with
both the view and the underlying model is represented in the sequence diagram of
Fig. 11.10. The user presses the delete button, and the landscape view asks which
application should be deleted. The user clicks on an application, which we
abstractly describe by *use(a,b,c)*. Now for the system to delete this relation from

Fig. 11.9 Interaction with
landscape view

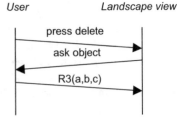

Fig. 11.10 More complex interaction with landscape view and underlying model

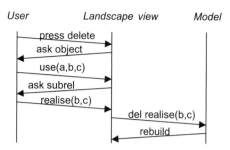

the model, it can, due to the construction of our relation, use from *support* and *realise*, either delete *support(a,b)* or *realise(b,c)*. When the user has selected *realise (b,c)*, the action *del* in the model is called, and finally the landscape map is rebuilt.

Actions may be interpreted in different ways, depending on the stakeholder and his or her role. The user in Fig. 11.9 is presumably allowed to change the underlying model. However, we can block this permission by updating the action in the view such that the *del-realise(b,c)* is not triggered by the *delete* action. Since the actions are specified in the view, and not in the landscape map tool, this blocking can be realised by another landscape map action.

11.5.4 Example: The Landscape Map Tool

The first contours of a landscape map are usually drawn on a whiteboard, flip-over, or piece of paper. Together with the stakeholders the architect tries to address their concerns. The map should be such that it concentrates on the choices that must be made. The drawing must also be such that consequences are visible. In this interaction the architect chooses the concepts on the axes and the plane, and the level of detail, leaving out the facts that are less important. For the sake of readability and acceptance the architect juggles a little bit with the (unwritten) rules of the landscape map. With pen and paper this can obviously be done.

Back at the desk and using the tool we envisage, the landscape map must be constructed in a more formal way. First, the architect needs to select the type of concepts used on the X-axis, on the Y-axis and on the plane (see Fig. 11.11). In our ArchiSurance example, the X-axis contains products, the Y-axis signifies business functions, and the plane holds applications.

Next, the objects on these axes must be chosen (the $X_1, \ldots, X_m$ and $Y_1, \ldots, Y_n$ in the figure). If a landscape map is used to define a new architecture, these objects can be freely chosen (of course conforming to the type of the axes). Alternatively, if an existing model is visualised they may be selected from this model. By choosing the concepts for the axes the playing field is defined.

After this, the architect must choose the type of assertions that are made by putting an object Z_k somewhere on the plane, i.e., the relations R_1 and R_2. In our example, the architect chooses business functions on the vertical axis, products on the horizontal

Fig. 11.11 Elements of a
landscape map

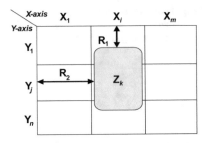

axis, and applications on the plane. The most obvious, intuitive assertion is that an
application is used by activities required within the business function in realising the
product, giving us $R_1 = support$ and $R_2 = realise$. For every object the architect
places on the plane, these relations between X_i, Y_j, and Z_k are instantiated.

Furthermore, if the rectangle of the application Z_k is not exactly aligned within a
row and/or column, then the relations with the X and Y elements are in a sense
'incomplete'. For example, an application may deliver only some of the functionality needed to support a business function.

The landscape map editor can be described in terms of a number of basic actions
that can be performed on the map. The initial state of the landscape map editor is an
empty canvas. However, the landscape map view is not empty. It contains actions
for selecting the type of concepts on the X-axis, on the Y-axis, and on the plane.
Once these have been selected, a new view is created which contains actions that
allow the user to select and draw the applications, such as the following:

- Draw a rectangle (rubber band) covering one or more cells of the map. A user
  may choose the colour and assign an object (instance of a concept) to the
  rectangle.
- Extend an existing rectangle with another rectangle that overlaps the original.
  Colour and label are inherited.
- Modify a rectangle, e.g., its coverage, colour, and value.
- Delete a rectangle.

In this way, the landscape map actions work as a kind of bootstrapping mechanism for the landscape map editor. All interaction mechanisms are defined in the
actions, not in the editor itself. In other words, the editor is generic, and can be used
for any other task as well.

Generating a Landscape Map from the Model Moreover, a landscape map can
be generated from a model. In Fig. 11.12 a model is shown together with its
landscape map. The left canvas visualises five products on the left, five business
functions on the right, and ten application components in the middle. The right
canvas visualises a landscape map as before.

Each canvas has its own set of actions. Only the actions of the active canvas can
be invoked. Most actions are invoked by buttons on the left side of the figure, where
inactive buttons are shown in grey. If an action is invoked that changes the
underlying mode, such as deleting a component, then both views are regenerated
and redrawn.

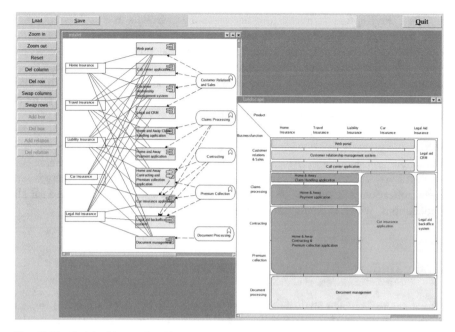

Fig. 11.12 Model with associated landscape map view

The user can add actions by adding them to the XML file that represents the view; for example, by adding a viewpoint rule with the desired effect. Thus, the user interface of the tool can be configured by the viewpoint being visualised, adding an extra layer of flexibility not normally present in typical modelling and visualisation tools.

11.5.5   Comparison with Model–View–Controller Architecture

If we compare our visualisation and interaction model with the popular model–view–controller or MVC architecture used in user interface frameworks, we see a number of differences. Consider an MVC architecture in which a model contains a description of the architecture, and the view is a landscape map. Moreover, assume that removing an object from the landscape map leads to several updates of the underlying model, maybe involving the same object, maybe involving only other objects. The effect of this interaction is defined in the controller. The point of the MVC pattern is that it is good software engineering practice to separate these concerns of storing a model in a database, and updating the database.

According to Eriksson and Penker (1998, pp. 219–222), the MVC architecture may be seen as an instance of the Core-Representation pattern used in business modelling:

The Core-Representation pattern structures the essentials in a problem domain with the purpose of building well-structured and easily changeable models. The core objects of a business, such as debt, agreement, customer, product, delivery, and order, are objects that rarely change fundamentally; conversely, the representations of these objects often change or are extended. A modeller should take this into consideration and separate the core objects from their representations. This process is added by the Core-Representation pattern.

Summarising, in the MVC and CR patterns, one rightly discriminates among the model, the view (which contains both the selection and visualisation aspects), and the interaction. However, the interaction in the controller is typically domain- or application-specific. Our approach departs from this assumption in that there is not a controller for each application, but there is a generic controller to be used for all applications, which is configured by the actions in the views.

11.6   Impact-of-Change Analysis Tool

The impact-of-change analysis tool illustrates the way in which structural impact analysis of an architecture can be done. By 'impact analysis', we mean the following: given an entity within the architecture which is considered to be modified or changed, which other entities in the description are possibly influenced by this change?

Users can use the analysis tool for these kinds of analyses. They can open different views of an architecture and select a model element within one of these views. After that, the tool shows the impact a change to this model element would have on the architecture. It does this by analysing the direct and indirect relations between the selected model element and other model elements within the architecture.

Within the ArchiMate language, there are many different relations between concepts. The tool allows the user to select a subset out of the entire set of relation types. If a subset of relation types is selected, only relations of the types within the subset are involved in the impact analysis. By including or excluding certain relation types, architects gain insight into the mutual dependencies between the entities within an architecture.

The core of this analysis tool is the Rule Markup Language (RML) (Jacob 2004; de Boer et al. 2005). RML is an XML-based language for transforming XML documents. Whereas the existing transformation techniques for XML such as XSLT (W3C 1999) are geared towards syntactic transformation, RML is aimed at expressing mathematical and logical rules and transformations. It consists of a set of XML constructs that can be added to an existing XML vocabulary in order to define RML rules for that XML vocabulary. These rules can then be executed by RML tools to transform the input XML according to the rule definition.

Rules defined in RML consist of an antecedent and a consequence. The antecedent defines a pattern and variables in the pattern. Without the RML constructs for variables this pattern would consist only of elements from the chosen XML vocabulary. The pattern in the antecedent is matched against the input XML. The variables specified with RML constructs are much like the wildcard patterns like * and + and ? as used in well-known tools like grep, but the RML variables also have a *name* that is used to remember the matching input. If the matching of the pattern in the antecedent succeeds, the variables are bound to parts of the input XML, and they can be used in the consequence of an RML rule to produce output XML.

The main benefit of RML is its ease of use. In XSLT, for example, it is very hard to specify that the XML expression

```
<apply>
    <and/>
    <ci>P</ci>
    <ci>P</ci>
</apply>
```

meaning 'P AND P' in MathML, should be transformed into

```
<ci>P</ci>
```

according to the logic rule of 'AND-elimination'. This is because XSLT is targeted at transformations of single XML elements, not element patterns. In RML+MathML the antecedent of the 'AND-elimination' rule above is expressed as

```
<apply>
    <and/>
    <rml-tree name='A' />
    <rml-use name='A' />
</apply>
```

and the consequence as

```
<rml-use name='A' />
```

where the tool applying this rule binds an XML tree to the variable 'A' at `<rml-tree name='A' />` and then later uses that variable to match and reproduce. In the above example variable A will be bound to `<ci>P</ci>`.

Rules for static analyses such as those described in Sect. 9.3.1 can be expressed in RML, and the RML rules engine embedded in the impact-of-change analysis tool applies these to an XML representation of the architecture to arrive at the analysis results. As in the ArchiMate workbench described in Sect. 11.4, the analysis tool is viewpoint based, and RML specifications of viewpoints are used to extract the relevant views from an underlying architecture model.

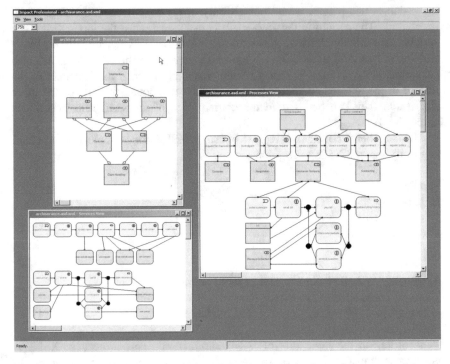

Fig. 11.13 The impact-of-change analysis tool showing multiple views of the same model

The following two figures illustrate the use of the analysis tool. Within Fig. 11.13, three different views of a certain architecture are shown. Note that the views overlap, which is allowed: the same model elements can be included in more than one view.

If we select one of the model elements, we get the picture of Fig. 11.14. Within this figure, all instances that are directly or indirectly related to the selected model element are coloured red. The selected model element itself is coloured dark red, in order to distinguish it from the model elements on which it has impact.

11.7   Quantitative Analysis Tool

To validate the quantitative analysis techniques described in Chap. 9, a prototype was built and applied in practice. This quantitative analysis prototype consists of two components:

– The *analysis component* implements the analysis algorithms. It reads an input model, normalises and analyses this model, and returns the original model extended with the values that resulted from the calculations. It can accept input models from file or from internal memory (string objects). The analysis logic is separated from the data source format by letting the logic operate on an

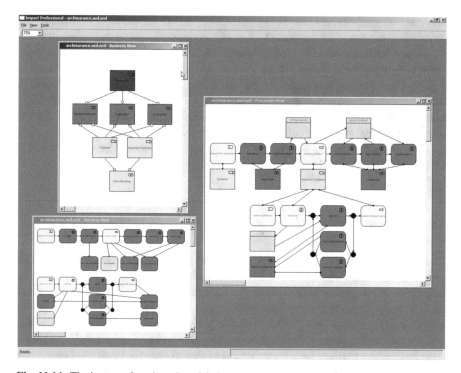

Fig. 11.14 The impact of a selected model element

interface that represents a model. Different data sources require different implementations of this interface, but the analysis logic is not affected.

– The *Web service component* wraps the analysis component into a web service that can be accessed remotely on the Internet by other applications. A user can start an analysis from the workbench by opening a model and selecting the 'Analyse content' menu item. The workbench submits the model to the Web service. This returns the analysis results, and the workbench presents the results to the user.

11.8 Commercial Tool Support for ArchiMate

Over the last years, we have seen a steady progression in the maturity of the enterprise architecture tool market. Although the vision outlined in the previous sections has yet not been realised fully, many available tools contain elements of this vision. The most prominent aspect in which they are still lacking is interoperability: most tools are relatively good at importing other file formats, but their support for exporting to (standardised) formats is often weaker. Hopefully, the ongoing standardisation efforts in this field will improve this situation.

We will not go into a detailed comparison of commercially available tools. Overviews of the enterprise architecture tool market are published by, for example,

Gartner (James 2008) and Matthes et al. (2008, 2014). At the time of writing, the ArchiMate language is supported in many commercially available architecture modelling tools, provided by companies such as Avolution, BiZZdesign, Corso, Orbus, Visual Paradigm and others.

The Open Group is responsible for certification of these tools with respect to their correct implementation of the language. There are other tools providing non-certified implementations, and there are also several open source implementations, of which Archi by the University of Bolton in particular deserves to be mentioned. Free sets of symbols for drawing tools such as Microsoft Visio and Omnigraffle are available from various sources.

11.9   Summary

In our vision, enterprise architecture will become a real-time tool for management and redesign of the enterprise for better performance, flexibility, and agility. The alignment of business and IT will be managed through a series of integrated views of the enterprise, each covering an appropriate set of concerns for the stakeholder addressed. To realise this vision, tool integration is of critical importance. We believe that tool support for enterprise architecture will not be realised by a single tool, but will be realised by a combination of domain-specific tools and enterprise architecture tools that add the enterprise architecture concepts and establish relations between domain-specific models.

The tool integration workbench we have presented is such an enterprise architecture tool that is able to integrate domain-specific models. Leaving existing modelling environments intact, the workbench allows the concurrent design of enterprise architecture domains: each domain may still be designed using its own languages, tools, and techniques. More importantly, with the ability to reason across domain boundaries the workbench introduces an instrument for collaborative design.

By adopting the ArchiMate modelling language, the workbench not only allows the integration of existing modelling languages, but provides a language to communicate across domain boundaries as well. Moreover, the workbench serves as a starting point for the analysis of enterprise architectures using generic analysis techniques that rely on the ArchiMate modelling language.

The view designer we described serves as a proof of concept of the separation of concerns, as it distinguishes the model, views of the model, visualisation, and interaction aspects. Moreover, it also serves as proof of concept for embedding of actions in models or views, which describe the dynamics of a model as an integral part of its semantics. These dynamics must be represented explicitly. The tool illustrates also that it is feasible to develop a very generic and therefore very powerful visualisation engine, which separates interaction from visualisation aspects. Moreover, the actions in models and views demonstrate the feasibility of interactive visualisation. In the tool these dynamic changes, such as hiring a new employee, are used via the visual interface. However, the changes could also be used by other programs.

The future of tool support for enterprise architecture requires better integration between the various tools used in the enterprise architecture field. The success of this integration depends heavily on standardisation organisations and tool vendors. Vendors of modelling tools need to standardise their modelling languages and concepts and also their interfaces and storage formats. Repository vendors need to offer 'model-intelligent' repositories and standardised interfaces and exchange formats for models.

Important steps in this direction have been taken, e.g. the MOF standard for repositories (Object Management Group 2015d) and the ArchiMate Model Exchange File Format (The Open Group 2015), but there is still a long way to go. Nevertheless, we see a clear evolution of the tools market and many tool suites are moving in a similar direction, with an increasing focus on the use of enterprise architectures for management purposes.

Chapter 12
Case Studies

Hans Bosma, Henk Jonkers, Math J. Cuvelier, Peter G.M. Penders, Saco F. Bekius, and Maria-Eugenia Iacob

12.1 Process and Application Visualisation at ABP

ABP is a pension fund for employees of the Dutch government and the educational sector. ABP is one of the largest pension funds in Europe with total assets of more than 156 billion euros serving more than two million customers.

In the year 1998, triggered by the millennium problem, ABP realised that a better grip was needed on the increasing complexity of the ICT situation. ABP decided to start an information planning and architecture program. Several products came out of this project, as follows:

– Architecture principles, such as:

   • a process starts with a client and ends with a client;
   • every process has a process owner;
   • the organisation works client-oriented;

H. Bosma
Ordina, Nieuwegein, The Netherlands

H. Jonkers (✉)
BiZZdesign, Enschede, The Netherlands
e-mail: h.jonkers@bizzdesign.com

M.J. Cuvelier
Retired, Heerlen, The Netherlands

P.G.M. Penders
Crescimento Universal, Amsterdam, The Netherlands

S.F. Bekius
Dutch Tax and Customs Administration, Apeldoorn, The Netherlands

M.-E. Iacob
University of Twente, Enschede, The Netherlands

© Springer-Verlag Berlin Heidelberg 2017
M. Lankhorst et al., *Enterprise Architecture at Work*, The Enterprise Engineering
Series, DOI 10.1007/978-3-662-53933-0_12

- ABP should not ask for certain information from clients if this information is already available within the organisation.
– An architecture vocabulary.
– An information systems blueprint to guide ICT development.

Some of the examples below are in Dutch, because they are taken from real-life data, but they serve to illustrate the type of diagram we are discussing.

12.1.1   ABP Meta-model

ABP divides the architectural universe of discourse into five domains: business, process, application, data and technology (Fig. 12.1). A further detailing in the form of a conceptual meta-model is shown in Fig. 12.2. Notice that the technology domain has not yet been covered by this meta-model.

From a first rough comparison with the ArchiMate meta-model (see also Fig. 5.4), the following differences can be identified:

– ABP uses a fixed decomposition of processes and systems, while ArchiMate uses a variable decomposition mechanism.
– The service concept is not used by ABP (although the *process implementation* concept comes close).
– The data domain of ABP has a more extensive set of concepts than the data domain of ArchiMate.
– ABP has no organisational concepts in its meta-model.

12.1.2   Case Essentials

ABP realised that keeping track of the current situation is an important requisite for disciplined ICT management. For that reason, ABP selected a repository in order to store metadata about ICT and in a later phase about other domains. The meta-model of Fig. 12.2 is used as the database scheme of this repository.

Fig. 12.1 ABP architecture domain model

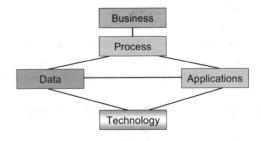

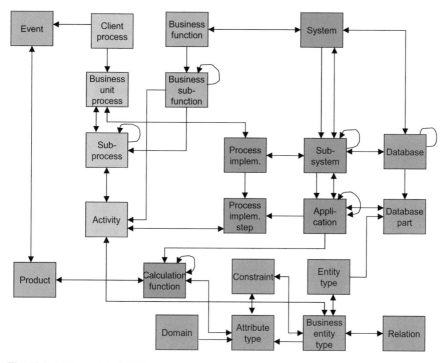

Fig. 12.2 Meta-model of ABP

The repository data is disclosed via a Web portal. However, a graphical presentation of the contents was missing, impeding the wider use of this information. Presentations could be made manually of course, but this requires a considerable effort. Therefore, ABP recognised a need for automatic generation of visualisations. To this end, a tool was built that generates visualisations of the data about information systems, interfaces, and databases. A typical example of such a diagram is shown in Fig. 12.3. For more information about this first ArchiMate case, we refer to Iacob and Leeuwen (2004).

Being able to visualise system information, ABP's next wish was to connect systems data with process data. However, information about processes was not yet stored in the repository: this process data was stored in a process modelling tool and in a workflow tool. Thus, the goal of the case was to integrate data from different sources and subsequently generate visualisations. The tool infrastructure was to be based on the generic ArchiMate concepts; hence an extra requirement was added, namely to map the (relevant parts of the) ABP meta-model to the ArchiMate meta-model.

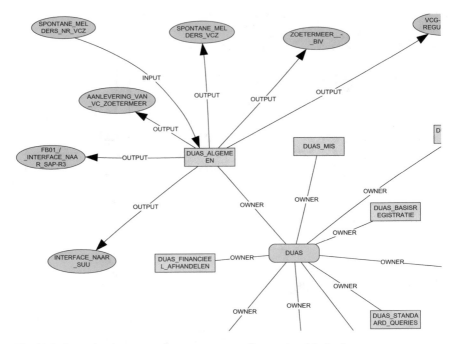

Fig. 12.3 Example of a generated system structure diagram (partial view)

12.1.3   Concepts

To connect system and process information, only part of the ABP meta-model was relevant (Fig. 12.4). The mapping of the ABP meta-model to the ArchiMate meta-model was achieved via an intermediary bridging level, a specialisation of the ArchiMate meta-model. Subtypes of *process* and *application component* are introduced, and the service concept is mapped onto *process implementation.*[1]

The concept mapping is depicted in Fig. 12.5. Note that the horizontal *use* relations are derived relations, based on the more detailed usage of *services* of an *application component* by a *business activity*.

12.1.4   Viewpoints

From the four types of design viewpoints identified in Sect. 8.5, the *Composition* and *Support* viewpoints are relevant to visualise the integrated process and system information.

---

[1]Actually, the relation between the concept *process implementation step* and the ArchiMate concept of a *service* is an indirect relation: the existence of a *process implementation step* is only an indicator that an *application service* is provided by an *application component*.

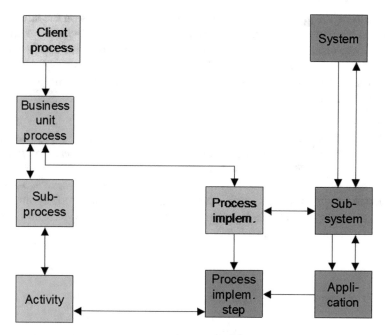

Fig. 12.4   Relevant parts of the ABP meta-model

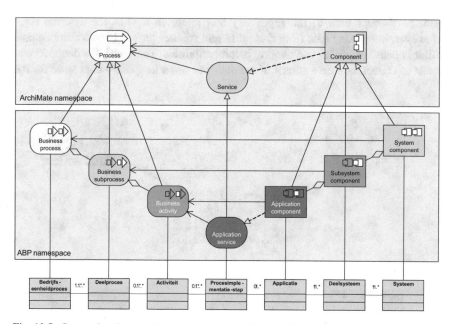

Fig. 12.5   Connecting the ArchiMate meta-model with the ABP meta-model

Composition Viewpoints The Composition viewpoints focus on the structure of processes and systems. The 'System component composition' viewpoint shows a *system component* or *subsystem component* and the *subsystem components* or *application components* it consists of (Fig. 12.6). The 'Business process composition' viewpoint shows a *business process* or *sub-process* and the *sub-processes* or *activities* it consists of (Fig. 12.7).

Support Viewpoints The Support viewpoints show the usage relations between processes and applications. The 'Business process dependencies' viewpoint shows a *business process*, *sub-process* or *activity* and the *system, subsystem* or *application components* it uses (Fig. 12.8). The 'Application component use' viewpoint shows a *system, subsystem* or *application component* and the *business process, sub-process* or *activities* it uses (Fig. 12.9). The 'Process–component relation' viewpoint zooms in on a particular *use* relation between a *system, subsystem* or *application component* and a *business process, sub-process* or *activity* (Fig. 12.10).

12.1.5 Design of the Visualiser

The overall design of the visualisation tool for ABP was based on the general workbench architecture described in Sect. 11.4. A logical first step in the integration of the different data sources mentioned in the previous section would have been to add the process data to the repository and integrate it with the systems data. However, integrating data from these different sources proved to be a cumbersome affair because of model and naming incompatibilities. Therefore, the decision was made to concentrate on a subset of the data and use a temporary data store for the

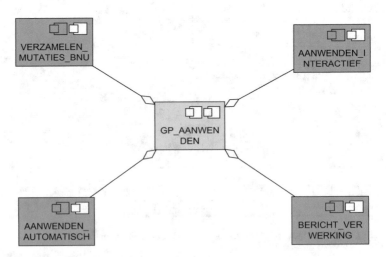

Fig. 12.6 A 'system component composition' view

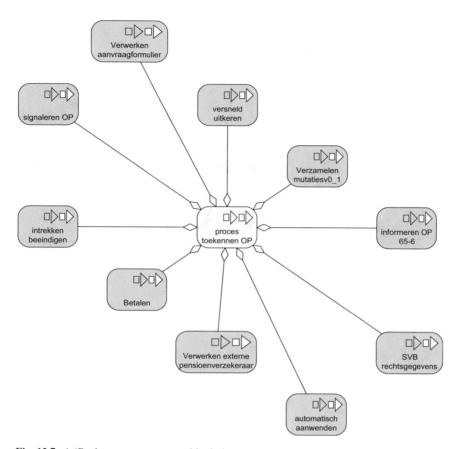

Fig. 12.7   A 'Business process composition' view

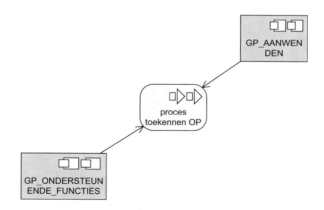

Fig. 12.8   A 'Business process dependencies' view

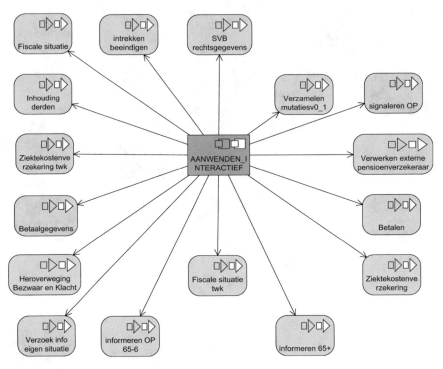

Fig. 12.9   An 'Application component use' view

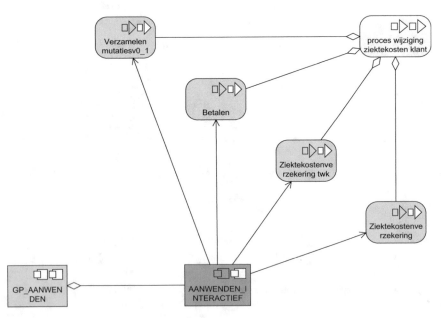

Fig. 12.10   A 'Process–component relation' view

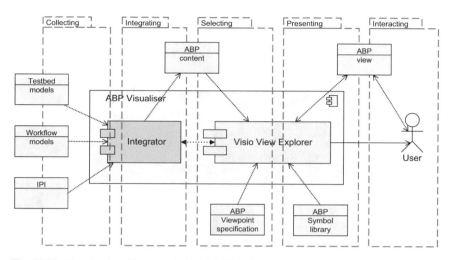

Fig. 12.11 High-level architecture of the ABP Visualiser

integrated data. The data integration itself was done by a technical integration component with data matching algorithms.

Collecting and integrating data are the first two steps of the process. Subsequently, data is selected and presented by the Visio View Explorer on the basis of user specifications. The high-level architecture of the visualiser is depicted in Fig. 12.11. In this figure, the different phases in creating a visualisation are shown. The Visio View Explorer is worked out in Fig. 12.12. The viewpoints are specified in an XML viewpoint configuration file. Together, these two figures are a specialisation of the generic architecture of the ArchiMate workbench shown in Figs. 11.4 and 11.7.

An important part of the generation of visualisations is creating the layout of diagrams. Diagram layout addresses the problem of positioning (possibly nested) boxes and connections on a canvas such that the resulting diagram becomes intuitively acceptable.

In our approach we confined the layout space to a two-dimensional grid. Such an approach is appropriate, because (1) a limited layout space speeds up the layout algorithm, and (2) using a grid causes the resulting diagram to have nicely arranged boxes. Roughly, our diagram layout strategy consists of (1) the estimation of the necessary grid size and (2) the actual positioning of boxes on the grid.

The actual positioning of boxes on the grid was done via a special purpose optimisation strategy.[2] It generates a layout by minimising the number of crossing connections, box–connection intersections, and the total length of all connections.

---

[2]The layout can also be created using general-purpose optimisation technology (e.g., genetic algorithms). We experimented with both the former and the latter, and finally opted for the latter. The main reason for opting for our own optimisation strategy was the problem of level interference: the quality of the visualisation is influenced by the layout of nested boxes.

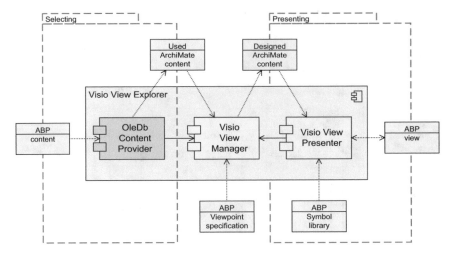

Fig. 12.12 Detailed design of the Visio View Explorer

Furthermore, it is possible to fix boxes in a certain position. In this way we realised a 'centred' diagram with one centre box and a 'flow' diagram with source and destination boxes.

A typical result is shown in Fig. 12.13: the use of a system component by business processes. A user then can navigate through the visualisations. For example, Fig. 12.13 shows a user zooming in on a particular relation, resulting in Fig. 12.14.

12.1.6   Case Study Results

The results of both case studies were received positively by ABP. Also, ABP's repository vendor recognised the added value of the case results and enhanced its (newly released) visualisation engine with the insights gained. Via the new repository functionality, ABP's system owners are now presented with visual representations of the systems for which they are responsible.

12.2   Application Visualisation at ABN AMRO

ABN AMRO is a global bank with a staff of more than 100,000 working in over 3000 branches in more than 60 countries. The bank has a federated, regionally distributed structure with its headquarters in the Netherlands.

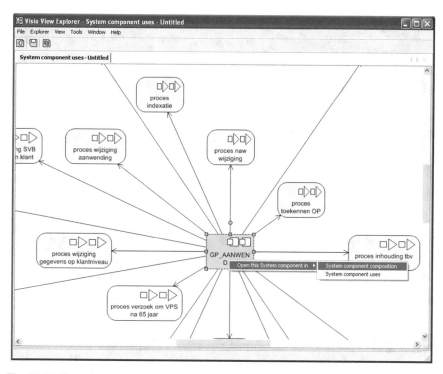

Fig. 12.13 Example: the use of a system component by business processes

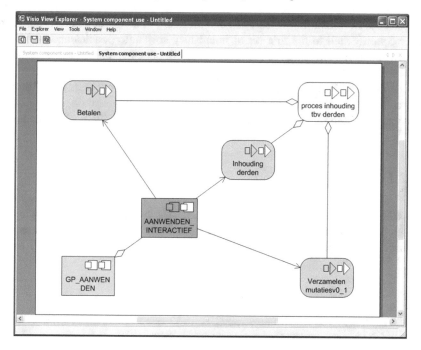

Fig. 12.14 Zooming in on a usage relation between a process and a system

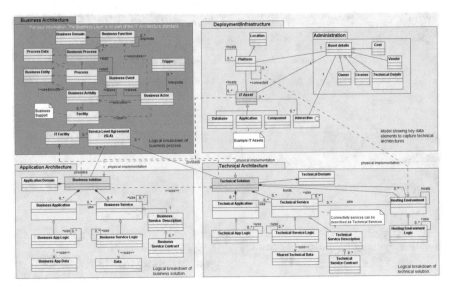

Fig. 12.15   ABN AMRO CITA meta-model

The bank started working with architecture in the middle of the 1990s. In 2000 this resulted in the first version of the Corporate IT Architecture (CITA) method, which primarily defines the organisation of architecture processes and a mandatory set of architecture concepts (in the form of an architecture meta-model). Soon after, a large-scale implementation of this method took place in the Netherlands. The experiences from that implementation and the setup of architecture departments in other countries led to the first set of mandatory corporate policies and standards (P&S) on IT Architecture, called CITA 2003. In 2004 implementation projects started in the USA and Brazil.

One of the P&S of CITA 2003 defines a set of architecture concepts in the form of an architecture meta-model. Another P&S specifies the communication of architecture deliverables, based on viewpoints and views (derived from the IEEE 1471 standard).

12.2.1   CITA Meta-model

The CITA meta-model is shown in Fig. 12.15.[3] The overall structure of this meta-model is very similar to the ArchiMate meta-model, with the service concept having a prominent role.

---

[3] Actually, the business process quadrant is not yet mandatory.

Table 12.1 Mapping of CITA meta-model to ArchiMate meta-model

CITA concept	ArchiMate concept
Business process	Business process
Business activity	Business activity
Business actor	Business actor
IT facility	Application service
Organisational domain	Grouping relation
Application domain	Grouping relation
Business solution	Application service
Business application	Application component + (External) service
Business service	Application component + (Internal) service
Business application logic	Application function
Business service logic	Application function
Business application data	Data object
(Enterprise) data	Data object

Several differences from ArchiMate are also apparent. For example, although in both meta-models the service concept is used, the meaning is subtly different. In ArchiMate a *service* is a conceptual notion; it does not have to correspond to a particular piece of software. In the CITA meta-model a *service* is an *invokable* piece of external functionality. The ArchiMate *service* concept resembles more the CITA *Business solution* concept and also its counterpart *IT facility*. Finally, the *domain concept* is important to assign domain owners and to group *business solutions* and *technical solutions*. In ArchiMate one would use a *grouping* relation to achieve this.

The case study described here primarily focuses on the business and application architectures. Based on the above explanation, a mapping between the CITA concepts and the ArchiMate concepts is presented for these quadrants in Table 12.1.

12.2.2 Case Essentials

The case study has been carried out in close association with the CITA architecture standard initiative and the work that the Business Unit C&CC (Consumer & Commercial Clients) Brazil, locally known as Banco Real, is doing in the architecture area.

The BU C&CC Brazil is in the process of setting up the architecture profession within the organisation. Currently, it has the following initiatives:

- Introduce the domain architecture function within the organisation.
- Create an application architecture strategy.
- Create a migration plan for this strategy.
- Make an inventory of the 'as is' situation from an application architectural point of view.

To support this last effort, BU C&CC Brazil collected information about its information systems using a comprehensive questionnaire. To improve the maintainability and accessibility of this data, a joint effort called CABRI, was set up by the Corporate Centre of ABN AMRO Bank between BU Brazil and ArchiMate. The target for CABRI was to capture essential architectural data from the questionnaire using CITA concept definitions, store them in a database, and generate visualisations based on predefined viewpoints.

12.2.3   Concepts

The CITA standard incorporates the basic principle of a service-oriented environment (SOE) in its meta-model by distinguishing *general-purpose* service components from *specific* business application components. In general this SOE is not yet implemented in full. The goal of applying the CITA meta-model to describe the current state of affairs in the BU Brazil was to identify the gap between the current state and the new application architecture strategy. Several adjustments to the CITA meta-model had to be introduced to show these potential areas for improvement (e.g., reusable functionality and data, ownership of business applications and business services).

Therefore, functionality of systems is split into external usable functionality (*services*) and internal functionality (*application logic*), and the databases are divided into two groups, namely those that contain general-purpose data (*enterprise data*) and those that contain local data (*business application data*). In making this distinction, one has the situation that *business applications* access *enterprise data*, and that *business services* access local *application data*, a situation that the CITA meta-model does not allow. In order not to lose this information, these two access relations need to be added temporarily to the CITA meta-model. The extended subset of the CITA meta-model used in this case study is shown in Fig. 12.16.

In the BU Brazil questionnaire, the primary concepts used were *Systems, Macro Functionality, Database, Domain,* and *Subdomain*. The mapping of these inventory concepts to the extended CITA meta-model is shown in Fig. 12.17. This mapping was used to translate the inventory concepts into CITA concepts, and also to facilitate communication with the Brazilian employees.

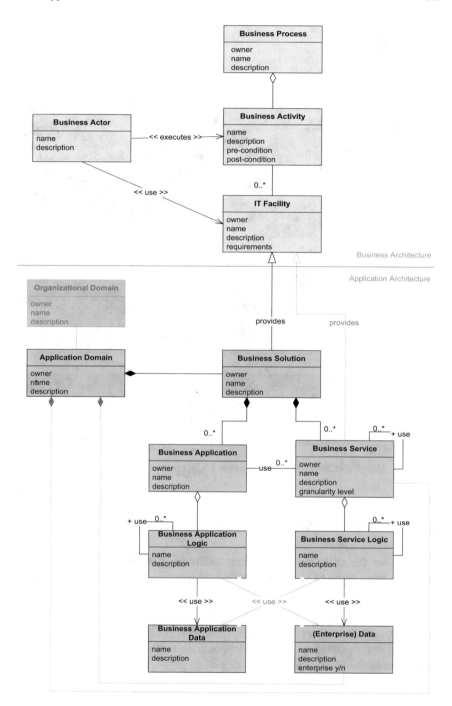

Fig. 12.16 Extended meta-model used in the case study

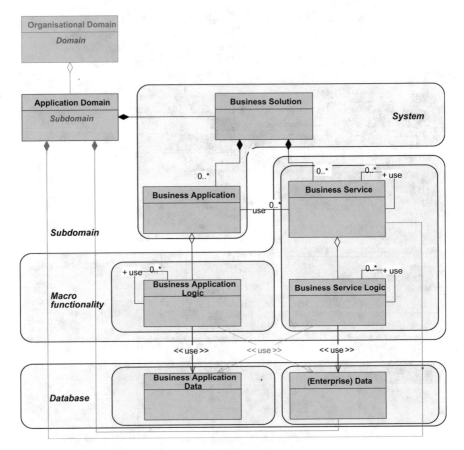

Fig. 12.17 Mapping of inventory concepts to the CABRI meta-model

12.2.4   *Visualisation*

To visualise the collected architectural information about the IT systems, the
following three types of viewpoints have been identified:

1. A global overview of the services and application components (landscape
   viewpoint).
2. Insight into the support of processes (process support viewpoint).
3. Insight into the relations between applications, services, logic, and data (coherence and dependency viewpoint).

Table 12.2 Concepts and their visual representation

Concept	Symbol	Concept	Symbol
Business process		Business solution	
Business actor		Business application	
Organisational domain		Multiple business applications	
Application domain		Business service	
Business application data		Business application logic	
(Enterprise) data		Business service logic	

The viewpoint description consists of a textual explanation accompanied by an example visualisation. The set of slightly modified ArchiMate symbols used is shown in Table 12.2.[4]

Since the examples used to illustrate these viewpoints in the next subsections are taken from real-life data, some of the text is in Brazilian Portuguese.

Landscape Viewpoints Landscape viewpoints show the overall application architecture, while abstracting from detailed information within these applications. Three different viewpoints have been used: Application domain landscape, Business service landscape, and Business solution landscape.

- The 'Application domain landscape' viewpoint shows *Organisational domains* and their containing *Application domains*. This viewpoint is mainly concerned with visualising (levels of) ownership (Fig. 12.18).
- The 'Business service landscape' viewpoint shows one *organisational domain*, with all its *application domains*, and all their *business services* (Fig. 12.19).
- The 'Business solution landscape' shows one *organisational domain*, with all its *application domains*, with all their *business solutions* (not shown here, but analogous to the previous figures).

---

[4]The concepts for business activity and IT facility are not used in these visualisations.

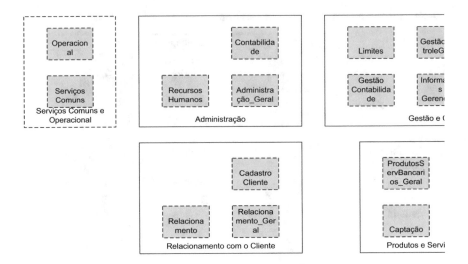

Fig. 12.18 An 'Application domain landscape' view (partial)

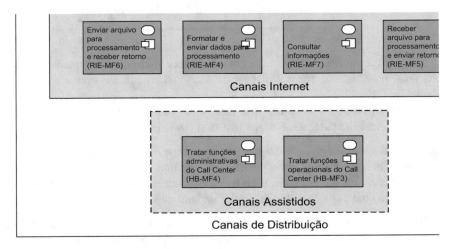

Fig. 12.19 A 'Business service landscape' view (partial)

Process Support Viewpoints Process support viewpoints facilitate insight into the relation between processes and applications.

Currently, only one viewpoint has been identified and worked out: the 'Business activity–business service alignment' viewpoint. This viewpoint shows one central *Business process*, together with the *Business activities* involved in that *Business process*. Each *Business activity* depicts the *Business services* that are used by it (Fig. 12.20).

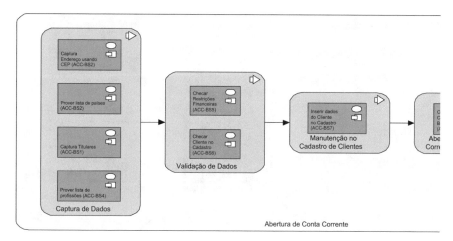

Fig. 12.20   A 'Business activity–business service alignment' view (partial)

Coherence Viewpoints   Coherence viewpoints facilitate insight into the coherence of the application architecture. They show how a particular element is used by other elements. Three coherence viewpoints have been worked out: Business service uses, Business application data uses, (Enterprise) data uses.

- The 'Business service usage' viewpoint shows one central *business service* surrounded by the *business applications* and *business actors* that use it (Fig. 12.21).
- The 'Business application data usage' viewpoint shows one central *business application data* entity surrounded by the *business application logic* entities and *business service logic* entities that use it (Fig. 12.22).
- The '(Enterprise) data usage' viewpoint shows one central *(enterprise) data* entity surrounded by the *Business application logic* entities and *Business service logic* entities that use the central data entity (not shown here, but analogous to Fig. 12.22).

Dependency Viewpoints   Dependency viewpoints facilitate insight into the dependencies of the application architecture. They show a central entity together with certain entities on which this central entity depends. The following viewpoints have been identified: Business application dependencies, Business application logic dependencies, and Business service dependencies.

- The 'Business application dependencies' viewpoint shows one central *Business application* surrounded by the *Business services* that are used by that central *Business application* (Fig. 12.23).
- The 'Business application logic dependencies' viewpoint shows one central *Business application logic* entity surrounded by the *Business application logic* entities, *Business application data* entities and *(Enterprise) data* entities that are used by the central entity (analogous to Fig. 12.23).

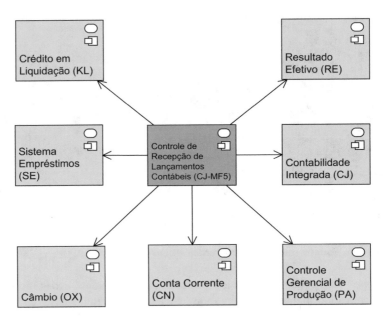

Fig. 12.21   A 'Business service usage' view

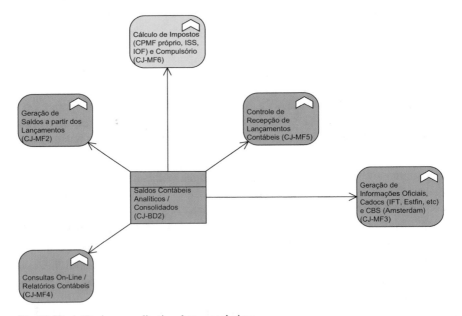

Fig. 12.22   A 'Business application data usage' view

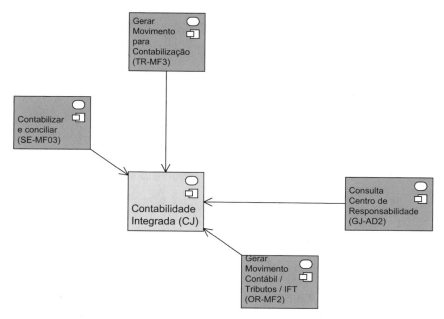

Fig. 12.23 A 'Business application dependencies' view

– The 'Business service dependencies' viewpoint shows one central *Business service* entity surrounded by the *Business service* entities, *Business application data* entities and *(Enterprise) data* entities that are used by the central entity (analogous to Fig. 12.23).

12.2.5 Tool Design and Results

As in the case of ABP, the ABN AMRO case study uses the generic tooling infrastructure described in Chap. 11. The way the tool is used in this case is shown in Fig. 12.24. Input of system information is not yet automated, since this is only available in the form of textual documents.

The practical results obtained with this visualisation infrastructure helped to clarify various misunderstandings and inconsistencies in the systems landscape. The visualisations are widely and interactively used in discussions about the current and future application architecture.

ABN AMRO BU Brazil decided to keep using the tool and implement it in the development organisation. It will capture systems that have not yet been assessed and will maintain the data already captured.

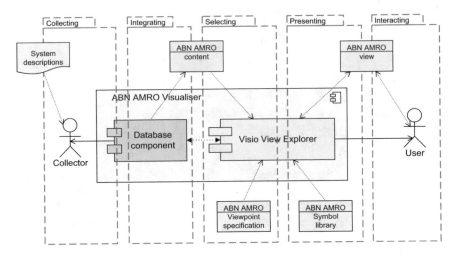

Fig. 12.24 Tool design

12.3 Design and Analysis at the Dutch Tax and Customs Administration

The Dutch Tax and Customs Administration (abbreviated TCA in the sequel) has a long history of continuously improving its organisation of process and ICT development. As early as the beginning of the 1980s, the ICT department started working with architecture. In the TCA architecture plays a prominent role, which is also exemplified by a total staff of over 100 architects. The importance of architecture has also increased the need for an enterprise architecture language to connect different architecture domains.

12.3.1 Case Essentials

In recent years, the organisation of social security in the Netherlands has changed dramatically. The goal is to arrive at a situation with a central contact point for organisations and citizens, and with unique 'authentic' data sources.

Within this context, the collection of employees' social security premiums is transferred from UWV (the central social security organisation) to the TCA. This joint project of TCA and UWV is called SUB ('Samenwerking UWV–Belastingdienst').

A major challenge in this project is to handle enormous flows of data within and among the different organisations. This concerns more than 600,000 payroll tax returns each month, a large proportion of which arrive within a peak period of a couple of days. Moreover, it is expected that a substantial proportion of these tax returns need to be sent back for correction. Such requirements need to be addressed early on in the project.

These aspects of this case study made it an ideal proving ground for the modelling language, viewpoints, and performance analysis techniques described in previous chapters. In the next subsections, we will show how the different aspects of the business processes, applications, and infrastructure were modelled in a coherent and consistent way, and also show how the quantitative analysis techniques were used in the capacity planning of the infrastructure.

12.3.2   Views

By means of a number of different views, based on the design viewpoints described in Sect. 8.5, the SUB information system architecture is presented from the perspective of the TCA. We have chosen not to show a model of SUB as a whole; instead, we start with a broad perspective and go into detail for a number of specific processes.

Subsequently, models are presented that describe the SUB business processes (viewpoint Process cooperation), the SUB application support for these processes (viewpoint Application usage), and the infrastructure support for the applications (viewpoint Infrastructure support).[5]

Process Cooperation: Client-to-Client Processes   The process architecture, depicted in Fig. 12.25, shows the most important client-to-client processes within the scope of SUB. Each process is initiated by a *trigger*. These triggers fall in one the following categories:

- *time* triggers, indicating that a process is executed periodically;
- *message* triggers, indicating that an incoming message initiates a process;
- *signal* triggers, indicating that an incoming signal initiates a process.

For each trigger, a *frequency* is specified, expressed in terms of the average number of 'firings' per month. Furthermore, the process architecture shows the most important messages that flow between the processes.

Obviously, each of the above-mentioned client-to-client processes can be described in more detail by further specifying the sub-processes of which they consist, the actors that are involved, the incoming and outgoing messages and the databases that are being used. Next, we present a more detailed decomposition of the process 'Payroll tax return' (Fig. 12.26) from the overall SUB process architecture. The model shows, among others, which part of the process is executed by the TCA and which by UWV.

---

[5]The actual design of SUB further evolved after completion of the case study.

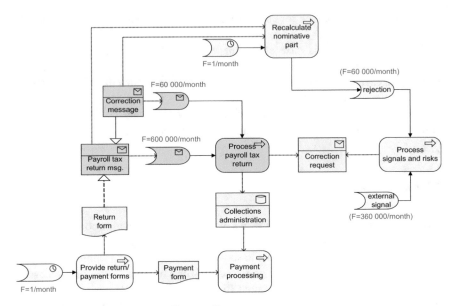

Fig. 12.25 Overview of the SUB client-to-client processes

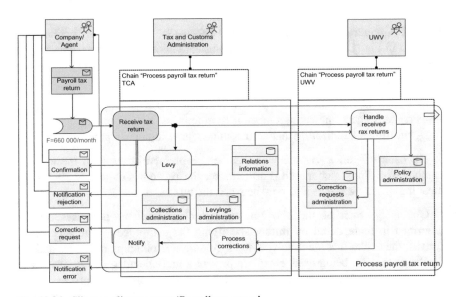

Fig. 12.26 Client-to-client process 'Payroll tax return'

Application Usage Going one level of detail deeper, we now zoom in on the 'Receive tax return' sub-process. The model of this sub-process and the corresponding application support are shown in Fig. 12.27. A payroll tax return (PTR) can be submitted in two main formats: on paper or electronically. The

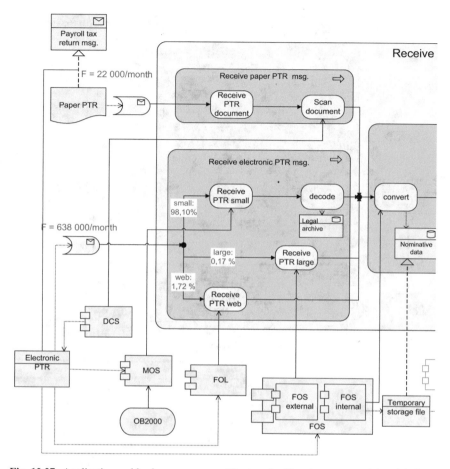

Fig. 12.27 Application and business process architecture for 'Receive tax return' (partial view)

electronic tax returns have three possible formats: Web-based messages, small messages sent via SMTP, and large messages sent via FTP. The model shows the expected distribution of the total number of messages over these different formats. The first part of the 'Receive tax return' process transforms these formats into a common, medium-independent format. We will refer to this phase of the process as 'Medium-specific processing'. The second phase of the 'Receive tax return' process, 'Medium-independent processing', processes all the payroll tax returns in the same way, irrespective of their original format.[6]

---

[6]The applications shown in Fig. 12.27 with a lighter colour, i.e. BvR, BBA, WCA and Notification, are mainly databases that are used in the processes, but play a secondary role. They are omitted in the more detailed models and the analysis.

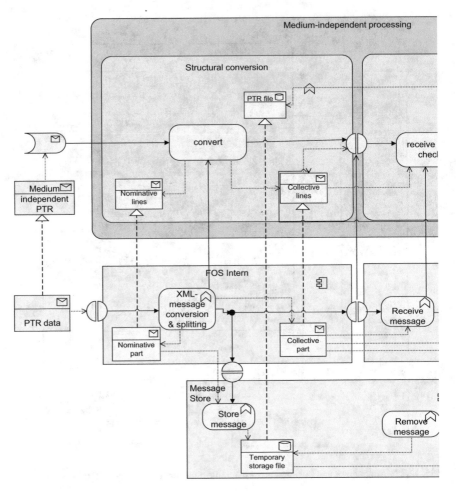

Fig. 12.28 Application support for 'Medium-independent processing' (partial view)

First, we detail the 'Medium-independent processing' phase. In the application architecture, the behaviour of each application component is partitioned into one or more *application functions* (denoting units of functionality used within the business processes) and *application interactions* to model communication between application components, as well as the data stores involved. Part of the resulting model is shown in Fig. 12.28.

Infrastructure Usage The next step is to take a closer look at the infrastructure support for the application architecture. We first illustrate the modelling approach for the 'Medium-independent processing'. A layer of infrastructure services supports the various application functions. We distinguish three types of infrastructural services:

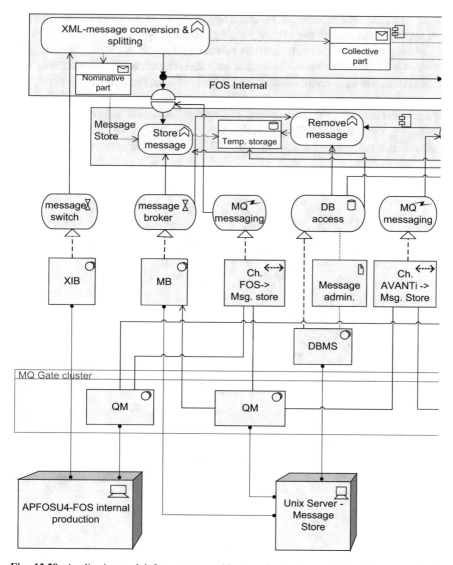

Fig. 12.29 Application and infrastructure architecture for 'Medium independent processing' (partial view)

- data storage and access services;
- processing services;
- communication services.

Data storage and access services are realised by, for example, a database management system. Processing services are typically realised by an execution environment or application server. Communication services support messaging between applications which is realised by, for instance, message queuing software (Fig. 12.29).

In this case, WebSphere MQ technology is used, where message brokers and message switches make use of functionality provided by queue managers. In MQ, communication services are realised by so-called *channels*. A channel between two devices is modelled as a communication path that represents a collaboration of two QM system software components, one for the sender and one for the receiver.

As mentioned above, the first part of the 'Return tax returns' process, 'Medium-specific processing', receives payroll tax returns from four information sources. Following the same modelling guidelines as in the case of the 'Medium-specific processing' part, we present in Fig. 12.30 the whole layered architecture

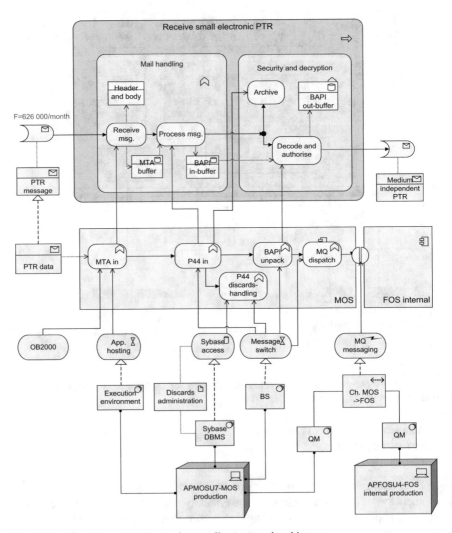

Fig. 12.30 'Receiving small electronic payroll tax returns' architecture

(i.e. business process, application and infrastructure architecture) of 'Receiving small electronic payroll tax returns'.

The models for the other three sources of tax returns will not be shown here, but they can be constructed in a similar way.

Infrastructure Support So far, we have adopted a top-down approach: starting with the business processes, we first identified the needed application support; then, we specified the infrastructure needed to run the applications. In this view, we work bottom-up: we show the complete infrastructure within the scope of the 'Receive tax return' process for SUB, and show which of the infrastructure services are used by which of the applications. Part of this view for the 'Receive tax return' process is shown in Fig. 12.31.

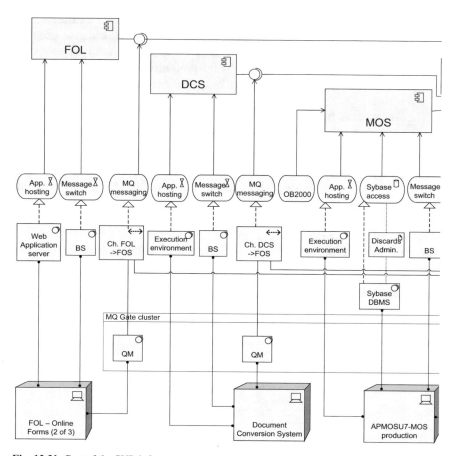

Fig. 12.31 Part of the SUB infrastructure support for applications (partial view)

12.3.3   Performance Analysis

This section illustrates the quantitative analysis of the model presented in the views in the previous sections, using the analysis approach described in Chap. 9. The results can be used to get an indication of the capacity that is required for the different resources in the infrastructure layer.

Analysis Approach For the given type of analysis, the following input data is required:

– For each trigger the *arrival frequency* (average and possibly also peaks).
– For each process, function, or service the average *service time*.
– For each actor, component, or device the *capacity*.

   Given these inputs, we can estimate the following performance measures:
– For each concept in the model (service, process, function, and resource) the *throughput*: the number of inputs/outputs that is to be processed per time unit. This is the *workload* that is imposed by the processes.
– For each actor, component, and device its *utilisation*: the percentage of time that it is active.
– For each process, function, and service the average *processing time* and *response time*.
– For each client-to-client process the average *completion time*.

   The analysis approach is portrayed in Fig. 12.32. Starting with the arrival frequencies on the business process level, the workload (throughput) for all model elements in the layers below is calculated (top-down analysis). Together with the given service time of the infrastructure services, the utilisation of the resources, and the processing and response times of the processes, functions, and services are calculated (bottom-up analysis). In Sect. 9.2 there is a detailed description of the analysis algorithms.

Workload Calculations (Top-Down) Some of the results of the workload calculations are shown in Fig. 12.33 (in italics). These figures reflect the workload of applications and infrastructure imposed by the sub-process *Medium-independent*

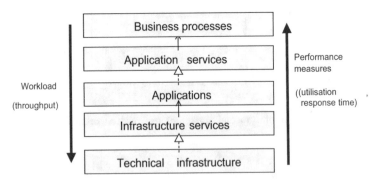

Fig. 12.32 Overview of the analysis approach

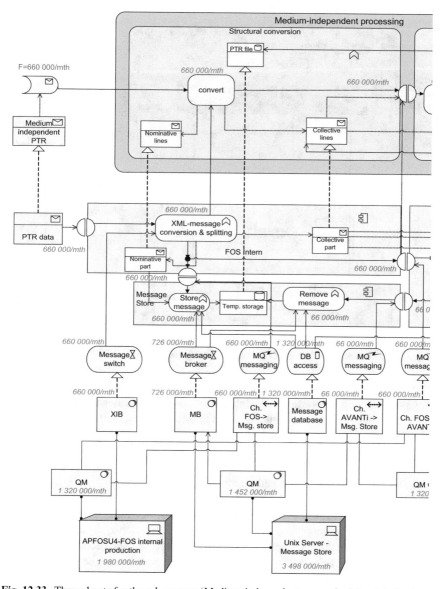

Fig. 12.33 Throughputs for the sub-process 'Medium-independent processing' (partial view)

processing, given an average monthly supply of 660,000 payroll tax returns. This workload is the basis for further performance analysis.

To obtain estimates of the total required infrastructure capacities, the same calculations also have to be made for the different *Medium-specific processing* parts of the *Receive tax return* process. The sum of the workloads from all the sub-processes results in a total workload for the SUB infrastructure, part of which is shown in Fig. 12.34. Similar calculations could be carried out for peak situations.

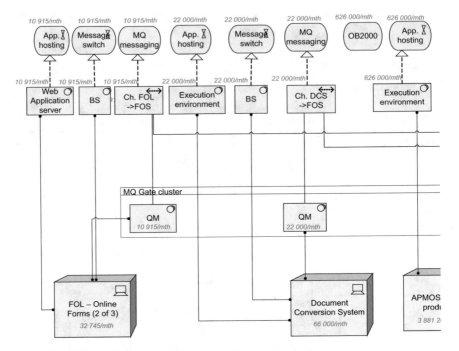

Fig. 12.34 Total workload of the SUB infrastructure (partial view)

Performance Measure Calculations (Bottom-Up) To calculate performance measures such as response times and utilisation, service times are also needed as input data. These figures are often difficult to establish, especially in a design phase of a project when systems are not yet operational. Nevertheless, based on technical documentation and available historical information (e.g., performance tests) of existing system components, and together with experts on the matter, reasonable estimates of these numbers could be made.

The numerical results of the bottom-up analysis of the process 'Receiving small electronic payroll tax returns' are given in Fig. 12.35. According to these figures the utilisation of the resources for an average workload is already quite high; this means that at peak loads the resources will almost certainly be overloaded. A solution to this problem may be to add additional resources or to increase the capacity of the resources. Further analysis can help to determine by how much the capacity needs to be increased.

12.3.4   Case Study Results

This case study shows that the ArchiMate language is suitable for modelling the relevant aspects of the technical architecture, as well as the relations of this

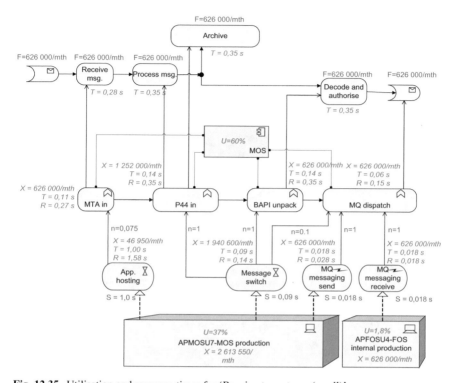

Fig. 12.35 Utilisation and response times for 'Receive tax returns (small)'

architecture to other architectures. The resulting models make the realisation of generic infrastructure services explicit. Quantitative analysis offered a clear view of how activities at the business process impose a workload on the application and infrastructure levels, thus providing a basis for capacity planning of the infrastructure. Performing these quantitative analyses at an early stage, considerably helps the realisation of the desired performance characteristics of the target system.

12.4 Summary

The case studies discussed in the previous sections represent only a small part of all the applications and validations of the methods and techniques presented in this book. However, they clearly show the feasibility and practical value of these results in various real-life settings. Both the modelling language and the visualisation and analysis techniques have shown their merit in providing more insight into complex, wide-ranging enterprise architectures.

Chapter 13
Beyond Enterprise Architecture

Wil P.M. Janssen and Marc M. Lankhorst

In the previous chapters we have discussed enterprise architecture modelling and analysis, its roots and foundations, and have seen enterprise architecture being applied in a number of industrial cases. The practice and possible added value have clearly been put forward. But what is next in the field of enterprise architecture?

13.1 The World Before Enterprise Architecture

This book is on enterprise architecture. Although the term has become quite common, enterprise architecture has only relatively recently reached a level where it is well understood and practically applicable. As we discussed in Chap. 2, Zachman (1987) can be seen as one of the first authors to define the concept in its full richness. But it took until the end of the twentieth century for enterprise architecture to be widely accepted. Why did this take so long?

Enterprise architecture is very much a holistic approach to the design of organisations. All different domains in enterprise design meet: organisation, information, systems, products, processes, and applications. Understanding the individual domains is complicated in itself, let alone their interdependencies. We have to look at this from both a business and a technical perspective.

The 1980s and 1990s of the last century have seen a focus on changing the way businesses operate. Business process redesign and business process re-engineering were used to rationalise processes and products. In the past, the industrial revolution

W.P.M. Janssen
Innovalor, Enschede, The Netherlands

M.M. Lankhorst (✉)
BiZZdesign, Capitool 15, 7521 PL Enschede, The Netherlands
e-mail: m.lankhorst@bizzdesign.com

© Springer-Verlag Berlin Heidelberg 2017
M. Lankhorst et al., *Enterprise Architecture at Work*, The Enterprise Engineering
Series, DOI 10.1007/978-3-662-53933-0_13

automated many production activities in companies. Work shifted from 'blue-collar work' to 'white-collar work'. Improving the performance of white-collar work cannot be achieved by simply automating it, but by working smarter, enabled by information technology. As Hammer (1990) stated in the title of his provocative article on business process reengineering: 'Don't automate, obliterate', i.e., radically rethink illogical business activities, which are there because nobody dares to challenge them. Introduce new information technology hand in hand with new business process ideas. The capabilities of information technology enable this smarter way of working (Davenport and Short 1990).

Another reason for changing business processes was customer focus. Companies need to compete and excel to keep and expand their customer base. The customer demands fast services, cost-efficiency, high, standardised quality, and flexibility. Ultimately, cost, flexibility, improvement, and standardisation of quality need a process focus. Looking at the business activities serving the end customer, they appeared to be partitioned on the basis of, amongst others, historical evolution and political power structures, existing departmental boundaries, and physical location and geographical borders.

Given the complexity and risks involved in changing an organisational way of working, a business process engineering approach is needed. Dealing with design complexity demands abstraction using architectural methods and tools. By the end of the last century, different methods and tools had been developed to assist organisations in optimising processes and introducing customer focus. Business process redesign has moved from an ill-understood skill, with a substantial failure rate, to a repeatable exercise (see, e.g., Franken et al. 2000), in which business process modelling and business process architecture play an important role.

From a technical perspective, modelling and architecture have a longer history. In hardware design, the notion of architecture has been in use since the 1960s, pioneered by the likes of Amdahl, Blaauw, and Brooks in their design of the IBM S/360 mainframe (IBM Corp. 1964). In their research note Amdahl et al. (1964) give probably the first definition of architecture in the IT world:

The term *architecture* is used here to describe the attributes of a system as seen by the programmer, i.e., the conceptual structure and functional behavior, as distinct from the organization of the data flow and controls, the logical design, and the physical implementation.

Information modelling has also been a common practice for a long time. Entity–relationship diagrams were developed in the 1970s. Nowadays, the class diagrams of UML form a crucial element in object-oriented analysis and design. Beyond information modelling, the picture is less clear. The UML standard, as was discussed in Chap. 2, provides many ingredients for this, but in practice we come across many proprietary and informal techniques.

Nevertheless, the role of architecture has been much more important on the technical side than from an organisational or business perspective. One reason for this is that the importance of architecture in this field is much more obvious than in business processes: the performance and suitability of applications and systems is immediately visible, and can lead to bad publicity and unsatisfied users; it is always convenient to blame 'the computer'. In the press we regularly see evidence of this phenomenon. Therefore, robustness, scalability, reliability, and feasibility have become key concepts in system analysis and design.

For business processes, bad performance is much more accepted. When does the fact that it takes 12–18 weeks to settle a building permit, or that some insurers have a backlog of almost half a year in their pension administrations, get into a newspaper? Oddly enough, this type of performance was accepted for ages, and hence the need for business process architecture was barely felt. But times have changed.

13.2 The Advent of Enterprise Architecture

Architecture is progressively seen not just as a tactical instrument for designing an organisation's systems and processes, but as a strategic tool for enterprise governance. Yet, the architecture practice within most organisations is still focused on design and has not yet progressed to the level of coordination, let alone to the level of enterprise governance. Furthermore, the term 'architecture' and the role of the 'architect' are heavily overloaded and have faced serious inflation.

To really profit from the strategic potential of enterprise architecture, an organisation needs to optimise the skills, methods, and tools of its architects, and give them the right position in the organisation. In this book, we have mainly concentrated on the first issue. However, without a proper organisational embedding of architectural practice, the enterprise will reap none of its potential benefits.

Many organisations struggle with this problem. On the one hand, a close relationship with business units and systems' development is crucial for a detailed understanding of the organisation. On the other hand, a certain distance and external authority is important to keep an overview of different projects, processes, and changes: the essence of architecture. In many companies, this has resulted in organisational units such as 'corporate architecture' or 'enterprise architecture' that are either overwhelmed by the continuous interaction with business units, or, worse, considered an 'ivory tower' and play a marginal role.

The acceptance of the role of the enterprise architect depends directly on its perceived added value. As Fowler (2003) states, this added value does not come from 'drawing pictures', but is based on shortened development times, reduced budget overspending, and increased flexibility in the organisation as a whole. Fowler shows that is it possible to play such a role, if skilled architects, supported by effective tools, apply the right techniques. We are very close to that stage, but have not reached it yet.

The organisations that participate in the ArchiMate project are to a certain extent forerunners in this new era, and already face the difficulties of this struggle. In the end, there is no real choice: the complexity and speed of change of society requires enterprise architecture in order to keep up with that pace. Enterprise architects will have to play a leading role, unless organisations are willing to spend too much money or not to live up to their customers' expectations.

A key element in the recognition of the role of enterprise architecture is that we should be able to quantify the impact of architecture, both financially as well as in terms of the organisational performance. Unfortunately, it is difficult to quantify precisely the benefits of a method of working that is so wide ranging as enterprise architecture. Until recently, hard evidence for the value of enterprise architecture has been hard to come by, beyond a certain 'gut feeling' and qualitative arguments. But has anyone ever asked a CEO to quantify his or her added value for an organisation? And evidence is mounting, as more and more case studies become available that show real added value (see e.g. Garret (2004) for an early example), and analysts such as Gartner and Forrester increasingly focus on enterprise architecture as an indispensable management practice. Furthermore, enterprise architectures themselves are increasingly used as an instrument to assess the benefits of IT projects (see, e.g., Romani 2003).

13.3   The Business Ecosystem

So enterprise architecture is here to stay, even though it may change its name or become part of a larger discipline of 'business design'. Architecture and architects have become well established and have shown serious added value in many organisations. Increasingly, their role is becoming that of both enterprise visionary and enterprise supervisor. Such an architect acts as a linking pin between CIO, CTO and CEO and the organisation, translator of strategic choices to tactical decisions and changes, protector of the conceptual integrity of the enterprise's processes and systems and guardian of the relationship between the enterprise and its environment: he or she will be both guard and guardian angel. However, new challenges for enterprise architects are just beyond the horizon.

Customers have become increasingly demanding and product innovation rates are high. Globalisation of markets and the availability of new electronic media lead to new players entering existing markets, disintermediation, and an ever higher competitive pressure to work more effectively, reduce costs, and become more flexible. The advent of e-business and e-government has definitely changed the way organisations and cross-organisational processes function.

E-business introduced new business models and new ways of thinking. According to Venkatraman (1995), IT-enabled business transformation can take place at different levels, ranging from local optimisations to radical business change or even business network redefinition, in e-business-like transformations (Fig. 13.1).

E-business has changed our view of organisations, moving from an enterprise perspective to a network and ecosystem perspective (e.g. see Dai and Kauffman 2002). The scope of an enterprise architect is increasingly the extended enterprise, or business network, in which the enterprise operates (Kalakote and Robinson 2001; Hoque 2000). Business ecosystem architecture has become a new playing field, determining the borders of business models and business network design.

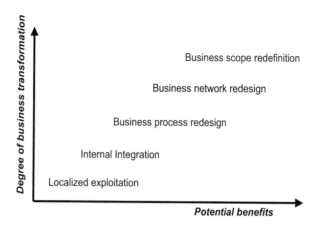

Fig. 13.1 Transformation levels according to Venkatraman (1995)

Modelling techniques for this type of architecture may change, but more in the sense that different views will be used rather than entirely new concepts. The ArchiMate modelling language was originally inspired by business network concepts, such as those described in Steen et al. (2002).

In several respects, networked business architecture and design differ from 'traditional' enterprise architecture (if there is such a thing). As stated in Janssen et al. (2003), the networked business architect should:

– Start the development of business services supporting cross-company cooperation from a *business network perspective*, not from the perspective of a single organisation. This implies that in principle many different actors involved can fulfil different roles at the same time, and that many relationships co-exist within the network.
– Emphasise the *roles of organisations* in the business ecosystem with respect to each other, instead of the actual actors themselves.
– *Link* cooperation between companies to internal business processes and existing (legacy) systems.
– Assess the *consequences and prerequisites of technology* for business processes and cross-company cooperation.
– Effectively allow knowledge on *standards* and available components to be gathered and *reused*, preferably supporting component-based development and reuse, designing for flexibility.

A specific issue in the design of such collaborative networks is that of *transparency* (Janssen et al. 2008). An organisation needs to make its architectures transparent to its partners (up to a certain level) to be able to cooperate, and compliance with various regulations (e.g. SOX, Solvency II and Basel II and III in finance, HACCP and ISO 22000 in the food industry, data retention policies from the US government or the EU) also requires organisations to be increasingly transparent. This makes the need for a standard architecture language as described in this book even more apparent.

However, disclosing business strategies or private customer data might be distinctly unwise or even illegal. Architectures of business networks need to accommodate these conflicting requirements. Especially in public-private or cross-border cooperation between government agencies and commercial organisations, with their often conflicting goals and requirements, we expect this to become a crucial element in architectural design.

Moreover, organisations must deal with rapidly changing environments, adapt their way of working and increase their capabilities to anticipate and respond to such developments: they must become *agile enterprises*. Agile enterprises embrace change as a positive force and harnesses it for the organisation's competitive advantage. This requires a combination of adaptive methods and flexible solutions (Lankhorst 2012).

Models play a prominent role in achieving agility. By using declarative, rule-based, and executable models instead of software code, systems can be adapted much more quickly, in many cases by business experts instead of software developers. Moreover, architecture models help you to create a coherent, holistic approach, relating high-level business goals and requirements, via the design of the business operations, to the actual implementation and execution. This direct connection between strategy and execution greatly improves the speed of action of the enterprise.

However, this ever faster pace of change, the growing complexity of business ecosystems and the limited span of control of each actor in such networks imply that an architect can no longer pretend to provide complete designs for situations in the distant future. Rather, architects will increasingly be pointing the way, creating the conditions, and setting the boundaries for self-organisation and evolution of the enterprise. In this complicated, networked and rapidly changing world, the role of the enterprise architect as a 'great communicator' needs to grow, and even enter the realm of the 'great negotiator', as architectural decisions move beyond the reach of a single organisational unit or managerial entity. This will have serious consequences for the skills and tools needed for the 'agile business ecosystem architect'. He or she will have to guard the interests of the different organisations involved, balancing cooperation in the network, organisational impact, regulatory compliance, speed of change, and individual benefits. The enterprise architect's role between guard and guardian angel will provide a decisive competitive edge to organisations in this dynamic world.

Appendix: Graphical Notation

The symbols of the ArchiMate Core language are shown in Fig. A.1. Note that several concepts can be denoted either by a 'box' with an icon, or by the icon by itself. The symbols of the other concepts are shown in Fig. A.2, and the notation for relationships is depicted in Fig. A.3.

© Springer-Verlag Berlin Heidelberg 2017
M. Lankhorst et al., *Enterprise Architecture at Work*, The Enterprise Engineering Series, DOI 10.1007/978-3-662-53933-0

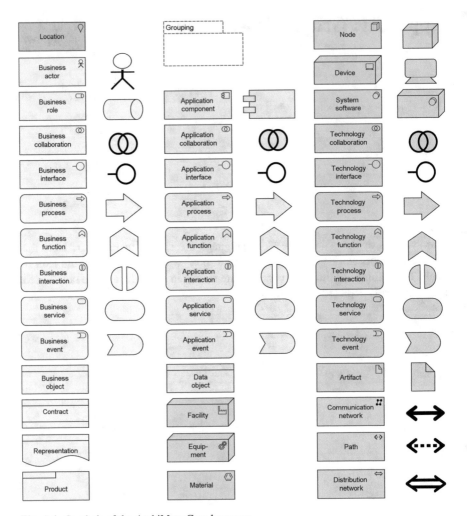

Fig. A.1 Symbols of the ArchiMate Core language

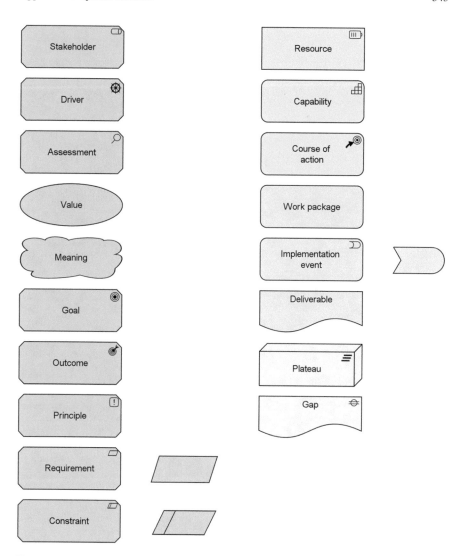

Fig. A.2 Symbols of motivation, strategy and implementation and migration concepts

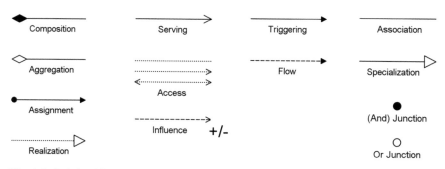

Fig. A.3 Relationships

References

Acme (1998), http://www-2.cs.cmu.edu/~acme/.

Aldea A, Iacob M-E, Hillegersberg J van, Quartel DAC, Franken HM (2015), Capability-based Planning with ArchiMate - Linking Motivation to Implementation. Proc. 17th International Conference on Enterprise Systems (ICEIS), pp. 352–359.

Alter S, Ein-Dor P, Lynne Markus M, Scott J, Vessey I (2001), Does the Trend Toward E-Business Call for Changes in The Fundamental Concepts of Information Systems? A Debate. Communications of AIS, 5(10):1–59, April.

Ambler SW (2002), Agile Modeling – Effective Practices for Extreme Programming and the Unified Process. Wiley, New York.

Amdahl GM, Blaauw GA, Brooks Jr FP (1964), Architecture of the IBM System/360, IBM Journal of Research and Development, 8(2):21–36.

Aquilani F, Balsamo S, Inverardi P (2001), Performance Analysis at the Software Architectural Design Level. Performance Evaluation, 45(2–3), July.

Arbab F, Boer F de, Bonsangue M, Lankhorst MM, Proper HA, Torre L van der (2007), Integrating Architectural Models: Symbolic, Semantic and Subjective Models in Enterprise Architecture, International Journal of Enterprise Modelling and Information Systems Architectures (EMISA), 2(1):44–57.

Baeten JCM, Weijland WP (1990), Process Algebra. Cambridge Tracts in Theoretical Computer Science 18. Cambridge University Press, Cambridge.

Band I, Engelsman W, Feltus C, González Paredes S, Hietala J, Jonkers H, Massart S (2015), Modeling Enterprise Risk Management and Security with the ArchiMate Language. White Paper, The Open Group.

Basel II (2004), Basel II: International Convergence of Capital Measurement and Capital Standards: A Revised Framework, Basel Committee Publications No. 107, June. http://www.bis.org/publ/bcbs107.htm.

Bass L, Clements P, Kazman R (1998), Software Architecture in Practice. Addison-Wesley, Reading, Massachusetts.

Bergstra JA, Ponse A, Smolka SA (eds.) (2001), Handbook of Process Algebra. Elsevier, Amsterdam.

Biemans FPM, Lankhorst MM, Teeuw WB, Van de Wetering RG (2001), Dealing with the Complexity of Business Systems Architecting. Systems Engineering, 4(2):118–133.

Blanchard BS, Fabrycky WJ (1990), Systems Engineering and Analysis. Prentice Hall, Englewood Cliffs, New Jersey.

Bon J van (ed.) (2002), IT Service Management – An Introduction – Based on ITIL. Van Haren Publishing, Zaltbommel.

© Springer-Verlag Berlin Heidelberg 2017
M. Lankhorst et al., *Enterprise Architecture at Work*, The Enterprise Engineering Series, DOI 10.1007/978-3-662-53933-0

Booch G, Rumbaugh J, Jacobson I (1999), The Unified Modeling Language User Guide. Addison-Wesley, Reading, Massachusetts.

Bosch J, Grahn H (1998), Characterising the Performance of Three Architectural Styles. Proc. First International Workshop on Software and Performance, Santa Fe, New Mexico.

Brooks FP (1975), The Mythical Man-Month: Essays on Software Engineering. Addison-Wesley, Reading, Massachusetts.

Buschmann F, Meunier R, Rohnert H, Sommerlad P, Stal M (1996), A System of Patterns: Pattern-Oriented Software Architecture. Wiley, New York.

Business Architecture Guild (2016), A Guide to the Business Architecture Body of Knowledge® (BIZBOK® Guide), Version 5.0, Business Architecture Guild.

Buuren R van, Jonkers H, Iacob, M-E, Strating P (2004), Composition of Relations in Enterprise Architecture Models. In Ehrig H et al. (eds.), Graph Transformations. Proc. Second International Conference on Graph Transformation (ICGT 2004), Rome, Italy, LNCS 3256, pp. 39–53. Springer, Berlin.

C4ISR Architecture Working Group (1997), C4ISR Architecture Framework Version 2.0, US Department of Defense, December 18, 1997. http://www.c3i.osd.mil/org/cio/i3/AWG_Digital_Library/pdfdocs/fw.pdf.

Chen P (1976), The Entity-Relationship Model – Toward a Unified View of Data. ACM Transactions on Database Systems 1(1):9–36.

CIO Council (2004), Federal Enterprise Architecture Framework (FEAF), http://www.cio.gov.

Clinger–Cohen Act (1996), Information Technology Management Reform Act, August 8. http://wwwoirm.nih.gov/policy/itmra.html.

CMMI Product Team (2002), Capability Maturity Model Integration (CMMI), Version 1.1, Staged Representation, CMU/SEI-2002-TR-029, ESC-TR-2002-029, Software Engineering Institute, Carnegie Mellon University, Pittsburgh, Pennsylvania.

Conway ME (1968), How Do Committees Invent? Datamation, 14(4):28–31.

Creasy PN, Ellis G (1993), A Conceptual Graph Approach to Conceptual Schema Integration. In Proc. ICCS'93, Conceptual Graphs for Knowledge Representation: First International Conference on Conceptual Structures, Quebec, Canada.

Cruse DA (2000), Meaning in Language – An Introduction to Semantics and Pragmatics. Oxford University Press, New York.

Crystal D (1997), The Cambridge Encyclopedia of Language, 2nd edition. Cambridge University Press, Cambridge, UK.

Dai Q, Kauffman R (eds.) (2002), B2B e-commerce revisited: revolution or evolution. Guest Editors' Preface to the Special section in Electronic Markets, 12(2):64–66.

Davenport T, Short JE (1990), The New Industrial Engineering: Information Technology and Business Process Redesign, Sloan Management Review, Summer:309–330.

De Boer F, Bonsangue M, Jacob J, Stam A, Van der Torre L (2004), A Logical Viewpoint on Architectures. Proc. 8th IEEE International Enterprise Distributed Object Computing Conference (EDOC'04), Monterey, California, September 20–24.

De Boer F, Bonsangue M, Jacob J, Stam A, Van der Torre L (2005), Enterprise Architecture Analysis with XML. Proc. 38th Hawaii International Conference on System Sciences (HICSS'05), Hawaii, January.

De Kinderen S, Gaaloul K, Proper HE (2012), Integrating Value Modelling into ArchiMate. In Snene M, Exploring Services Science. Proc. Third International Conference (IESS 2012), Geneva, Switzerland, February 15–17, pp. 125–139.

Di Marco A, Inverardi P (2004), Compositional Generation of Software Architecture Performance QN Models. In Magee J, Szyperski C, Bosch J (eds.), Proc. Fourth Working IEEE/IFIP Conference on Software Architecture, pp. 37–46, Oslo, Norway.

Department of Defense (2007), DoD Architecture Framework Version 1.5, Volume I: Definitions and Guidelines. Department of Defense, Washington DC.

Dietz JLG (2006), Enterprise Ontology: Theory and Methodology. Springer, Berlin.

Dijkstra EW (1968), Structure of the 'THE'-Multiprogramming System, Communications of the ACM, 11(5):341–346.

Eager D, Sevcik K (1986), Bound hierarchies for multiple-class queuing networks. Journal of the ACM, 33:179–206.

Eck PAT van, Blanken H, Wieringa RJ (2004), Project GRAAL: Towards Operational Architecture Guidelines. International Journal of Cooperative Information Systems, 13(3):235–255.

Eertink H, Janssen W, Oude Luttighuis P, Teeuw W, Vissers C (1999), A Business Process Design Language. Proc. 1st World Congress on Formal Methods, Toulouse, France.

EFQM (2003), EFQM Excellence Model, EFQM Brussels Representative Office, Brussels. http://www.efqm.org/model_awards/model/excellence_model.htm

Eriksson H-E, Penker M (1998), Business Modeling with UML: Business Patterns at Work. Wiley, New York.

Falkenberg ED, Hesse W, Lindgreen P, Nilsson BE, Oei JLH, Rolland C, Stamper RK, Van Assche FJM, Verrijn-Stuart AA, Voss K (eds.) (1998), A Framework of Information Systems Concepts, IFIP WG 8.1 Task Group FRISCO.

Ferris C, Farrell J (2003), What are Web Services? Communications of the ACM, 46(6):31.

Finkelstein A, Kramer J, Nuseibeh B, Finkelstein L, Goedicke M (1992), Viewpoints: A Framework for Integrating Multiple Perspectives in System Development, International Journal of Software Engineering and Knowledge Engineering, Special issue on Trends and Research Directions in Software Engineering Environments, 2(1):31–58.

Fitzsimmons JA, Fitzsimmons MJ (2000), New Service Development: Creating memorable experiences. Sage, Thousand Oaks, California.

Fowler M (2003), Who Needs an Architect? IEEE Software, July–August:2–4.

Fowler M, Scott K (1999), UML Distilled: A Brief Guide to the Standard Object Modeling Language, 2nd edition. Addison-Wesley, Springfield, Virginia.

Franckson M, Verhoef TF (eds.) (1999), Information Services Procurement Library. Ten Hagen & Stam, Den Haag.

Frankel DS (2003), Model Driven Architecture: Applying MDA to Enterprise Computing. Wiley, New York.

Franken H, Bal R, Van den Berg H, Janssen W, De Vos H (2000), Architectural Design Support for Business Process and Business Network Engineering. International Journal of Services Technology and Management, 1(1):1–14.

Gamma E, Helm R, Johnson R, Vlissides J (1995), Design Patterns: Elements of Reusable Object-Oriented Software, 1st edition. Addison-Wesley, Reading, Massachusetts.

Garrett GR (2004), Volkswagen of America's Enterprise Architecture Story, Presentation at the ACT/IAC Enterprise Architecture (EA) Best Practices Seminar, July 23.

Goldstein SM, Johnston R, Duffy J, Rao J (2002), The Service Concept: The Missing Link in Service Design Research? Journal of Operations Management, 20(2):121–134.

Gordijn J (2002), Value-based Requirements Engineering: Exploring Innovative e-Commerce Ideas. PhD thesis. Vrije Universiteit Amsterdam.

Greefhorst D, Proper HA (2011), Architecture Principles: The Cornerstones of Enterprise Architecture. Springer.

Grice HP (1975), Logic and Conversation. In Cole P, Morgan JL (eds.), Syntax and Semantics III: Speech Acts. pp. 41–58. Academic Press, New York.

Hall AD (1962), A Methodology for Systems Engineering. Van Nostrand, Princeton, New Jersey.

Hall AD (1969), Three-Dimensional Morphology of Systems Engineering. IEEE Transactions on System Science and Cybernetics, SSC-5(2):156–160.

Hammer M (1990), Reengineering Work: Don't Automate, Obliterate, Harvard Business Review, July–August:109–144.

Hanna A, Windebank J, Adams S, Sowerby J, Rance S, Cartlidge A (2008), ITIL V3 Foundation Handbook. The Stationary Office, Norwich, UK.

Hardjono TW, Bakker RJM (2001), Management van processen: Identificeren, besturen, beheersen en vernieuwen. Kluwer, Dordrecht (in Dutch).

Harel D, Pnueli A (1985), On the development of reactive systems. In Apt K (ed.), Logics and Models of Concurrent Systems, pp. 477–498. NATO ASI Series. Springer, Berlin.

Harel D, Rumpe B (2004), Meaningful Modeling: What's the Semantics of 'Semantics'? IEEE Computer, October:64–72.

Harrison P, Patel N (1992), Performance Modelling of Communication Networks and Computer Architectures. Addison-Wesley, Reading, Massachusetts.

Henderson JC, Venkatraman N (1993), Strategic Alignment: Leveraging Information Technology for Transforming Operations, IBM Systems Journal, 32(1):4–16.

Hermanns H, Herzog U, Katoen J-P (2002), Process Algebra for Performance Evaluation, Theoretical Computer Science, 274(1–2):43–87.

Hoque F (2000), e-Enterprise: Business Models, Architecture, and Components. Cambridge University Press, Cambridge.

Horton W (1991), Illustrating Computer Documentation, Wiley, New York.

Iacob M-E, Jonkers H (2005), Quantitative Analysis of Enterprise Architectures. Proc. INTEROP-ESA 2005 Conference, 23–25 February, Geneva.

Iacob M-E, Leeuwen D (2004), View Visualisation for Enterprise Architecture. Proc. 6th International Conference on Enterprise Information Systems (ICEIS 2004), 14–17 April, Porto, Portugal.

IBM Corp. (1964), IBM System/360 Principles of Operation. IBM Systems Reference Library, File No. S360-01, Form A22-6821-0. Poughkeepsie, New York.

IDEF (1993), Integration Definition for Function Modeling (IDEF0) Draft, Federal Information Processing Standards Publication FIPSPUB 183. U.S. Department of Commerce, Springfield, Virginia.

IEEE Computer Society (2000), IEEE Std 1471-2000: IEEE Recommended Practice for Architecture description of Software-Intensive Systems. IEEE, New York.

IFIP-IFAC Task Force (1999), GERAM: Generalised Enterprise Reference Architecture and Methodology, Version 1.6.3, March (Published also as Annex to ISO WD15704). http://www.fe.up.pt/~jjpf/isf2000/v1_6_3.html.

Illeris S (1997), The Service Economy: A Geographical Approach. Wiley, New York.

Insurance Frameworks (2013), Panorama 360 Enterprise Business Architecture Framework. Insurance Frameworks. http://www.insuranceframeworks.com.

ISO (2000), Quality Management Systems – Requirements, ISO 9000:2000. International Organization for Standardization, Geneva.

ISO/IEC/IEEE (2011), Systems and software engineering – Architecture description, ISO/IEC/IEEE FDIS 42010:2011. International Organization for Standardization, Geneva.

ITU (1995a), Open Distributed Processing – Reference Model – Part 2: Foundations, ITU Recommendation X.902 | ISO/IEC 10746-2. International Telecommunication Union, Geneva.

ITU (1995b), Open Distributed Processing – Reference Model – Part 3: Architecture, ITU Recommendation X.903 | ISO/IEC 10746-3. International Telecommunication Union, Geneva.

ITU (1996), Open Distributed Processing – Reference Model – Part 1: Overview, ITU Recommendation X.901 | ISO/IEC 10746-1. International Telecommunication Union, Geneva.

ITU (1997), Open Distributed Processing – Reference Model – Part 4: Architectural Semantics, ITU Recommendation X.904 | ISO/IEC 10746-4. International Telecommunication Union, Geneva.

Jacob J (2004), The RML Tutorial. CWI, Amsterdam. http://homepages.cwi.nl/~jacob/rml/

Jacobson I, Booch G, Rumbaugh J (1999), The Unified Software Development Process. Addison-Wesley, Reading, Massachusetts.

Jagannathan R (1995), Data flow Models. In Zomaya EY (ed.), Parallel and Distributed Computing Handbook. McGraw-Hill, New York.

James GA (2008), Magic Quadrant for Enterprise Architecture Tools. Gartner, June 17.

Janssen WPM, Fielt E, Lankhorst, MM (2008) Transparency in Services Networks, Combining Choice and Obligation. In Bouwman H, Bons R, Hoogeweegen M, Janssen M, Pronk H (eds.), Let a Thousand Flowers Bloom: Essays in commemoration of prof.dr. René Wagenaar. IOS Press, Amsterdam.

Janssen WPM, Steen MWA, Franken H (2003), Business Process Engineering versus E-Business Engineering: a summary of case experiences. Proc. 36th Hawaii International Conference on System Sciences (HICCS'03), IEEE Computer Society Press, Silver Spring, Maryland.

Jonkers H, Boekhoudt P, Rougoor M, Wierstra E (1999), Completion Time and Critical Path Analysis for the Optimisation of Business Process Models. In Obaidat M, Nisanci A, Sadoun B (eds.), Proc. 1999 Summer Computer Simulation Conference, pp. 222–229, Chicago, Illinois.

Jonkers H, Iacob M-E (2009), Performance and Cost Analysis of Service-Oriented Enterprise Architectures. In Gunasekaran A (ed.), Global Implications of Modern Enterprise Information Systems: Technologies and Applications, IGI Global.

Jonkers H, Lankhorst MM, Buuren R van, Hoppenbrouwers S, Bonsangue M, Van der Torre L (2004), Concepts for Modelling Enterprise Architectures, International Journal of Cooperative Information Systems, special issue on Architecture in IT, Vol. 13, No. 3, Sept. 2004, pp. 257-287.

Jonkers H, Swelm M van (1999), Queuing Analysis to Support Distributed System Design. Proc. 1999 Symposium on Performance Evaluation of Computer and Telecommunication Systems, pp. 300–307, Chicago, Illinois.

Kalakote R, Robinson M (2001), e-Business 2.0. Addison-Wesley, Reading, Massachusetts.

Kaplan R, Norton D (1992), The Balanced Scorecard – Measures That Drive Performance, Harvard Business Review, January–February:71–79.

Kaplan R, Norton D (2004), Strategy Maps, Converting Intangible Assets into Tangible Outcomes, Harvard Business School Publishing.

Kazman R, Bass L, Abowd G, Webb M (1994), SAAM: A Method for Analyzing the Properties of Software Architectures. Proc. 16th International Conference on Software Engineering, pp. 81–90, Sorento, Italy.

Koning H (2002), Guidelines Concerning Readability of IT-Architecture Diagrams version 1.0, May 17, 2002, http://www.cs.vu.nl/~henk/research/via/guidelines-readability-020517b.doc.

Kotonya G, Sommerville I (1992), Viewpoints for Requirements Definition. IEE/BCS Software Engineering Journal, 7(6):375–387.

Krogstie J, Lindland OI, Sindre G (1995), Defining Quality Aspects for Conceptual Models. In Falkenberg ED, Hesse W, Olive A (eds.), Information Systems Concepts: Towards a consolidation of views. Proc. IFIP international working conference on information system concepts, pp. 216–231. Chapman & Hall, London.

Kruchten P (1995), Architectural Blueprints – The '4+1' View Model of Software Architecture, IEEE Software, 12(6):42–50.

Kruchten P (2000), The Rational Unified Process: An Introduction, 2nd edition. Addison-Wesley, Reading, Massachusetts.

Labovitz G, Rosansky V (1997), The Power of Alignment. Wiley, New York.

Lamsweerde A van (2004), Goal-Oriented Requirements Engineering: A Roundtrip from Research to Practice. Proceedings of the 12th IEEE International Requirements Engineering Conference, 4–7.

Lankhorst MM, Buuren R van, Leeuwen D van, Jonkers H, Doest HWL ter (2005), Enterprise Architecture Modelling – The Issue of Integration, Advanced Engineering Informatics, special issue Enterprise Modelling and System Support, 18(4):205–216.

Lankhorst MM, Proper HA, Jonkers H (2010), The Anatomy of the ArchiMate Language. International Journal of Information Systems Modeling and Design (IJISMD), 1(1):1–32, January–March.

Lankhorst MM (ed.) (2012), Agile Service Development – Combining Adaptive Methods and Flexible Solutions. Springer, Berlin Heidelberg.

Leeuwen D van, Doest HWL ter, Lankhorst MM (2004), A Tool Integration Workbench for Enterprise Architecture. Proc. 6th International Conference on Enterprise Information Systems (ICEIS 2004), Porto, Portugal, 14–17 April 2004.

Lindland OI, Sindre G, Sølvberg A (1994), Understanding Quality in Conceptual Modeling, IEEE Software, 11(2):42–49.

Lung C-H, Jalnapurkar A, El-Rayess A (1998), Performance-Oriented Software Architecture Analysis: An Experience Report. Proc. First International Workshop on Software and Performance, Santa Fe, New Mexico.

Martin J (1982), Strategic Data-Planning Methodologies. Prentice Hall, Englewood Cliffs, New Jersey.

Martin J (1989), Information Engineering (3 vols.). Prentice Hall, Englewood Cliffs, New Jersey.

Martin RC (2002), Agile Software Development Principles, Patterns, and Practices. Prentice Hall, Englewood Cliffs, New Jersey.

Matthes F, Buckl S, Leitel J, Schwerda CM (2008), EAMTS2008 - Enterprise Architecture Management Tool Survey 2008. TU Munich.

Matthes F, Hauder M, Katinsky N (2014), EAMTS2014 - Enterprise Architecture Management Tool Survey 2014 Update. TU Munich.

Mayer RJ, Menzel CP, Painter MK, deWitte PS, Blinn T, Perakath B (1995), Information Integration for Concurrent Engineering (IICE), IDEF3 Process Description Capture Method Report, Interim Technical Report April 1992–September 1995. Knowledge Based Systems, College Station, Texas.

McGovern J, Ambler SW, Stevens ME, Linn J, Sharan V, Elias KJ (2004), A Practical Guide to Enterprise Architecture. Pearson Education, Upper Saddle River, New Jersey.

Medvidovic N, Taylor RN (2000), A Classification and Comparison Framework for Software Architecture Description Languages, IEEE Transactions on Software Engineering, 26 (1):70–93.

Menzel C, Mayer RJ (1998), The IDEF Family of Languages. In Bernus P, Mertins K, Schmidt G (eds.), Handbook on Architectures of Information Systems, vol. 1 of International Handbooks on Information Systems, Chap. 10, pp. 209–241. Springer, Berlin.

Miller GA (1956), The Magical Number Seven, Plus or Minus Two: Some Limits on Our Capacity for Processing Information. Psychological Review, 63:81–97.

Nadler DA, Gerstein MS, Shaw RB (1992), Organizational Architecture: Designs for Changing Organizations. Jossey-Bass, San Francisco.

NASCIO (2003), NASCIO Enterprise Architecture Maturity Model Version 1.3, National Association of State Chief Information Officers. https://www.nascio.org/hotIssues/EA/EAMM.pdf

Nonaka I, Takeuchi H (1991), The Knowledge-Creating Company. Harvard Business Review, November–December:97–130.

Nuseibeh BA (1994), A Multi-Perspective Framework for Method Integration. PhD thesis, Imperial College, University of London.

Object Management Group (2013), Business Process Modeling Notation (BPMN), Version 2.0.2 (formal/2013-12-09), Object Management Group. http://www.omg.org/spec/BPMN/.

Object Management Group (2014), Model Driven Architecture (MDA) MDA Guide Revision 2.0 (ormsc/2014-06-01), Object Management Group. http://www.omg.org/mda/.

Object Management Group (2015a), OMG Unified Modeling Language™ (OMG UML) Version 2.5 (formal/2015-03-01), Object Management Group. http://www.omg.org/spec/UML/.

Object Management Group (2015b), Business Motivation Model (BMM), Version 1.3 (formal/2015-05-19), Object Management Group. http://www.omg.org/spec/BMM/.

Object Management Group (2015c), XML Metadata Interchange (XMI) Specification, Version 2.5.1 (formal/2015-06-07). Object Management Group. http://www.omg.org/spec/XMI/.

Object Management Group (2015d), Meta Object Facility (MOF) Core Specification, Version 2.5 (formal/2015-06-05), Object Management Group. http://www.omg.org/spec/MOF/.

Object Management Group (2015e), OMG Systems Modeling Language (OMG SysML, Version 1.4 (formal/2015-06-03), Object Management Group. http://www.omg.org/spec/SysML/.

Object Management Group (2015f), Value Delivery Metamodel, Version 1.0 (formal/2015-10-05), Object Management Group. http://www.omg.org/spec/VDML/.

Object Management Group (2015g), Semantics of Business Vocabulary and Business Rules (SBVR) Version 1.3 (formal/2015-05-07), Object Management Group. http://www.omg.org/spec/SBVR/.

Object Management Group (2016a), Decision Model and Notation (DMN) Version 1.1 (formal/2016-06-01), Object Management Group. http://www.omg.org/spec/DMN/.

Object Management Group (2016b), Meta Object Facility (MOF) 2.0 Query/View/Transformation Specification Version 1.3 (formal/2016-06-03), Object Management Group. http://www.omg.org/spec/QVT/.

ODMG (2000), Using XML as an Object Interchange Format, Object Data Management Group. http://www.odmg.org/.

Olle TW, Hagelstein J, Macdonald IG, Rolland C, Sol HG, van Assche FJM Verrijn-Stuart AA (1988), Information Systems Methodologies: A Framework for Understanding. Addison-Wesley, Reading, Massachusetts.

Op 't Land M, Proper E, Waage M, Cloo J, Steghuis C (2008), Enterprise Architecture: Creating Value by Informed Governance. Springer, Berlin.

Osterwalder A (2004), The Business Model Ontology – A Proposition in a Design Science Approach. PhD Thesis, University of Lausanne.

Osterwalder A, Pigneur Y (2010), Business Model Generation: A Handbook for Visionaries, Game Changers, and Challengers. Wiley.

Pahl G, Beitz W (1986), Konstruktionslehre. Handbuch für Studium und Praxis. Springer, Berlin.

Parker MM, Benson RJ (1989), Enterprise-wide Information Management: State-of-the-Art Strategic Planning, Journal of Information Systems Management, 6(3):14–23.

Paulk M, Curtis B, Chrissis M, Weber C (1993), Capability Maturity Model for Software (Version 1.1), Technical Report CMU/SEI-93-TR-024, Software Engineering Institute, Carnegie Mellon University, Pittsburgh, Pennsylvania.

Peirce CS (1969a), Volumes I and II – Principles of Philosophy and Elements of Logic. Collected Papers of C.S. Peirce. Harvard University Press, Boston, Massachusetts.

Peirce CS (1969b), Volumes III and IV – Exact Logic and The Simplest Mathematics. Collected Papers of C.S. Peirce. Harvard University Press, Boston, Massachusetts.

Peirce CS (1969c), Volumes V and VI – Pragmatism and Pragmaticism and Scientific Metaphysics. Collected Papers of C.S. Peirce. Harvard University Press, Boston, Massachusetts.

Peirce CS (1969d), Volumes VI and VIII – Science and Philosophy and Reviews, Correspondence and Bibliography. Collected Papers of C.S. Peirce. Harvard University Press, Boston, Massachusetts.

Pols R van der, Backer Y (2006), Application Services Library – A Management Guide. ASL Foundation/Van Haren Publishing.

Porter ME (1985), Competitive Advantage: Creating and Sustaining Superior Performance. Simon and Schuster, New York.

Proper HA (ed.) (2001), ISP for Large-Scale Migrations, Information Services Procurement Library. Ten Hagen & Stam, Den Haag.

Proper HA (2004), Da Vinci – Architecture-Driven Information Systems Engineering. Nijmegen Institute for Information and Computing Sciences, University of Nijmegen.

Putman JR (1991), Architecting with RM-ODP. Prentice Hall, Englewood Cliffs, New Jersey.

Quartel DAC, Steen MWA, Lankhorst MM (2010), IT Portfolio Valuation: Using Enterprise Architecture and Business Requirements Modeling. Proc. 14th IEEE International Enterprise Distributed Object Computing Conference (EDOC 2010), 25–29 October 2010, Vitoria, Brazil, pp. 3–13. IEEE Computer Society.

Rechtin E, Maier MW (1997), The Art of Systems Architecting. CRC Press, Boca Raton, Florida.

Reeves J, Marashi M, Budgen D (1995), A Software Design Framework or How to Support Real Designers, IEE/BCS Software Engineering Journal, 10(4):141–155.

Rittgen P (2000), A Modelling Method for Developing Web-Based Applications. Proc. International Conference IRMA 2000, Anchorage, Alaska, pp. 135–140.

Romani MB (2003), Using the Enterprise Architecture to Quantify the Benefits of Information Technology Projects, IR204L2/March 2003. Logistics Management Institute, McLean, Virginia.

Roozenburg NFM, Eekels J (1995), Product Design: Fundamentals and Methods. Wiley, New York.

Ross JW, Weill P, Robertson DC (2006), Enterprise Architecture As Strategy: Creating a Foundation for Business Execution. Harvard Business School Press.

Rueping A (2003), Agile Documentation: A Pattern Guide to Producing Lightweight Documents for Software Projects. Wiley, New York.

Sanden WAM van der, Sturm BJAM (1997), Informatiearchitectuur, de infrastructurele benadering. Panfox, Rosmalen (in Dutch).

Sarbanes–Oxley Act (2002), http://www.law.uc.edu/CCL/SOact/toc.html.

Schefstroem D, Broek G van den (1993), Tool Integration: Environments and Frameworks. Wiley, New York.

Schomig A, Rau H (1995), A Petri Net Approach for the Performance Analysis of Business Processes. Technical Report 116, Lehrstuhl für Informatik III, Universitat Wurzburg.

Schuurman P, Berghout EW, Powell P (2008), Calculating the Importance of Information Systems: The Method of Bedell Revisited, CITER WP/010/PSEBPP, University of Groningen, June 2008. Sprouts Working Papers on Information Systems, http://sprouts.aisnet.org/8-37.

Sherwood J, Clark A, Lynas D (2009), Enterprise Security Architecture. White Paper, SABSA Institute.

Shostack GL (1984), Designing Services that Deliver, Harvard Business Review, 62(1):133–139.

Smith C (1990), Performance Engineering of Software Systems. Addison-Wesley, Reading, Massachusetts.

Smith JM, Smith DCP (1977), Database Abstractions: Aggregation and Generalization, ACM Transactions on Database Systems, 2(2):105–133.

Sowa JF, Zachman JA (1992), Extending and Formalizing the Framework for Information Systems Architecture, IBM Systems Journal, 31(3):590–616.

Spitznagel B, Garlan D (1998), Architecture-based Performance Analysis. Proc. 1998 Conference on Software Engineering and Knowledge Engineering, San Francisco Bay.

Stam A, Jacob J, De Boer F, Bonsangue M, Van der Torre L (2004), Using XML transformations for Enterprise Architectures. Proc. 1st International Symposium on Leveraging Applications of Formal Methods (ISOLA'04), Paphos, Cyprus.

Steen MWA, Doest HWL ter, Lankhorst MM, Akehurst DH (2004), Supporting Viewpoint-Oriented Enterprise Architecture. Proc. 8th IEEE International Enterprise Distributed Object Computing Conference (EDOC'04), Monterey, California, September 20–24.

Steen MWA, Lankhorst MM, Wetering RG van de (2002), Modelling Networked Enterprises. In Proc. Sixth International Enterprise Distributed Object Computing Conference (EDOC'02), Lausanne, Switzerland, September, pp. 109–119.

Stevens M (2002), Service-Oriented Architecture Introduction, Part 1. www.developer.com/design/article.php/1010451, April.

Stroud RE (2012), Introduction to COBIT 5. ISACA. http://www.isaca.org/education/upcoming-events/documents/intro-cobit5.pdf.

Teeuw WB, Berg, H van den (1997), On the Quality of Conceptual Models. In Liddle SW (ed.), Proc. ER'97 Workshop on Behavioral Models and Design Transformations: Issues and Opportunities in Conceptual Modeling, UCLA, Los Angeles. http://osm7.cs.byu.edu/ER97/workshop4/tvdb.html.

The Open Group (2011), The Open Group Architectural Framework (TOGAF) Version 9.1. The Open Group, Reading, UK. http://www.opengroup.org/togaf/.

The Open Group (2013), Risk Taxonomy (O-RT) Version 2.0. The Open Group, Reading, UK. https://www2.opengroup.org/ogsys/catalog/C13K

The Open Group (2015), ArchiMate® Model Exchange File Format, Open Group Standard, The Open Group, Reading, UK.

The Open Group (2016a), ArchiMate® 3.0 Specification, Open Group Standard, The Open Group, Reading, UK. http://www.opengroup.org/archimate/.

The Open Group (2016b), Business Capabilities, Open Group Guide, The Open Group, Reading, UK. https://www2.opengroup.org/ogsys/catalog/G161

The Open Group (2016c), Open Business Architecture (O-BA) – Part I, Open Group Preliminary Standard, P161, The Open Group, Reading, UK.

Treacy M, Wiersema, F (1997), The discipline of market leaders. Perseus Publishing, Reading, Massachusetts.

Turner KJ (1987), An Architectural Semantics for LOTOS. Proc. 7th International Conf. on Protocol Specification, Testing, and Verification, pp. 15–28.

Ulrich, W, Rosen, M (2011), The Business Capability Map: The "Rosetta Stone" of Business/IT Alignment. Executive Report, March 8, 2011, Cutter Consortium.

UN/CEFACT (2011), UMM Foundation Module Version 2.0, http://www.unece.org/cefact/.

Velzen RCG van, Oosten JNA van, Snijders T, Hardjono TW (2002), Procesmanagement en de SqEME-benadering. Kluwer, Dordrecht.

Venkatraman N (1995), IT-enabled Business Transformation: From Automation to Business Scope Redefinition, Sloan Management Review, Fall:32–42.

Veryard R (2004), Business-Driven SOA 2 – How business governs the SOA process, CBDI Journal, June.

W3C (1999), XSL Transformations 1.0, World Wide Web Consortium. http://www.w3.org/TR/xslt.

W3C (2004), XML Schema 1.1, W3C Recommendation 28 October 2004, World Wide Web Consortium. http://www.w3.org/TR/xmlschema-0/.

W3C (2008), XML 1.0, W3C Recommendation 26 November 2008, World Wide Web Consortium. http://www.w3.org/TR/xml/.

Weill P, Vitale M (2002), What IT Infrastructure Capabilities Are Needed to Implement E-Business Models? MIS Quarterly Executive, 1(1):17–34.

Weinberg GM (1988), Rethinking Systems Analysis & Design. Dorset House Publishing, New York.

White House (2013), Federal Enterprise Architecture Framework, Version 2.0. https://www.whitehouse.gov/sites/default/files/omb/assets/egov_docs/fea_v2.pdf

Wieringa RJ (1996), Requirements Engineering: Frameworks for Understanding. Wiley, New York.

Wieringa RJ (1998a), Postmodern Software Design with NYAM: Not Yet Another Method. In Broy M, Rumpe B (eds.), Requirements Targeting Software and Systems Engineering, LNCS 1526, pp. 69–94. Springer, Berlin.

Wieringa RJ (1998b), A Survey of Structured and Object-Oriented Software Specification Methods and Techniques, ACM Computing Surveys, 30(4):459–527.

Wieringa RJ (2003), Design Methods for Reactive Systems: Yourdon, Statemate and the UML. Morgan Kaufmann, San Francisco.

Wieringa RJ, Blanken HM, Fokkinga MM, Grefen PWPJ (2003), Aligning application architecture to the business context. Proc. Conference on Advanced Information System Engineering (CaiSE'03), LNCS 2681, pp. 209–225. Springer, Berlin.

Wieringa R, Eck P van, Steghuis C, Proper E (2008), Competences of IT Architects. Sdu Uitgevers, The Hague.

Wijers GM, Heijes H (1990), Automated Support of the Modelling Process: A view based on experiments with expert information engineers. In Steinholtz B, Sølvberg A, Bergman L (eds.), Proc. Second Nordic Conference on Advanced Information Systems Engineering (CaiSE'90), LNCS 436, pp. 88–108. Springer, Berlin.

Williams LG, Smith CU (1998), Performance Evaluation of Software Architectures. Proc. First International Workshop on Software and Performance, Santa Fe, New Mexico, October, pp. 164–177.

Wood-Harper AT, Antill L, Avison DE (1985), Information Systems Definition: The Multiview Approach. Blackwell Scientific, Oxford, UK.

Woods WA, Schmolze JG (1992), The KL-ONE family, Computers & Mathematics with Applications, 23(2/5):133–177.

Yu ESK (1997), Towards Modelling and Reasoning Support for Early-Phase Requirements Engineering, Proceedings of the 3rd IEEE International Symposium on Requirements Engineering, 226–235.

Zachman JA (1987), A Framework for Information Systems Architecture, IBM Systems Journal, 26(3):276–292.

Zee H van der, Laagland P, Hafkenscheid B (eds.) (2000), Architectuur als Management Instrument – Beheersing en Besturing van Complexiteit in het Netwerktijdperk. Ten Hagen & Stam, Den Haag (in Dutch).

Trademarks

TOGAF®, ArchiMate® and The Open Group® are registered trademarks of The Open Group.

MDA®, Model Driven Architecture®, OMG®, SysML® and UML® are registered trademarks and BPMN™, Business Process Modeling Notation™, MOF™, Decision Model and Notation™, DMN™, Semantics of Business Vocabulary and Rules™, SBVR™, VDML™ and Unified Modeling Language™ are trademarks of the Object Management Group.

CMM® and CMMI® are registered trademarks of the Carnegie Mellon Software Engineering Institute.

ITIL® is a registered trademark of the Office of Government Commerce.

COBIT® is a registered trademark of the Information Systems Audit and Control Association and the IT Governance Institute.

BIZBOK® and A Guide to the Business Architecture Body of Knowledge® are registered trademarks of the Business Architecture Guild®.

There may be other brand, company, and product names used in this document that may be covered by trademark protection. We advise the reader to verify these independently.

© Springer-Verlag Berlin Heidelberg 2017
M. Lankhorst et al., *Enterprise Architecture at Work*, The Enterprise Engineering Series, DOI 10.1007/978-3-662-53933-0

Index

© Springer-Verlag Berlin Heidelberg 2017
M. Lankhorst et al., *Enterprise Architecture at Work*, The Enterprise Engineering
Series, DOI 10.1007/978-3-662-53933-0

Printed in the United States
By Bookmasters